MYTHS
and
FACTS

A GUIDE TO THE
Arab-Israeli Conflict

By *Mitchell G. Bard*

American-**I**sraeli **C**ooperative **E**nterprise (AICE)

2810 Blaine Dr.
Chevy Chase, MD 20815

http://www.JewishVirtualLibrary.org

ISBN: 1537152726

ISBN 13: 9781537152721

Printed in the United States of America

American Israeli Cooperative Enterprise (AICE)
2810 Blaine Dr.
Chevy Chase, MD 20815
Tel.: 301-565-3918
Fax: 301-587-9056
E-mail: aiceresearch@gmail.com
http://www.JewishVirtualLibrary.org

Other studies available from AICE (all are now available on our website)**:**

■ **Israel Studies:** An Anthology
■ **Partners for Change:** How U.S.- Israel Cooperation Can Benefit America
■ **Learning Together:** Israeli Innovations in Education That Could Benefit Americans
■ **Breakthrough Dividend:** Israeli Innovations in Biotechnology That Could Benefit Americans
■ **Experience Counts:** Innovative Programs for the Elderly in Israel That Can Benefit Americans
■ **Building Bridges:** Lessons for America from Novel Israeli Approaches to Promote Coexistence
■ **Good Medicine:** Israeli Innovations in Health Care That Could Benefit Americans
■ **Rewriting History in Textbooks**
■ **On One Foot:** A Middle East Guide for the Perplexed or How to Respond on Your Way to Class, When Your Best Friend Joins an Anti-Israel Protest
■ **Tenured or Tenuous:** Defining the Role of Faculty in Supporting Israel on Campus

Production, new cover art by CreateSpace
Original book logo design, cover concept, typography, map illustration: *Danakama / Nick Moscovitz / NYC.*
Additional maps by North Market Street Graphics and the media and public affairs division in the Israeli Ministry of Foreign Affairs.

Contents

Preface

The great enemy of truth is very often not the lie—deliberate, contrived and dishonest—but the myth—persistent, persuasive and repeated.

—President John F. Kennedy*

"Everyone is entitled to his own opinion, but not his own facts."

—Daniel Patrick Moynihan†

"The Israeli-Palestinian conflict has several dimensions—national, political, territorial, cultural and religious," Israeli journalist Yossi Melman observed. "In the worst case scenarios drawn by Israeli analysts, the most feared and dangerous one is that the religious aspect will take over and dominate the conflict, thus turning it into a religious war, which might draw the billions of Muslims around the globe against Israel."‡

Melman has proved prophetic. While there has always been a religious component to the conflict in the Middle East, the conflict was primarily between Israel and the Arab states for at least thirty years, hence the subtitle of this book. Today, however, the Arab-Israeli conflict no longer exists. Israel still has peace treaties with only two Arab states, Egypt and Jordan; however, none of the other states considers themselves at war with Israel. The Gulf States were never a major factor in the conflict, and for a brief period following the Oslo agreement, ties became more formal. Today, those relations are less overt but still exist. Israel's two major Arab antagonists had been Saddam Hussein and the Assad family. Hussein, of course, is gone, and Iraq is too preoccupied with internal issues and threats from its neighbors to pose a threat to Israel. Bashar Assad, meanwhile, is fighting for his regime, and probably his life, in the Syrian civil war. Even before the dissolution of Syria began, Assad and his father, since being routed in the 1973 war, effectively kept the border with Israel quiet. The one border nation that remains a threat to Israel is Lebanon, but danger comes from the Hezbollah terrorists—radical Muslims determined to

---

*President John F. Kennedy, Commencement Address at Yale University (June 11, 1962).

†Daniel Patrick Moynihan, Steven R. Weisman, Ed. *Daniel Patrick Moynihan: A Portrait in Letters of an American Visionary* (PublicAffairs, October 12, 2010), 2.

‡Yossi Melman, "A Price Tag for Jewish Terror," *Jerusalem Report* (May 6, 2013), 18.

annihilate the Jews—who dominate the country rather than the virtually nonexistent government and passive army.

Israel is now threatened almost exclusively by radical Muslims from Gaza, the West Bank, Lebanon and, especially, Iran. These Muslims, as opposed to most living in the Middle East, are not interested in a political agreement; they seek the elimination of the Jewish state.

Meanwhile, Israel's detractors outside the region are engaged in a global campaign to delegitimize Israel with their anti-Semitic boycott, divestment, and sanctions (BDS) campaign. Though often portrayed as a human rights movement to help the Palestinians, it actually shares the radical Muslim objective of destroying Israel.

Even the Palestinian-Israeli dispute, which has typically been referred to as a fight between two peoples over one land, has become a primarily religious conflict. The popularity of Hamas influenced the Islamization of the conflict with the Palestinians. Hamas cast itself as the defender of Muslim land and the group that could liberate Palestine from the Zionist usurpers. Not to be outdone, the supposedly secular PLO leaders now use Islamic themes and rhetoric to inspire and incite the Palestinian population.

Not all Muslims hold extreme views; however, enough believe that a Jewish state cannot exist in the Muslim heartland, and that Jews should never rule over Muslims, to ensure the religious conflict continues whether or not negotiations achieve political agreements.

People often ask me to name the most prevalent myth about the Middle East. The answer is the suggestion, in one form or another, that Israelis do not want peace.

No one craves peace more desperately than Israelis, who have lived through seven wars and an ongoing campaign of terror for more than six decades. Each time a new peace initiative is launched, our hopes are raised that we will not need to publish another edition of *Myths and Facts*, which was first printed more than fifty years ago. In the meantime, old myths continue to be recycled and new calumnies invented. These must not be allowed to go unanswered if we are to progress toward coexistence.

We do not pretend that Israel is perfect. *Myths and Facts* pulls no punches when it comes to addressing Israel's responsibility for events and policies that tarnish its image. We have no desire to whitewash the truth, but context is needed to understand complex policies and events. When friends criticize Israel, it is because they want the country to improve; by contrast, Israel's detractors are only interested in delegitimizing the country, placing a wedge between Israel and its allies, and working toward its destruction.

This book should be treated as an introduction to the issues. We encourage you to study different perspectives to reach your own conclusions. You can find the complete text of this book and much more information in the **Jewish Virtual Library (www.JewishVirtual Library.org)**. We continually update the online edition of *Myths*, archive older facts, and post material we could not fit in the book.

We anticipate offering translations online as well. For now, previous editions are available in Mandarin, Spanish, German, Portuguese, Russian, French, Polish, Swedish, and Hebrew. In addition, we have a listserv for weekly myths/facts and other periodic updates. To sign up, visit the Library.

I would like to acknowledge the contributions of the distinguished group of past editors: Sheila Segal, Wolf Blitzer, Alan Tigay, Moshe Decter, M. J. Rosenberg, Jeff Rubin, Eric Rozenman, Lenny Davis, and Joel Himelfarb. I would also like to thank Rafi Danziger, Rebecca Weiner, Isaac Wolf, David Shyovitz, Alden Oreck, Elihai Braun, Sarah Szymkowicz, Avi Hein, Joanna Sloame, Stephanie Persin, Ariel Scheib, David Krusch, Jonathan Lord, Allison Krant, Yariv Nornberg, Jennifer Feinberg, Elie Berman, Sybil Ottenstein, Stephanie Kogan, Zachary Scheinerman, Brett Boren, and Jason Levine for their invaluable assistance in the AICE editions.

AICE is especially grateful to the sponsors of this edition: Evelyn and Dr. Shmuel Katz from Bal Harbour, Florida, who contributed in loving memory of the AUSCH and KATZ family members O.B.M. H.Y.D. who perished during the Holocaust in Europe. May their greatness be an inspiration to all people of good will.

"Facts are stubborn things," observed John Adams, "and whatever may be our wishes, our inclinations, or the dictates of our passion, they cannot alter the state of facts and evidence."*

The following pages lay out the stubborn facts about the conflict between Israel and the Arab states and radical Islam. Facts are the best weapons we have to ensure that truth triumphs over fiction.

Mitchell G. Bard, PhD
September 2016

---

*John Adams, "Argument in Defense of the Soldiers in Boston Massacre Trial," (December 1770).

1. Israel's Roots

The Jews have no claim to the land they call Israel.

Palestine was always an Arab country.

The Palestinians are descendants of the Canaanites.

The Palestinians have aboriginal rights to Palestine.

The Balfour Declaration did not give Jews a right to a homeland in Palestine.

Arabs in Palestine suffered because of Jewish settlement.

Zionism is racism.

The Zionists could have chosen another country besides Palestine.

The Zionists were colonialist tools of Western imperialism.

The British promised the Arabs independence in Palestine.

MYTH

The Jews have no claim to the land they call Israel.

FACT

A common misperception is that all the Jews were forced into the Diaspora by the Romans after the destruction of the Second Temple in Jerusalem in the year 70 CE, and then, 1,800 years later, the Jews suddenly returned to Palestine demanding their country back. In reality, the Jewish people have maintained ties to their historic homeland for more than 3,700 years.

The Jewish people base their claim to the land of Israel on at least four premises: 1) the Jewish people settled and developed the land, 2) the international community granted political sovereignty in Palestine to the Jewish people, 3) the territory was captured in defensive wars, and 4) God promised the land to the patriarch Abraham.

Even after the destruction of the Second Temple in Jerusalem, and the beginning of the exile, Jewish life in the land of Israel continued and often flourished. Large communities were reestablished in Jerusalem and Tiberias by the ninth century. In the eleventh century, Jewish communities grew in Rafah, Gaza, Ashkelon, Jaffa, and Caesarea. The Crusaders massacred many Jews during the twelfth century, but the community rebounded in the next two centuries as large numbers of rabbis and Jewish pilgrims immigrated to Jerusalem and the Galilee. Prominent rabbis established communities in Safed, Jerusalem, and elsewhere during the following three hundred years.

By the early nineteenth century—years before the birth of the modern Zionist movement—more than ten thousand Jews lived throughout what is today Israel.[1] The seventy-eight years of nation-building, beginning in 1870, culminated in the reestablishment of the Jewish State.

Israel's international "birth certificate" was validated by the promise of the Bible; uninterrupted Jewish settlement from the time of Joshua onward; the Balfour Declaration of 1917; the League of Nations Mandate, which incorporated the Balfour Declaration; the United Nations partition resolution of 1947; Israel's admission to the UN in 1949; the recognition of Israel by most other states; and—most of all—the society created by Israel's people in decades of thriving, dynamic national existence.

Nobody does Israel any service by proclaiming its "right to exist." Israel's right to exist, like that of the United States, Saudi Arabia and 152 other states, is axiomatic and unreserved. Israel's legitimacy is not suspended in midair awaiting acknowledgement... There is certainly no other state, big or small, young or old, that would consider mere recognition of its "right to exist" a favor, or a negotiable concession.

—Abba Eban[2]

MYTH

Palestine was always an Arab country.

FACT

The term "Palestine" is believed to be derived from the Philistines, an Aegean people who, in the twelfth century BCE, settled along the Mediterranean coastal plain—now Israel and the Gaza Strip. In the second century CE, after crushing the last Jewish revolt, the Romans first applied the name *Palaestina* to Judea (the southern portion of what is now called the West Bank) in an attempt to minimize Jewish identification with the land of Israel. The Arabic word *Filastin* is derived from this Latin name.[3]

The Hebrews entered the land of Israel about 1300 BCE, living under a tribal confederation until being united under the first monarch, King Saul. The second king, David, established Jerusalem as the capital around 1000 BCE. David's son, Solomon, built the Temple soon thereafter and consolidated the military, administrative, and religious functions of the kingdom. The nation was divided under Solomon's son, with the northern kingdom (Israel) lasting until 722 BCE, when the Assyrians destroyed it, and the southern kingdom (Judah) surviving until the Babylonian conquest in 586 BCE. The Jewish people enjoyed brief periods of sovereignty afterward until most Jews were finally driven from their homeland in 135 CE.

Jewish independence in the land of Israel lasted for more than four hundred years. This is much longer than Americans have enjoyed independence in what has become known as the United States.[4] In fact, if not for foreign conquerors, Israel would be more than three thousand years old today.

Palestine was never an exclusively Arab country, although Arabic gradually became the language of most of the population after the Muslim invasions of the seventh century. No independent Arab or Palestinian state ever existed in Palestine. When the distinguished Arab-American historian, Princeton University professor Philip Hitti, testified against partition before the Anglo-American Committee in 1946, he said, "There is no such thing as 'Palestine' in history, absolutely not."[5]

Prior to partition, Palestinian Arabs did not view themselves as having a separate identity. When the First Congress of Muslim-Christian Associations met in Jerusalem in February 1919 to choose Palestinian representatives for the Paris Peace Conference, they adopted the following resolution:

> We consider Palestine as part of Arab Syria, as it has never been separated from it at any time. We are connected with it by national, religious, linguistic, natural, economic, and geographical bonds.[6]

Similarly, the King-Crane commission found that Christian and Muslim Arabs opposed any plan to create a country called "Palestine," because it was viewed as recognition of Zionist claims.[7] In 1937, a local Arab leader, Auni Bey Abdul Hadi, told the Peel Commission, which ultimately suggested the partition of Palestine: "There is no such country as Palestine! 'Palestine' is a term the Zionists invented! There is no Palestine in the Bible. Our country was for centuries part of Syria."[8]

The representative of the Arab Higher Committee to the United Nations echoed this view in a statement to the General Assembly in May 1947, which said Palestine was part of the Province of Syria and the Arabs of Palestine did not comprise a separate political entity. A few years later, Ahmed Shuqeiri, later the chairman of the PLO, told the Security Council: "It is common knowledge that Palestine is nothing but southern Syria."[9]

Palestinian Arab nationalism is largely a post–World War I phenomenon that did not become a significant political movement until after the 1967 Six-Day War. Today, the Palestinian people have international recognition and claim the rights to self-determination, independence, and territory. "Urgently required is a peaceful process that respects the dignity of both peoples," wrote Allen Hertz, a former Canadian government official, "and [that] effects a reconciliation of the subsequent rights of the newly emerged Palestinian people with the prior rights of the ancient Jewish people."[10]

MYTH

The Palestinians are descendants of the Canaanites.

FACT

Palestinian claims to be related to the Canaanites are a recent phenomenon and contrary to historical evidence. The Canaanites disappeared three millennia ago, and no one knows if any of their descendants survived or, if they did, who they would be.

Over the last two thousand years, there have been massive invasions (e.g., the Crusades), migrations, the plague, and other manmade or natural disasters that killed off most of the local people. The entire local population has been replaced many times over. During the British Mandate alone, more than one hundred thousand Arabs emigrated from neighboring countries and are today considered Palestinians.

Sherif Hussein, the guardian of the Islamic Holy Places in Arabia, said the Palestinians' ancestors had only been in the area for one thousand years.[11] Even the Palestinians themselves have acknowledged their association with the region came long after the Jews. In testimony before the Anglo-American Committee in 1946, for example, they claimed a connection to Palestine of more than one thousand years, dating back no further than the conquest of Muhammad's followers in the seventh century.[12]

By contrast, no serious historian questions the more than three-thousand-year-old Jewish connection to the land of Israel, or the modern Jewish people's relation to the ancient Hebrews.

We know that some of those who live in our villages are Jews who converted to Islam after the Muslim conquests beginning in the 7th century, and most of us are the descendants of foreign workers who came to British Mandate of Palestine from the various Arab countries in the wake of the Zionist enterprise. By trying to trace our "ancestry" to the Canaanites, we lie to ourselves and demonstrate our silliness and self-deception to the world. And when we try to claim that Jesus was a Palestinian, we make ourselves an international laughing stock.

—Bassam Tawil[13]

MYTH

The Palestinians have aboriginal rights to Palestine.

FACT

The Jews are often depicted by Israel's detractors as newcomers to "Palestine" who are displacing the aboriginal Arab people. The truth is quite different, however, as it is the Jews who are the aboriginal tribe based on their presence in the Holy Land for more than two thousand years. Of all the people who lived in the area at that time, such as Phoenicians, Moabites, Philistines, only the Jews remain today.

The Arabs, however, are not native to "Palestine"; they are aboriginal to Arabia. "Judaism, the Hebrew language, and the Jewish people were established in the Holy Land for about a thousand years" before the emergence of Islam. It is "the Arab people," who are "the interloping settler[s] populating [the Holy Land], including newer waves of Arab immigration in the 19th and 20th centuries."[14]

MYTH

The Balfour Declaration did not give Jews the right to a homeland in Palestine.

FACT

On November 2, 1917, Britain issued the Balfour Declaration:

> His Majesty's Government views with favour the establishment in Palestine of a national home for the Jewish people, and will use their best endeavours to facilitate the achievement of this object, it being clearly understood that nothing shall be done which may prejudice the civil and religious rights of existing non-Jewish communities in Palestine, or the rights and political status enjoyed by Jews in any other country.

Emir Faisal, son of Sherif Hussein, the leader of the Arab revolt against the Turks, signed an agreement with Chaim Weizmann and other Zionist leaders during the 1919 Paris Peace Conference supporting the implementation of Balfour. It acknowledged the "racial kinship and ancient bonds existing between the Arabs and the Jewish people" and concluded that "the surest means of working out the consummation of their national aspirations is through the closest possible collaboration in the development of the Arab states and Palestine." Furthermore, the agreement called for all necessary measures " . . . to encourage and stimulate immigration of Jews into Palestine on a large scale, and as quickly as possible to settle Jewish immigrants upon the land through closer settlement and intensive cultivation of the soil."[15]

Faisal had conditioned his acceptance of the Balfour Declaration on the fulfillment of British wartime promises of independence to the Arabs. These were not kept.

Critics dismiss the Weizmann-Faisal agreement because it was never enacted; however, the fact that the leader of the Arab nationalist movement and the Zionist movement could reach an understanding is significant because it demonstrated that Jewish and Arab aspirations were not necessarily mutually exclusive.

The international community accepted the Balfour Declaration, as evident from its inclusion in the Mandate for Palestine, which specifically referred to "the historical connections of the Jewish people with Palestine" and to the moral validity of "reconstituting their National Home in that country." The term "reconstituting" shows recognition of the fact that Palestine had been the Jews' home. Furthermore, the British were instructed to "use their best endeavours to facilitate" Jewish immigration, to encourage settlement on the land, and to "secure" the Jewish National Home. The word "Arab" does not appear in the Mandatory award.[16]

The Mandate was formalized by the fifty-two governments at the League of Nations on July 24, 1922.

MYTH

Arabs in Palestine suffered because of Jewish settlement.

FACT

For many centuries, Palestine was a sparsely populated, poorly cultivated, and widely neglected expanse of eroded hills, sandy deserts, and malarial marshes. As late as 1880, the American consul in Jerusalem reported the area was continuing its historic decline. "The population and wealth of Palestine has not increased during the last forty years," he said.[17]

The Report of the Palestine Royal Commission quotes an account of the Maritime Plain in 1913:

> The road leading from Gaza to the north was only a summer track suitable for transport by camels and carts . . . no orange groves, orchards or vineyards were to be seen until one reached [the Jewish village of] Yabna [Yavne . . . Houses were all of mud. No windows were anywhere to be seen . . . The ploughs used were of wood . . . The yields were very poor . . . The sanitary conditions in the village were horrible. Schools did not exist . . . The western part, towards the sea, was almost a desert . . . The villages in this area were

few and thinly populated. Many ruins of villages were scattered over the area, as owing to the prevalence of malaria, many villages were deserted by their inhabitants.[18]

Surprisingly, many people who were not sympathetic to the Zionist cause believed the Jews would improve the condition of Palestinian Arabs. For example, Dawood Barakat, editor of the Egyptian paper *Al-Ahram,* wrote: "It is absolutely necessary that an entente be made between the Zionists and Arabs, because the war of words can only do evil. The Zionists are necessary for the country: The money which they will bring, their knowledge and intelligence, and the industriousness which characterizes them will contribute without doubt to the regeneration of the country."[19]

Even a leading Arab nationalist believed the return of the Jews to their homeland would help resuscitate the country. According to Sherif Hussein, the guardian of the Islamic Holy Places in Arabia:

> The resources of the country are still virgin soil and will be developed by the Jewish immigrants. One of the most amazing things until recent times was that the Palestinian used to leave his country, wandering over the high seas in every direction. His native soil could not retain a hold on him, though his ancestors had lived on it for 1000 years. At the same time, we have seen the Jews from foreign countries streaming to Palestine from Russia, Germany, Austria, Spain, [and] America. The cause of causes could not escape those who had a gift of deeper insight. They knew that the country was for its original sons (*abna'ihi-l-asliyin*), for all their differences, a sacred and beloved homeland. The return of these exiles (*jaliya*) to their homeland will prove materially and spiritually [to be] an experimental school for their brethren who are with them in the fields, factories, trades and in all things connected with toil and labor.[20]

As Hussein foresaw, the regeneration of Palestine, and the growth of its population, came only after Jews returned in massive numbers.

A desolate country whose soil is rich enough, but is given over wholly to weeds—a silent mournful expanse . . . A desolation is here that not even imagination can grace with the pomp of life and action . . . We never saw a human being on the whole route . . . There was hardly a tree or a shrub anywhere. Even the olive and the cactus, those fast friends of the worthless soil, had almost deserted the country.

—Mark Twain's description of Palestine in 1867[21]

MYTH

Zionism is racism.

FACT

In 1975, the UN General Assembly adopted a resolution slandering Zionism by equating it with racism. Zionism is the national liberation movement of the Jewish people, which holds that Jews, like any other nation, are entitled to self-determination in their homeland—Israel.

Zionism recognizes that Jewishness is defined by shared origin, religion, culture, and history. The realization of the Zionist dream is exemplified by more than six million Jews, from more than one hundred countries, who are Israeli citizens.

Israel's Law of Return grants automatic citizenship to Jews, but non-Jews are also eligible to become citizens under naturalization procedures similar to those in other countries. For example, Germany, Greece, Ireland, and Finland have special categories of people who are entitled to citizenship.

More than one million Muslim and Christian Arabs, Druze, Baha'is, Circassians, and other ethnic groups also are represented in Israel's population. The presence in Israel of thousands of Jews "of color" from Ethiopia, Yemen, and India is the best refutation of the calumny against Zionism.

Zionism does not discriminate against anyone. Israel's open and democratic character, and its scrupulous protection of the religious and political rights of Christians and Muslims, rebuts the charge of exclusivity. Moreover, anyone—Jew or non-Jew, Israeli, American, Chinese, black, white, or purple—can be a Zionist.

By contrast, the Arab states define citizenship strictly by native parentage. It is almost impossible to become a naturalized citizen in Arab states such as Algeria, Saudi Arabia, and Kuwait. Several Arab nations have laws that facilitate the naturalization of foreign Arabs, with the specific exception of Palestinians. Jordan, on the other hand, instituted its own "law of return" in 1954, according citizenship to all former residents of Palestine, *except for Jews* and Gazans.[22] In 2004, however, Jordan began revoking the citizenship of Palestinians who lacked Israeli permits to reside in the West Bank.[23]

The 1975 UN resolution was part of the Soviet-Arab Cold War anti-Israel campaign. Almost all the former non-Arab supporters of the resolution have apologized and changed their positions. When the General Assembly voted to repeal the resolution in 1991, only some Arab and Muslim states, as well as Cuba, North Korea, and Vietnam were opposed.

For the first time in history, thousands of black people are being brought to a country not in chains but in dignity, not as slaves but as citizens.

—William Safire writing after "Operation Moses" rescued black Jews from Ethiopia[24]

MYTH

The Zionists could have chosen another country besides Palestine.

FACT

In the late nineteenth century, the rise of anti-Semitism led to a resurgence of pogroms in Russia and Eastern Europe, shattering promises of equality and tolerance. This stimulated Jewish immigration to Palestine from Europe.

Simultaneously, a wave of Jews immigrated to Palestine from Yemen, Morocco, Iraq, and Turkey. These Jews were unaware of Theodor Herzl's political Zionism or of European pogroms. They were motivated by the centuries-old dream of the "Return to Zion" and a fear of intolerance. Upon hearing that the gates of Palestine were open, they braved the hardships of travel and went to the land of Israel.

The Zionist ideal of a return to Israel has profound religious roots. Many Jewish prayers speak of Jerusalem, Zion, and the land of Israel. The injunction not to forget Jerusalem, the site of the Temple, is a major tenet of Judaism. The Hebrew language, the Torah, laws in the Talmud, the Jewish calendar, and Jewish holidays and festivals all originated in Israel and revolve around its seasons and conditions. Jews pray toward Jerusalem and every Passover recite the words "next year in Jerusalem." Jewish religion, culture, and history make clear that it is only in the land of Israel that the Jewish commonwealth can be built.

In 1897, Jewish leaders formally organized the Zionist political movement, calling for the restoration of the Jewish national home in Palestine, where Jews could find sanctuary and self-determination, and work for the renascence of their civilization and culture.

Due to the urgency of the plight of Jews in Russia, at the Sixth Zionist Congress at Basel on August 26, 1903, Herzl proposed the creation of a Jewish state in Uganda as a *temporary emergency refuge*. While Herzl made it clear that this program would not affect the ultimate aim of Zionism, a Jewish entity in the land of Israel, the proposal aroused a storm of protest at the congress and nearly led to a split in the Zionist movement. The Uganda Program, which never had much support, was formally rejected by the Zionist movement at the Seventh Zionist Congress in 1905.

Our settlers do not come here as do the colonists from the Occident to have natives do their work for them; they themselves set their shoulders to the plow and they spend their strength and their blood to make the land fruitful. But it is not only for ourselves that we desire its fertility. The Jewish farmers have begun to teach their brothers, the Arab farmers, to cultivate the land more intensively; we desire to teach them further: together with them we want to cultivate the land—to "serve" it, as the Hebrew has it. The more fertile this soil becomes, the more space there will be for us and for them. We have no desire to dispossess them: we want to live with them.

—**Martin Buber**[25]

MYTH

The Zionists were colonialist tools of Western imperialism.

FACT

"Colonialism means living by exploiting others," Yehoshafat Harkabi has written. "But what could be further from colonialism than the idealism of city-dwelling Jews who strive to become farmers and laborers and to live by their own work?"[26]

Moreover, as British historian Paul Johnson noted, Zionists were hardly tools of imperialists given the powers' general opposition to their cause. "Everywhere in the West, the foreign offices, defense ministries and big business were against the Zionists."[27]

Emir Faisal saw the Zionist movement as a companion to the Arab nationalist movement, fighting against imperialism, as he explained in a letter to Harvard law professor and future Supreme Court Justice Felix Frankfurter on March 3, 1919, one day after Chaim Weizmann presented the Zionist case to the Paris conference. Faisal wrote:

> The Arabs, especially the educated among us, look with deepest sympathy on the Zionist movement . . . We will wish the Jews a hearty welcome home . . . We are working together for a reformed and revised Near East and our two movements complete one another. *The Jewish movement is nationalist and not imperialist.* And there is room in Syria for us both. Indeed, I think that neither can be a real success without the other (emphasis added).[28]

In the 1940s, the Jewish underground movements waged an *anticolonial* war against the British. The Arabs, meanwhile, were concerned primarily with fighting the Jews rather than expelling the British imperialists.

MYTH

The British promised the Arabs independence in Palestine.

FACT

The central figure in the Arab nationalist movement at the time of World War I was Hussein ibn 'Ali, the Sherif of Mecca in 1908. As Sherif, Hussein was responsible for the custody of Islam's shrines in the Hejaz and was one of the Muslims' spiritual leaders.

In July 1915, Hussein sent a letter to Sir Henry MacMahon, the High Commissioner for Egypt, informing him of the terms for Arab participation in the war against the Turks. The letters between Hussein and MacMahon that followed outlined the areas that Britain was prepared to cede to the Arabs in exchange for their help.

The Hussein-MacMahon correspondence conspicuously fails to mention Palestine. The British argued the omission had been intentional, thereby justifying their refusal to grant the Arabs independence in Palestine after the war.[29] MacMahon explained:

> I feel it my duty to state, and I do so definitely and emphatically, that it was not intended by me in giving this pledge to King Hussein to include Palestine in the area in which Arab independence was promised. I also had every reason to believe at the time that the fact that Palestine was not included in my pledge was well understood by King Hussein.[30]

Notes, Chapter 1

1. Dan Bahat, ed., *Twenty Centuries of Jewish Life in the Holy Land* (Jerusalem: The Israel Economist, 1976), 61–63.
2. Abba Eban, "The Saudi Text," *New York Times* (November 18, 1981).
3. Yehoshua Porath, *The Emergence of the Palestinian-Arab National Movement, 1918-1929* (London: Frank Cass, 1974), 4.
4. Max Dimont, *Jews, God, and History* (NY: Signet, 1962), 49–53.
5. Moshe Kohn, "The Arabs' 'Lie' of the Land," *Jerusalem Post* (October 18, 1991).
6. Randall Price, *Fast Facts on the Middle East Conflict* (Harvest House Publishers: 2003), 25.
7. Allen Z. Hertz, "Aboriginal Rights of the Jewish People," *American Thinker* (October 30, 2011).
8. Moshe Kohn, "The Arabs' 'Lie' of the Land," *Jerusalem Post* (October 18, 1991).
9. Avner Yaniv, *PLO* (Jerusalem: Israel Universities Study Group of Middle Eastern Affairs, August 1974), 5.
10. Allen Z. Hertz, "Aboriginal Rights of the Jewish People," *American Thinker* (October 30, 2011).
11. *Al-Qibla* (March 23, 1918), quoted in Samuel Katz, *Battleground-Fact and Fantasy in Palestine* (NY: Bantam Books, 1977), 126.
12. British Government, "Report of the Anglo-American Committee of Enquiry, 1946, Part VI" (April 20, 1946).
13. Bassam Tawil, "Muslim Blood and Al-Aqsa," Gatestone Institute (October 31, 2015).

14. Allen Z. Hertz, "Aboriginal Rights of the Jewish People," American Thinker (October 30, 2011).

15. Howard Sachar, *A History of Israel: From the Rise of Zionism to Our Time* (NY: Alfred A. Knopf, 1979), 129.

16. Ben Halpern, *The Idea of a Jewish State* (MA: Harvard University Press, 1969), 108.

17. Melvin Urofsky, *American Zionism from Herzl to the Holocaust* (Bison Books: 1995), 29.

18. Palestine Royal Commission Report, 233.

19. Neville Mandel, *The Arabs and Zionism before World War I* (University of California Press: 1976), 8.

20. *Al-Qibla* (March 23, 1918), quoted in Samuel Katz, *Battleground: Fact and Fantasy in Palestine* (NY: Bantam Books, 1977), 126.

21. Mark Twain, *The Innocents Abroad* (London, 1881).

22. Jordanian Nationality Law, Article 3(2) of Law No. 6 of 1954, Official Gazette, No. 1171, January 1, 1954.

23. Michael Slackman, "Some Palestinian Jordanians Lose Citizenship," *New York Times* (March 13, 2010).

24. William Safire, "Interrupted Exodus," *The New York Times* (January 7, 1985).

25. From an open letter from Martin Buber to Mahatma Gandhi in 1939, accessed at GandhiServe.com.

26. Yehoshafat Harkabi, *Palestinians and Israel* (Jerusalem: Keter, 1974), 6.

27. Paul Johnson, *Modern Times: The World from the Twenties to the Nineties* (NY: Harper & Row, 1983), 485.

28. Naomi Comay, *Arabs Speak Frankly on the Arab-Israeli Conflict* (Printing Miracle Ltd., 2005), 8.

29. George Kirk, *A Short History of the Middle East* (NY: Frederick Praeger Publishers, 1964), 314.

30. "Report of a Committee Setup to Consider Certain Correspondence between Sir Henry McMahon and the Sharif of Mecca in 1915/1916," UK Parliament (March 16, 1939).

2. The British Mandate Period

The British helped the Jews displace the native Arab population
   of Palestine.

The British allowed Jews to flood Palestine while Arab immigration was
   tightly controlled.

The British changed their policy after World War II to allow Holocaust
   survivors to settle in Palestine.

As the Jewish population in Palestine grew, the plight of the Palestinian
   Arabs worsened.

Jews stole Arab land.

The British helped the Palestinians to live peacefully with the Jews.

The Mufti was not anti-Semitic.

The bombing of the King David Hotel was part of a deliberate terror
   campaign against civilians.

MYTH

*The British helped the Jews displace the
native Arab population of Palestine.*

FACT

Herbert Samuel, a British Jew who served as the first High Commissioner of Palestine, placed restrictions on Jewish immigration "in the 'interests of the present population' and the 'absorptive capacity' of the country."[1] The influx of Jewish settlers was said to be forcing the Arab fellahin (native peasants) from their land. This was at a time when less than a million people lived in an area that now supports more than nine million.

The British actually limited the absorptive capacity of Palestine when, in 1921, Colonial Secretary Winston Churchill severed nearly four-fifths of Palestine—some thirty-five thousand square miles—to create a brand new Arab entity, Transjordan. As a consolation prize for the Hejaz and Arabia (which are both now Saudi Arabia) going to the Saud family, Churchill rewarded Sherif Hussein's son Abdullah for his contribution to the war against Turkey by installing him as Transjordan's emir.

The British went further and placed restrictions on Jewish land purchases in what remained of Palestine, contradicting the provision of the Mandate (Article 6) stating that "the Administration of Palestine . . . shall encourage, in cooperation with the Jewish Agency . . .

Map 1 — Great Britain's Division of the Mandated Area, 1921–1923

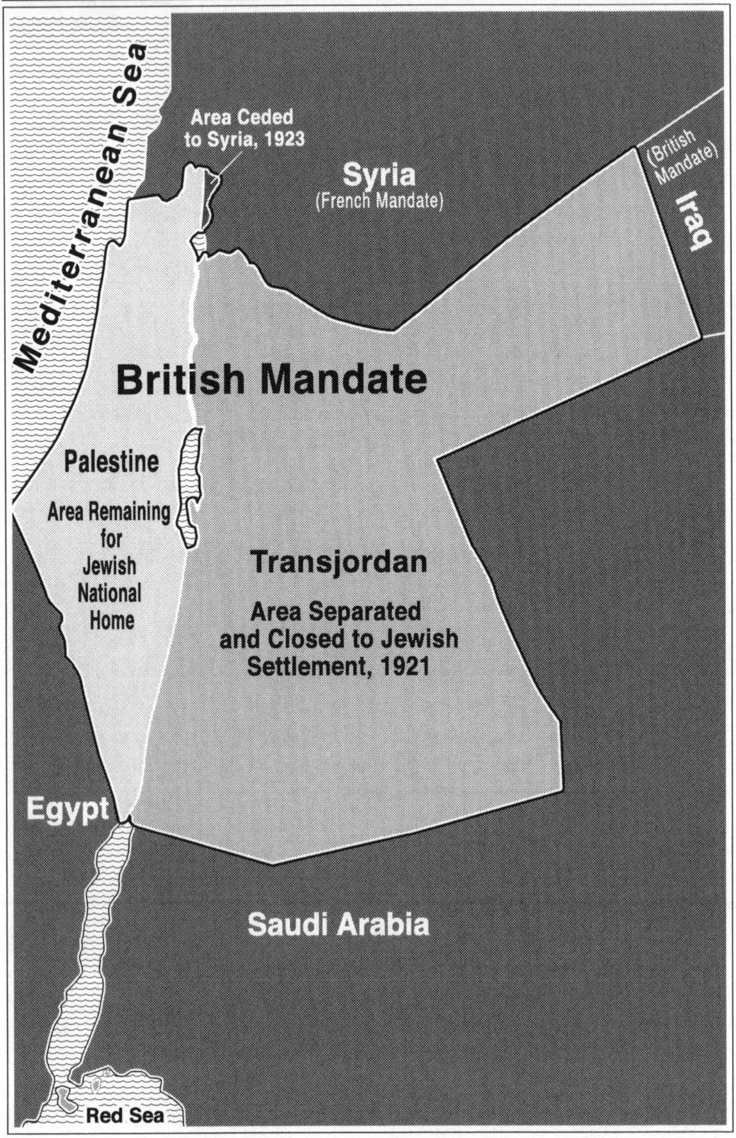

Mediterranean Sea

Area Ceded to Syria, 1923

Syria (French Mandate)

Iraq (British Mandate)

British Mandate

Palestine

Area Remaining for Jewish National Home

Transjordan

Area Separated and Closed to Jewish Settlement, 1921

Egypt

Saudi Arabia

Red Sea

close settlement by Jews on the land, including State lands and waste lands not acquired for public purposes." By 1949, the British had allotted 87,500 acres of the 187,500 acres of cultivable land to Arabs and only 4,250 acres (2 percent) to Jews.[2]

Ultimately, the British admitted that the argument about the absorptive capacity of the country was specious. The Peel Commission said, "The heavy immigration in the years 1933–36 would seem to show that the Jews have been able to enlarge the absorptive capacity of the country for Jews."[3]

MYTH

The British allowed Jews to flood Palestine while Arab immigration was tightly controlled.

FACT

The British response to Jewish immigration set a precedent of appeasing the Arabs, which was followed for the duration of the Mandate. The British placed restrictions on Jewish immigration while allowing Arabs to enter the country freely. Apparently, London did not feel that a flood of Arab immigrants would affect the country's "absorptive capacity."

During World War I, the Jewish population in Palestine declined because of the war, famine, disease, and expulsion by the Turks. In 1915, approximately 83,000 Jews lived in Palestine among 590,000 Muslim and Christian Arabs. According to the 1922 census, the Jewish population was 84,000, while the Arabs numbered 643,000.[4] Thus, the Arab population grew exponentially while that of the Jews stagnated.

In the mid-1920s, Jewish immigration to Palestine increased primarily because of anti-Jewish economic legislation in Poland and Washington's imposition of restrictive quotas.[5]

The record number of immigrants in 1935 (see table) was a response to the growing persecution of Jews in Nazi Germany. The British administration considered this number too large, however, so the Jewish Agency was informed that less than one-third of the quota it asked for would be approved in 1936.[6]

The British gave in further to Arab demands by announcing in the 1939 White Paper that an independent Arab state would be created within ten years, and that Jewish immigration was to be limited to seventy-five thousand for the next five years, after which it was to cease altogether. It also forbade land sales to Jews in 95 percent of the territory of Palestine. The Arabs, nevertheless, rejected the proposal.

Jewish Immigrants to Palestine[7]

1919	1,806	1931	4,075
1920	8,223	1932	12,533
1921	8,294	1933	37,337
1922	8,685	1934	45,267
1923	8,175	1935	66,472
1924	13,892	1936	29,595
1925	34,386	1937	10,629
1926	13,855	1938	14,675
1927	3,034	1939	31,195
1928	2,178	1940	10,643
1929	5,249	1941	4,592
1930	4,944		

By contrast, throughout the Mandatory period, Arab immigration was unrestricted. In 1930, the Hope Simpson Commission, sent from London to investigate the 1929 Arab riots, said the British practice of ignoring the uncontrolled illegal Arab immigration from Egypt, Transjordan, and Syria had the effect of displacing the prospective *Jewish* immigrants.[8]

The British governor of the Sinai from 1922 to 1936 observed, "This illegal immigration was not only going on from the Sinai, but also from Transjordan and Syria, and it is very difficult to make a case out for the misery of the Arabs if at the same time their compatriots from adjoining states could not be kept from going in to share that misery."[9]

The Peel Commission reported in 1937 that the "shortfall of land is . . . due less to the amount of land acquired by Jews than to the increase in the Arab population."[10]

MYTH

The British changed their policy after World War II to allow Holocaust survivors to settle in Palestine.

FACT

The gates of Palestine remained closed for the duration of the war, stranding hundreds of thousands of Jews in Europe, many of whom became victims of Hitler's "Final Solution." After the war, the British refused to allow the survivors of the Nazi nightmare to find sanctuary in Palestine. On June 6, 1946, President Truman urged the British gov-

Map 2

The Balfour Declaration
Britain's Promise to the Jews

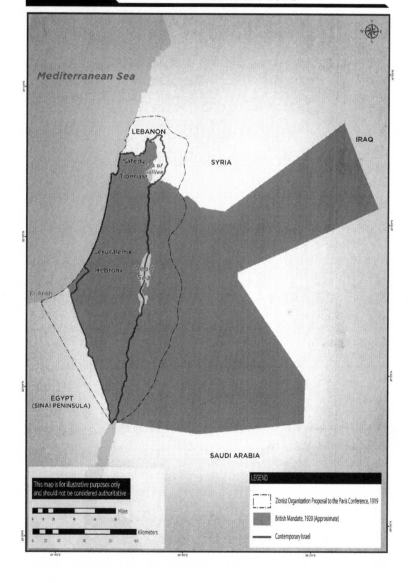

Mediterranean Sea

LEBANON

IRAQ

Safed

Sea of Galilee

SYRIA

Tiberias

Jerusalem★

Hebron★

Dead Sea

El-Arish

EGYPT
(SINAI PENINSULA)

SAUDI ARABIA

This map is for illustrative purposes only
and should not be considered authoritative

Miles

Kilometers

LEGEND

Zionist Organization Proposal to the Paris Conference, 1919

British Mandate, 1920 (Approximate)

Contemporary Israel

ernment to relieve the suffering of the Jews confined to displaced persons camps in Europe by immediately accepting a hundred thousand Jewish immigrants. Britain's foreign minister Ernest Bevin replied sarcastically that the United States wanted displaced Jews to immigrate to Palestine "because they did not want too many of them in New York."[11]

Some Jews reached Palestine, many smuggled in on dilapidated ships organized by the Haganah. Between August 1945 and the establishment of the State of Israel in May 1948, sixty-five "illegal" immigrant ships, carrying 69,878 people, arrived from European shores. In August 1946, however, the British began to intern those they caught in camps on Cyprus. Approximately fifty thousand people were detained in the camps, twenty-eight thousand of whom were still imprisoned when Israel declared independence.[12]

MYTH

As the Jewish population in Palestine grew, the plight of the Palestinian Arabs worsened.

FACT

In July 1921, Hasan Shukri, the mayor of Haifa and president of the Muslim National Associations, sent a telegram to the British government in reaction to a delegation of Palestinians that went to London to try to stop the implementation of the Balfour Declaration. Shukri wrote:

> We are certain that without Jewish immigration and financial assistance there will be no future development of our country as may be judged from the fact that the towns inhabited in part by Jews such as Jerusalem, Jaffa, Haifa, and Tiberias are making steady progress while Nablus, Acre, and Nazareth where no Jews reside are steadily declining.[13]

The Jewish population increased by 470,000 between World War I and World War II, while the non-Jewish population rose by 588,000.[14] In fact, the permanent Arab population increased 120 percent between 1922 and 1947.[15]

This rapid growth of the Arab population was a result of several factors. One was immigration from neighboring states—constituting 37 percent of the total immigration to prestate Israel—by Arabs who wanted to take advantage of the higher standard of living the Jews had made possible.[16] The Arab population also grew because of the improved living conditions created by the Jews as they drained malarial swamps and brought improved sanitation and health care to the region. Thus, for example, the Muslim infant mortality rate fell from 201 per thousand in 1925 to ninety-four per thousand in 1945, and life expectancy rose from thirty-seven years in 1926 to forty-nine in 1943.[17]

The Arab population increased the most in cities where large Jewish populations had created new economic opportunities. From 1922–1947, the non-Jewish population increased 290 percent in Haifa, 131 percent in Jerusalem, and 158 percent in Jaffa. The growth in Arab towns was more modest: 42 percent in Nablus, 78 percent in Jenin, and 37 percent in Bethlehem.[18]

MYTH

Jews stole Arab land.

FACT

Despite the growth in their population, the Arabs continued to assert they were being displaced. From the beginning of World War I, however, part of Palestine's land was owned by absentee landlords who lived in Cairo, Damascus, and Beirut. About 80 percent of the Palestinian Arabs were debt-ridden peasants, seminomads, and Bedouins.[19]

Jews actually went out of their way to avoid purchasing land in areas where Arabs might be displaced. They sought land that was largely uncultivated, swampy, cheap, and—most important—without tenants. In 1920, Labor Zionist leader David Ben-Gurion expressed his concern about the Arab *fellahin,* whom he viewed as "the most important asset of the native population." Ben-Gurion said "under no circumstances must we touch land belonging to *fellahs* or worked by them." He advocated helping liberate them from their oppressors. "Only if a *fellah* leaves his place of settlement," Ben-Gurion added, "should we offer to buy his land, at an appropriate price."[20]

It was only after the Jews had bought all of the available uncultivated land that they began to purchase cultivated land. Many Arabs were willing to sell because of the migration to coastal towns and because they needed money to invest in the citrus industry.[21]

When John Hope Simpson arrived in Palestine in May 1930, he observed, "They [the Jews] paid high prices for the land and, in addition, they paid to certain of the occupants of those lands a considerable amount of money which they were not legally bound to pay."[22]

In 1931, Lewis French conducted a survey of landlessness for the British government and offered new plots to any Arabs who had been "dispossessed." British officials received more than three thousand applications, of which 80 percent were ruled invalid by the government's legal adviser because the applicants were not landless Arabs. This left only about six hundred landless Arabs, one hundred of whom accepted the government land offer.[23]

In April 1936, a new outbreak of Arab attacks on Jews was instigated by local Palestinian leaders who were later joined by Arab volunteers led by a Syrian guerrilla named Fawzi al-Qawukji, the commander of the Arab Liberation Army. By November, when the British finally sent a new commission headed by Lord Peel to investigate, eighty-nine Jews had been killed and more than three hundred wounded.[24]

The Peel Commission's report found that Arab complaints about Jewish land acquisition were baseless. It pointed out that "much of the land now carrying orange groves was sand dunes or swamp and uncultivated when it was purchased . . . [T]here was at the time of the earlier sales little evidence that the owners possessed either the resources or training needed to develop the land."[25] Moreover, the Commission found the shortage was "due less to the amount of land acquired by Jews than to the increase in the Arab population." The report concluded that the presence of Jews in Palestine, along with the work of the British administration, had resulted in higher wages, an improved standard of living, and ample employment opportunities.[26]

> *It is made quite clear to all, both by the map drawn up by the Simpson Commission and by another compiled by the Peel Commission, that the Arabs are as prodigal in selling their land as they are in useless wailing and weeping (emphasis in the original).*
>
> **—Transjordan's King Abdullah**[27]

Even at the height of the Arab revolt in 1938 (which began in April 1936 with the murder of two Jews by Arabs and the subsequent murder of two Arab workers by members of the Jewish underground[28]), the British high commissioner to Palestine believed the Arab landowners were complaining about sales to Jews to drive up prices for lands they wished to sell. Many Arab landowners had been so terrorized by Arab rebels they decided to leave Palestine and sell their property to the Jews.[29]

The Jews were paying exorbitant prices to wealthy landowners for small tracts of arid land. "In 1944, Jews paid between $1,000 and $1,100 per acre in Palestine, mostly for arid or semiarid land; in the same year, rich black soil in Iowa was selling for about $110 per acre."[30]

By 1947, Jewish holdings in Palestine amounted to about 463,000 acres. Approximately forty-five thousand of these acres were acquired from the mandatory government, thirty thousand were bought from various churches, and 387,500 were purchased from Arabs. Analyses of land purchases from 1880 to 1948 show that 73 percent of Jewish plots were purchased from large landowners, not poor *fellahin*.[31] Those who sold land included the mayors of Gaza, Jerusalem, and

Jaffa. As'ad el-Shuqeiri, a Muslim religious scholar and father of Palestine Liberation Organization chairman Ahmed Shuqeiri, took Jewish money for his land. Even King Abdullah leased land to the Jews. In fact, many leaders of the Arab nationalist movement, including members of the Muslim Supreme Council, sold land to Jews. [32]

MYTH

The British helped the Palestinians to live peacefully with the Jews.

FACT

In 1921, Haj Amin el-Husseini first began to organize *fedayeen* ("one who sacrifices himself") to terrorize Jews. Haj Amin hoped to duplicate the success of Kemal Atatürk in Turkey by driving the Jews out of Palestine just as Kemal had driven the invading Greeks from his country.[33] Arab radicals were able to gain influence because the British administration was unwilling to take effective action against them until they began a revolt against British rule.

Colonel Richard Meinertzhagen, former head of British military intelligence in Cairo, and later chief political officer for Palestine and Syria, wrote in his diary that British officials "incline towards the exclusion of Zionism in Palestine." In fact, the British encouraged the Palestinians to attack the Jews. According to Meinertzhagen, Col. Bertie Harry Waters-Taylor (financial adviser to the military administration in Palestine 1919–23) met with Haj Amin a few days before Easter, in 1920, and told him that "he had a great opportunity at Easter to show the world . . . that Zionism was unpopular not only with the Palestine administration but in Whitehall." He added that "if disturbances of sufficient violence occurred in Jerusalem at Easter, both General [Louis] Bols [chief administrator in Palestine, 1919–20] and General [Edmund] Allenby [commander of the Egyptian force, 1917–19, then high commissioner of Egypt] would advocate the abandonment of the Jewish Home. Waters-Taylor explained that freedom could only be attained through violence."[34]

Haj Amin took the colonel's advice and instigated a riot. The British withdrew their troops and the Jewish police from Jerusalem, allowing the Arab mob to attack Jews and loot their shops. Because of Haj Amin's overt role in instigating the pogrom, the British decided to arrest him. Haj Amin escaped, however, and was sentenced to ten years imprisonment in absentia.

A year later, some British Arabists convinced High Commissioner Herbert Samuel to pardon Haj Amin and to appoint him Mufti (a cleric in charge of Jerusalem's Islamic holy places). By contrast, Vladimir

Jabotinsky and several of his followers, who had formed a Jewish defense organization during the unrest, were sentenced to fifteen years' imprisonment but released a few months later.[35]

Samuel met with Haj Amin on April 11, 1921, and was assured "that the influences of his family and himself would be devoted to tranquility." Three weeks later, riots in Jaffa and elsewhere left forty-three Jews dead.[36]

Haj Amin consolidated his power and took control of all Muslim religious funds in Palestine. He used his authority to gain control over the mosques, the schools, and the courts. No Arab could reach an influential position without being loyal to the Mufti. His power was so absolute "no Muslim in Palestine could be born or die without being beholden to Haj Amin."[37] The Mufti's henchmen also ensured he would have no opposition by systematically killing Palestinians from rival clans who were discussing cooperation with the Jews.

As the spokesman for Palestinian Arabs, Haj Amin did not ask that Britain grant them independence. On the contrary, in a letter to Churchill in 1921, he demanded that Palestine be reunited with Syria and Transjordan.[38]

The Arabs found rioting to be an effective political tool because of the lax British response toward violence against Jews. In handling each riot, the British prevented Jews from protecting themselves, but made little or no effort to prevent the Arabs from attacking them. After each outbreak, a British commission of inquiry would try to establish the cause of the violence. The conclusion was always the same: The Arabs were afraid of being displaced by Jews. To stop the rioting, the commissions would recommend that restrictions be placed on Jewish immigration. Thus, the Arabs came to recognize that they could always stop the influx of Jews by staging a riot.

This cycle began after a series of riots in May 1921. After failing to protect the Jewish community from Arab mobs, the British appointed the Haycraft Commission to investigate the cause of the violence. Although the panel concluded the Arabs had been the aggressors, it rationalized the cause of the attack: "The fundamental cause of the riots was a feeling among the Arabs of discontent with, and hostility to, the Jews, due to political and economic causes, and connected with Jewish immigration, and with their conception of Zionist policy."[39] One consequence of the violence was the institution of a temporary ban on Jewish immigration.

The Arab fear of being "displaced" or "dominated" was used as an excuse for their merciless attacks on peaceful Jewish settlers. Note, too, that these riots were not inspired by nationalistic fervor—nationalists would have rebelled against their British overlords—they were motivated by racial strife, the radical Islamic views of the Mufti, and misunderstanding.

In 1929, Arab provocateurs succeeded in convincing the masses that the Jews had designs on the Temple Mount (a tactic still used today). A Jewish religious observance at the Western Wall, which forms a part of the Temple Mount, served as a pretext for rioting by Arabs against Jews, which spilled out of Jerusalem into other villages and towns, including Safed and Hebron.

Again, the British administration made no effort to prevent the violence and, after it began, the British did nothing to protect the Jewish population. After six days of mayhem, the British finally brought troops in to quell the disturbance. By this time, virtually the entire Jewish population of Hebron had fled or been killed. In all, 133 Jews were killed and 399 wounded in the pogroms.[40]

After the riots were over, the British ordered an investigation, which resulted in the Passfield White Paper. It said the "immigration, land purchase and settlement policies of the Zionist Organization were already, or were likely to become, prejudicial to Arab interests. It understood the mandatory government's obligation to the non-Jewish community to mean that Palestine's resources must be primarily reserved for the growing Arab economy."[41] This meant it was necessary to place restrictions on Jewish immigration and land purchases.

MYTH

The Mufti was not anti-Semitic.

FACT

In 1941, Haj Amin al-Husseini, the Mufti of Jerusalem, fled to Germany and met with Adolf Hitler, Heinrich Himmler, Joachim Von Ribbentrop, and other Nazi leaders. He wanted to persuade them to extend the Nazis' anti-Jewish program to the Arab world.

The Mufti sent Hitler fifteen drafts of declarations he wanted Germany and Italy to make concerning the Middle East. One called on the two countries to declare the illegality of the Jewish home in Palestine. He also asked the Axis powers to "accord to Palestine and to other Arab countries the right to solve the problem of the Jewish elements in Palestine and other Arab countries in accordance with the interest of the Arabs, and by the same method that the question is now being settled in the Axis countries."[42]

In November 1941, the Mufti met with Hitler, who told him the Jews were his foremost enemy. The Nazi dictator rebuffed the Mufti's requests for a declaration in support of the Arabs, however, telling him the time was not right. The Mufti offered Hitler his "thanks for the sympathy which he had always shown for the Arab and especially Palestinian cause, and to which he had given clear expression in his public speeches . . . The Arabs were Germany's natural friends because they had the same enemies as had Germany, namely . . . the Jews." Hitler told the Mufti he opposed the creation of a Jewish state and that Germany's objective was the destruction of the Jewish element residing in the Arab sphere.[43]

In 1945, Yugoslavia sought to indict the Mufti as a war criminal for his role in recruiting twenty thousand Muslim volunteers for the SS, who participated in the killing of Jews in Croatia and Hungary. He escaped from French detention in 1946, however, and continued his fight against the Jews from Cairo and later Beirut where he died in 1974.

MYTH

The bombing of the King David Hotel was part of a deliberate terror campaign against civilians.

FACT

British troops seized the Jewish Agency compound on June 29, 1946, and confiscated large quantities of documents. At about the same time, more than twenty-five hundred Jews from all over Palestine were placed under arrest. A week later, news of a massacre of forty Jews in a pogrom in Poland reminded the Jews of Palestine how Britain's restrictive immigration policy had condemned thousands to death.

As a response to what it viewed as British provocations, and a desire to demonstrate that the Jews' spirit could not be broken, the United Resistance Movement planned to target the King David Hotel, which housed the British military command and the Criminal Investigation Division in addition to hotel guests. The Haganah pulled out of the plot and left it to the Irgun to carry out the action.

Irgun leader Menachem Begin stressed his desire to avoid civilian casualties and the plan was to warn the British so they would evacuate the building before it was blown up. Three telephone calls were placed on July 22, 1946, one to the hotel, another to the French Consulate, and a third to the *Palestine Post,* warning that explosives in the King David Hotel would soon be detonated.

The call into the hotel was apparently received and ignored. Begin quotes one British official who supposedly refused to evacuate the building, saying, "We don't take orders from the Jews."[44] As a result, when the bombs exploded, the casualty toll was high: a total of ninety-one killed and forty-five injured. Among the casualties were fifteen Jews. Few people in the hotel proper were injured by the blast.[45]

For decades, the British denied they had been warned. In 1979, however, a member of the British Parliament introduced evidence that the Irgun had indeed issued the warning. He offered the testimony of a British officer who heard other officers in the King David Hotel bar joking about a Zionist threat to the headquarters. The officer who overheard the conversation immediately left the hotel and survived.[46]

In contrast to Arab attacks against Jews, which were widely hailed by Arab leaders as heroic actions, the Jewish National Council denounced the bombing of the King David.[47]

Notes, Chapter 2

1. Aharon Cohen, *Israel and the Arab World* (NY: Funk and Wagnalls, 1970), 172; Howard Sachar, *A History of Israel: From the Rise of Zionism to Our Time* (NY: Alfred A. Knopf, 1979), 146.
2. Moshe Aumann, "Land Ownership in Palestine 1880-1948," in Michael Curtis, et al., *The Palestinians* (New Brunswick, NJ: Transaction Books, 1975), 25.
3. *Palestine Royal Commission Report* (the Peel Report), (London: 1937), 300. Henceforth, Palestine Royal Commission Report.
4. Arieh Avneri, *The Claim of Dispossession* (Tel Aviv: Hidekel Press, 1984), 28; Yehoshua Porath, *The Emergence of the Palestinian-Arab National Movement, 1918-1929* (London: Frank Cass, 1974), 17-18.
5. Porath (1974), 18.
6. Aharon Cohen, 53.
7. Yehoshua Porath, *Palestinian Arab National Movement, 1929-1939: From Riots to Rebellion*, vol. 2 (London: Frank Cass and Co., Ltd., 1977), 17-18, 39.
8. John Hope Simpson, *Palestine: Report on Immigration, Land Settlement and Development*, (London, 1930), 126.
9. C. S. Jarvis, "Palestine," *United Empire* (London), vol. 28 (1937), 633.
10. *Palestine Royal Commission Report*, 242.
11. George Lenczowski, *American Presidents and the Middle East* (NC: Duke University Press, 1990), 23.
12. Aharon Cohen, 174.
13. Hillel Cohen, *Army of Shadows* (Berkeley: University of California Press, 2008), 15.
14. Dov Friedlander and Calvin Goldscheider, *The Population of Israel* (NY: Columbia Press, 1979), 30.
15. Avneri, 254.
16. Curtis, 38.
17. Avneri, 264; Aharon Cohen, 60.
18. Avneri, 254-55.
19. Aumann, 8-9.
20. Shabtai Teveth, *Ben-Gurion and the Palestinian Arabs: From Peace to War* (London: Oxford University Press, 1985), 32.
21. Porath, 80, 84; See also Hillel Cohen, *Army of Shadows: Palestinian Collaboration with Zionism, 1917-1948* (Berkeley: University of California Press, 2008).
22. Hope Simpson Report, 51.
23. Avneri, 149-158; Aharon Cohen, 37; based on the Report on Agricultural Development and Land Settlement in Palestine by Lewis French (December 1931, Supplementary; Report, April 1932) and material submitted to the Palestine Royal Commission.
24. Netanel Lorch, *One Long War* (Jerusalem: Keter, 1976), 27; Sachar, 201.
25. *Palestine Royal Commission Report* (1937), 242.
26. *Palestine Royal Commission* (1937), 241-42.
27. King Abdallah, *My Memoirs Completed* (London, Longman Group, Ltd., 1978), 88-89.
28. Porath (77), 86-87.
29. Hillel Cohen, 95.
30. Aumann, 13.

31. Abraham Granott, *The Land System in Palestine,* (London: Eyre and Spottiswoode, 1952), 278.

32. Avneri, 179-180, 224-25, 232-34; Porath (77), 72-73; See also Hillel Cohen, *Army of Shadows: Palestinian Collaboration with Zionism, 1917-1948,* (Berkeley: University of California Press, 2008).

33. Jon Kimche, *There Could Have Been Peace: The Untold Story of Why We Failed with Palestine and Again with Israel,* (England: Dial Press, 1973), 189.

34. Richard Meinertzhagen, *Middle East Diary 1917-1956,* (London: The Cresset Press, 1959), 49, 82, 97.

35. Samuel Katz, *Battleground: Fact and Fantasy in Palestine,* (NY: Bantam Books, 1977), 63-65; Howard Sachar, *A History of Israel: From the Rise of Zionism to Our Time* (NY: Alfred A. Knopf, 1979), 97.

36. Paul Johnson, *Modern Times: The World from the Twenties to the Nineties* (NY: Harper & Row, 1983), 438.

37. Larry Collins and Dominique Lapierre, *O Jerusalem!* (NY: Simon and Schuster, 1972), 52.

38. Kimche, 211.

39. Ben Halpern, *The Idea of a Jewish State* (Cambridge, MA: Harvard University Press, 1969), 323.

40. Sachar, 174.

41. Halpern, 201.

42. "Grand Mufti Plotted to Do Away with All Jews in Mideast," *Response* (Fall 1991), 2-3.

43. Record of the Conversation between the Führer and the Grand Mufti of Jerusalem on November 28, 1941, in the Presence of Reich Foreign Minister and Minister Grobba in Berlin, *Documents on German Foreign Policy, 1918-1945,* Series D, Vol. XIII, London, 1964, 881ff in Walter Lacquer and Barry Rubin, *The Israel-Arab Reader* (NY: Penguin Books, 2001), 51-55.

44. Menachem Begin, *The Revolt* (NY: Nash Publishing, 1977), 224.

45. J. Bowyer Bell, *Terror Out of Zion* (NY: St. Martin's Press), 172.

46. Benjamin Netanyahu, ed., "International Terrorism: Challenge and Response," Proceedings of the Jerusalem Conference on International Terrorism, July 2-5, 1979, (Jerusalem: The Jonathan Institute, 1980), 45.

47. Anne Sinai and I. Robert Sinai, *Israel and the Arabs: Prelude to the Jewish State* (NY: Facts on File, 1972), 83.

3. Partition

The United Nations unjustly partitioned Palestine.

The partition plan gave the Jews most of the land, including all the fertile areas.

Israel usurped all of Palestine in 1948.

Prior to 1948, the Palestinian Arabs were never offered a state.

The majority of the population in Palestine was Arab; therefore, a unitary Arab state should have been created.

The Arabs were prepared to compromise to avoid bloodshed.

MYTH

The United Nations unjustly partitioned Palestine.

FACT

As World War II ended, the magnitude of the Holocaust became known. This accelerated demands for a resolution to the question of Palestine so the Displaced Persons, survivors of Hitler's Final Solution, might find sanctuary in a homeland of their own. The existing Jewish community, the yishuv, was also thriving and ready for independence.

The British tried to work out an agreement acceptable to both Arabs and Jews, but their insistence on the former's approval guaranteed failure because the Arabs would not make any concessions. The British subsequently turned the issue over to the UN in February 1947.

The UN established a Special Commission on Palestine (UNSCOP) to devise a solution. Delegates from eleven nations[1] went to the area and found what had long been apparent: the conflicting national aspirations of Jews and Arabs could not be reconciled.

When they returned, the delegates of seven nations—Canada, Czechoslovakia, Guatemala, The Netherlands, Peru, Sweden, and Uruguay—recommended the establishment of two separate states, Jewish and Arab, to be joined by economic union, with Jerusalem an internationalized enclave. Three nations—India, Iran, and Yugoslavia—recommended a unitary state with Arab and Jewish provinces. Australia abstained.

The Jews of Palestine were not satisfied with the small territory allotted to them by the Commission, nor were they happy that Jerusalem was severed from the Jewish State; nevertheless, they welcomed the compromise. The Arabs rejected UNSCOP's recommendations.

The ad hoc committee of the UN General Assembly rejected the Arab demand for a unitary Arab state. The majority recommendation

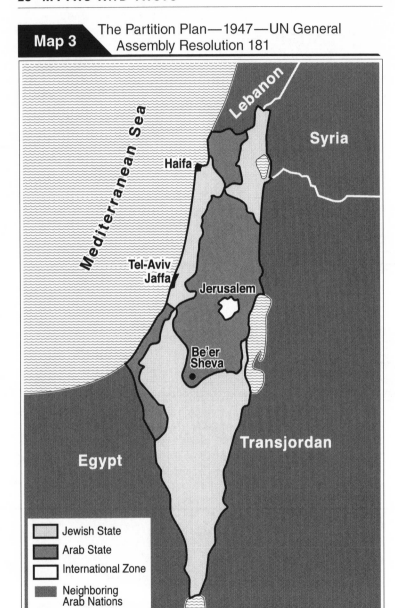

Mediterranean Sea

Lebanon

Syria

Haifa

Tel-Aviv
Jaffa

Jerusalem

Be'er
Sheva

Transjordan

Egypt

Jewish State
Arab State
International Zone
Neighboring
Arab Nations

for partition was viewed as a more just solution and subsequently ad-opted by a vote of thirty-three to thirteen with ten abstentions on November 29, 1947.[2]

It is hard to see how the Arab world, still less the Arabs of Palestine, will suffer from what is mere recognition of accomplished fact—the pres-ence in Palestine of a compact, well organized, and virtually autono-mous Jewish community.

—*London Times* **editorial**[3]

MYTH

The partition plan gave the Jews most of the land, including all the fertile areas.

FACT

The partition plan took on a checkerboard appearance largely be-cause Jewish towns and villages were spread throughout Palestine. This did not complicate the plan as much as the fact that the high living standards in Jewish cities and towns had attracted large Arab populations, which ensured that any partition would result in a Jew-ish state that included a substantial Arab population. Recognizing the need to allow for additional Jewish settlement, the majority proposal allotted the Jews land in the northern part of the country, the Galilee, and the large, arid Negev Desert in the south. The remainder was to form the Arab state.

These boundaries were based solely on demographics. The borders of the Jewish State were arranged with no consideration of security; hence, the new state's frontiers were virtually indefensible. Overall, the Jewish State was to be comprised of roughly fifty-five hundred square miles (about 55 percent of Palestine), and the population was to be 538,000 Jews and 397,000 Arabs. Approximately 92,000 Arabs lived in Tiberias, Safed, Haifa, and Bet Shean, and another forty thou-sand were Bedouins, most of whom were living in the desert. The remainder of the Arab population was spread throughout the Jewish state. The Arab State was to be forty-five hundred square miles with a population of 804,000 Arabs and 10,000 Jews.[4]

Critics claim the UN gave the Jews fertile land while the Arabs were allotted hilly, arid land. To the contrary, approximately 60 per-cent of the Jewish state was to be the desert in the Negev, while the Arabs occupied most of the agricultural land.[5]

Further complicating the situation was the UN majority's insistence that Jerusalem remain apart from both states and be administered as an international zone. This arrangement left more than 100,000 Jews in Jerusalem isolated from their country and circumscribed by the Arab state.

According to British statistics, more than 70 percent of the land in what would become Israel belonged to the mandatory government. Those lands reverted to Israeli control after the departure of the British. Another 9 percent of the land was owned by Jews, and about 3 percent by Arabs who became citizens of Israel. That means only about 18 percent belonged to Arabs who left the country before and after the Arab invasion of Israel.[6]

MYTH

Israel usurped all of Palestine in 1948.

FACT

Nearly 80 percent of what was the historic land of Palestine and the Jewish National Home, as defined by the League of Nations, was severed by the British in 1921 and allocated to what became Transjordan. Jewish settlement there was barred. The UN partitioned the remaining 20-odd percent of Palestine into two states. With Transjordan's annexation of the West Bank in 1950 and Egypt's occupation of Gaza, Arabs controlled more than 80 percent of the territory of the Mandate while the Jewish State held a bare 17.5 percent.[7]

MYTH

Prior to 1948, the Palestinian Arabs were never offered a state.

FACT

The Peel Commission in 1937 concluded the only logical solution to resolving the contradictory aspirations of the Jews and Arabs was to partition Palestine into separate Jewish and Arab states. The Jews would have received only 15 percent of Western Palestine between the Jordan River and the Mediterranean. A small area, including Jerusalem, was to remain under British control, but 80 percent of the land was to be united with Transjordan and become independent.

The Arabs rejected the plan because it forced them to accept the creation of a Jewish state, and required some Palestinians to live under "Jewish domination." Muslim religious leaders said supporters of the plan were heretics while the political machine controlled by the Mufti labeled them traitors.[8]

The Zionists opposed the Peel Plan's boundaries because they would have been confined to nineteen hundred out of the 10,310 square miles remaining in Palestine. Nevertheless, the Zionists de-

Map 4 Peel Commission Partition Plan, July 1937

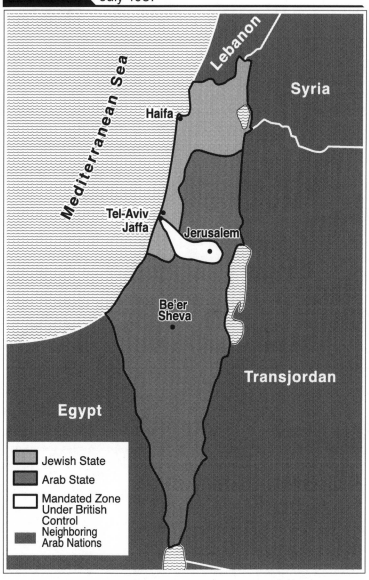

Mediterranean Sea

Lebanon

Syria

Haifa

Tel-Aviv
Jaffa

Jerusalem

Be'er
Sheva

Transjordan

Egypt

Jewish State

Arab State

Mandated Zone
Under British
Control

Neighboring
Arab Nations

cided to negotiate with the British, while the Arabs refused to consider any compromises.

In 1939, the British White Paper called for the establishment of an Arab state in Palestine within ten years, and for limiting Jewish immigration to no more than seventy-five thousand over the following five years. Afterward, no one would be allowed in without the consent of the Arab population. Though the Arabs had been granted a concession on Jewish immigration, and been offered independence—the goal of Arab nationalists—they repudiated the White Paper.

With partition, the Palestinians were given a state and the opportunity for self-determination. This, too, was rejected.

MYTH

The majority of the population in Palestine was Arab; therefore, a unitary Arab state should have been created.

FACT

At the time of the 1947 partition resolution, the Arabs did have a majority in western Palestine as a whole—1.2 million Arabs versus six hundred thousand Jews.[9] But the Jews were a majority *in the area allotted to them* by the resolution, and in Jerusalem.

The Jews never had a chance of reaching a majority in the country given the restrictive immigration policy of the British. By contrast, Palestine's Arab population, which had been declining prior to the Mandate in 1922, grew exponentially because Arabs from all the surrounding countries were free to come—and thousands did—to take advantage of the rapid economic development and improved health conditions stimulated by Zionist settlement.

The decision to partition Palestine was not determined solely by demographics; it was based on the conclusion that the territorial claims of Jews and Arabs were irreconcilable, and that the most logical compromise was the creation of two states. Ironically, that same year, 1947, the Arab members of the United Nations supported the partition of the Indian subcontinent and the creation of the new, predominantly Muslim state of Pakistan.

MYTH

The Arabs were prepared to compromise to avoid bloodshed.

FACT

As the partition vote approached, it became clear that little hope existed for a political solution to a problem that transcended politics:

the Arabs' unwillingness to accept a Jewish state in Palestine and the refusal of the Zionists to settle for anything less.

The implacability of the Arabs was evident when Jewish Agency representatives David Horowitz and Abba Eban made a last-ditch effort to reach a compromise in a meeting with Arab League secretary Abd al-Rahman Azzam Pasha on September 16, 1947. Pasha told them bluntly:

> The Arab world is not in a compromising mood. It's likely, Mr. Horowitz, that your plan is rational and logical, but the fate of nations is not decided by rational logic. Nations never concede; they fight. You won't get anything by peaceful means or compromise. You can, perhaps, get something, but only by the force of your arms. We shall try to defeat you. I am not sure we'll succeed, but we'll try. We were able to drive out the Crusaders, but on the other hand we lost Spain and Persia. It may be that we shall lose Palestine. But it's too late to talk of peaceful solutions.[10]

Meanwhile, the Mufti and his henchmen made sure to silence supporters of partition. According to one of the Mufti's associates who spied for the Haganah, "The opposition, which was prepared to agree to partition, had to go along with the opponents of partition after they learned of the decision to murder everyone who supported that opinion, even if they were among the greatest [leaders.]"[11]

Notes, Chapter 3

1. Australia, Canada, Czechoslovakia, Guatemala, India, Iran, the Netherlands, Peru, Sweden, Uruguay, and Yugoslavia. United Nations Special Committee on Palestine (May 15, 1947).
2. **Voting in *favor* of partition:** Australia, Belgium, Bolivia, Brazil, Byelorussian SSR, Canada, Costa Rica, Czechoslovakia, Denmark, Dominican Republic, Ecuador, France, Guatemala, Haiti, Iceland, Liberia, Luxembourg, Netherlands, New Zealand, Nicaragua, Norway, Panama, Paraguay, Peru, Philippines, Poland, Sweden, Ukrainian SSR, Union of South Africa, USSR, USA, Uruguay, and Venezuela. **Voting *against* partition:** Afghanistan, Cuba, Egypt, Greece, India, Iran, Iraq, Lebanon, Pakistan, Saudi Arabia, Syria, Turkey, and Yemen. ***Abstained***: Argentina, Chile, China, Columbia, El Salvador, Ethiopia, Honduras, Mexico, UK, and Yugoslavia. *Yearbook of the United Nations, 1947-48* (NY: United Nations, 1949), 246–47.
3. *London Times* (December 1, 1947).
4. Howard Sachar, *A History of Israel: From the Rise of Zionism to Our Time* (NY: Alfred A. Knopf, 1998), 292.
5. Aharon Cohen, *Israel and the Arab World* (Boston: Beacon Press, 1976), 238.
6. Moshe Aumann, "Land Ownership in Palestine, 1880–1948" (Academic Committee on the Middle East: Israel, 1974), 18.
7. Historic Palestine comprised what is today Jordan (approximately 35,640 square miles), Israel (8,019 square miles), Gaza (139 square miles), and the West Bank (2,263 square miles).

8. Hillel Cohen, *Army of Shadows* (Berkeley: University of California Press, 2008), 122-23.
9. Arieh Avneri, *The Claim of Dispossession* (New Brunswick, NJ: Transaction Books, 1984), 252.
10. David Horowitz, *State in the Making* (NY: Alfred A. Knopf, 1953), 233.
11. Hillel Cohen, *Army of Shadows* (Berkeley: University of California Press, 2008), 124.

4. The War of 1948

The Jews started the first war with the Arabs.

The United States was the only nation that criticized the Arab attack on Israel.

The West's support of Israel allowed the Jews to conquer Palestine.

The Arab economic boycott was imposed in response to the creation of Israel.

MYTH

The Jews started the first war with the Arabs.

FACT

The Arabs made clear they would go to war to prevent the establishment of a Jewish state. The chairman of the Arab Higher Committee said the Arabs would "fight for every inch of their country."[1] Two days later, the holy men of Al-Azhar University in Cairo called on the Muslim world to proclaim a *jihad* (holy war) against the Jews.[2] Jamal Husseini, the Arab Higher Committee's spokesman, had told the UN prior to the partition vote that the Arabs would drench "the soil of our beloved country with the last drop of our blood."[3]

Husseini's prediction began to come true almost immediately after the UN adopted the partition resolution on November 29, 1947. The Arabs declared a protest strike and instigated riots that claimed the lives of sixty-two Jews and thirty-two Arabs. Violence continued to escalate through the end of the year.[4]

The first large-scale assaults began on January 9, 1948, when approximately one thousand Arabs attacked Jewish communities in northern Palestine. By February, the British said so many Arabs had infiltrated that they lacked the forces to run them back.[5]

In the first phase of the war, lasting from November 29, 1947, until April 1, 1948, the Palestinian Arabs took the offensive, with help from volunteers from neighboring countries. The Jews suffered severe casualties, and passage along most of their major roadways was disrupted.

On April 26, 1948, Transjordan's King Abdullah said:

> All our efforts to find a peaceful solution to the Palestine problem have failed. The only way left for us is war. I will have the pleasure and honor to save Palestine.[6]

On May 4, 1948, Abdullah's Arab Legion attacked Kfar Etzion. The defenders drove them back, but the Legion returned a week later. After two days, the ill-equipped and outnumbered settlers were overwhelmed. Many defenders were massacred after they had surren-

Map 5 The Arab Invasion, May 15,1948

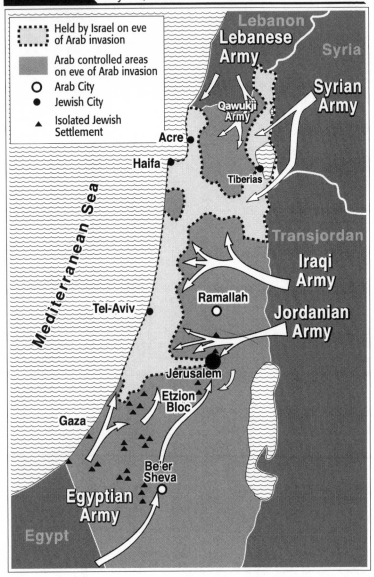

Held by Israel on eve of Arab invasion

Arab controlled areas on eve of Arab invasion

○ Arab City

● Jewish City

▲ Isolated Jewish Settlement

Lebanon

Lebanese Army

Syria

Syrian Army

Qawukji Army

Acre

Haifa

Tiberias

Mediterranean Sea

Transjordan

Iraqi Army

Tel-Aviv

Ramallah

Jordanian Army

Jerusalem

Etzion Bloc

Gaza

Be'er Sheva

Egyptian Army

Egypt

dered.[7] This was prior to the invasion by the regular Arab armies that followed Israel's declaration of independence.

The UN Palestine Commission, which was never permitted by the Arabs or British to go to Palestine to implement the resolution, reported to the Security Council on February 16, 1948, that "powerful Arab interests, both inside and outside Palestine, are defying the resolution of the General Assembly and are engaged in a deliberate effort to alter by force the settlement envisaged therein."[8]

The Arabs were blunt in taking responsibility for the war. Jamal Husseini told the Security Council on April 16, 1948:

> The representative of the Jewish Agency told us yesterday that they were not the attackers, that the Arabs had begun the fighting. We did not deny this. We told the whole world that we were going to fight.[9]

The British commander of Jordan's Arab Legion, John Bagot Glubb, admitted:

> Early in January, the first detachments of the Arab Liberation Army began to infiltrate into Palestine from Syria. Some came through Jordan and even through Amman . . . They were in reality to strike the first blow in the ruin of the Arabs of Palestine.[10]

Despite the disadvantages in numbers, organization, and weapons, the Jews began to take the initiative in the weeks from April 1 until the declaration of independence on May 14. The Haganah captured several major towns, including Tiberias and Haifa, and temporarily opened the road to Jerusalem.

The partition resolution was never suspended or rescinded. Thus, Israel, the Jewish State in Palestine, was born on May 14, as the British finally left the country. Five Arab armies (Egypt, Syria, Transjordan, Lebanon, and Iraq) immediately invaded Israel. Their intentions were declared by Abd al-Rahman Azzam Pasha, secretary-general of the Arab League: "It will be a war of annihilation. It will be a momentous massacre in history that will be talked about like the massacres of the Mongols or the Crusades."[11]

MYTH

The United States was the only nation that criticized the Arab attack on Israel.

FACT

The United States, the Soviet Union, and most other states recognized Israel soon after it declared independence on May 14, 1948, and imme-

Map 6 Armistice Lines, 1949

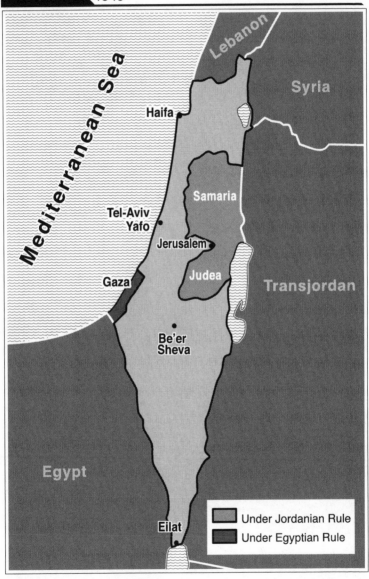

diately condemned the Arabs for their aggression. The United States urged a resolution charging the Arabs with breach of the peace.

Soviet delegate Andrei Gromyko told the Security Council on May 29, 1948:

> This is not the first time that the Arab states, which orga-
> nized the invasion of Palestine, have ignored a decision of
> the Security Council or of the General Assembly. The USSR
> delegation deems it essential that the council should state
> its opinion more clearly and more firmly with regard to this
> attitude of the Arab states toward decisions of the Security
> Council.[12]

On July 15, the Security Council threatened to cite the Arab governments for aggression under the UN Charter. By this time, the Israel Defense Forces (IDF) had succeeded in stopping the Arab offensive, and the initial phase of the fighting ended.

MYTH

The West's support of Israel allowed the Jews to conquer Palestine.

FACT

The Jews won their war of independence with minimal help from the West. In fact, they won despite actions that undermined their military strength.

Although President Harry Truman supported the partition resolution, many officials in the State Department did not and tried to sabotage the plan. Some of these officials—often referred to as "Arabists"—were anti-Semitic. Others feared supporting partition would harm our relations with the Arab states (especially the oil producers), and the early Cold Warriors worried that the new Jewish state might side with the Communists or provide an opening for the Soviet Union to spread its influence in the region.

The Arabists decided to prevent the Jews from obtaining the means to defend themselves. "Otherwise," Undersecretary of State Robert Lovett argued, "the Arabs might use arms of U.S. origin against Jews, or Jews might use them against Arabs."[13] Consequently, on December 5, 1947, the United States imposed an arms embargo on the region.

Truman did not recognize the embargo as an impediment to partition and went along because he hoped it could avert bloodshed. This was naive given Britain's rejection of Lovett's request to suspend weapons shipments to the Arabs and subsequent agreements to provide additional arms to Iraq and Transjordan.[14]

The Arabs had no difficulty obtaining all the arms they needed. In fact, Jordan's Arab Legion was armed and trained by the British, and led by a British officer. At the end of 1948, and beginning of 1949, British RAF planes flew with Egyptian squadrons over the Israel-Egypt border.[15]

Meanwhile, the Jews were forced to smuggle weapons, principally from Czechoslovakia. When Israel declared its independence in May 1948, the army did not have a single cannon or tank, and its air force consisted of nine obsolete planes.

Although outgunned, Israel was not outmanned, despite the exponentially larger populations of the Arab invaders. The Haganah had sixty thousand trained fighters, but the newly formed Israel Defense Forces (IDF) could only arm and mobilize 32,500, which was roughly the size of the enemy forces.[16] On the eve of the war, Chief of Operations Yigael Yadin told David Ben-Gurion: "The best we can tell you is that we have a 50–50 chance."[17]

The lack of participation by Palestinians in the war was particularly striking. Though Palestinians claim a close connection to the land going back centuries, and a fervent desire for independence, a surprisingly low percentage fought in 1948. In village after village, Arab residents defied the call to arms, and those who joined often did so "to obtain free weapons for their personal protection and then return home." The small number who joined the fight often deserted; one commander complained the Palestinians were "unreliable, excitable, and difficult to control, and in organized warfare virtually unemployable."[18]

The Arab war to destroy Israel failed. Indeed, because of their aggression, the Arabs wound up with less territory than if they had accepted partition.

The cost to Israel, however, was enormous. "Many of its most productive fields lay gutted and mined. Its citrus groves, for decades the basis of the Yishuv's Jewish community economy, were largely destroyed."[19] Military expenditures totaled approximately $500 million. Worse yet, 6,373 Israelis were killed, nearly 1 percent of the Jewish population of 650,000. Approximately 10,000 Arabs were killed.[20]

Had the West enforced the partition resolution or given the Jews the capacity to defend themselves, many lives might have been saved.

The Arab countries signed armistice agreements with Israel in 1949, starting with Egypt (Feb. 24), followed by Lebanon (March 23), Jordan (April 3), and Syria (July 20). Iraq was the only country that did not sign an agreement with Israel, choosing instead to withdraw its troops and hand over its sector to Jordan's Arab Legion. None of the Arab states would negotiate a peace agreement.

Meanwhile, forty of the fifty-nine member states of the UN recognized Israel by the end of 1949.[21]

MYTH

The Arab economic boycott was imposed in response to the creation of Israel.

FACT

The Arab boycott was formally declared by the newly formed Arab League Council on December 2, 1945: "Jewish products and manufactured goods shall be considered undesirable to the Arab countries." All Arab "institutions, organizations, merchants, commission agents and individuals" were called upon "to refuse to deal in, distribute, or consume Zionist products or manufactured goods."[22] As is evident in this declaration, the terms "Jewish" and "Zionist" were used synonymously. Thus, even before the establishment of Israel, the Arab states had declared an economic boycott against the Jews of Palestine.

The boycott, as it evolved after 1948, is divided into three components. The primary boycott prohibits direct trade between Israel and the Arab nations. The secondary boycott is directed at companies that do business with Israel. The tertiary boycott involves the blacklisting of firms that trade with other companies that do business with Israel.[23]

The objective of the boycott has been to isolate Israel from its neighbors and the international community, and deny it trade that might be used to augment its military and economic strength. While undoubtedly isolating Israel and separating the Jewish State from its most natural markets, the boycott failed to undermine Israel's economy to the degree intended. Instead, Israel flourished and enjoyed one of the world's highest growth rates for many years.

After learning the extent to which US companies were cooperating with the boycott, and the number of firms on the Arab blacklist, Congress voted in 1977 to prohibit US companies from cooperating with the Arab boycott. When President Carter signed the law, he said the "issue goes to the very heart of free trade among nations" and that it was designed to "end the divisive effects on American life of foreign boycotts aimed at Jewish members of our society."[24]

The boycott has gradually crumbled, and few countries outside the Middle East comply with it. The primary boycott—prohibiting direct relations between Arab countries and Israel—cracked when nations such as Qatar, Oman, and Morocco negotiated deals with Israel. Saudi Arabia and some other Arab states have also engaged in quiet diplomacy in response to the shared concern over Iran's nuclear program. This mutual interest has not changed the Saudis' adherence to the economic boycott, which they had pledged to end as a condition for membership in the World Trade Organization.[25]

The Arab League boycott remains technically in force. In August

2016, for example, the ninetieth conference of boycott officers was held in Cairo. Kuwait and the UAE were among the participants who reiterated their commitment to boycotting Israel.[26] In addition, a global campaign by individuals, organizations, and some governments—the anti-Semitic boycott, divestment, and sanctions (BDS) movement—seeks to isolate and, ultimately, destroy Israel.

Notes, Chapter 4

1. *New York Times* (December 1, 1947).
2. *Facts on File Yearbook* (NY: Facts on File, Inc., 1948), 48.
3. J. C. Hurewitz, *The Struggle for Palestine* (NY: Shocken Books, 1976), 308.
4. *Palestine Post* (January 2, 7, 27; April 1; May 1, 1948).
5. *Facts on File 1947*, 231.
6. Howard Sachar, *A History of Israel: From the Rise of Zionism to Our Time*, (NY: Alfred A. Knopf, 1979), 322.
7. Netanel Lorch, *One Long War*, (Jerusalem: Keter Books, 1976), 47; Ralph Patai, ed., *Encyclopedia of Zionism and Israel* (NY: McGraw Hill, 1971), 307-8.
8. Security Council Official Records, Special Supplement (1948), 20.
9. Security Council Official Records, S/Agenda/58 (April 16, 1948), 19.
10. John Bagot Glubb, *A Soldier with the Arabs* (London: Staughton and Hodder, 1957), 79.
11. "Interview with Abd al-Rahman Azzam Pasha," *Akhbar al-Yom* (Egypt) (October 11, 1947), translated by R. Green.
12. Security Council Official Records, SA/Agenda/77 (May 29, 1948), 2.
13. *Foreign Relations of the United States 1947* (DC: GPO, 1948), 1249. Henceforth, FRUS.
14. Mitchell Bard, *The Water's Edge and Beyond* (New Brunswick, NJ: Transaction Books, 1991), 171-75; *FRUS*, 537-39; Robert Silverberg, *If I Forget Thee, O Jerusalem: American Jews and the State of Israel* (NY: William Morrow and Co., Inc., 1970), 366, 370; Shlomo Slonim, "The 1948 American Embargo on Arms to Palestine," *Political Science Quarterly* (Fall 1979), 500.
15. Sachar, 345.
16. Larry Collins and Dominique Lapierre, *O Jerusalem!*, (NY: Simon and Schuster, 1972), 352; undated letter from Professor Meron Medzini to the author.
17. Golda Meir, *My Life* (NY: Dell, 1975), 213, 222, 224.
18. Efraim Karsh, "1948, Israel, and the Palestinians—The True Story," *Commentary online* (May 2008).
19. Sachar, 452.
20. "Total Casualties, Arab-Israeli Conflict," Jewish Virtual Library.
21. Undated letter from Professor Meron Medzini to the author.
22. Terence Prittie and Walter Nelson, *The Economic War against The Jews* (London: Corgi Books, 1977); Dan Chill, *The Arab Boycott of Israel* (NY: Praeger, 1976), 10.
23. Prittie and Nelson, 47-48; Sol Stern, "On and Off the Arabs' List," *New Republic*, (March 27, 1976), 9; Kennan Teslik, *Congress, the Executive Branch, and Special Interests*, (CT: Greenwood Press, 1982), 11.
24. Bard, 91-115.
25. "Saudis Flout Vow to End Israel Boycott," *Jerusalem Post* (May 29, 2006).
26. "UAE Participates in Israel Boycott Meeting," *Gulf News* (August 2, 2016); "Kuwait Adherent to Israel's Boycott—Official," *Kuwait News Agency* (August 2, 2016).

5. The 1956 Suez War and the 1967 Six-Day War

Arab governments were prepared to accept Israel after the 1948 war.
Israel's military strike in 1956 was unprovoked.
The United States' blind support for Israel was apparent during the Suez War.
Arab governments recognized Israel after the Suez War.
Israel's military strike in 1967 was unprovoked.
Nasser had the right to close the Straits of Tiran to Israeli shipping.
The United States helped Israel defeat the Arabs in six days.
During the 1967 War, Israel deliberately attacked the USS *Liberty*.
Israel attacked Jordan to capture Jerusalem.
Israel did not have to fire the first shot in June 1967.
Israel expelled peaceful Arab villagers from the West Bank and prevented their return.

MYTH

Arab governments were prepared to accept Israel after the 1948 war.

FACT

In the fall of 1948, the UN Security Council called on Israel and the Arab states to negotiate armistice agreements. Thanks to UN mediator Ralph Bunche's insistence on direct bilateral talks between Israel and each Arab state, armistice agreements between Israel and Egypt, Jordan, and Syria were concluded by the summer of 1949. Iraq, which had also fought against Israel, refused to follow suit.

Later, on December 11, 1948, the General Assembly adopted a resolution calling on the parties to negotiate peace; all Arab delegations voted against it. After 1949, the Arabs insisted that Israel accept the borders in the 1947 partition resolution and repatriate the Palestinian refugees before they would negotiate an end to the war they had initiated. This was a novel approach that they would use after subsequent defeats: the doctrine of the limited-liability war. Under this theory, aggressors may reject a compromise settlement and gamble on war to win everything in the comfortable knowledge that, even if they fail, they may insist on reinstating the status quo ante.

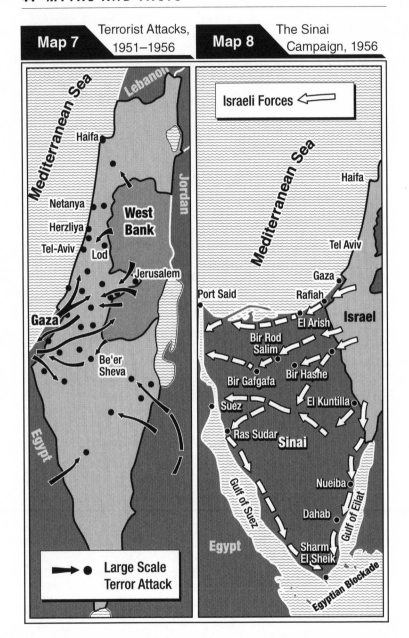

Map 7 Terrorist Attacks, 1951–1956

Map 8 The Sinai Campaign, 1956

Israeli Forces ⟵

Mediterranean Sea

Lebanon

Haifa

Netanya

Herzliya

Tel-Aviv

Lod

West Bank

Jordan

Jerusalem

Gaza

Be'er Sheva

Egypt

➡● **Large Scale Terror Attack**

Mediterranean Sea

Haifa

Tel Aviv

Gaza

Port Said

Rafiah

El Arish

Israel

Bir Rod Salim

Bir Hashe

Bir Gafgafa

El Kuntilla

Suez

Ras Sudar

Sinai

Gulf of Suez

Egypt

Nueiba

Dahab

Gulf of Eilat

Sharm El Sheik

Egyptian Blockade

MYTH

Israel's military strike in 1956 was unprovoked.

FACT

Egypt had maintained its state of belligerency with Israel after the armistice agreement had been signed. The first manifestation of this was the closing of the Suez Canal to Israeli shipping. On August 9, 1949, the UN Mixed Armistice Commission upheld Israel's complaint that Egypt was illegally blocking the canal. UN negotiator Ralph Bunche declared: "There should be free movement for legitimate shipping and no vestiges of the wartime blockade should be allowed to remain, as they are inconsistent with both the letter and the spirit of the armistice agreements."[1]

On September 1, 1951, the Security Council ordered Egypt to open the Canal to Israeli shipping. Egypt refused to comply.

Egypt was equally obdurate in refusing to lift a blockade Egyptian president Gamal Abdel Nasser imposed on the Straits of Tiran, which interfered with Israel's access to the Red Sea and the Indian Ocean, impeded communication with Asia and East Africa, and violated Israel's right to freedom of navigation.

The Egyptian foreign minister Muhammad Salah al-Din said early in 1954:

> The Arab people will not be embarrassed to declare: We shall not be satisfied except by the final obliteration of Israel from the map of the Middle East.[2]

In 1955, Nasser began to import arms from the Soviet Bloc to build his arsenal for a future confrontation with Israel. In the short term, however, he employed a new tactic to prosecute Egypt's war with Israel. He announced it on August 31, 1955:

> Egypt has decided to dispatch her heroes, the disciples of Pharaoh and the sons of Islam and they will cleanse the land of Palestine . . . There will be no peace on Israel's border because we demand vengeance, and vengeance is Israel's death.[3]

These "heroes" were Arab terrorists, or *fedayeen*, trained and equipped by Egyptian Intelligence to engage in hostile action on the border, and to infiltrate Israel to commit acts of sabotage and murder. The *fedayeen* operated mainly from bases in Jordan, so that Jordan would bear the brunt of Israel's retaliation, which inevitably followed. The terrorist attacks violated the armistice agreement provision that prohibited the initiation of hostilities by paramilitary forces; nevertheless, the UN Security Council condemned Israel for its counterattacks.

The escalation continued with the Egyptian blockade of Israel's shipping lane in the Straits of Tiran, and Nasser's nationalization of the Suez Canal in July 1956. On October 14, Nasser made clear his intent:

> I am not solely fighting against Israel itself. My task is to deliver the Arab world from destruction through Israel's intrigue, which has its roots abroad. Our hatred is very strong. There is no sense in talking about peace with Israel. There is not even the smallest place for negotiations.[4]

Less than two weeks later, on October 25, Egypt signed a tripartite agreement with Syria and Jordan placing Nasser in command of all three armies.

The blockade of the Suez Canal and Gulf of Aqaba to Israeli shipping, combined with the increased *fedayeen* attacks and the bellicosity of Arab statements, prompted Israel, with the backing of Britain and France, to attack Egypt on October 29, 1956. The Israeli attack on Egypt was successful, with Israeli forces capturing the Gaza Strip, much of the Sinai, and Sharm al-Sheikh. Estimates of casualties range from 171 to 231 Israelis and three thousand Egyptians.

Israeli ambassador to the UN Abba Eban explained the provocations to the Security Council on October 30:

> During the six years during which this belligerency has operated in violation of the Armistice Agreement there have occurred 1,843 cases of armed robbery and theft, 1,339 cases of armed clashes with Egyptian armed forces, 435 cases of incursion from Egyptian controlled territory, [and] 172 cases of sabotage perpetrated by Egyptian military units and fedayeen in Israel. As a result of these actions of Egyptian hostility within Israel, 364 Israelis were wounded and 101 killed. In 1956 alone, as a result of this aspect of Egyptian aggression, 28 Israelis were killed and 127 wounded.[5]

MYTH

The United States' blind support for Israel was apparent during the Suez War.

FACT

President Eisenhower was upset by the fact that Israel, France, and Great Britain had secretly planned the campaign to evict Egypt from the Suez Canal. Israel's failure to inform the United States of its intentions, combined with ignoring American entreaties not to go to war, sparked tensions between the countries. The United States subsequently joined the Soviet Union (ironically, just after the Soviets invaded Hungary) in a campaign to force Israel to withdraw. This included a threat to discontinue all US assistance, UN sanctions, and expulsion from the UN.[6]

US pressure resulted in an Israeli withdrawal from the areas it conquered without obtaining any concessions from the Egyptians. This sowed the seeds of the 1967 War.

One reason Israel did give in to Eisenhower was the assurance he gave to Prime Minister David Ben-Gurion. Before evacuating Sharm al-Sheikh, the strategic point guarding the Straits of Tiran, Israel elicited a promise that the United States would maintain the freedom of navigation in the waterway.[7] In addition, Washington sponsored a UN resolution creating the United Nations Emergency Force (UNEF) to deter future hostilities, assure freedom of navigation of the Straits of Tiran, and prevent *fedayeen* raids from Gaza.

The war temporarily ended the activities of the *fedayeen;* however, they were renewed a few years later by a loosely knit group of terrorist organizations that became known as the Palestine Liberation Organization (PLO).

MYTH

Arab governments recognized Israel after the Suez War.

FACT

Israel consistently expressed a desire to negotiate with its neighbors. In an address to the UN General Assembly on October 10, 1960, Foreign Minister Golda Meir challenged Arab leaders to meet with Prime Minister David Ben-Gurion to negotiate a peace settlement. Egyptian president Nasser answered on October 15, saying that Israel was trying to deceive the world, and reiterating that his country would never recognize the Jewish State.[8]

The Arabs were equally adamant in their refusal to negotiate a separate settlement for the refugees. Nasser made clear that solving the refugee issue was not his concern. "The danger of Israel," he said, "lies in the very existence of Israel as it is in the present and in what she represents."[9]

Meanwhile, Syria used the Golan Heights, which tower three thousand feet above the Galilee, to shell Israeli farms and villages. Syria's attacks grew more frequent in 1965 and 1966, while Nasser's rhetoric became increasingly bellicose: "We shall not enter Palestine with its soil covered in sand," he said on March 8, 1965. "We shall enter it with its soil saturated in blood."[10]

A few months later, Nasser expressed the Arabs' aspiration as: "the full restoration of the rights of the Palestinian people. In other words, we aim at the destruction of the State of Israel. The immediate aim:

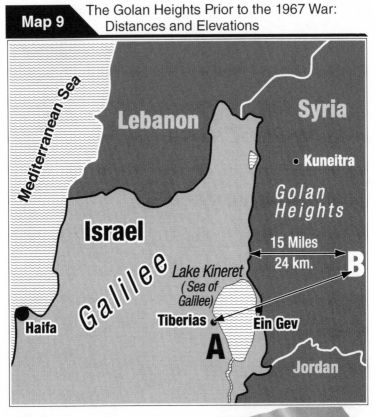

Map 9 The Golan Heights Prior to the 1967 War: Distances and Elevations

Mediterranean Sea

Syria

Lebanon

• **Kuneitra**

Golan Heights

Israel

15 Miles
24 km.

B

Galilee

Lake Kineret (Sea of Galilee)

Tiberias

Ein Gev

A

Haifa

Jordan

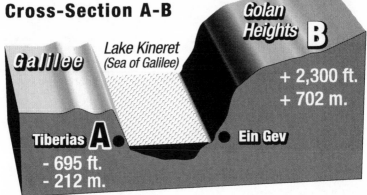

Cross-Section A-B

Golan Heights **B**

Lake Kineret (Sea of Galilee)

Galilee

+ 2,300 ft.
+ 702 m.

Tiberias A

Ein Gev

- 695 ft.
- 212 m.

perfection of Arab military might. The national aim: the eradication of Israel."[11]

MYTH

Israel's military strike in 1967 was unprovoked.

FACT

A combination of bellicose Arab rhetoric, threatening behavior, and—ultimately—an act of war left Israel no choice but preemptive action. To do this successfully, Israel needed the element of surprise. Had it waited for an Arab invasion, Israel would have been at a potentially catastrophic disadvantage.

In addition to Nasser's verbal threats, Israel was under actual attack from Arab terrorists. In 1965, thirty-five raids were conducted against Israel. In 1966, the number increased to forty-one. In just the first four months of 1967, thirty-seven attacks were launched.[12]

Meanwhile, Syria's attacks on Israeli kibbutzim from the Golan Heights provoked a retaliatory strike on April 7, 1967, during which Israeli planes shot down six Syrian MiGs. Shortly thereafter, the Soviet Union—which had been providing military and economic aid to both Syria and Egypt—gave Damascus and Cairo information alleging a massive Israeli military buildup in preparation for an attack. Despite Israeli denials, Syria decided to invoke its defense treaty with Egypt.

On May 15, Israel's Independence Day, Egyptian troops began moving into the Sinai and massing near the Israeli border. By May 18, Syrian troops were prepared for battle along the Golan Heights.

Nasser ordered the UN Emergency Force, stationed in the Sinai since 1956, to withdraw on May 16. Without bringing the matter to the attention of the General Assembly, as his predecessor had promised, Secretary-General U Thant complied with the demand. After the withdrawal of the UNEF, the Voice of the Arabs proclaimed (May 18, 1967):

> As of today, there no longer exists an international emergency force to protect Israel. We shall exercise patience no more. We shall not complain any more to the UN about Israel. The sole method we shall apply against Israel is total war, which will result in the extermination of Zionist existence.[13]

An enthusiastic echo was heard on May 20 from Syrian defense minister Hafez Assad:

> Our forces are now entirely ready not only to repulse the aggression, but [also] to initiate the act of liberation itself, and

Map 10   Israel before June 1967

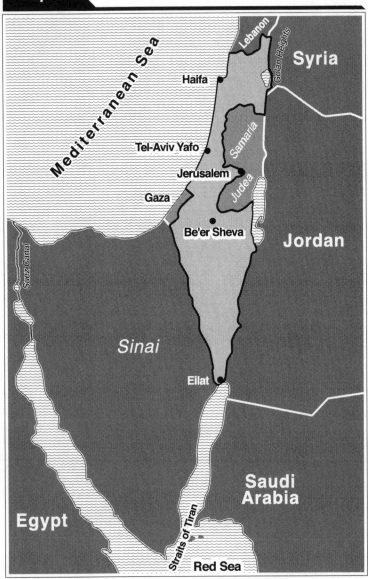

to explode the Zionist presence in the Arab homeland. The Syrian army, with its finger on the trigger, is united . . . I, as a military man, believe that the time has come to enter into a battle of annihilation.[14]

On May 22, Egypt closed the Straits of Tiran to all Israeli shipping and all ships bound for Eilat. This blockade cut off Israel's only supply route with Asia and stopped the flow of oil from its main supplier, Iran. The following day, President Johnson declared the blockade illegal and tried, unsuccessfully, to organize an international flotilla to test it.

Nasser was fully aware of the pressure he was exerting to force Israel's hand. The day after the blockade was set up, he said defiantly: "The Jews threaten to make war. I reply: Welcome! We are ready for war."[15]

Nasser challenged Israel to fight almost daily. "Our basic objective will be the destruction of Israel. The Arab people want to fight," he said on May 27.[16] The following day, he added, "We will not accept any . . . coexistence with Israel . . . Today the issue is not the establishment of peace between the Arab states and Israel . . . The war with Israel [has been] in effect since 1948."[17]

King Hussein of Jordan signed a defense pact with Egypt on May 30. Nasser then announced:

The armies of Egypt, Jordan, Syria and Lebanon are poised on the borders of Israel . . . to face the challenge, while standing behind us are the armies of Iraq, Algeria, Kuwait, Sudan and the whole Arab nation. This act will astound the world. Today they will know that the Arabs are arranged for battle [and that] the critical hour has arrived. We have reached the stage of serious action and not declarations.[18]

President Abdur Rahman Aref of Iraq joined in the war of words: "The existence of Israel is an error which must be rectified. This is our opportunity to wipe out the ignominy which has been with us since 1948. Our goal is clear—to wipe Israel off the map."[19] On June 4, Iraq joined the military alliance with Egypt, Jordan, and Syria.

The Arab rhetoric was matched by the mobilization of Arab forces. Approximately 250,000 troops (nearly half in Sinai), more than two thousand tanks, and seven hundred aircraft ringed Israel.[20]

By this time, Israeli forces had been on alert for three weeks. The country could not remain fully mobilized indefinitely, nor could it allow its sea-lane through the Gulf of Aqaba to be interdicted. Israel's best option was to strike first. On June 5, 1967, the order was given to attack Egypt.

MYTH

*Nasser had the right to close the Straits
of Tiran to Israeli shipping.*

FACT

In 1956, the United States gave Israel assurances that it recognized the
Jewish State's right of access to the Straits of Tiran. In 1957, at the UN,
seventeen maritime powers declared that Israel had a right to tran-
sit the Strait. Moreover, the blockade violated the Convention on the
Territorial Sea and Contiguous Zone, which was adopted by the UN
Conference on the Law of the Sea on April 27, 1958.[21]

The closure of the Strait of Tiran was the *casus belli* in 1967. Israel's
attack was a reaction to this Egyptian first strike.

President Johnson acknowledged as much after the war (June 19,
1967):

> If a single act of folly was more responsible for this explo-
> sion than any other, it was the arbitrary and dangerous an-
> nounced decision that the Strait of Tiran would be closed.
> The right of innocent maritime passage must be preserved
> for all nations.[22]

MYTH

The United States helped Israel defeat the Arabs in six days.

FACT

The United States tried to prevent the war through negotiations, but
it could not persuade Nasser or the other Arab states to cease their
belligerent statements and actions. Still, right before the war, President Johnson warned, "Israel will not be alone unless it decides to go
alone."[23] Then, when the war began, the State Department announced,
"Our position is neutral in thought, word, and deed."[24]

Moreover, while the Arabs were falsely accusing the United States
of airlifting supplies to Israel, Johnson imposed an arms embargo on
the region (France, Israel's other main arms supplier, also embargoed
arms to Israel).

By contrast, the Soviets were supplying massive amounts of arms to
the Arabs. Simultaneously, the armies of Kuwait, Algeria, Saudi Arabia,
and Iraq were contributing troops and arms to the Egyptian, Syrian,
and Jordanian fronts.[25]

Map 11 Events Leading to the Six-Day War, May 25–30, 1967

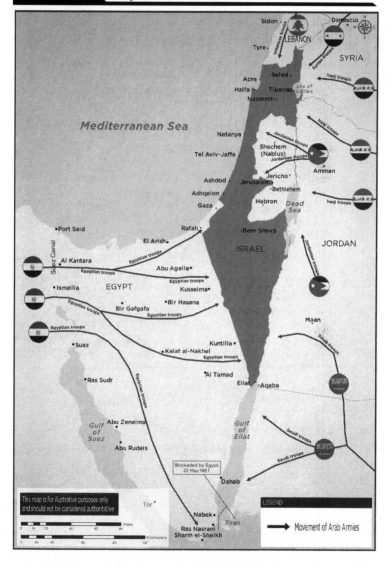

This map is for illustrative purposes only and should not be considered authoritative

LEGEND

⟶ Movement of Arab Armies

MYTH

During the 1967 War, Israel deliberately attacked the USS Liberty.

FACT

Besides not aiding Israel in the war, the United States and Israel actually came into direct military conflict as a result of a series of errors. On June 8, 1967, the fourth day of the war, the Israeli high command received reports that Israeli troops in El Arish were being fired upon from the sea, presumably by an Egyptian vessel, as they had a day before. The United States had announced that it had no naval forces within hundreds of miles of the battlefront; however, the USS *Liberty,* an American intelligence ship under the dual control of the Defense Intelligence Agency/Central Intelligence Agency and the Sixth Fleet, was assigned to monitor the fighting. As a result of a series of US communication failures, whereby messages directing the ship not to approach within one hundred miles were not received by the *Liberty,* the ship sailed to within fourteen miles off the Sinai coast. The Israelis mistakenly thought this was the ship shelling its soldiers and warplanes, and torpedo boats attacked, killing thirty-four members of the *Liberty*'s crew and wounding 171.

The Israeli attack on the USS *Liberty* was a grievous error, largely because it occurred in the "fog of war." Ten official US investigations, and three official Israeli inquiries, all concluded the attack was a tragic mistake. Israel apologized and paid nearly $13 million in humanitarian reparations to the United States and to the families of the victims. The matter was officially closed between the two governments by an exchange of diplomatic notes on December 17, 1987.[26]

MYTH

Israel attacked Jordan to capture Jerusalem.

FACT

Prime Minister Levi Eshkol sent a message to King Hussein saying Israel would not attack Jordan unless he initiated hostilities. When Jordanian radar picked up a cluster of planes flying from Egypt to Israel, however, the Egyptians convinced Hussein the planes were theirs prompting the king to order the shelling of West Jerusalem. It turned out the planes were Israel's, and were returning from destroying the Egyptian air force on the ground. Had Jordan not attacked, the status of Jerusalem would not have changed during the course of the war. Once the city came under fire, however, Israel needed to defend it, and, in doing so, took the opportunity to unify the city, ending Jordan's nineteen-year occupation of the eastern part.

Map 12 The Egyptian Front,
June 5–8, 1967

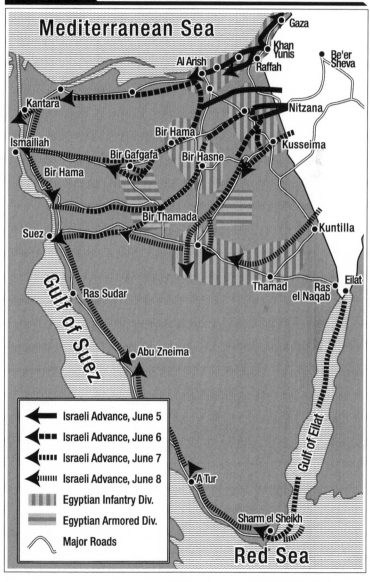

MYTH

Israel did not have to fire the first shot in June 1967.

FACT

By using the element of surprise, Israeli forces managed to break through the enemy lines after just six days of fighting and were in a position to march on Cairo, Damascus, and Amman. A cease-fire was invoked on June 10.

The victory came at a very high cost. In storming the Golan Heights, Israel suffered 115 dead—roughly the number of Americans killed during Operation Desert Storm. Altogether, Israel lost twice as many men—777 dead and 2,586 wounded—in proportion to her total population as the United States lost in eight years of fighting in Vietnam (approximately eighteen thousand Arab fighters died).[27] Additionally, despite the incredible success of the air campaign, the Israeli Air Force lost forty-six of its two hundred fighters.[28] Had Israel waited for the Arabs to strike first, as it did in 1973, and not taken preemptive action, the cost would certainly have been much higher, and victory could not have been assured.

MYTH

Israel expelled peaceful Arab villagers from the West Bank and prevented their return.

FACT

After Jordan launched its attack on June 5, approximately 325,000 Palestinians living in the West Bank fled.[29] These were Jordanian citizens who moved from one part of what they considered their country to another, primarily to avoid being caught in the cross fire of a war.

A Palestinian refugee who was an administrator in a UNRWA camp in Jericho said Arab politicians had spread rumors in the camp. "They said all the young people would be killed. People heard on the radio that this is not the end, only the beginning, so they think maybe it will be a long war and they want to be in Jordan."[30]

Some Palestinians who left preferred to live in an Arab state rather than under Israeli military rule. Members of various PLO factions fled to avoid capture by the Israelis. Nils-Göran Gussing, the person appointed by the UN secretary-general to investigate the situation, found that many Arabs also feared they would no longer be able to receive money from family members working abroad.[31]

Israeli forces ordered a handful of Palestinians to move for "strategic and security reasons." In some cases, they were allowed to return in a few days; in others, Israel offered to help them resettle elsewhere.[32]

Map 13 The Battle for Jerusalem,
        June 5–7, 1967

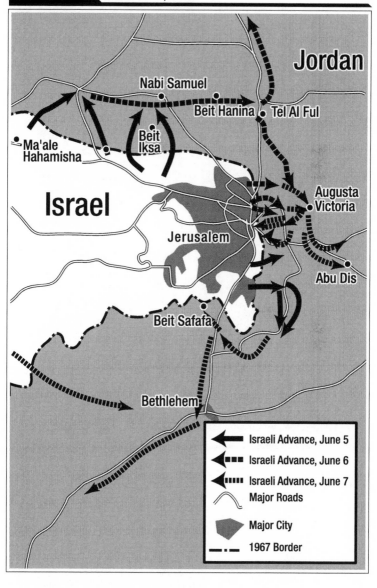

Following the war, Israel ruled more than three-quarters of a million Palestinians—most of whom were hostile to the government. Nevertheless, more than nine thousand Palestinian families were reunited in 1967. Ultimately, more than sixty thousand Palestinians were allowed to return.[33]

After the Six-Day War ended, President Johnson announced his view of what was required next to end the conflict:

Certainly, troops must be withdrawn; but there must also be recognized rights of national life, progress in solving the refugee problem, freedom of innocent maritime passage, limitation of the arms race and respect for political independence and territorial integrity.[34]

Notes, Chapter 5

1. "Israel's Complaint to the U.N. Security Council on the Suez Canal Blockade; S-2241," Israel Ministry of Foreign Affairs (July 11, 1951).
2. Yehoshafat Harkabi, *Arab Attitudes to Israel* (Jerusalem: Keter Publishing House, 1972), 28.
3. *Middle Eastern Affairs* (December 1956), 461.
4. *Middle Eastern Affairs* (December 1956), 460.
5. *Security Council Official Records,* S/3706, (October 30, 1956), 14.
6. "President Eisenhower & PM Ben-Gurion on Israeli Withdrawal from Sinai (November 7-8, 1956)," Jewish Virtual Library, http://www.jewishvirtuallibrary.org/jsource/History/ikewarn.html.
7. Janice Gross Stein and Raymond Tanter, *Rational Decision Making: Israel's Security Choices* (Columbus: Ohio State University, 1976), 163.
8. *Encyclopedia Americana Annual 1961* (NY: Americana Corporation, 1961), 387.
9. Speech by Nasser to the United Arab Republic National Assembly, March 26, 1964, quoted in Harkabi, 27.
10. Howard Sachar, *A History of Israel: From the Rise of Zionism to Our Time* (NY: Alfred A. Knopf, 1979), 616.
11. Samuel Katz, *Battleground: Fact and Fantasy in Palestine* (NY: Bantam Books, 1985), 10-11, 185.
12. Netanel Lorch, *One Long War* (Jerusalem: Keter, 1976), 110.
13. Isi Leibler, *The Case for Israel* (Australia: The Globe Press, 1972), 60-61.
14. Ibid.
15. Abba Eban, *Abba Eban* (NY: Random House, 1977), 331.
16. Leibler, 60.
17. Leibler, 18.
18. Leibler, 60.
19. Leibler, 61.
20. Chaim Herzog, *The Arab-Israeli Wars* (NY: Random House, 1982), 149.
21. *United Nations Conference on the Law of the Sea* (Geneva: UN Publications, 1958), 132-34.
22. Yehuda Lukacs, *Documents on the Israeli-Palestinian Conflict, 1967-1983* (NY: Cambridge University Press, 1984), 7-18; Eban, 358.

23. Eban, 358.
24. Lyndon B. Johnson, *The Vantage Point: Perspectives of the Presidency 1963-1969* (NY: Holt, Rinehart, and Winston, 1971), 299.
25. Sachar, 629.
26. Hirsh Goodman, "Messrs. Errors and No Facts," *Jerusalem Report*, (November 21, 1991); Arieh O'Sullivan, "Exclusive: Liberty Attack Tapes Revealed," *Jerusalem Post*, (June 3, 2004); "Attack on a SIGINT Collector, the U.S.S. Liberty," "Special Series Crisis Collection," National Security Agency, 64; Dan Kurzman, *Soldier of Peace: The Life of Yitzhak Rabin* (NY: HarperCollins, 1998), 224-27; Yitzhak Rabin, *The Rabin Memoirs* (Boston, MA: Little, Brown, and Co., 1979), 109-11; Rowland Evans and Robert Novak, "Remembering the Liberty," *Washington Post*, (November 6, 1991); L. Wainstain, "Some Aspects of the U.S. Involvement in the Middle East Crisis, May-June 1967," Institute for Defense Analysis, (February 1968); "Pilot Who Bombed 'Liberty' Talks to Post," *Jerusalem Post* (October 10, 2003); *Jerusalem Post* (January 13, 2004). See also, Nathan Guttman, "Memos Show Liberty Attack Was an Error," *Haaretz* (July 9, 2003); Hirsh Goodman and Zeev Schiff, "The Attack on the *Liberty*," *Atlantic Monthly*, (September 1984); The Larry King Show" (radio), (February 5, 1987); *Washington Times*, (January 12, 2004). For a detailed discussion, see "The USS Liberty Incident," in the Jewish Virtual Library. http://www.jewishvirtuallibrary.org/jsource/History/libertytoc.html.
27. Katz, 3.
28. Gerald M. Steinberg, "The Palestinian Time Machine," *Jerusalem Post* (April 23, 1999).
29. *Encyclopedia Americana Annual 1968*, 366.
30. George Gruen, "The Refugees of Arab-Israeli Conflict" (NY: American Jewish Committee, March 1969), 5.
31. Gruen, 5.
32. Gruen, 4.
33. *Encyclopedia Americana Annual 1968*, 366.
34. Lyndon B. Johnson, *Public Papers of the President* (DC: GPO 1968), 683.

6. The War of Attrition (1967–1970) and the 1973 Yom Kippur War

After the 1967 war, Israel refused to negotiate a settlement with the Arabs.

The Palestinians were willing to negotiate a settlement after the Six-Day War.

Israel was responsible for the War of Attrition.

Israel rejected Sadat's reasonable peace offer.

Israel was responsible for the 1973 War.

Egypt and Syria were the only Arab states involved in the 1973 war.

MYTH

After the 1967 war, Israel refused to negotiate a settlement with the Arabs.

FACT

By the end of the war, Israel had captured enough territory to more than triple the size of the area it controlled, from eight thousand to twenty-six thousand square miles. The victory enabled Israel to unify Jerusalem as well as capture the Sinai, the Golan Heights, the Gaza Strip, and the West Bank. Israel hoped the Arab states would enter peace negotiations. On June 19, 1967, Israel signaled to the Arab states its willingness to relinquish virtually all the territories it acquired in exchange for peace. As Moshe Dayan put it, Jerusalem was waiting only for a telephone call from Arab leaders to start negotiations.[1]

But these hopes were dashed in August 1967 when Arab leaders meeting in Khartoum adopted a formula of three noes: "no peace with Israel, no negotiations with Israel, no recognition of Israel."[2]

As former Israeli president Chaim Herzog wrote, "Israel's belief that the war had come to an end and that peace would now reign along the borders was soon dispelled. Three weeks after the conclusion of hostilities, the first major incident occurred on the Suez Canal."[3]

MYTH

The Palestinians were willing to negotiate a settlement after the Six-Day War.

FACT

The Arab League created the Palestine Liberation Organization (PLO) in Cairo in 1964 as a weapon against Israel. Until the Six-Day War, the

Map 14 — Israel after the Six-Day War, June 10, 1967

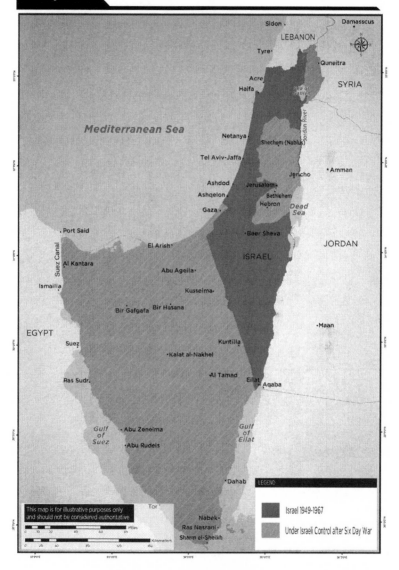

PLO engaged in terrorist attacks that contributed to the momentum toward conflict. Neither the PLO nor any other Palestinian groups campaigned for Jordan or Egypt to create an independent Palestinian state in the West Bank and Gaza. The focus of Palestinian activism was on the destruction of Israel.

After the Arab states were defeated in 1967, the Palestinians did not alter their basic objective. With one million Arabs coming under Israeli rule, some Palestinians believed the prospect for waging a popular war of liberation had grown. Toward that end, Yasser Arafat instigated a campaign of terror from the West Bank. During September through December 1967, sixty-one attacks were launched, most against civilian targets such as factories, movie theaters, and private homes.[4]

Israeli security forces gradually became more effective in thwarting terrorist plans inside Israel and the territories. Consequently, the PLO began to pursue a different strategy—attacking Jews and Israeli targets abroad. In early 1968, the first aircraft was hijacked by Palestinian terrorists.

The Arabs say they want their territory back, but they don't want to talk to us, and they don't want to negotiate with us, and they don't want to recognize us. They want peace by immaculate conception.

—Abba Eban[5]

MYTH

Israel was responsible for the War of Attrition.

FACT

Egypt's president Gamal Abdel Nasser thought that because most of Israel's army consisted of reserves, it could not withstand a lengthy war of attrition. He believed Israel would be unable to endure the economic burden and that Israeli morale would be undermined by the relentless casualties. To pursue this strategy of slowly weakening Israel, Nasser ordered attacks on Israel that were calibrated so that they would not provoke an all-out Israeli war in response.

As early as July 1, 1967, Egypt began shelling Israeli positions near the Suez Canal. On October 21, 1967, Egypt sank the Israeli destroyer *Eilat,* killing forty-seven. A few months later, Egyptian artillery began to shell Israeli positions along the Suez Canal, and Israeli military patrols were ambushed.

In the summer of 1970, the United States persuaded Israel and

Egypt to accept a cease-fire. This cease-fire was designed to lead to negotiations under UN auspices.

On August 7, however, the Soviets and Egyptians deployed sophisticated ground-to-air missiles in the restricted thirty-two-mile-deep zone along the west bank of the Suez Canal. This was a violation of the cease-fire agreement, which barred the introduction or construction of any military installations in this area. The "most massive anti-aircraft system ever created" provided air coverage for Egypt's surprise attack against Israel in 1973.[6] Despite Egypt's provocative action, the cease-fire held.

This bloody War of Attrition, as it became known, lasted three years. The Israeli death toll between June 15, 1967, and August 8, 1970, when a cease-fire was declared, was 1,424 soldiers and more than one hundred civilians. Another two thousand soldiers and seven hundred civilians were wounded. Egypt suffered approximately five thousand dead.[7]

MYTH

Israel rejected Sadat's reasonable peace offer.

FACT

Despite the Egyptian violations, UN-sponsored negotiations resumed—additional evidence that Israel was anxious to make progress toward peace. The talks were swiftly short-circuited, however, by UN Special Envoy Gunnar Jarring, when he accepted the Egyptian interpretation of Resolution 242 and called for Israel's total withdrawal to the pre–June 5, 1967, demarcation lines.

On that basis, Anwar Sadat, Egypt's new president expressed his willingness "to enter into a peace agreement with Israel" in a February 20, 1971, letter to Jarring. But this seeming moderation masked an unchanging Egyptian irredentism and unwillingness to accept a real peace, as shown by the letter's sweeping reservations and preconditions. The crucial sentences about a "peace agreement with Israel" were neither published nor broadcast in Egypt. Moreover, Egypt refused to enter direct negotiations. Israel attempted to transform the struggling Jarring mission into bilateral discussions by addressing all letters not to Jarring, but to the Egyptian government. Egypt refused to accept them.

Contrary to revisionist histories suggesting that Israel missed a chance to make peace and avoid the 1973 war by failing to respond favorably to Sadat's initiatives, Sadat did not sound like a leader interested in peace. He threatened to go to war if a political solution was not achieved and demanded Israel's complete withdrawal from the Sinai and a resolution of the Palestinian refugee problem, while at the same time declaring he would never establish diplomatic relations with Israel. He also was unwilling to negotiate because of fears he would anger his financial patrons in Libya and Saudi Arabia and possibly lose power. Furthermore, Sadat could not have made peace in 1971 because it would have been from a point of weakness and dishonor.[8]

Five days after Sadat suggested he was ready to make peace with Israel, Mohammed Heikal, a Sadat confidant and editor of the semiofficial *Al-Ahram,* wrote:

> Arab policy at this stage has but two objectives. The first, the elimination of the traces of the 1967 aggression through an Israeli withdrawal from all the territories it occupied that year. The second objective is the elimination of the traces of the 1948 aggression, by the means of the elimination of the State of Israel itself. This is, however, as yet an abstract, undefined objective, and some of us have erred in commencing the latter step before the former.[9]

Sadat was only willing to sign a peace agreement if Israel capitulated to all his demands. This was unacceptable to Israel. Moreover, Israelis questioned Sadat's sincerity after the Egyptian president promised the Palestine National Council meeting in Cairo in 1971 that he would support the PLO "until victory," and declared that Egypt would not accept Resolution 242.[10]

In 1972, after Israel rejected his offer, Sadat said war was inevitable and that he was prepared to sacrifice one million soldiers in the showdown with Israel.[11] He carried out his threat a year later.

MYTH

Israel was responsible for the 1973 War.

FACT

Throughout 1972, and for much of 1973, Egyptian president Anwar Sadat threatened war unless the United States forced Israel to accept his interpretation of Resolution 242—total Israeli withdrawal from territories taken in 1967. In an April 1973 interview, Sadat warned he would renew the war with Israel.[12] But it was the same threat he had made in 1971 and 1972, and most observers remained skeptical.

On October 6, 1973—Yom Kippur, the holiest day in the Jewish calendar—Egypt and Syria opened a coordinated surprise attack against Israel. The equivalent of the total forces of NATO in Europe was mobilized on Israel's borders.[13] On the Golan Heights, approxi-

Map 15
Egyptian Attack, Oct. 6, 1973
Syrian Attack, Oct. 6, 1973

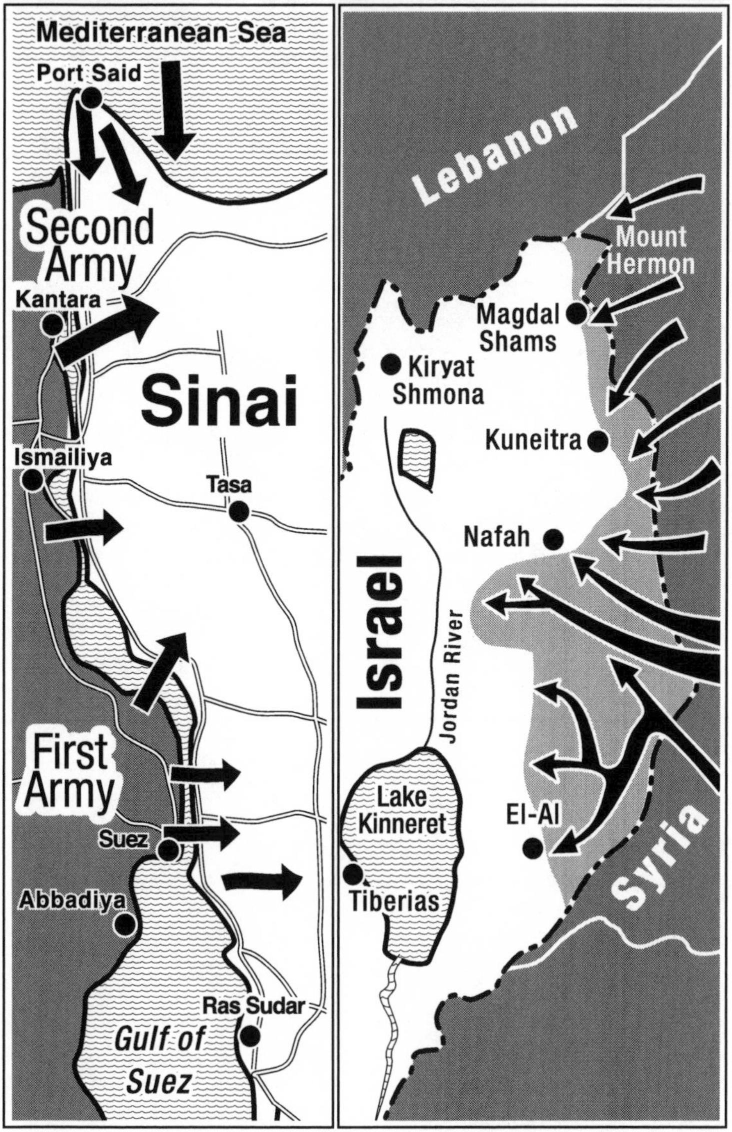

Mediterranean Sea
Port Said
Second Army
Kantara
Sinai
Ismailiya
Tasa
First Army
Suez
Abbadiya
Ras Sudar
Gulf of Suez

Lebanon
Mount Hermon
Magdal Shams
Kiryat Shmona
Kuneitra
Nafah
Israel
Jordan River
Nafah
Lake Kinneret
El-Al
Tiberias
Syria

mately 180 Israeli tanks faced an onslaught of fourteen hundred Syrian tanks. Along the Suez Canal, fewer than five hundred Israeli defenders were attacked by eighty thousand Egyptians.

Thrown onto the defensive during the first two days of fighting, Israel mobilized its reserves and eventually repulsed the invaders and carried the war deep into Syria and Egypt. The Arab states were swiftly resupplied by sea and air from the Soviet Union, which rejected US efforts to work toward an immediate cease-fire. As a result, the United States belatedly began its own airlift to Israel. Two weeks later, Egypt was saved from a disastrous defeat when the Soviets invited Secretary of State Henry Kissinger to Moscow and negotiated the terms for ending the war through a UN Security Council Resolution. The UN, which had failed to act while the tide was in the Arabs' favor, now acted to save them at the behest of the superpowers.

On October 22, 1973, the Security Council adopted Resolution 338 calling for "all parties to the present fighting to cease all firing and terminate all military activity immediately." The vote came on the day that Israeli forces cut off and isolated the Egyptian Third Army and were in a position to destroy it.[14]

Despite the Israel Defense Forces' ultimate success on the battlefield, the war was considered a diplomatic and military failure. A total of 2,688 Israeli soldiers and approximately nineteen thousand Arabs were killed.

All countries should wage war against the Zionists, who are there to destroy all human organizations and to destroy civilization and the work which good people are trying to do.

—King Faisal of Saudi Arabia[15]

MYTH

Egypt and Syria were the only Arab states involved in the 1973 war.

FACT

At least nine Arab states, including four non-Middle Eastern nations, actively aided the Egyptian-Syrian war effort.

A few months before the Yom Kippur War, Iraq transferred a squadron of Hunter jets to Egypt. During the war, an Iraqi division of some eighteen thousand men and several hundred tanks was deployed in the central Golan and participated in the October 16 attack against Israeli positions.[16] Iraqi MiGs began operating over the Golan Heights as early as October 8, the third day of the war.

Besides serving as financial underwriters, Saudi Arabia and Kuwait committed men to battle. A Saudi brigade of approximately three thousand troops was dispatched to Syria, where it participated in fighting along the approaches to Damascus. Additionally, violating Paris's ban on the transfer of French-made weapons, Libya sent Mirage fighters to Egypt.[17]

Other North African countries responded to Arab and Soviet calls to aid the frontline states. Algeria sent three aircraft squadrons of fighters and bombers, an armored brigade and 150 tanks. Approximately one thousand to two thousand Tunisian soldiers were positioned in the Nile Delta. The Sudan stationed thirty-five hundred troops in southern Egypt, and Morocco sent three brigades to the front lines, including twenty-five hundred men to Syria.

Lebanese radar units were used by Syrian air defense forces. Lebanon also allowed Palestinian terrorists to shell Israeli civilian settlements from its territory. Palestinians fought on the southern front with the Egyptians and Kuwaitis.[18]

The least enthusiastic participant in the October fighting was probably Jordan's King Hussein. He had actually warned Golda Meir that a war was coming, but couldn't tell her when because he had been kept uninformed of Egyptian and Syrian war plans.[19] After the war began, Hussein did send two of his best units—the fortieth and sixtieth armored brigades—to Syria. This force took positions in the southern sector, defending the main Amman-Damascus route and attacking Israeli positions along the Kuneitra-Sassa road on October 16. Three Jordanian artillery batteries also participated in the assault, carried out by nearly one hundred tanks.[20]

Notes, Chapter 6

1. Walter Lacquer, *The Road to War* (London: Weidenfeld and Nicolson, 1968), 297.
2. "Khartoum Resolutions," Jewish Virtual Library, (September 1, 1967), www.Jewish-VirtualLibrary.org/jsource/Peace/three_noes.html.
3. Chaim Herzog, *The Arab-Israeli Wars* (NY: Random House, 1982), 195.
4. Netanel Lorch, *One Long War* (NY: Herzl Press, 1976), 139-46.
5. Quoted in Alfred Leroy Atherton, Jr., Foreign Affairs Oral History Collection of the Association for Diplomatic Studies and Training (Summer 1990).
6. "World: Buildup on the Suez," *Time* (September 14, 1970); John Pimlott, *The Middle East Conflicts from 1945 to the Present* (NY: Crescent Books, 1983), 99.
7. Some historians consider the starting date of the War of Attrition in 1968 or 1969. We are using Chaim Herzog's time frame. Chaim Herzog, *The Arab-Israeli Wars* (NY: Random House, 1984), 195-221; Nadav Safran, *Israel, the Embattled Ally,* (MA: Harvard University Press, 1981), 266.
8. Shlomo Aronson, "On Sadat's Peace Initiatives in the Wake of the Yom Kippur War"; Mitchell Bard, *Will Israel Survive* (NY: Palgrave, 2007), 8-9.
9. Cited in Anwar Sadat, *The Public Diary of President Sadat, Vol 2.* (BRILL: 1978), 33-34.
10. *Al-Ahram* (February 25, 1971).

11. Howard Sachar, *A History of Israel: From the Rise of Zionism to Our Time* (NY: Alfred A. Knopf, 1979), 747.
12. *Newsweek* (April 9, 1973).
13. Herzog, 230.
14. Herzog, 280.
15. *Beirut Daily Star* (November 17, 1972).
16. Trevor Dupuy, *Elusive Victory: The Arab-Israeli Wars, 1947-1974* (NY: Harper & Row, 1978), 462.
17. Dupuy, 376; Herzog, 278; Safran, 1981), 499.
18. Herzog, 278, 285, 293; Dupuy, 534.
19. Bernard Avishai, "An Unlikely King: Hussein in War and Peace," *The Nation* (September 3, 2008).
20. Herzog, 300.

7. Borders and Boundaries

Israel has been an expansionist state since its creation.
Israel seized the Golan Heights and illegally annexed the area.
The Golan has no strategic significance for Israel.
Israel can withdraw from the West Bank as easily as from Sinai.
Defensible borders are unrealistic in an era of ballistic missiles.
Israel "occupies" the West Bank.
Israel's security fence is meant to create a Palestinian ghetto.
Israel is the only country that has a fence to secure its borders.
The security fence should be built along the pre-1967 border.
Israel's security fence is comparable to the Berlin Wall.

MYTH

Israel has been an expansionist state since its creation.

FACT

Israel's boundaries were determined by the United Nations when it adopted the partition resolution in 1947. In a series of defensive wars, Israel captured additional territory. Israel has withdrawn from more than 90 percent of the area it won in these wars and has repeatedly offered to give up additional lands it now controls in exchange for peace and security.

As part of the 1974 disengagement agreement, Israel returned territories captured in the 1967 and 1973 wars to Syria.

Under the terms of the 1979 Israeli-Egyptian peace treaty, Israel withdrew from the Sinai peninsula for the third time. It had already withdrawn from large parts of the desert area it captured in its War of Independence. After capturing the entire Sinai in the 1956 Suez conflict, Israel relinquished the peninsula to Egypt a year later.

In September 1983, Israel withdrew from large areas of Lebanon to positions south of the Awali River. In 1985, all troops were withdrawn with the exception of a small force holding a narrow "security zone" just north of the Israeli border. In 2000, Israel evacuated completely from Lebanon.

After signing the Oslo agreements with the Palestinians, and a treaty with Jordan, Israel agreed to withdraw from most of the territory in the West Bank captured from Jordan in 1967. A small area was returned to Jordan, and more than 40 percent was ceded to the Palestinian Authority. The agreement with the Palestinians also involved

Map 16   Peace with Egypt

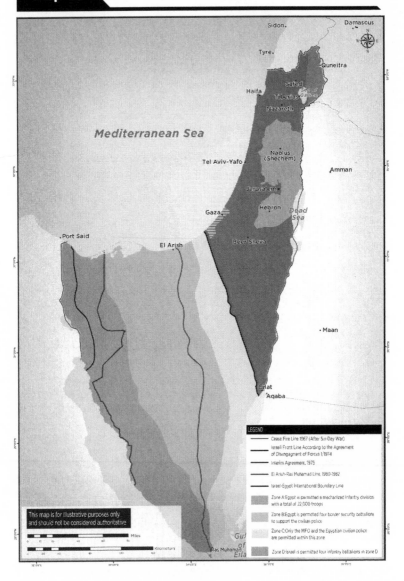

Israel's withdrawal in 1994 from most of the Gaza Strip, which had been captured from Egypt in 1973.

In 2000, Israeli prime minister Ehud Barak offered to withdraw from 97 percent of the West Bank and 100 percent of the Gaza Strip in a final settlement. In addition, Prime Minister Yitzhak Rabin and his successors offered to withdraw from virtually all of the Golan Heights in exchange for peace with Syria. These offers were rejected.

In August 2005, all Israeli troops and civilians were evacuated from the Gaza Strip and the territory was turned over to the control of the Palestinian Authority. In addition, four communities in Northern Samaria that covered an area larger than the entire Gaza Strip were evacuated as part of the disengagement plan. As a result, Israel has now withdrawn from approximately 94 percent of the territory it captured in 1967.

Today, the only question is the final disposition of the remaining 6 percent of the disputed territories in Israel's possession (about 136 square miles, roughly the size of Las Vegas). The Palestinians have turned down multiple offers in which Israel agreed to withdraw from nearly all the remaining land in exchange for lands swaps. (That is, in exchange for retaining, say, 4 percent of the land in the West Bank, Israel would give the Palestinians an equivalent amount of land now controlled by Israel, such as a swath of territory adjacent to the Gaza Strip).

Israel's willingness to make territorial concessions in exchange for security proves its goal is peace, not expansion.

MYTH

Israel seized the Golan Heights and illegally annexed the area.

FACT

Between 1948 and 1967, Syria controlled the Golan Heights and used it as a military stronghold from which its troops randomly sniped at Israeli civilians in the Hula Valley below, forcing children living on kibbutzim to sleep in bomb shelters. In addition, many roads in northern Israel could be crossed only after being cleared by mine-detection vehicles. In late 1966, a youth was blown to pieces by a mine while playing soccer near the Lebanon border. In some cases, attacks were carried out by Yasser Arafat's Fatah, which Syria allowed to operate from its territory.[1]

Israel repeatedly, and unsuccessfully, protested the Syrian bombardments to the UN Mixed Armistice Commission, which was charged with enforcing the cease-fire. For example, Israel went to the UN in October 1966 to demand a halt to the Fatah attacks. The re-

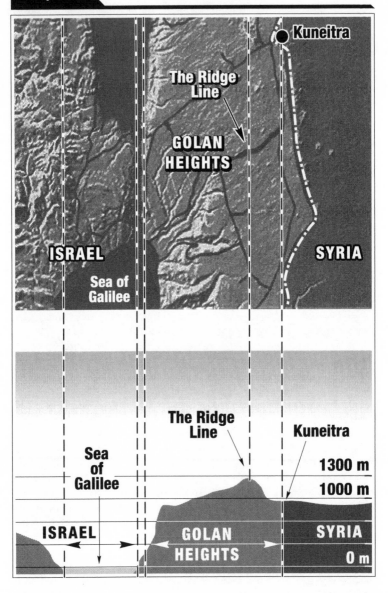

Map 17 The Golan Heights Ridge Line

sponse from the Syrian ambassador was defiant: "It is not our duty to stop them, but to encourage and strengthen them."[2]

Nothing was done to stop Syria's aggression. A mild Security Council resolution expressing "regret" for such incidents was vetoed by the Soviet Union. Meanwhile, Israel was condemned by the UN when it retaliated. "As far as the Security Council was officially concerned," historian Netanel Lorch wrote, "there was an open season for killing Israelis on their own territory."[3]

After the Six-Day War began, the Syrian air force attempted to bomb oil refineries in Haifa. While Israel was fighting in the Sinai and West Bank, Syrian artillery bombarded Israeli forces in the eastern Galilee, and armored units fired on villages in the Hula Valley below the Golan Heights.

On June 9, 1967, Israel moved against Syrian forces on the Golan. By late afternoon, June 10, Israel was in complete control of the plateau. Israel's seizure of the strategic heights occurred only after nineteen years of provocation from Syria, and after unsuccessful efforts to get the international community to act against the aggressors.

On December 14, 1981, the Knesset voted to annex the Golan Heights. The statute extended Israeli civilian law and administration to the residents of the Golan, replacing the military authority that had ruled the area since 1967. The law does not foreclose the option of negotiations on the final status of the territory.

Following the Knesset's approval of the law, Professor Julius Stone of Hastings College of the Law wrote, "There is no rule of international law which requires a lawful military occupant, in this situation, to wait forever before [making] control and government of the territory permanent . . . Many international lawyers have wondered, indeed, at the patience which led Israel to wait as long as she did."[4]

MYTH

The Golan has no strategic significance for Israel.

FACT

Syria—deterred by an IDF presence within artillery range of Damascus—kept the Golan quiet since 1974 with the exception of a few cross-border attacks that spilled over in 2015–16 during the Syrian civil war. Syria has supported and provided a haven for numerous terrorist groups that attacked Israel from Lebanon and other countries. These include the Democratic Front for the Liberation of Palestine (DFLP), the Popular Front for the Liberation of Palestine (PFLP), Hezbollah, and the Popular Front for the Liberation of Palestine-General Command (PFLP-GC). From the western Golan, it is only about sixty

Map 18 Relative Size of the Golan Heights

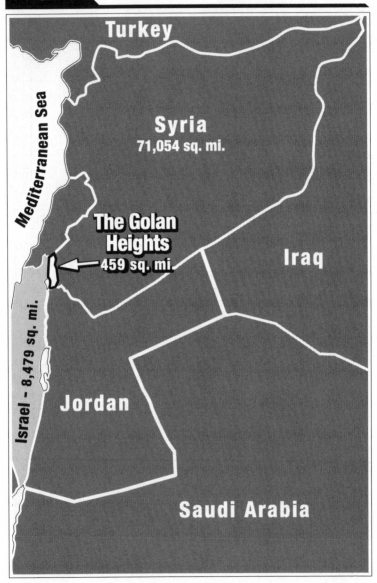

miles—without major terrain obstacles—to Haifa and Acre, Israel's industrial heartland.

The Golan—rising from four hundred to seventeen hundred feet in the western section bordering on pre-1967 Israel—overlooks the Hula Valley, Israel's richest agricultural area. In the hands of a friendly neighbor, the escarpment has little military importance. If controlled by a hostile country, however, the Golan has the potential to again become a strategic nightmare for Israel.

Before the Six-Day War, when Israeli agricultural settlements in the Galilee came under fire from the Golan, Israel's options for countering the Syrian attacks were constrained by the geography of the Heights. "Counterbattery fire was limited by the lack of observation from the Hula Valley; air attacks were degraded by well-dug-in Syrian positions with strong overhead cover, and a ground attack against the positions . . . would require major forces with the attendant risks of heavy casualties and severe political repercussions," US Army Col. (Ret.) Irving Heymont observed.[5]

When Israel eventually took these risks and stormed the Syrian positions in 1967, it suffered 115 dead—roughly the number of Americans killed during Operation Desert Storm.

Israel held talks with the Syrians in hopes of reaching an agreement to permanently secure the peace. Syria insisted, however, that Israel completely withdraw from the entire Golan Heights before even discussing what Syria might do in return. President Hafez Assad and his son never expressed any willingness to make peace even if Israel met this demand.

Israel was equally adamant that it would not give up any territory without knowing what Syria was prepared to concede, and insisted that Syria agree to normalize relations and sign an agreement that would bring about an end to the state of war Syria says exists between them. These points are now moot because of the Syrian civil war.

During the best of times, relinquishing the Golan to Syria without adequate security arrangements could jeopardize Israel's early-warning system against surprise attack. Israel has built radar systems on Mt. Hermon, the highest point in the region. If Israel withdrew from the Golan and had to relocate these facilities to the lowlands of the Galilee, they would lose much of their strategic effectiveness.

Israel's unwillingness to give up the Golan looks even more prescient today as fighters from Iran, Hezbollah, and ISIS have fought a war that is so destructive that Syria may never be reconstituted as a single nation with its previous borders. It now appears likely that whoever takes control of the area abutting the Golan Heights will be more radical, adventurous, and hostile than the Assad regime and pose the most serious security threat to Israel since 1973. Unless a future leader of Syria (or whoever emerges from the civil war in control of the area along the Golan) dramatically changes the country's orientation, and accepts Israel as a neighbor, it is difficult to imagine any new talks regarding the status of the Golan Heights for the foreseeable future.

From a strictly military point of view, Israel would require the retention of some captured territory in order to provide militarily defensible borders.

**—Memorandum for the secretary of defense
from the joint chiefs of staff, June 29, 1967**

MYTH

Israel can withdraw from the West Bank as easily as from Sinai.

FACT

Several pages of Israel's peace treaty with Egypt are devoted to security arrangements. For example, Article III of the treaty's annex concerns the areas where reconnaissance flights are permitted, and Article V allows the establishment of early-warning systems in specific zones.

The security guarantees, which were required to give Israel the confidence to withdraw, were only possible because the Sinai was demilitarized. They provide Israel a large buffer zone of more than one hundred miles of sparsely populated desert. Today, the Egyptian border is sixty miles from Tel Aviv and seventy from Jerusalem, the nearest major Israeli cities.

The situation in the territories is entirely different. More than two million Arabs live in the West Bank, many in crowded cities and at least nineteen refugee camps. Most of them are located close to Israeli cities such as Tel Aviv and Jerusalem. The Palestinians have rockets capable of threatening these cities as well as Ben-Gurion Airport.

The infiltration of terrorists from the Palestinian Authority, who have committed horrific acts, such as suicide bombings, illustrate the danger Israelis could face if they evacuate the West Bank. The 2011 uprisings in Egypt, and the ongoing civil war in Syria, are reminders of the risk involved in making permanent territorial concessions to leaders whose tenure is only temporary. Israel must consider the possibility of a hostile regime coming to power in the future and account for the likelihood that the Palestinians will have even more sophisticated weapons at their disposal in the future.

Despite the risks, Israel has withdrawn from more than 40 percent of the West Bank since Oslo and offered to give up 97 percent of it in return for a final settlement with the Palestinians. Israel will not, how-

Map 19 Range of Fire from Judea & Samaria
(West Bank)

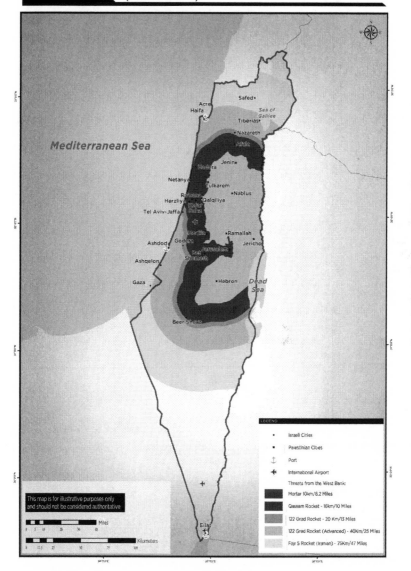

Map 20 Israel–PLO Interim Agreements since 1993

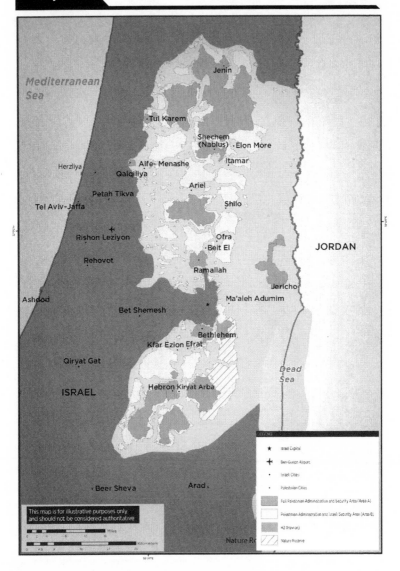

ever, return to the pre-1967 borders as demanded by the Palestinians and the Arab states.

It is impossible to defend Jerusalem unless you hold the high ground . . . An aircraft that takes off from an airport in Amman is going to be over Jerusalem in two-and-a-half minutes, so it's utterly impossible for me to defend the whole country unless I hold that land.

—**Lieutenant General (Ret.) Thomas Kelly,
director of operations for the
joint chiefs of staff during the Gulf War**[6]

MYTH

Defensible borders are unrealistic in an era of ballistic missiles.

FACT

History shows that aerial attacks have never defeated a nation. Countries are only conquered by troops occupying land. One example of this was Iraq's invasion of Kuwait, in which the latter nation was overrun and occupied in a matter of hours. Though the multinational force bombed Iraq for close to six weeks, Kuwait was not liberated until the Allied troops marched into that country in the war's final days. Defensible borders are those that would prevent or impede such a ground assault.

Israel's return to its pre-1967 borders, which the Arab states want to reimpose, would tempt potential aggressors to launch attacks on the Jewish State—as they did routinely before 1967. Israel would lose the extensive system of early-warning radars it has set up in the hills of Judea and Samaria. Were a hostile neighbor then to seize control of these mountains, its army could split Israel in two: from there, it is only about fifteen miles—without any major geographic obstacles—to the Mediterranean.

At their narrowest point, these 1967 lines are within nine miles of the Israeli coast, eleven miles from Tel Aviv, ten from Be'er Sheva, twenty-one from Haifa, and one foot from Jerusalem.

To defend Jerusalem, the US joint chiefs concluded in a 1967 report to the secretary of defense, Israel would need to have its border "positioned to the east of the city."[7]

Control over the Jordan River Valley is also critical to Israeli security because it "forms a natural security barrier between Israel and Jordan, and effectively acts as an anti-tank ditch," military analyst Anthony Cordesman noted. "This defensive line sharply increases the amount of time Israel has to mobilize and its ability to ensure control

Map 21 Flying Times to Israel

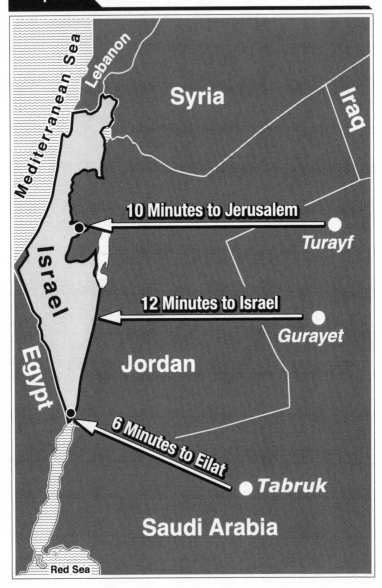

over the West Bank in the event of a war." He added that sacrificing control over the routes up to the heights above the West Bank makes it more difficult for the IDF to deploy and increases the risk of Jordanian, Syrian, or Palestinian forces deploying on the heights.[8]

Even in the era of ballistic missiles, strategic depth matters. The Jaffee Center for Strategic Studies, an Israeli think tank considered dovish, concluded: "Early-warning stations and the deployment of surface-to-air missile batteries can provide the time needed to sound an air-raid alert, and warn the population to take shelter from a missile attack. They might even allow enemy missiles to be intercepted in mid-flight . . . As long as such missiles are armed with conventional warheads, they may cause painful losses and damage, but they cannot decide the outcome of a war."[9]

MYTH

Israel "occupies" the West Bank.

FACT

In politics, words matter, and, unfortunately, the misuse of words applying to the Arab-Israeli conflict has shaped perceptions to Israel's disadvantage. As in the case of the term "West Bank," the word "occupation" has been hijacked by those who wish to paint Israel in the harshest possible light. It also gives apologists an excuse to describe terrorism as "resistance to occupation," as if the women and children killed by suicide bombers in buses, pizzerias, and shopping malls were responsible for the plight of the Palestinians.

Given the negative connotation of an "occupier," it is not surprising that Israel's detractors use the word, or some variation, as many times as possible in their propaganda and when interviewed by the press. The more accurate description of the territories in Judea and Samaria, however, is "disputed" territories.

Nonetheless, the European Union has fallen for the propaganda and accepted the fallacious terminology. In July 2013, the EU published guidelines severely limiting interaction with Israeli entities beyond the pre-1967 lines. The new rules enforce the union's "long-held position that bilateral agreements with Israel do not cover the territory that came under Israel's administration in June 1967." This means the EU has banned funding and cooperation with Israeli institutions that operate beyond the "Green Line."[10]

In 2015, the EU imposed additional punitive measures against Israel by recommending that all goods originating from the disputed territories carry a label indicating they were from an "Israeli settlement."[11] Goods from other disputed territories around the world do not require labeling; thus, Israel is singled out for special treatment reminiscent of the Nazi boycott against Jews in Germany.

The EU action also undermines the prospect for a negotiated peace by giving the Palestinians the false hope that the international community will pressure Israel to make concessions without the Palestinians having to negotiate or compromise.

The hypocrisy of critics of Israel's administration of the West Bank is compounded by the fact that other disputed territories around the world are not referred to as being occupied by the party that controls them. This is true, for example, of the hotly contested regions of Kashmir, Cyprus, and Tibet. Yet rarely does the international community make a fuss over these territories.[12]

Occupation typically refers to foreign control of an area that was under the previous sovereignty of another state. In the case of the West Bank, there was no legitimate sovereign because the territory had been illegally occupied by Jordan from 1948 to 1967. Only two countries—Britain and Pakistan—recognized Jordan's action. The Palestinians never demanded an end to Jordanian occupation and the creation of a Palestinian state.

For a Texan, a first visit to Israel is an eye-opener. At the narrowest point, it's only 8 miles from the Mediterranean to the old Armistice line: That's less than from the top to the bottom of Dallas-Ft. Worth Airport. The whole of pre-1967 Israel is only about six times the size of the King Ranch near Corpus Christi.

—President George W. Bush[13]

It is also necessary to distinguish the acquisition of territory in a war of conquest as opposed to a war of self-defense. A nation that attacks another and then retains the territory it conquers is an occupier. One that gains territory in the course of defending itself is not in the same category. This is the situation with Israel, which specifically told King Hussein that if Jordan stayed out of the 1967 War, Israel would not fight against him. Hussein ignored the warning and attacked Israel. While fending off the assault, and driving out the invading Jordanian troops, Israel came to control the West Bank.

By rejecting Arab demands that Israel be required to withdraw from all the territories won in 1967, UN Security Council Resolution 242 acknowledged that Israel was entitled to claim at least part of these lands for new defensible borders.

Since Oslo, the case for tagging Israel as an occupying power has been further weakened by the fact that Israel transferred virtually all civilian authority in the West Bank to the Palestinian Authority. Israel retained the power to control its own external security and that of its citizens, but 98 percent of the Palestinian population in the West Bank, and 100 percent in Gaza, came under the PA's authority.

The extent to which Israel has been forced to maintain a military presence in the territories has been governed by the Palestinians' unwillingness to end violence against Israel. The only way to resolve the dispute over the territories is for the Palestinians to negotiate a final settlement. Until now, the intransigence of the Palestinian Authority's leadership has prevented the resumption of peace talks, which offer the only route to an agreement that will lead to a sustainable future for Israelis and Palestinians alike.

MYTH

Israel's security fence is meant to create a Palestinian ghetto.

FACT

Israel did not want to build a fence, and resisted doing so for more than thirty-five years. If anyone is to blame for the construction, it is Hamas, Islamic Jihad, and the other Palestinian terrorists.

Following the 1967 War, the frontier separating Israel from the West Bank had no physical obstacles to prevent the infiltration of terrorists. In response to dozens of suicide bombings and daily terrorist attacks against its civilians, Israel decided to construct a security fence near the "Green Line" (the 1949 armistice line) to prevent Palestinian terrorists from crossing the border.

A large majority of Israelis support the construction of the security fence. Israelis living along the Green Line, both Jews and Arabs, were happy because the fence helps prevent penetration by thieves and vandals as well as terrorists. In fact, the fence caused a revolution in the daily life of some Israeli Arab towns because it has brought quiet, which allowed a significant upsurge in economic activity.[14]

The fence is not impregnable. It is possible that some terrorists will manage to get past the barrier; nevertheless, the obstacle makes it far more difficult for incursions and thereby minimizes the number of attacks. During the thirty-four months from the beginning of the violence in September 2000 until the construction of the first continuous segment of the security fence at the end of July 2003, Samaria-based terrorists carried out seventy-three attacks in which 293 Israelis were killed and 1,950 wounded. In the eleven months between the erection of the first segment at the beginning of August 2003 and the end of June 2004, only three attacks were successful, and all three occurred in the first half of 2003. The value of the fence in saving lives is clear: in 2002, the year before construction started, 457 Israelis were murdered. From 2004 through 2014, 339 Israelis were killed in Israel.[15]

This is still far too many lives lost and reflects the unremitting threat posed by Palestinian terrorists who continue to be incited to violence by their leaders.

MYTH

Israel is the only country that has a fence to secure its borders.

FACT

It is not unreasonable or unusual to build a fence for security purposes. Before building the security fence, Israel already had fences along the frontiers with Lebanon, Syria, and Jordan, so building a barrier to separate Israel from the Palestinian Authority was not revolutionary. Most nations have fences to protect their borders, and several use barriers in political disputes:

- The United States is building a fence to keep out illegal Mexican immigrants.

- Spain built a fence to separate its enclaves of Ceuta and Melilla from Morocco to prevent people from sub-Saharan Africa from entering Europe.

- India constructed a 460-mile barrier in Kashmir to halt infiltrations supported by Pakistan.

- Saudi Arabia built a sixty-mile barrier along an undefined border zone with Yemen to halt arms smuggling, and, subsequently, erected new barriers in response to the escalation of the civil war in Yemen. The Saudis also built a nearly six-hundred-mile fence on the border with Iraq.

- Turkey built a barrier in the southern province of Alexandretta, which was formerly in Syria and is an area that Syria claims as its own. In 2015, Turkey announced plans to further fortify its border with Syria after a suicide bombing.

- In Cyprus, the UN sponsored a security fence reinforcing the island's de facto partition.

- Tunisia began to construct a fence to guard its border with Libya after an attack on a Tunisian beach hotel killed thirty-eight foreign tourists.

- The British built barriers to separate Catholic and Protestant neighborhoods in Belfast.[16]

- Ironically, after condemning Israel's barrier, the UN announced plans to build its own fence to improve security around its New York headquarters.[17]

- Even ISIS has built barriers to defend its territory in Iraq and to keep people from escaping.[18]

■ Three decades before any of these fortifications were built, Morocco built the oldest and longest security barrier to separate areas controlled by Morocco and the Polisario. In 2014, Morocco began construction of a new divider along its border with Algeria.

Only Israel's security fence has been the subject of UN condemnation and a ruling by the International Court of Justice; one more example of the double standard applied to Israel.

MYTH

The security fence should be built along the pre-1967 border.

FACT

Critics have complained that the fence is being built beyond Israel's pre-1967 border, but the so-called "Green Line" was not an internationally recognized border, it was an armistice line between Israel and Jordan pending the negotiation of a final border. As Israel's Supreme Court noted in its ruling on the route of the barrier, building the fence along that line would have been a political statement and would not accomplish the principal goal of the barrier, namely, the prevention of terror.

The route of the fence must take into account topography, population density, and threat assessment of each area. To be effective in protecting the maximum number of Israelis, it also must incorporate some of the settlements in the West Bank.

Most of the fence runs roughly along the "Green Line." In some places, the fence is *inside* this line. One of the most controversial questions has been whether to build the fence around Ariel, a town of approximately twenty thousand people. To incorporate Ariel, the fence would have to extend approximately twelve miles into the West Bank. In the short run, Israel decided to build a separate fence around Ariel.

Palestinians complain that the fence creates "facts on the ground," but most of the area incorporated within the fence is expected to be part of Israel in any peace agreement with the Palestinians. Israeli negotiators have always envisioned the future border to be the 1967 frontier with modifications to minimize the security risk to Israel and maximize the number of Jews living within the state.

The original route has been repeatedly modified. As a result of the June 2004 supreme court decision, the barrier was moved closer to the 1967 cease-fire line to make it less burdensome to the Palestinians. The fence is now expected to cover approximately five hundred miles and incorporate just 7 percent of the West Bank—less than 160 square miles—on its "Israeli side," while twenty-one hundred square miles will be on the "Palestinian side." To date, more than 320 miles of the fence have been completed.

Approximately 99 percent of West Bank Palestinians are on the Palestinian side of the fence. Every effort is being made to exclude Palestinian villages from the area within the fence, and no territories are being annexed. The land used in building the security fence is seized for military purposes, not confiscated, and it remains the property of the owner. Legal procedures allow every owner to file an objection to the seizure of their land. In addition, Israel budgeted $22 million to compensate Palestinians for the use of their land.

Israel is doing its best to minimize the negative impact on Palestinians in the area of construction and is providing agricultural passageways to allow farmers to continue to cultivate their lands, and crossing points to allow the movement of people and the transfer of goods. Moreover, property owners are offered compensation for the use of their land and for any damage to their trees. Contractors are responsible for carefully uprooting and replanting the trees. So far, more than sixty thousand olive trees have been relocated in accordance with this procedure.

Despite Israel's best efforts, the fence has caused some injury to residents near the fence. Israel's supreme court took up the grievances of Palestinians (who are allowed to petition the court without being Israeli citizens) and ruled the government had to reduce the infringement upon local inhabitants by altering the path of the fence in an area near Jerusalem. Though the court's decision made the government's job of securing the population from terrorist threats more difficult, costly, and time consuming, the prime minister immediately accepted the ruling.

If and when the Palestinians decide to negotiate an end to the conflict, the fence may be torn down or moved (as occurred after Israel's withdrawal from Lebanon). Even without any change, a Palestinian state could now theoretically be created in 93 percent of the West Bank (Hamas now controls 100 percent of the Gaza Strip) if Israel evacuated entirely without any land swaps. This is very close to the 97 percent Israel offered to the Palestinians at Camp David in 2000, which means that while other difficult issues remain to be resolved, the territorial aspect of the dispute has been reduced to a negotiation over roughly ninety square miles (93 percent vs. 97 percent).

MYTH

Israel's security fence is comparable to the Berlin Wall.

FACT

Although critics have sought to portray the security fence as a kind of "Berlin Wall," it is nothing of the sort. First, unlike the Berlin Wall, the fence does not separate one people, Germans from Germans, or deny freedom to those on one side. Israel's security fence separates two peoples, Israelis and Palestinians, and offers freedom and security for both. Second, while Israelis are fully prepared to live with Palestinians, and 20 percent of the Israeli population is already Arab, it is the Palestinians who say they do not want to live with any Jews and call for the West Bank to be *judenrein*. Third, the fence is not being constructed to prevent the citizens of one state from escaping; it is designed solely to keep terrorists out of Israel. Fourth, there are no guard towers with machine-gun toting guards to shoot anyone who approaches the fence.

Finally, most of the barrier is a chain-link type fence, similar to those used all over the United States, combined with underground and long-range sensors, unmanned aerial vehicles, trenches, landmines, and guard paths. Less than 3 percent (about fifteen miles) is a thirty-foot-high concrete wall, built in areas where it will prevent Palestinian snipers from shooting at Israeli cars, as they did for three years along the Trans-Israel Highway, one of the country's main roads.

Notes, Chapter 7

1. Netanel Lorch, *One Long War* (Jerusalem: Keter, 1976), 106-10.
2. Anne Sinai and Allen Pollack, *The Syrian Arab Republic* (NY: American Academic Association for Peace in the Middle East, 1976), 117.
3. Lorch, 111.
4. *Near East Report* (January 29, 1982).
5. Sinai and Pollack, 130-31.
6. Justus Reid Weiner and Diane Morrison, "Linking the Gaza Strip with the West Bank: Implications of a Palestinian Corridor across Israel," *JCPA* (2007).
7. Memorandum for the Secretary of Defense, June 29, 1967, cited in Dore Gold, "Defensible Borders for Israel," JCPA (June 15, 2003).
8. Anthony Cordesman, "Escalating to Nowhere: The Israeli-Palestinian War—The Final Settlement Issues" (DC: CSIS, January 13, 2005), 15.
9. *Israel's Options for Peace* (Tel Aviv: The Jaffee Center for Strategic Studies, 1989), 171-72.
10. Herb Keinon, "EU Officially Publishes Settlement Guidelines despite Israeli Objections," *Jerusalem Post*, (July 19, 2013).
11. Malcolm Lowe, "The EU's Embarrassing Little Secret in Labeling Israeli Products," Gatestone Institute (November 19, 2015).
12. Douglas Murray, "'Occupied Territories': What about Cyprus, Kashmir, Tibet?" *Gatestone Institute* (July 23, 2013).
13. Speech to the American Jewish Committee (May 3, 2001).
14. Yair Ettinger, "Highway, Fence Spur Growth in Wadi Ara," *Haaretz* (July 14, 2004).
15. Israel Ministry of Foreign Affairs.
16. Ben Thein, "Is Israel's Security Barrier Unique?" *Middle East Quarterly* (Fall 2004), 25-32.
17. United Nations (May 6, 2004).
18. Salma Wardany and Caroline Alexander, "Fences Rise across Middle East as Jihadi Threat Escalates," *Bloomberg* (July 23, 2015).

8. Israel and Lebanon

The PLO posed no threat to Israel in 1982 when Israel attacked Lebanon.

Israel was responsible for the massacre of Palestinian refugees at Sabra and Shatila.

Israel instigated a second war in Lebanon without provocation.

Lebanon poses no direct threat to Israel.

Israeli forces deliberately targeted civilians during the war instigated by Hezbollah.

The media fairly and accurately covered the second war in Lebanon.

MYTH

The PLO posed no threat to Israel in 1982 when Israel attacked Lebanon.

FACT

The PLO repeatedly violated a cease-fire agreement reached in July 1981. By June 1982, when the IDF went into Lebanon, the PLO had made life in northern Israel intolerable through its repeated shelling of Israeli towns.

In the ensuing eleven months, the PLO staged 270 terrorist actions in Israel, the West Bank, and Gaza, and along the Lebanese and Jordanian borders. Twenty-nine Israelis died, and more than three hundred were injured in the attacks.[1] The frequency of attacks in the Galilee forced thousands of residents to flee their homes or to spend large amounts of time in bomb shelters.

A force of some fifteen to eighteen thousand PLO members was encamped in scores of locations in Lebanon. About five to six thousand were foreign mercenaries, coming from countries such as Libya, Iraq, India, Sri Lanka, Chad, and Mozambique.[2] The PLO had an arsenal that included mortars, Katyusha rockets, and an extensive antiaircraft network.[3] The PLO also brought hundreds of T-34 tanks into the area.[4] Syria, which permitted Lebanon to become a haven for the PLO and other terrorist groups, brought surface-to-air missiles into that country, creating yet another danger for Israel.

Israeli strikes and commando raids were unable to stem the growth of this PLO army. Israel was not prepared to wait for more deadly attacks to be launched against its civilian population before acting against the terrorists. The final straw actually occurred abroad on June 3, 1982, when Israel's ambassador to London, Shlomo Argov, was shot and critically wounded by an assassin from the Abu Nidal faction of the PLO. Israel retaliated by launching an assault on PLO positions in Lebanon on June 4 and 5, and the PLO responded with a massive artillery and mortar barrage on the Israeli population of the Galilee. On June 6, the IDF moved into Lebanon to drive out the terrorists.

Former secretary of state Henry Kissinger defended the Israeli operation: "No sovereign state can tolerate indefinitely the buildup along its borders of a military force dedicated to its destruction and implementing its objectives by periodic shellings and raids."[5]

MYTH

Israel was responsible for the massacre of Palestinian refugees at Sabra and Shatila.

FACT

The Lebanese Christian Phalangist militia was responsible for the massacres that occurred at the two Beirut-area refugee camps on September 16–17, 1982. Israeli troops allowed the Phalangists to enter Sabra and Shatila to root out terrorist cells believed to be located there. It had been estimated that there might have been up to two hundred armed men in the camps working out of the countless bunkers built by the PLO over the years, and stocked with generous reserves of ammunition.[6]

When Israeli soldiers ordered the Phalangists out, they found hundreds dead (the Lebanese police estimated the number to be 460 while Israeli intelligence believed the figure was 700–800). The dead, according to the Lebanese account, included thirty-five women and children. The rest were men: Palestinians, Lebanese, Pakistanis, Iranians, Syrians, and Algerians.[7] The killings were perpetrated to avenge the murders of Lebanese president Bashir Gemayel and twenty-five of his followers, killed in a bomb attack earlier that week.[8]

Israel had allowed the Phalange to enter the camps as part of a plan to transfer authority to the Lebanese, and accepted responsibility for that decision. The Kahan Commission of Inquiry, formed by the Israeli government in response to public outrage and grief, found that Israel was indirectly responsible for not anticipating the possibility of Phalangist violence. Subsequently, Defense Minister Ariel Sharon resigned, and the term of army chief of staff Gen. Raful Eitan was not extended.

The Kahan Commission, declared former secretary of state Henry Kissinger, was "a great tribute to Israeli democracy . . . There are very few governments in the world that one can imagine making such a public investigation of such a difficult and shameful episode."[9]

Ironically, while three hundred thousand Israelis protested the killings, little or no reaction occurred in the Arab world. Outside the Middle East, a major international outcry against Israel erupted over the massacres. The Phalangists, who perpetrated the crime, were spared the brunt of the condemnations for it.

By contrast, few voices were raised in May 1985, when Muslim militiamen attacked the Shatila and Burj-el Barajneh Palestinian refugee camps. According to UN officials, 635 were killed and twenty-five hundred wounded. During a two-year battle between the Syrian-backed Shiite Amal militia and the PLO, more than two thousand people, including many civilians, were reportedly killed. No outcry was directed at the PLO or the Syrians and their allies over the slaughter. International reaction was also muted in October 1990 when Syrian forces overran Christian-controlled areas of Lebanon. In the eight-hour clash, seven hundred Christians were killed—the worst single battle of Lebanon's Civil War.[10] These killings came on top of an estimated ninety-five thousand deaths that had occurred from 1975–1982.[11]

Our goal is to liberate the 1948 borders of Palestine ... [Jews] can go back to Germany or wherever they came from.

—Hezbollah spokesperson Hassan Ezzedin[12]

MYTH

Israel instigated a second war in Lebanon without provocation.

FACT

Though this particular conflict officially began on July 12, 2006, the context of the war was set by disputes stemming from the preceding twenty-four years dating back to the start of the first war in Lebanon. Following the IDF invasion of Lebanon in 1982, during which they sought to destroy the base of operations for the Palestinian Liberation Organization, Iran sent fighters to assist in the creation of a revolutionary Islamic movement in Lebanon, soon called Hezbollah, or "Party of God." As the Israeli presence in Lebanon lingered, Hezbollah drew manpower support from those in the southern part of the country who wanted Israel to withdraw, and its organizational and military infrastructure developed through the help of Iranian and Syrian donations.

Hezbollah attacks against the IDF eventually forced Israel to evacuate its personnel from the buffer zone it had created in southern Lebanon and, on May 24, 2000, Israel ended its eighteen-year military presence there in cooperation with the United Nations and in compliance with the obligations set down by Security Council Resolution 425. Nevertheless, Hezbollah used Israel's withdrawal as a sign of victory and subsequently took over southern Lebanon, creating a veritable "state within a state" while amassing thousands of tons of weaponry and entrenching themselves in civilian areas with a network of bunkers and fortified bases.

Following Israel's withdrawal, Hezbollah initiated numerous cross-border raids to both kill and abduct Israeli soldiers. In October 2000, mere months after Israel's evacuation of Lebanon, Hezbollah guerrillas kidnapped three Israeli soldiers—Benny Avraham, Omar Sawad, and Adi Avitan—and held them as hostages for nearly four years before returning their bodies to Israel in a prisoner exchange deal. From 2000 to 2006, Hezbollah carried out several attacks against northern Israel that killed both civilians and military personnel.

On the morning of July 12, 2006, Hezbollah attacked an IDF patrol. The terrorists killed three soldiers, severely wounded another three, and abducted two—Eldad Regev and Ehud Goldwasser. An IDF merkava tank sent over the border to pursue the guerrillas after this attack was struck by a large land mine and exploded, killing all four soldiers within. Later, another IDF soldier was killed during an attempted rescue operation to recover the bodies of the tank crew.

Israel responded with air and artillery raids against Hezbollah and Lebanese army targets. Hezbollah responded by launching rocket barrages into northern Israel, some reaching as far south as Haifa. The situation would have been worse if the Israeli Air Force had not destroyed Hezbollah's most sophisticated and long-range rockets in the first hours of the fighting.

Under the circumstances it faced—two kidnapped soldiers being held in Lebanon, and Hezbollah firing hundreds of rockets on a daily basis against Israeli cities—Prime Minister Ehud Olmert decided to launch a ground attack on July 22 codenamed Operation Change of Direction. By July 25, fifteen Israeli civilians, among them a number of Israeli Arabs, had been killed from Hezbollah rockets, and dozens more had been wounded.

The fighting ended on August 14 with the signing of a United Nations–brokered ceasefire, and the war was officially ended when Israel lifted its naval blockade of Lebanon on September 8, 2006. After thirty-four days of fighting, Israel lost 121 soldiers, including the two kidnapped soldiers, with more than six hundred injured. In addition, forty-four civilians were killed and nearly fifteen hundred injured. Though estimates vary, Israel claims to have killed more than five hundred Hezbollah fighters. More than eleven hundred Lebanese civilians were killed, many because they were being used as human shields by Hezbollah.

Map 22   2nd Lebanon War

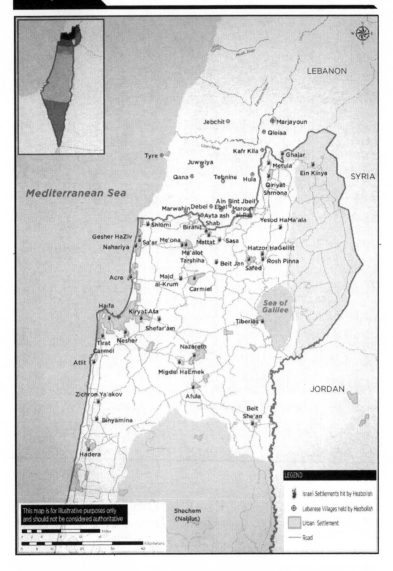

LEBANON

SYRIA

JORDAN

Mediterranean Sea

Jebchit ⊕

⊕ Marjayoun
⊕ Qleiaa

Tyre ⊕

Kafr Kila ⊕

Ghajar

Juwwiya

Metula

Ein Kinya

Qana ⊕

Tebnine ⊕

Hula

Qiriyat
Shmona

Marwahin

Debel ⊕ Ebel ⊕
Ayta ash
Shab

Ain Bint Jbeil
Maroun
al-Ras

Shlomi

Biranit

Yesod HaMa'ala

Gesher HaZiv

Sa'ar

Me'ona

Mattat

Sasa

Nahariya

Ma'alot
Tarshiha

Beit Jan

Hatzor HaGelilit

Rosh Pinna

Acre

Majd
al-Krum

Carmiel

Safed

*Sea of
Galilee*

Haifa

Kiryat Ata

Shefar'am

Tiberias

Tirat
Carmel

Nesher

Nazareth

Atlit

Migdal HaEmek

Zichron Ya'akov

Afula

Beit
She'an

Binyamina

Hadera

Shechem
(Nablus)

This map is for illustrative purposes only
and should not be considered authoritative

Miles

Kilometers

LEGEND

Israeli Settlements hit by Hezbollah

⊕ Lebanese Villages held by Hezbollah

Urban Settlement

Road

Meanwhile, the terrorists fired at least forty-five rockets into Israel forcing thousands of Israelis to live in bomb shelters for more than a month, and tens of thousands to move out of rocket range. Hundreds of thousands of Lebanese civilians also fled the fighting, which left billions of dollars in damage on both sides of the border.[13]

MYTH

Lebanon poses no direct threat to Israel.

FACT

On August 11, 2006, the UN Security Council adopted Resolution 1701 in response to the Israel-Hezbollah war. The resolution called upon the Lebanese government "to secure its borders and other entry points to prevent the entry in Lebanon without its consent of arms and related materials."

In May 2007, United Nations secretary general Ban Ki-moon established the Lebanon Independent Border Assessment Team (LIBAT) to evaluate Lebanon's compliance with Resolution 1701. The committee concluded that "the performance of the (Lebanese inspection) agencies in stopping ongoing arms smuggling, which is generally accepted as a fact, can only be described as not up to what can be expected."[14]

The committee discovered widespread corruption among Lebanese border police and described the ease by which missiles and militants moved across the Syrian-Lebanese border. The report illustrated the United Nations' skepticism of Lebanese attempts to end the flow of illegal arms into Lebanon when it said "one would have expected that an occasional seizure of arms . . . would have taken place. If by nothing else, then by pure chance. This lack of performance is worrying."[15]

Lebanon's failure to implement Resolution 1701 poses a direct threat to Israel and to Lebanese stability. Since the war in 2006, large quantities of weapons (including rockets capable of striking as far south as Tel Aviv and southern Israel), have been smuggled into Lebanon from Syria and Iran.

Hezbollah leader Hassan Nasrallah has openly declared that "Israel is a cancer" and that the "ultimate goal should be to remove it."[16] He has pledged that Hezbollah will not disarm so long as Israel remains a threat. Meanwhile, the Israeli military estimates at least one hundred thousand Hezbollah rockets are aimed at Israel.[17] The UN's failure to ensure the implementation of its resolution increases the risk of renewed violence between Israel and Hezbollah. This risk has been heightened by Hezbollah's involvement in the Syrian civil war and the possibility of the group gaining a strategic foothold near the Golan Heights.

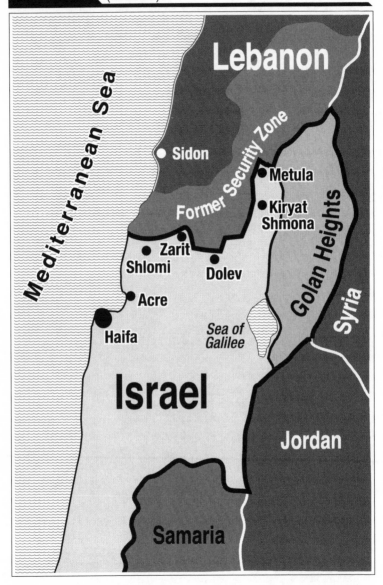

Map 23 Israel's Border with Lebanon (in 2000)

MYTH

*Israeli forces deliberately targeted civilians
during the war instigated by Hezbollah.*

FACT

Throughout the war initiated by Hezbollah on July 12, 2006, the media reported casualty totals offered by Lebanese officials as facts with no apparent effort to verify them. When the number of Hezbollah terrorists killed was mentioned at all, it was invariably with a qualifier such as "Israel says" or "Israel claims." The evidence suggests, however, that it is likely that half or more of the casualties were not innocent civilians, but Hezbollah fighters.

According to Lebanon's Higher Relief Council, the total number of Lebanese who died in the war was 1,191.[18] No distinctions were made between civilians and terrorists. Press reports usually ignored the fact that it was in Hezbollah and the Lebanese government's interest to exaggerate the number of civilian casualties to blacken the image of Israel and support their contention that Israeli attacks were disproportionate and indiscriminate. Simultaneously, Hezbollah sought to conceal its casualties to enhance its prestige and make propagandistic claims about the damage it was inflicting on Israel while suffering few losses of its own.

Human Rights Watch (HRW) issued a report that charged Israel with indiscriminate attacks against civilians in Lebanon."[19] Nothing in the report was based on firsthand knowledge by HRW; rather, it was gathered from interviews with "eye-witnesses and survivors" of Israeli strikes who "told HRW that neither Hezbollah fighters nor other legitimate military targets were in the area that the IDF attacked."

"There was no dependable method by which HRW could assess the veracity of what it was told by the 'witnesses,' many of whom were in areas where the population was sympathetic to, or intimidated by Hezbollah," analyst Joshua Muravchik observed. "Indeed, there was no means by which it could be sure that they were not Hezbollah cadres, since members of the group do not ordinarily wear uniforms or display identity badges."[20]

HRW also had no evidence for the scurrilous accusation that civilians were "deliberately" killed. On the contrary, a great deal of evidence was available showing the efforts Israel made to avoid harming noncombatants, such as dropping leaflets to warn civilians to evacuate locations before they were attacked, pinpoint attacks on buildings in neighborhoods that could more easily have been carpet-bombed, and reports of Israeli pilots and others who withheld fire because of the presence of civilians in target areas.

Anyone watching television saw the images of rockets being fired

Map 24 Range of Fire from Lebanon

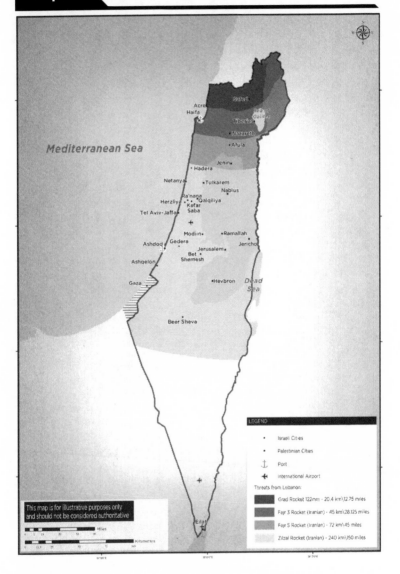

Mediterranean Sea

Acre
Haifa
Safed
Tiberias
Qalukh
Nazareth
Afula
Jenin
Hadera
Netanya
Tulkarem
Nablus
Ra'nana
Herzliya
Qalqiliya
Kefar
Saba
Tel Aviv-Jaffa
Modiin
Ramallah
Ashdod
Gedera
Jericho
Jerusalem
Bet
Shemesh
Ashqelon
Gaza
Hevbron
Dead Sea
Beer Sheva

Eilat

This map is for illustrative purposes only
and should not be considered authoritative

Miles
Kilometers

LEGEND

• Israeli Cities

• Palestinian Cities

⌁ Port

✈ International Airport

Threats from Lebanon:

Grad Rocket 122mm - 20.4 km\12.75 miles

Fajr 3 Rocket (Iranian) - 45 km\28.125 miles

Fajr 5 Rocket (Iranian) - 72 km\45 miles

Zilzal Rocket (Iranian) - 240 km\150 miles

of the city's mostly *Christian* eastern district" that killed ten people. In the next paragraph, however, the report says Israel hit "a building *near a mosque.*"[30]

Photographs can be especially powerful, but they can also be misleading or outright fakes. A photo of a baby pulled from the rubble of a building in Qana that appeared on front pages around the world, for example, was exposed as a fake.[31] One of the photographers involved, Adnan Hajj, was discovered to have doctored at least two photographs, one of which was changed to show more and darker smoke rising from buildings in Beirut bombed by Israel, and the other altered the image of an Israeli jet so it showed three flares being discharged instead of one. Reuters admitted the photos had been falsified, suspended the photographer, and removed all of his photographs from its database.[32]

Reporters in Lebanon exaggerated the destruction in Beirut and elsewhere by showing tight shots of buildings hit in Israeli air strikes and rebroadcasting the same images repeatedly. "You would think Beirut has begun to resemble Dresden and Hamburg in the aftermath of Second World War air raids," observed former *Sunday Telegraph* correspondent Tom Gross. But, Gross notes, "a careful look at aerial satellite photos of the areas targeted by Israel in Beirut shows that certain specific buildings housing Hezbollah command centers in the city's southern suburbs have been singled out. Most of the rest of Beirut, apart from strategic sites such as airport runways used to ferry Hezbollah weapons in and out of Lebanon, has been left pretty much untouched."[33]

While an Israeli strike that killed UN observers drew headlines, little attention was given to reports that Hezbollah was using the UN posts as shields. A Canadian soldier with UNIFIL, for example, reported that his team could observe "most of the Hezbollah static positions in and around our patrol base," and noted that Israeli ordnance that fell near the base was not a result of deliberate targeting, but "has rather been due to tactical necessity."[34]

Over the years, Arab propagandists have learned that one surefire way to get media attention is to scream "massacre" when Israelis are in the neighborhood. On August 7, news outlets repeated Lebanese prime minister Fouad Siniora's claim that Israel had committed a "massacre" by killing forty people in an air raid on the village of Houla. Later, it was learned that one person had died.[35]

Here are some facts the media neglected during the war:

- Two million Israelis lived under threat of rockets, including approximately seven hundred thousand Israeli Arabs.

- More than three hundred thousand Israelis were displaced from their homes.

- Fifteen percent of the entire Israeli population lived in bomb shelters.

- Approximately fifty-five hundred homes were damaged by Hezbollah rockets.

- Israel's tourist industry, which had finally started to recover from the Palestinian War, was again devastated.

- Towns that are home to important sites of the three major religions came under fire, including Tiberias, Nazareth, and Safed.

- Fires sparked by rockets destroyed 16,500 acres of forests and grazing fields in Israel.

Wars are never easy to cover, and each side of a conflict wants to make its case through the media. A responsible press, however, does not simply repeat whatever it hears; it first makes every effort to ensure the accuracy of its reporting.

Notes, Chapter 8

1. Jillian Becker, *The PLO* (London: Weidenfeld and Nicolson, 1984), 205.
2. Becker, 205.
3. *Jerusalem Post* (June 28, 1982).
4. Quoted in Raphael Israeli, ed., *PLO in Lebanon* (London: Weidenfeld and Nicolson, 1983), 7.
5. Henry Kissinger, "From Lebanon to the West Bank to the Gulf," *Washington Post,* (June 16, 1982).
6. Zeev Schiff and Ehud Yaari, *Israel's Lebanon War* (NY: Simon and Schuster, 1984), 70.
7. Becker, 212.
8. Schiff and Yaari, 257.
9. *Washington Post* (February 8, 1983).
10. *New York Times* (October 19, 1990).
11. Becker, 212.
12. Jeffrey Goldberg, "In the Party of God," *New Yorker* (October 14, 2002).
13. "Operation Change of Direction," Globalsecurity.org, (no date).
14. Lebanon wire, Independent Border Assessment Team Report (June 2007).
15. Ibid.
16. Ariel Ben Solomon, "Nasrallah: Israel Is a Cancer and the Ultimate Goal Should Be to Remove It," *Jerusalem Post* (August 15, 2014).
17. Yossi Melman, "Analysis: Hezbollah's 100,000 Rockets and Israel's New Missile Defense System," *Jerusalem Post* (December 23, 2015).
18. Lebanese Higher Relief Council (December 6, 2006).
19. Human Rights Watch, "Fatal Strikes: Israel's Indiscriminate Attacks against Civilians in Lebanon," vol. 18, no. 3 (August 2006), 3.
20. Joshua Muravchik, "Human Rights Watch vs. Human Rights: The Cynical Manipulation of a Worthy Cause Has a History," *The Weekly Standard* (September 11, 2006).
21. Alan Dershowitz, "What Are They Watching?" *New York Sun* (August 23, 2006).
22. Dr. Reuven Erlich (Col. Ret.), "Hezbollah's Use of Lebanese Civilians as Human Shields: The Extensive Military Infrastructure Positioned and Hidden in Populated Areas. From within the Lebanese Towns and Villages, Deliberate Rocket Attacks Were Directed against Civilian Targets in Israel." Intelligence and Terrorism Information Center at the Center for Special Studies (C.S.S) (November 2006).

23. Con Coughlin, "Teheran Fund Pays War Compensation to Hezbollah Families," *Daily Telegraph* (August 4, 2006).

24. *Kuwait Times* (August 30, 2006).

25. John Keegan, "Why Israel Will Go to War Again—Soon," *Daily Telegraph* (November 3, 2006).

26. *CNN* (July 23, 2006). Also, corrected transcripts from broadcast.

27. Anderson Cooper, "Our Very Strange Day with Hezbollah," AC 360 (CNN), (July 23, 2006).

28. Tom Gross, "The Media War against Israel: The Jewish State Is Fighting Not One Enemy but Two: Hezbollah, and Those Who Peddle Its Propaganda," *National Post* (August 2, 2006).

29. *CNN* (August 6, 2006).

30. *CNN* (August 7, 2006).

31. Reuven Koret, "Hezbollywood Horror: 'Civil Defense Worker' Doubles as Traveling Mortician," *Israelinsider.com* (August 3, 2006) and "Hezbollywood? Evidence Mounts that Qana Collapse and Deaths Were Staged," *Israelinsider.com* (July 31, 2006); EU Referendum (July 31, August 1, August 5, 2006).

32. Ricki Hollander, "A Reprise: Media Photo Manipulation," CAMERA (August 9, 2006).

33. Tom Gross, "The Media War against Israel: The Jewish State Is Fighting Not One Enemy but Two: Hezbollah, and Those Who Peddle Its Propaganda," *National Post* (August 2, 2006).

34. "A Canadian Soldier's Report from South Lebanon," *CTV.ca* (July 26, 2006).

35. Associated Press (August 7, 2006) and Amos Harel, "One Dead in IDF Strike in Beirut Southern Suburb," *Haaretz,* (August 7, 2006).

9. Terrorism

Ariel Sharon's visit to the Temple Mount caused the Palestinian War.
Israel created Hamas.
Palestinians do not encourage children to engage in terror.
Palestinian women become suicide bombers to liberate Palestine.
Palestinians are allowed freedom of speech by the Palestinian Authority.
Israel's policy of targeted killings is immoral and counterproductive.
Israel indiscriminately murders terrorists and Palestinian civilians.
Israel was guilty of war crimes in the 2014 Gaza War.
Israel praises terrorists who attack Palestinians.
The Palestinian Authority prevents and condemns terrorism.
Palestinians resort to terrorism out of frustration with their plight.
Palestinian terrorists only attack Israelis; they never assault Americans.
Palestinian violence is only directed at Israeli "settlers."
Terrorism directed at Israel is motivated by politics, not religion.
Palestinians oppose terrorism.
Groups such as Hezbollah, Islamic Jihad, and Hamas are freedom fighters.

MYTH

Ariel Sharon's visit to the Temple Mount caused the Palestinian War.

FACT

To believe Palestinian spokesmen, the five-year Palestinian War—or Al-Aqsa intifada—was caused by the desecration of a Muslim holy place: *Haram al-Sharif* (the Temple Mount) by Likud leader Ariel Sharon and the "thousands of Israeli soldiers" who accompanied him for a visit in September 2000. The violence was carried out through unprovoked attacks by Israeli forces, which invaded Palestinian-controlled territories and "massacred" defenseless Palestinian civilians, who merely threw stones in self-defense. The only way to stop the violence, then, was for Israel to enter a cease-fire and remove its troops from the Palestinian areas.

The truth is dramatically different.

Imad Faluji, the Palestinian Authority communications minister, admitted months after Sharon's visit that the violence had been planned in July, far in advance of Sharon's "provocation." He said the violence "had been planned since Chairman Arafat's return from Camp David, when he turned the tables on the former US president and rejected the

American conditions."[1] Similarly, in 2010, Mahmoud Zahar of Hamas said that Arafat instructed his organization to launch terror attacks against Israel after the failure of peace negotiations.[2]

Yasser Arafat's widow, Suha, also admitted that Arafat had planned the uprising. "Immediately after the failure of the Camp David [negotiations], I met him in Paris upon his return . . . Camp David had failed, and he said to me, 'You should remain in Paris.' I asked him why, and he said, 'Because I am going to start an intifada.'"[3]

The Sharon visit did not cause the "Al-Aqsa Intifada."

—Conclusion of the Mitchell Report (May 4, 2001)[4]

The violence started before Sharon's September 28, 2000, visit to the Temple Mount. The day before, for example, an Israeli soldier was killed at the Netzarim Junction. The next day, in the West Bank city of Kalkilya, a Palestinian police officer working with Israeli police on a joint patrol opened fire and killed his Israeli counterpart.

Official Palestinian Authority media exhorted the Palestinians to violence. On September 29, 2000, the Voice of Palestine, the PA's official radio station sent out calls "to all Palestinians to come and defend the Al-Aqsa Mosque." The PA closed its schools and bused Palestinian students to the Temple Mount to participate in the organized riots.

Arafat also secretly sent a representative to meet with a Hamas leader and told him, "I have no problem with Hamas carrying out operations." Arafat also arranged for the transfer of weapons to Hamas.[5]

Just prior to Rosh Hashanah (September 30), the Jewish New Year, when hundreds of Israelis were worshipping at the Western Wall, thousands of Arabs began throwing bricks and rocks at Israeli police and Jewish worshippers. Rioting then spread to towns and villages throughout Israel, the West Bank, and Gaza Strip.

Internal Security Minister Shlomo Ben-Ami permitted Sharon to go to the Temple Mount—Judaism's holiest place—only after calling Palestinian security chief Jibril Rajoub and receiving his assurance that if Sharon did not enter the mosques, no problems would arise. The need to protect Sharon arose when Rajoub later said that the Palestinian police would do nothing to prevent violence during the visit.[6]

Sharon did not enter any mosques and his thirty-four-minute visit to the Temple Mount was conducted during normal hours when the area is open to tourists. Palestinian youths—eventually numbering around fifteen hundred—shouted slogans in an attempt to inflame the situation. Some fifteen hundred Israeli police were present at the scene to forestall violence.

There were limited disturbances during Sharon's visit, mostly involving stone throwing. During the remainder of the day, outbreaks of stone throwing continued on the Temple Mount and in the vicinity, leaving twenty-eight Israeli policemen injured. There are no accounts of Palestinian injuries on that day. Significant and orchestrated violence was initiated by Palestinians the next day following Friday prayers.

MYTH

Israel created Hamas.

FACT

Israel had nothing to do with the creation of Hamas. The organization's leaders were inspired by the ideology and practice of the Islamic fundamentalist Muslim Brotherhood movement founded in Egypt in 1928.

Hamas was legally registered in Israel in 1978 as an Islamic Association by Sheik Ahmad Yassin. Initially, the organization engaged primarily in social welfare activities and soon developed a reputation for improving the lives of Palestinians, particularly the refugees in the Gaza Strip.

Though Hamas was committed from the outset to destroying Israel, it took the position that this was a goal for the future, and that the more immediate focus should be on winning the hearts and minds of the people through its charitable and educational activities. Its funding came primarily from Jordan and Saudi Arabia.

The PLO was convinced that Israel was helping Hamas in the hope of triggering a civil war. Since Hamas did not engage in terror at first, Israel did not see it as a serious short-term threat, and some Israelis believed the rise of fundamentalism in Gaza would have the beneficial impact of weakening the PLO, and this is what ultimately happened. The unintended consequence was to strengthen radical Islamists.

Hamas certainly didn't believe it was being supported by Israel. As early as February 1988, the group put out a primer on how its members should behave if confronted by the Shin Bet. Several more instructional documents were distributed by Hamas to teach followers how to confront the Israelis and maintain secrecy.

Israel's assistance was more passive than active; that is, it did not interfere with Hamas activities or prevent funds from flowing into the organization from abroad. Israel also may have provided some funding to allow its security forces to infiltrate the organization.[7] Meanwhile, Jordan was actively helping Hamas, with the aim of undermining the PLO and strengthening Jordanian influence in the territories.

Though some Israelis were very concerned about Hamas before

rioting began in December 1987, Israel was reluctant to interfere with an Islamic organization, fearing that it might trigger charges of violating the Palestinians' freedom of religion. It was not until early in the intifada, when Hamas became actively involved in the violence, that the group began to be viewed as a potentially greater threat than the PLO. The turning point occurred in the summer of 1988 when Israel learned that Hamas was stockpiling arms to build an underground force and that Hamas had issued its covenant calling for the destruction of Israel. At this point, it became clear that Hamas was not going to put off its *jihad* to liberate Palestine and was shifting its emphasis from charitable and educational activity to terrorism. Hamas has been waging a terror war against Israel ever since.[8]

MYTH

Palestinians do not encourage children to engage in terror.

FACT

Most Palestinians who adopt terror in the hope of either "ending the occupation" or destroying Israel do so because they freely choose murder over any other option. Palestinian terrorists also use children, however, to do their dirty work.

On March 15, 2004, Israeli security forces caught an eleven-year-old boy attempting to smuggle a bomb through a roadblock. The boy was promised a large sum of money by Tanzim activists in Nablus if he delivered a bag containing a bomb stuffed with bolts to a woman on the other side of the checkpoint. If the boy was stopped and searched, the terrorists who sent him planned to use a cell phone to immediately detonate the explosives he was carrying, murdering nearby soldiers as well as the boy. The plan was foiled by an alert Israeli soldier, and the bomb apparently malfunctioned when the terrorists tried to detonate it remotely. A week later, on March 24, 2004, a fourteen-year-old Palestinian child was found to be carrying explosives when attempting to pass through the Israeli army checkpoint at Hawara, at the entrance of the town of Nablus.[9]

Just over a year later, on May 22, 2005, a fourteen-year-old boy was again arrested at the Hawara checkpoint with two pipe bombs strapped to a belt he was wearing. A few days later, a fifteen-year-old tried to get through the checkpoint with two more pipe bombs. Yet another teen, a sixteen-year-old, was caught on July 4, 2005, attempting to smuggle a bomb and homemade handgun. In August, another fourteen-year-old boy was caught carrying three pipe bombs packed with explosives, shrapnel, and glass balls.[10]

These are a few examples of the cynical use of children by Palestinians waging war on Israel. Young Palestinians are routinely indoctrinated and coerced into the cult of martyrdom.

Using children to carry out or assist in armed attacks of any kind is an abomination. We call on the Palestinian leadership to publicly denounce these practices.

—**Amnesty International**[11]

Despite occasional claims that terror is only promoted by "extremists," the truth is that the Palestinian Authority has consistently incited its youth to violence. On the official PA television station, for example, the host of *Children's Talk*, told his young viewers that Israel "is all ours" and that it "will return to us."[12] In December 2015, Israeli customs seized four thousand Palestinian dolls wearing kaffiyehs covering their faces and holding up rocks so they resemble the young Arabs engaged in pelting Israelis. The intent is to teach young Palestinians that it is normal to throw rocks.[13] But not just rocks. In January 2016, to celebrate the anniversary of Fatah's fifty-one years of violence, children dressed as terrorists with masks, "toy" suicide belts, guns, and rocket-propelled grenade launchers marched through the streets of Bethlehem.[14]

Children are taught that the greatest glory is to die for Allah in battle as a *shahid* (martyr). The PA regularly broadcasts television shows that encourage children to embrace this concept. One film used the death of Muhammad al-Dura, the child most likely killed by Palestinians in the crossfire of a shootout between Palestinian gunmen and Israeli forces, to show that life after death is paradise. An actor playing al-Dura was shown in an amusement park, playing on the beach, and flying a kite. The al-Dura in the film invited viewers to follow his example. Similar messages extolling the virtue of the *shahid* can be found in school textbooks and sermons by Muslim clergy.[15]

The indoctrination is having an impact. According to one Palestinian newspaper, 79–80 percent of children told pollsters they were willing to be *shahids*.[16] Palestinian children now play death games, competing to see who will be the *shahid*. They also collect "terrorist cards" the way American kids collect baseball cards. The maker of the Palestinian cards sold six million in just over two years. "I take hundreds of these pictures from children every day and burn them," said Saher Hindi, a teacher at a Nablus elementary school. "They turn children into extremists."[17]

Many Palestinian youngsters have gone from pretending, to carrying out actual terrorist attacks. Dozens of minors have been involved in planning, attempting, and carrying out suicide bombings. According to one study, 5 percent of the suicide bombings between 2000 and 2015 were carried out by Palestinians aged seventeen or under.[18]

As Israel began to have greater success in preventing these heinous attacks, the Palestinians changed tactics and adopted a more low-tech approach to terror. During the wave of violence beginning in October 2015 that became known as the "stabbing intifada," at least forty stabbing, shooting, and car-ramming attacks were carried out against Israeli civilians and security forces by Palestinian individuals under the age of twenty. A nineteen-year-old Palestinian stabbed an eighty-year-old Israeli woman riding a bus on November 2, 2015, before exiting the vehicle and stabbing two more bystanders on the street.[19] On November 23, 2015, two Palestinian girls aged fourteen and sixteen attacked a seventy-year-old Arab-Israeli with scissors in Jerusalem's Mahane Yehuda Market, after mistaking the man for a Jew.[20] A seventeen-year-old Palestinian terrorist snuck into a home in the West Bank town of Kiryat Arba on June 30, 2016, and stabbed a sleeping thirteen-year-old American-Israeli girl to death.[21]

> *As one of the Islamic fanatics who inspired al-Qaida said: "We are not trying to negotiate with you. We are trying to destroy you" ... They wish to destroy the whole basis of Western society—secular democracy, individual liberty, equality before the law, toleration and pluralism—and replace it with a theocracy based on a perverted and dogmatic interpretation of the Koran ... The idea that we should try to appease the terrorists is wrong in every respect. It would not protect us, for nothing acts as a greater incentive to terrorists than the realization that their target is weak and frightened. And it would only weaken the institutions we are trying to protect, and demonstrate to the terrorists that we are—as they frequently allege—too decadent and craven to defend the way of life to which we claim to be attached.*
>
> *—London Daily Telegraph*[22]

The use of children for terrorist attacks finally led some Palestinian families to protest. The mother of one of three teenagers sent to carry out an attack in Afula said of the letter he had left behind, "My son doesn't know how to write such a letter and never belonged to any groups. Someone older wrote this letter for him." The boy's father added, "Nobody can accept to send his children to be slaughtered. I am sure that whoever recruits children in this kind of unlawful activity will not recruit his own children."[23]

Martin Fletcher interviewed the parents of a fifteen-year-old stopped at the Hawara checkpoint. His parents expressed their anger at the Al-Aqsa Martyrs Brigade, calling its operatives criminals and saying that Allah would punish them. The correspondent spoke with the boy and read him a letter from his mother asking him to confess and to give Israel all the information in his possession about the men who had sent him.[24]

Many of these attacks could be stopped if parents took action, but too often, they express pride in the heinous crimes their children commit.

MYTH

Palestinian women become suicide bombers to liberate Palestine.

FACT

It may be that some Palestinian women share the ideology of the terrorists who believe that blowing up innocent men, women, and children will achieve their political objective, but many others are blackmailed into carrying out suicide attacks by sadistic and manipulative Palestinian men.

More than twenty Palestinian women have engaged in suicide attacks. According to one study, 5 percent of these terrorist acts from 2000 to 2015 were carried out by women.[25] The terrorist organizations that recruit them do so in part because they believe women will generate less suspicion and that Israeli soldiers will be more reticent to search them.

Some of the women have been convinced to engage in terrorist attacks to rehabilitate their reputations in their community if they have acquired a bad name or done something to bring shame upon their families. Shame is a powerful force in Arab society, and women who are accused of "improper behavior," such as promiscuity, adultery, or becoming pregnant out of wedlock may be ostracized or severely punished (e.g., husbands may kill wives who shamed them in so-called "honor crimes").

Terrorist organizations have used emotional blackmail against these often vulnerable women to convince them that by carrying out a suicide attack against Jews, they may restore their honor or that of their families. Israeli intelligence declassified a report that said Fatah operatives went so far as to seduce women and then, after they became pregnant, used their condition to blackmail them into committing heinous crimes. The report cited two specific cases, one involved a twenty-one-year-old from Bethlehem who blew herself up in the Mahane Yehuda market in Jerusalem, killing six and wounding more than sixty, and the other was an eighteen-year-old from the Dehaishe refugee camp, who blew up a Jerusalem supermarket and killed two people and wounded twenty-two others.[26]

MYTH

*Palestinians are allowed freedom of speech
by the Palestinian Authority.*

FACT

One of the principal deterrents to speaking out against Palestinian irredentism and terror in the Palestinian Authority is the threat of being murdered. By the end of the first intifada in the early 1990s, more Palestinians were killed by their fellow Palestinians than died in clashes with Israeli security forces. During the Palestinian War, intimidation and murder were used to muzzle dissent. Usually those seeking peace or an end to terror are labeled "collaborators" and, if they are lucky, arrested by the Palestinian Authority. The unlucky ones are murdered, often in grisly and public ways, such as stringing them up from lamp posts in public squares to send the message that a similar fate awaits anyone who dares cross those seeking Israel's destruction.

> *If Muslims claim that we are against violence, why aren't we demonstrating in the streets against suicide bombings? Why is it so much easier to draw us into protest against a French ban on the hijab, but next to impossible to exorcise ourselves about slavery, stonings and suicide killings? Where's our collective conscience?*
>
> **—Muslim author Irshad Manji**[27]

A Palestinian need not be interested in peace to become a target of violence; one need only express opposition or offer a challenge to the ruling Fatah party. For example, after student elections at Bir Zeit University in Ramallah resulted in the Islamic Bloc of Hamas and Islamic Jihad receiving more votes than Fatah, Palestinian security forces and members of Fatah attacked members of the Islamic groups and their supporters. Security forces opened fire on the crowd and wounded more than one hundred students.[28] When the president of the Gaza-based National Institute of Strategic Studies, Riad al-Agha, criticized the Palestinian security forces on Palestine TV for failing to impose law and order after Israel's disengagement, he was arrested.[29]

There are no exact figures for the number of Palestinians killed in the internecine war; however, Amnesty International reported that "scores of Palestinians" had been unlawfully killed and that the PA "consistently failed to investigate these killings and none of the perpetrators was brought to justice."[30] The Independent Commission for Human Rights (ICHR), a Palestinian organization that monitors slayings of Palestinians by Palestinians, estimated that between January 2006 and June 2007, 616 Palestinians were killed during the civil war between Fatah and Hamas.[31] From January 2008 to March 2011, ICHR reported at least 570 Palestinians were killed as a result of murder, tribal fighting, gang violence, tunnel collapses (Egypt to Gaza), weapons misuse, torture, executions, revenge actions, and public safety.[32]

The media and pro-Palestinian activists rarely notice violence among Palestinians.

Perhaps the most vivid image of the Palestinian War was the film of a Palestinian father trying unsuccessfully to shield his son from gunfire. Israel was universally blamed for the death of twelve-year-old Mohammed al-Dura, but subsequent investigations found that the boy was most likely killed by Palestinian bullets.

Denis Jeambar, editor in chief of the French news weekly *l'Express*, and filmmaker Daniel Leconte, saw raw, unedited video of the shooting and said the boy could not have been shot by Israeli soldiers. "The only ones who could hit the child were the Palestinians from their position.[33]

An independent investigation by German ARD Television concluded that footage of al-Dura's death was censored by the Palestinians to look as if he had been killed by the Israelis when, in fact, his death was caused by Palestinian gunfire.[34] James Fallows revisited the story and found that "the physical evidence of the shooting was in all ways inconsistent with shots coming from the IDF outpost."[35]

I think when you are attacked by a terrorist and you know who the terrorist is and you can fingerprint back to the cause of the terror, you should respond.

—US secretary of state Colin Powell[36]

MYTH

Israel's policy of targeted killings is immoral and counterproductive.

FACT

Israel is faced with a nearly impossible situation in attempting to protect its civilian population from Palestinians who are prepared to blow themselves up to murder innocent Jews. One strategy for dealing with the problem has been to pursue negotiations; however, Palestinian

MYTH

*Israel indiscriminately murders terrorists
and Palestinian civilians.*

FACT

It is always a tragedy when innocent civilians are killed in a counter-terrorism operation. Civilians would not be at risk, however, if the Palestinian Authority arrested the terrorists, if the murderers did not choose to hide among noncombatants, and if the civilians refused to protect the killers.

Terrorists often disguise themselves as civilians and, if they are killed, it is often impossible to distinguish them from noncombatants, so they inevitably end up counted by the media and human rights organizations among the civilian casualties. In the 2014 Gaza War, for example, several hundred women participated in the fighting and may have been among the dead labeled as civilians.[44] This is a deliberate strategy to shape the narrative of the conflict and tarnish Israel's image as perhaps the world's most moral army. The Hamas Interior Ministry, for example, instructed social media activists never to post photos of rockets being fired from civilian population centers and to always refer to the dead as "innocent civilians."[45]

Israel does not attack Palestinian areas indiscriminately. On the contrary, the IDF takes great care to target people who are planning terrorist attacks against Israeli civilians. The United States has also adopted Israeli techniques in its campaign against ISIS, such as warning civilians before a bombing with a dud bomb—known as "roof knocking."

Israeli forces have a history of accuracy in such assaults; nevertheless, they sometimes make mistakes. Whereas the terrorists make no apology for their attacks on civilians, and purposely target them, Israel always investigates the reasons for any errors and takes steps to prevent them from reoccurring.

The IDF is not the only military that has inadvertently harmed people who are not targets. For example, on the same day that American officials were condemning Israel because a number of civilians died when Israel assassinated a leader of Hamas, news reports disclosed that the United States bombed a village in Afghanistan in an operation directed at a Taliban leader that instead killed forty-eight Afghan civilians at a wedding party. In both cases, flawed intelligence played a role in the tragic mistakes.

The terrorists themselves do not care about the lives of innocent Palestinians and are ultimately responsible for any harm that comes to them. The terrorists' behavior is a violation of international law, specifically, Article 51 of the 1977 amendment to the 1949 Geneva

Conventions, which prohibits the use of civilians to "shield, favor or impede military operations."[46]

MYTH

Israel was guilty of war crimes in the 2014 Gaza War.

FACT

On June 22, 2015, the United Nations Human Rights Council (HRC) released the findings of the commission it appointed to investigate the 2014 Gaza conflict, suggesting that both Israel and Hamas *may have* committed war crimes. Given the HRC's historical bias against Israel (e.g., a separate line item to discuss Israel during meetings), it was not surprising that the investigators equated the "firefighters" of the IDF with the Hamas "arsonists."

The HRC has a history of slandering Israel's human rights record while ignoring the world's worst violators of human rights. The council has condemned Israel in sixty-seven individual resolutions since its inception in 2006, more than half of the 128 total resolutions the council has considered.[47]

> *In Gaza last week, crowds of children reveled and sang while adults showered them with candies. The cause for celebration: the cold-blooded murder of at least seven people—five of them Americans—and the maiming of 80 more by a terrorist bomb on the campus of Jerusalem's Hebrew University.*
>
> **—Historian Michael Oren[48]**

The "investigation" into the 2014 Gaza conflict was designed to come to the predetermined conclusion that Israel was guilty of abuses. This was evident when the council appointed as head of this supposedly impartial commission William Schabas, who previously worked for the Palestine Liberation Organization. Schabas was forced to resign after his background was disclosed, but the objective of proving Israeli crimes remained unchanged.

The truly independent High Level International Military Group, comprised of eleven of the world's top generals and former diplomats, came to an entirely different conclusion than did the HRC. The group, led by former chairman of the NATO Military Committee, General Klaus Naumann, found that *"Israeli forces acted proportionately as required by the laws of armed conflict and often went beyond the required legal principles of proportionality, necessity and discrimination."* In some cases, their report said, *"Israel's scrupulous adher-*

ence to the laws of war cost Israeli soldiers' and civilians' lives" (emphasis added).

The generals did not dispute that the Palestinians suffered a high number of civilian casualties, and acknowledged that some were "caused by error and misjudgment." However, they concluded "the majority of deaths were the tragic inevitability of defending against an enemy that deliberately carries out attacks from within the civilian population."[49]

One member of the military group, Colonel Richard Kemp of Great Britain, submitted his own report to the HRC. He reiterated that "the IDF took exceptional measures to adhere to the Laws of Armed Conflict and to minimize civilian casualties in Gaza." He also criticized those who suggested that Israel make greater efforts to minimize civilian casualties in Gaza because none of them had any idea how to do this. "I conclude that this was because Israel was taking all feasible steps," stated Kemp. He also noted that Israel was investigating specific incidents where it is alleged that soldiers acted improperly. "I am not aware of any nation that has conducted more comprehensive or resolute investigations into its own military activities than Israel during and following the 2014 Gaza conflict," Kemp testified.

By contrast, Kemp said, Hamas flouted the Laws of Armed Conflict by "deliberately targeting the Israeli civilian population, using their own civilian population as human shields and seeking to entice the IDF to take military action that would kill large numbers of Gaza civilians for their own propaganda purposes. There was and is of course no accountability or investigation of any allegations against Hamas and other extremist groups in Gaza."[50]

In addition to these investigations, two American legal experts also examined Israel's conduct. Michael Schmitt and John Merriam lecture on the law of armed conflict at the US Naval War College, and Schmitt also advises on the topic at NATO, Harvard, and Exeter. They concluded that Israel's "approach to targeting is consistent with the law and, in many cases, worthy of emulation."[51]

General Charles Wald, USAF (ret.), former deputy commander of United States European Command (EUCOM), also participated in an investigation of Israel's conduct of the war. He asserted the HRC report was unbalanced and failed to accurately assess human rights violations perpetrated by Hamas. As a result, Wald said, "the international community should not accept this inaccurate and biased report and should instead rely on the balanced and accurate reports that are authored by actual experts on how to conduct combat operations in accordance with the Law of Armed Conflict."[52]

The Israeli Defense Forces have repeatedly showed unprecedented restraint when operating in densely populated combat zones full of civilians. According to one Israeli brigade commander, "There were instances where the extensive caution caused harm to soldiers."[53]

Even the Palestinian ambassador to the UN Human Rights Council, Ibrahim Khraishi, acknowledged that it was Hamas, not Israel, which had committed war crimes:

> I am not a candidate in any Palestinian elections, so I don't need to win popularity among the Palestinians. The missiles that are now being launched against Israel, each and every missile constitutes a crime against humanity, whether it hits or misses, because it is directed at civilian targets . . . Please note that many of our people in Gaza appeared on TV and said that the Israelis warned them to evacuate their homes before the bombardment. In such a case, if someone is killed, the law considers it a mistake rather than an intentional killing because [the Israelis] followed the legal procedures. As for the missiles launched from our side . . . We never warn anyone about where these missiles are about to fall, or about the operations we carry out.[54]

Hamas took advantage of Israel's concern for civilian casualties by locating their headquarters in the basement of a hospital. Nearly 250 rockets were launched from schools, 331 from mosques, forty-one from hospitals, and more than one hundred from other medical facilities. Rockets were also fired from churches, Red Cross and first aid stations, amusement parks, playgrounds, and graveyards.[55] The civilian shields served their purpose; Israel did not attack terrorist targets such as the Hamas command center in the al-Shifa hospital to avoid potential civilian casualties.

Hamas also stored weapons in mosques and facilities run by UNRWA; rockets were also fired from sites located near UNRWA schools. After the war, it was learned that Hamas threatened UNRWA officials at gunpoint and told them if they revealed what Hamas was doing in their facilities, they would be killed.[56]

Why don't they learn from the Israeli army, which tries, through great efforts, to avoid shelling areas populated by civilians in Lebanon and Palestine? Didn't Hezbollah take shelter in areas populated by civilians because it knows that the Israeli air force doesn't bomb these areas? Why doesn't the Syrian army respect the premises of universities, schools or inhabited neighborhoods?

—Faisal al-Qassem, moderating a discussion on Al-Jazeera regarding Syrian military tactics in its civil war.[57]

According to the chairman of the US joint chiefs of staff, Gen. Martin Dempsey, "Israel went to extraordinary lengths to limit collateral damage and civilian casualties." He was so impressed with Israel's conduct of the war that he sent a team to Israel to study Israel's strategies, including lessons about how to limit civilian casualties.[58]

A Brookings study of the UN report on the Gaza War found that it was a "bad piece of work" that was fatally flawed from the outset. "The commission all but admits that it lacked the information to draw the conclusions it drew."[59]

The HRC has consistently slandered Israel while shielding terrorists and their sponsoring countries. By equating Israel's democratic government defending its citizens with a terrorist organization whose goal is to destroy Israel, the HRC reveals its moral bankruptcy. Misleading reports such as the ones issued after the last two wars in Gaza will not curb human rights abuses since Hamas has no intention of changing its tactics of indiscriminately bombarding civilian areas in Israel and using its own people as human shields. Israel, despite its adherence to the laws of war, will nevertheless continue to be pilloried by the international community and the media, and will be forced to endanger its own soldiers out of fear of international scrutiny, scurrilous charges of abuse, and investigations meant to prove Israel's predetermined guilt.

MYTH

Israel praises terrorists who attack Palestinians.

FACT

On July 31, 2015, arsonists set fire to two Palestinian homes in the West Bank village of Duma. An eighteen-month-old boy died in the blaze at the Dawabsheh home, and his father and mother succumbed to their injuries a few days later. The boy's five-year-old brother survived. On January 3, 2016, a twenty-one-year-old Jewish settler, Amiram Ben-Uliel, was indicted for the murder, along with a Jewish minor for participation in planning the murder. In addition, along with two others, they were both charged with one count of membership in a terrorist organization. The motive, as stated in the indictment, was revenge for the murder of Israeli Malachi Rosenfeld by Palestinians near Duma about a month earlier.

Murderous attacks by Jews against Arabs are extremely rare and, when they occur, Israel's leaders and the public immediately denounce them. "This is an act of terrorism in every respect," Israeli prime minister Benjamin Netanyahu said of the Duma attack, pledging that Israel would "take firm action" against the perpetrators. His denunciation was echoed by Israel's president, Reuven Rivlin, and members of the opposition parties. The horrific attack was likewise condemned by Jews around the world.

In addition to words, Israel reacted with deeds, as the Israeli cabinet approved applying administrative detention measures to Israeli citizens suspected of participating in terror attacks against Palestinians. The public also reacted to the shocking attack by holding rallies attended by thousands of Israelis protesting hate crimes.[60]

Contrast the reaction of Israelis to the horrific attack in Duma with the behavior of Palestinians following terrorist attacks against Israelis. Rather than protests, the Palestinian public holds parades and celebrations. Rather than denounce the killers, the president of the Palestinian Authority, Mahmoud Abbas, and other Palestinian leaders laud them as "martyrs." The PA also rewards the families of deceased terrorists, and those with relatives in jail, with generous payments, even at a time when the PA is in financial shambles and cannot pay many of its bills or employees. The main financiers of the PA, donor nations such as the United States, who believe they are improving the welfare of the Palestinian people and promoting peace, are actually subsidizing support for terrorists.

In addition to money, terrorists also receive a variety of honors, especially those who killed the most Israelis. For example, the perpetrator of the Passover Seder massacre that killed thirty Jews had a soccer tournament named for him. The bus hijacker responsible for the deadliest terror attack in Israel's history, the 1978 slaughter of thirty-seven civilians, twelve of them children, "has had summer camps, schools, graduation ceremonies and sporting events named for her, as well as many TV documentaries honoring her." A monument in Nablus was erected to honor the commander of the local Al-Aqsa Martyrs Brigade. He was responsible for several terror attacks, including a double suicide bombing in Tel Aviv on January 5, 2003, which left twenty-three people dead and dozens injured. Streets, neighborhoods, and squares are also named after Palestinian terrorists. In school, Palestinian children are taught to aspire to death as a martyr. No fewer than twenty-five schools are named after terrorists, which makes the terrorists role models.[61]

So long as Palestinians praise murderers and preach hatred, they will find no common ground with Israelis who celebrate life and condemn intolerance. As Golda Meir said, "Peace will come when the Arabs will love their children more than they hate us."[62]

MYTH

The Palestinian Authority prevents and condemns terrorism.

FACT

Many people have forgotten, but one of the principal reasons that Israel decided to recognize the PLO and engage in peace talks was because Yasser Arafat renounced the use of terrorism and other acts of violence. Sadly, peace has not been achieved, primarily because terrorism has never ceased. Instead, during negotiations subsequent to the Oslo agreements, the Palestinians repeated their promise to end terror in an effort to extract additional concessions from Israel. This pattern has continued to the present day when Palestinians make new demands on Israel while, simultaneously, encouraging violence against Israelis.

Since the first Oslo agreement in September 1993, more than fifteen hundred Israelis have been murdered by Palestinian terrorists. Even after withdrawing from nearly half the West Bank and all of the Gaza Strip, the attacks continue. According to data compiled by the Israeli Shin Bet Security Agency, 2015 was the deadliest year for terrorism since 2008. The number of Israelis killed in terror attacks increased from a low of six in 2009 to twenty-eight in 2015.[63]

Violence escalated beginning in October 2015 as individuals began to shoot, stab, and run over Israelis. By July 2016, more than thirty Israelis had been killed, including two Americans, and hundreds more wounded.

The time has come for us to realize that using knives (shibrie) against the Jews will not yield us even a sliver of land (shiber), and we have to change our strategy. We need to talk to the Israelis and get our Palestinian state by peaceful means. They will give it to us: they have offered to do so many times already—otherwise we will not get it at all.

—Bassam Tawil[64]

Members of the Palestinian Authority governing cabinet placed condolence calls to families of Palestinians who were killed by Israeli police after stabbing, shooting, or ramming Israeli citizens with their cars.[65] Mahmoud Abbas referred to this wave of terrorism as a "peaceful, popular uprising" and praised the bravery of the attackers, prompting columnist Bassam Tawil to ask, "What is peaceful and popular about stabbing an 80-year-old lady named Ruti Malka in Rishon Lezion, and a 70-year-old Jewish woman [in] Jerusalem?"[66] Referring to the attackers who were killed during or after their assaults, Tawil says, Abbas wants to "deceive the world into believing that Israel's mighty security forces killed these poor innocent terrorists who were merely part of a peaceful protest against those awful Israeli 'occupiers.'" Tawil adds that Abbas "knows very well that the terrorists are 'lone wolves' whom he himself has whipped up to murder Jews for no other reason than that they are Jews."[67]

Since 2005, more than eleven thousand rockets and mortars fired from Gaza into Israel have hit Israeli civilian areas.[68] Hamas leader Khaled Meshaal reaffirmed the terrorist group's view that "the so-called peace process is futile. There is no peace. Only the path of *jihad*, sacrifice, and blood will bear fruit."[69]

MYTH

Palestinians resort to terrorism out of frustration with their plight.

FACT

While some commentators suggest that terrorists kill Jews out of frustration, the truth is that they are given financial incentives. The Palestinian Authority, which complains incessantly about the economic conditions in the West Bank, manages to pay $3–$7 million as salaries and financial rewards to terrorists and their families. According to a 2004 regulation, "prisoners serving up to five years in Israeli prisons receive 1,300 shekels per month; wives of married inmates receive another 300 shekels, and an additional 50 shekels a month is sent for each child in the family. After five years, the payments increase to 2,000 shekels. Inmates in prison longer than 25 years are paid 4,000 shekels." The PA makes many of these payments to mass murderers.[70]

In 2014 alone, the PA allocated $46 million for released prisoners in addition to payments made to terrorists still in jail and the families of "martyrs." Abbas and other senior officials, investigative journalist Edwin Black discovered, "scrutinize the details of each case, the specific carnage caused, and the personal details of each terrorist act before approving salaries and awarding honorary ranks in either the PA government or the military." Since the PA's budget relies on foreign donations, these payments to terrorists are essentially subsidized by Western nations, including the United States, despite laws on the books in many of these countries prohibiting support for terrorists.[71]

Martyrs also receive other types of recognition. Soccer teams, sports tournaments, and schools are named after terrorists. For example, a Palestinian table tennis tournament for women was named after a terrorist who hijacked a bus that led to the death of thirty-seven Israelis, and a soccer tournament was named after a suicide bomber who killed thirty-one people at a Passover seder.[72]

In addition, Abbas awarded the "Military Star of Honor" to a terrorist who placed a bomb in a movie theater in 1967 that was discovered before it detonated. The bomber subsequently spent ten years in prison.[73] On another occasion, Abbas issued a posthumous "medal of sacrifice" to the mother of three Palestinian murderers, including one who died during a 2002 suicide attack that killed five Israelis.[74] On

February 3, 2016, Abbas hosted the families of eleven terrorists who carried out attacks against Israelis in the previous four months. Abbas told them, "Your sons are martyrs." The meeting occurred shortly after three Palestinians killed nineteen-year-old Israeli Border Police Officer Hadar Cohen and injured a second young female officer in Jerusalem.[75]

Despite repeated assurances, the PA has not stopped terrorists from targeting Israel. If the Palestinians have not lived up to these promises in the past—or in the present—why should Israelis trust them to do so in the future? After giving up land and getting more terror rather than peace, is it surprising that Israelis are reluctant to make further concessions to the Palestinians or that Prime Minister Benjamin Netanyahu has insisted that security guarantees are a sine qua non for any new agreement?

MYTH

Palestinian terrorists only attack Israelis;
they never assault Americans.

FACT

The PLO has a long history of brutal violence against innocent civilians of many nations, including the United States. Palestinian Muslim terrorist groups are a more recent phenomenon, but they have not spared Americans either. Palestinian terrorist incidents involving American citizens goes back to at least 1970 when more than three dozen Americans were among the passengers who were held hostage when the Popular Front for the Liberation of Palestine (PFLP) hijacked four jets. There have been more than twenty other cases of Americans victimized by Palestinian terrorists. Here are a few recent examples:

- December 20, 2010, an American tourist hiking in the foothills of Jerusalem was stabbed to death by a Palestinian terrorist.

- June 30, 2014, Naftali Frankel (sixteen) was one of three Israeli teenagers kidnapped and murdered while hitchhiking from a yeshiva in Gush Etzion.

- October 22, 2014, three-month-old Chaya Zissel Braun was killed when a Palestinian rammed his car into a light-rail station.

- October 1, 2015, Eitan Henkin and his wife Naama were ambushed and murdered by Palestinian gunmen as they drove with their four children in the West Bank.

- October 13, 2015, Richard Lakin (seventy-six) was killed when Palestinians hijacked a bus in Jerusalem.

- November 19, 2015, a Palestinian terrorist opened fire on cars stuck in a traffic jam in Gush Etzion, killing an Israeli, an American tourist, and a Palestinian, and wounding seven others. Five of the wounded were American Yeshiva students. The American fatality was Ezra Schwartz (eighteen).

- March 9, 2016, a Palestinian attacker began stabbing random Israelis at the entrance to the Jaffa Port. One victim was an American tourist, Taylor Force (twenty-eight), a US Army veteran of Iraq and Afghanistan who was on a school-sponsored trip to Israel through Vanderbilt University. Palestinian Authority TV called Taylor a "settler," and his killer was honored as an Islamic martyr.[76]

The bombing yesterday [August 9, 2001] of a crowded pizza restaurant in downtown Jerusalem, which killed at least 14 people and injured around 100, was an atrocity of the sort that must be distinguished from everything else that goes on in the Palestinian-Israeli conflict. . . . [T]he deliberate targeting of civilians, including children . . . is a simple savagery that no country can reasonably be expected to tolerate. Israel's determination last night to respond was entirely legitimate.

—Washington Post Editorial[77]

An even more heinous crime was the murder of another American citizen, Hallel Yaffa Ariel (thirteen), in her bed on June 30, 2016. The response from the Palestinian Authority—the one committed by formal agreement to stop all terrorism—was to fund the mourning tent of the family whose son committed the murder, to send a representative to pay his respects, and to honor the killer as a martyr (making the family eligible for a monthly stipend from money paid by international donors).[78]

MYTH

Palestinian violence is only directed at Israeli "settlers."

FACT

One of the many ways to demonstrate that settlements are not the central issue in the dispute with Palestinians is that terrorists have targeted Jews around the world, most of whom have nothing to do with the settlements. Moreover, many terrorist attacks are indiscriminate; their goal is to maximize casualties. During the Palestinian War (or second intifada), suicide bombers and armed terrorists killed sixty foreigners including Americans, Europeans, Egyptians, and others. Rocket attacks have killed both Israeli and Palestinian civilians, such as the explosion of a Palestinian rocket inside the Al-Shati refugee camp in Gaza on July 28, 2014, which killed thirteen Palestinian civilians. Hamas attacks during the 2014 Gaza War killed five civilians in Israel, including four-year-old Daniel Tregerman, a Bedouin man, a Thai farmworker, and two other Israeli civilians.

During the so-called Stabbing Intifada, a Nigerian man named Samuel Ono was stabbed by a Palestinian in Ra'anana on October 16, 2015. On November 29, a Nepalese foreign worker was stabbed in her back by a seventeen-year-old Palestinian. In Bethlehem, on November 23, 2015, a seventy-year-old Palestinian man was stabbed by a Palestinian girl after she thought he was an Israeli.[79]

MYTH

Terrorism directed at Israel is motivated by politics, not religion.

FACT

For many years, terrorism against Jews in the Middle East was stimulated primarily by political concerns. The Arab states used terror as a tool of warfare against Israel, Arabs angry over Israeli policies were often moved to violence, terror attracted international attention to the Palestinian cause, and terror inflicted a human cost on Israelis for failing to capitulate to Palestinian demands.

At least since the days of the Mufti of Jerusalem in the 1920s, however, religion has played a major role in the incitement of violence against Jews.

The vast majority of Arabs are Muslims, but not all Muslims are Arabs. Many Muslims inside and outside the Middle East have been persuaded by spiritual leaders such as the Mufti, as well as their own interpretation of the Koran, that Jews are infidels who must submit to the will of Allah. Israeli Jews, moreover, are seen as the cells in the cancerous body of Israel that is infecting the heart of Islam. While never disappearing, the political conflict took precedence over the religious one for roughly thirty years following the establishment of Israel. The situation began to dramatically change, however, following the 1979 Iranian revolution when Ayatollah Khomeini and his successors began to publicly call for the destruction of Israel on religious grounds.[80] Iran's establishment of Hezbollah in Lebanon led to another escalation in anti-Semitic rhetoric, with the leaders of Hezbollah routinely calling for Israel's destruction.

The emergence of Hamas in the Gaza Strip represented yet another step toward the Islamization of the conflict. The Hamas covenant explicitly calls for the destruction of Israel—and Jews everywhere. For example, "Our struggle against the Jews is very great and very serious. It needs all sincere efforts. The Islamic Resistance Movement is but one squadron that should be supported . . . until the enemy is vanquished and Allah's victory is realized. It strives to raise the banner of Allah over every inch of Palestine."[81]

Anti-Semitic sermons against Jews are now a commonplace occurrence in Palestinian mosques, courses in schools preach hatred based on Islam, and the media is filled with Islamic incitement. To cite just a few examples:

- Sheikh Khaled al-Mugrahbi delivered a sermon captured on video from a mosque on the Temple Mount in which he said, "We will go after the Jews everywhere. They won't escape us. The Children of Israel will be wiped out."[82]

- Sheikh Omar Abu Sara offered a sermon at the Al-Aqsa Mosque in which he called Jews "the most evil of Allah's creations . . . the most evil creatures to have walked the earth." He said that Allah turned Jews into "apes and pigs" and repeated the Hadith of the Gharqad Tree, which says that a final battle with the Jews is approaching in which the trees will say: "Oh servant of Allah, oh Muslim, there is a Jew behind me. Come and kill him." To ensure that his call for genocide was understood, the sheikh added: "I say to the Jews loud and clear: The time for your slaughter has come." And he beseeched Allah to "hasten the day of their slaughter."[83]

- Palestinian children are encouraged to repeat Koranic slurs against Jews. A young Palestinian appeared on Palestinian Authority TV on September 12, 2014, for example, and recited a poem: "You have been condemned to humiliation and hardship O Sons of Zion, O most evil among creations, O barbaric apes, O wretched pigs."[84]

The popularity of Hamas also influenced a broader Islamization of the conflict with the Palestinians. Hamas cast itself as the defenders of Muslim land and the group that could liberate Palestine from the Zionist usurpers. Not to be outdone, the supposedly secular PLO leaders began to use Islamic themes and rhetoric to inspire and incite the Palestinian population. PA president Mahmoud Abbas, for example, has tried to rally support by accusing Israel of endangering the Al-Aqsa Mosque, a tactic used since the days of the Mufti to enrage Muslims around the world. "We are all ready to sacrifice ourselves for Al-Aqsa and for Jerusalem," Abbas said.[85]

Of course, not all Muslims hold such extreme views; however, enough believe a Jewish state cannot exist in the Muslim heartland and that Jews should never rule over Muslims to ensure radical Muslims will remain a threat to Jews and Israel whether a peace agreement is signed or not. In fact, an agreement that ceded land to Israel would give the extremists an excuse to continue their *jihad*.

MYTH

Palestinians oppose terrorism.

FACT

Let us stipulate that Palestinians are unhappy living under Israeli rule and that they face many hardships. The question they face is how to improve their situation and, ideally, achieve independence.

To their misfortune, Palestinian leaders have eschewed the one way to reach their goals, namely negotiation. Instead, since well before Israel's capture of the West Bank in 1967, Palestinians have chosen the path of violence in the misguided belief that they can either inflict enough pain on Israelis to force them to capitulate to their demands or draw enough sympathy to their plight that the international community will pressure Israel on their behalf. The failure of these strategies over nearly fifty years has not convinced them to eschew terror and embrace compromise.

Worse, Palestinian leaders have engaged in nonstop incitement through sermons, social and conventional media, education, and acculturation, which has inspired men, women, and even children to engage in terrorism. In recent years, they have been encouraged to seek martyrdom, and suicide bombing has become an all-too-routine feature of Palestinian "protest."

Politicians outside Israel have forgotten—or simply don't care—that Israel's agreement to negotiate with the PLO was predicated on Yasser Arafat's commitment to cease all violence. The promise of the Oslo agreements ultimately was sabotaged by Arafat's refusal to fulfill this obligation. Since then, the Palestinians have played the game in every agreement of offering this same concession to pocket new Israeli compromises (as they did, for example, in agreeing to the Road Map), knowing that they have no intention of abandoning violence.

The international community, which hardly blinks when Jews are murdered, holds the Palestinians blameless for the failure to achieve peace and focus instead on the red herring of settlements. The Quartet's July 2016 report continued this pattern of equating heinous atrocities committed against Jews with the peaceful construction of homes on land that Israel has an equal or better claim to than do the Palestinians.[86]

Whether it is wise for Israelis to exercise their claim to Judea and Samaria is a question of religion, politics, and security. The incessant violence originating from the West Bank, combined with the sour experience of evacuating Gaza and being rewarded with rocket bombardments and ongoing terror instead of peace, has hardened the positions of Israelis (or simply made them more realistic). Thus, for example, in the June 2016 Peace Index, a monthly survey of Israeli opinion, a majority of Jewish Israelis said they would vote against withdrawal from the West Bank if a referendum were held today. A plurality of Jews believes holding the West Bank has improved Israel's security situation (though 57 percent acknowledge it has worsened Israel's diplomatic situation).[87]

Israelis are also well aware of the incitement by the Palestinians and the widespread support that murdering Jews enjoys among Israel's "peace partners." In a December 2014 PCPO survey, for example, 58 percent of Palestinians agreed that firing missiles at Israel is a good idea. Perhaps more alarming are the results of a Pew survey of Muslims from September 2013, which found that *62 percent of Palestinian Muslims said that suicide bombing attacks are often or sometimes justified to defend Islam from its enemies* (emphasis added). Note, too, that the results were nearly equal in Hamas-ruled Gaza (64 percent) and the Fatah-governed West Bank (60 percent). By comparison, the country with the second highest level of support for suicide bombings was Lebanon (39 percent).[88]

In an analysis of polls conducted by the Palestinian Center for Policy and Survey Research (PSR), Daniel Polisar found a consistent pattern of approval for generic terror attacks against Israelis. What was more disturbing, however, is that when Palestinians were asked their opinions about specific assaults that resulted in the death of Jews, their level of support increased dramatically.[89]

In March 2016, for example, 60 percent of Palestinians supported "attacks against Israeli civilians within Israel." Note these respondents were not asked about attacks on soldiers or settlers, they approved the murder of civilians in Israel. In June 2016, PSR asked their opinion of an April suicide bombing on a Jerusalem bus that wounded more than twenty Israelis; Palestinians approved the attack 65 percent to 31 percent.

A majority of Palestinians has consistently supported attacks on civilians. In 2003, for example, 74 percent approved the bombing of a Haifa restaurant that killed twenty Israelis. The following year, 77 percent endorsed an attack in Beersheva that killed sixteen Israelis. In June 2006, after Israel's complete withdrawal from the Gaza Strip, 69 percent applauded a bombing in Tel Aviv that left eleven Israelis dead.

In March 2008, a record 68 percent of Palestinians supported attacks against Israeli citizens. When asked about a February 2008 bombing in Dimona that killed one Israeli woman, 78 percent approved. Respondents were also asked about the bombing of a religious school in Jerusalem in which eight Israeli students were killed; a record 84 percent of Palestinians supported that attack.

Polisar concludes that "would-be terrorists contemplating an attack can be reasonably confident that if they succeed in killing or injuring Israeli civilians, their actions will earn support and praise in their society—for themselves, their families and the militant group to which they belong, whether or not they live to enjoy it personally. Indeed, they will be seen as heroes, not only in the communiques of Hamas, but in the minds of rank-and-file Palestinians."

People looking for reasons why peace has not been achieved should recognize the role terrorism plays in reinforcing Israeli fears that no concessions will satisfy some Palestinians' bloodlust. The United States and other countries are enabling Palestinian violence by failing to penalize the Palestinian Authority, by refusing to insist on the cessation of incitement in all forms, and by providing aid that is used to pay terrorists and their families and to subsidize their heinous acts.

MYTH

Groups such as Hezbollah, Islamic Jihad, and Hamas are freedom fighters.

FACT

When the United States declared a war on terrorists and the nations that harbor them after September 11, Arab states and their sympathizers argued that many of the organizations that engage in violent actions against Americans and Israelis should not be targets of the new American war because they are "freedom fighters" rather than terrorists. This has been the mantra of the terrorists themselves, who claim that their actions are legitimate forms of resistance against the "Israeli occupation."

This argument is deeply flawed. First, the enemies of Israel rationalize any attacks as legitimate because of real and imagined sins committed by Jews since the beginning of the twentieth century. Consequently, the Arab bloc and its supporters at the United Nations have succeeded in preventing the condemnation of any terrorist attack against Israel. Instead, they routinely sponsor resolutions criticizing Israel when it acts in self-defense.

You can't say there are good terrorists and there are bad terrorists.

—US National Security Adviser Condoleezza Rice[90]

Second, nowhere else in the world is the murder of innocent men, women, and children considered a "legitimate form of resistance." The long list of heinous crimes includes snipers shooting infants, suicide bombers blowing up pizzerias and discos, hijackers taking and killing hostages, and infiltrators murdering Olympic athletes. Hezbollah,

Islamic Jihad, Hamas, and a number of other groups have engaged in these activities for decades and rarely been condemned or their members brought to justice. All of them qualify as terrorist groups according to the US government's own definition ("Terrorism is the unlawful use of force or violence against persons or property to intimidate or coerce a government, the civilian population, or any segment thereof, in furtherance of political or social objectives") and therefore should be targets of US efforts to cut off their funding, to root out their leaders, and to bring them to justice.[91]

Notes, Chapter 9

1. "Intelligence Briefs: Israel/Palestinians," *Middle East Intelligence Bulletin* (March 2001).
2. Khaled Abu Toameh, "Arafat Ordered Hamas Attacks against Israel in 2000," *Jerusalem Post* (September 28, 2010).
3. "Suha Arafat Admits Husband Premeditated Intifada," *Jerusalem Post* (December 29, 2012).
4. "Abd al-Bari Atwan: Arafat Ignited Second Intifada; Why Don't We Do the Same in West Bank?" *MEMRI* (August 4, 2014).
5. Elhanan Miller, "Arafat Gave Us Arms for Second Intifada Attacks, Hamas Official Says," *Times of Israel* (December 16, 2014).
6. Israel Radio (October 3, 2000), cited by *Independent Media Review & Analysis*.
7. Richard Sale, "Hamas History Tied to Israel," UPI (June 18, 2002).
8. Ze'ev Schiff and Ehud Yaari, *Intifada: The Palestinian Uprising—Israel's Third Front*, (NY: Simon and Schuster, 1990), 227–39.
9. "14-Year-Old Suicide Bomber Intercepted," Ministry of Foreign Affairs (March 24, 2004).
10. "Improvements at the Security Crossings and Roadblocks in the West Bank," Ministry of Foreign Affairs (June 14, 2005); "Terror Attack at the Hawara Crossing Near Nablus Thwarted," Ministry of Foreign Affairs (May 24, 2005); "Palestinian Terror Increases," CAMERA (August, 30, 2005).
11. Amnesty International, Press Release (March 24, 2004).
12. Nan Jacques Zilberdik, "Official PA TV to Kids: Israel Will Cease to Exist," *Palestinian Media Watch* (December 16, 2015).
13. Stuart Winer, "Israel Seizes Thousands of Rock-Thrower Dolls Headed for PA," *Times of Israel* (December 8, 2015).
14. Itamar Marcus and Nan Jacques Zilberdik, "Palestinian Children Wear 'Suicide Belts' to Celebrate Fatah's 51 Years of Violence," *Palestinian Media Watch* (January 11, 2016).
15. Itamar Marcus, "Ask for Death," World Security Network (March 2003).
16. Anna Geifman, "Who Is Killing Palestinian Children?" *The Jerusalem Post* (August 7, 2014).
17. "Palestinian Kids Collect Terrorist Cards," *The Jerusalem Post* (December 25, 2003).
18. "Palestinian Suicide Bombing in Israel Statistics," Statistic Brain (December 16, 2015).
19. Ben Hartman and Yaakov Lappin, "Palestinian Assailant Stabs Three People in Rishon Lezion Terror Attack," *Jerusalem Post* (November 2, 2015).
20. Ari Yashar, "Stabbing at Mahane Yehuda Market," Arutz Sheva (November 23, 2015).
21. Chaim Levinson, Gili Cohen, and Ido Efrati, "Palestinian Man Stabs and Kills 13-Year-Old Israeli Girl Asleep in Her West Bank Home," *Haaretz* (June 30, 2016).
22. "The World at War," *The Telegraph* (March 14, 2004).
23. Ali Daraghmeh, "Palestinians Shocked over Kids on Attack," Associated Press (March 1, 2004).

24. MSNBC (May 27, 2005), cited in "Public Outcry in Nablus against Use of Teenagers for Terrorist Missions," Intelligence and Terrorism Information Center at the Center for Special Studies (May 30, 2005).

25. "Palestinian Suicide Bombing in Israel Statistics," Statistic Brain (December 16, 2015).

26. "Blackmailing Young Women into Suicide Terrorism," Israel Ministry of Foreign Affairs (February 12, 2003).

27. Pearl Sheffy Gefen, "Irshad Manji, Muslim Refusenik," *Lifestyles Magazine* (Summer 2004), 29.

28. "Riots Follow Hamas Victory in Ramallah Student Elections—100 Wounded," *Jerusalem Center for Public Affairs* (December 12, 2003).

29. Khaled Abu Toameh, "PA Arrests Academic Voicing Criticism," *Jerusalem Post* (July 5, 2005).

30. *Country Reports on Human Rights Practices—2002,* US State Department (March 31, 2003); B'tselem, Amnesty International (January–December 2002).

31. "Over 600 Palestinians Killed in Internal Clashes since 2006," *Ynet News* (June 6, 2007); "Monthly Reports on Violations of HR," The Independent Commission for Human Rights.

32. Mohammed Daraghmeh, "Palestinian Vigilante Killings on the Rise," *Associated Press* (October 6, 2005).

33. Eva Cahen, "French TV Sticks by Story That Fueled Palestinian Intifada," *CNS News* (July 7, 2008).

34. "Backgrounder: Mohammed Al Dura, Anatomy of a French Media Scandal," *CAMERA* (May 20, 2013).

35. James Fallows, "Who Shot Mohammed Al Dura?" *The Atlantic* (June 2003).

36. Secretary Colin L. Powell, "On-the-Record Briefing," US Department of State Archive (September 12, 2001).

37. Christian Lowe and Barbara Opall-Rome, "Israel Air Force Seeks Expanded Anti-Terror Role," *Defense News* (March 28, 2005).

38. "American Opinion Polls: Opinions toward Terrorism," Jewish Virtual Library.

39. The Peace Index (October 2015).

40. News Conference (September 12, 2001).

41. Hirsh Goodman, "A Lesson Learned," *Jerusalem Report* (September 19, 2005).

42. "Targeted Killings," *Council on Foreign Relations* (May 23, 2013).

43. Amos Yadlin, "Ethical Dilemma's in Fighting Terrorism," vol. 4, no. 8, *Jerusalem Center for Public Affairs* (November 25, 2004).

44. Thomas Wictor, "Female Combatants in Gaza," Thomas Wictor (April 18, 2015).

45. Ariel Ben Solomon, "Hamas Tells Social Media Activists to Always Call the Dead Innocent Civilians," *Jerusalem Post* (July 21, 2014).

46. Customary International Humanitarian Law, "Practice Relating to Rule 97—Human Shields," *ICRC*, Additional Protocol #1.

47. "Reform or Regression? Ten Years of the UN Human Rights Council," Testimony of Hillel C. Neuer, Executive Director, United Nations Watch, Washington, DC (May 17, 2016).

48. Michael Oren, "Palestinians Cheer Carnage," *Wall Street Journal* (August 7, 2002).

49. "Top World Generals: No Israeli War Crimes in Gaza," *Israel Today* (June 15, 2015); Tovah Lazaroff, "Ex-Generals, Diplomats, Absolve Israel of War Crimes," *Jerusalem Post* (June 13, 2015).

50. Colonel Richard Kemp, "Submission to the United Nations Independent Commission of Inquiry on the 2014 Gaza conflict," *www.richard-kemp.com* (February 21, 2015).

51. Michael Schmitt and John Merriam, "A Legal and Operational Assessment of Israel's Targeting Practices," *Justsecurity.org* (April 24, 2015).

52. "US General Charles Wald, USAF (Retired): UNHRC Report on 2014 Gaza Conflict

Unbalanced, Fails to Accurately Assess Violations by Hamas," *BusinessWire* (June 22, 2015).

53. Amos Harel, "Israeli Brigade Commander: Excessive Caution in Gaza Caused Harm to Soldiers," *Haaretz* (June 24, 2015).

54. Ibrahim Khraishi, "Each and Every Missile Launched against Israel Constitutes a Crime against Humanity," UN Watch (July 13, 2014).

55. Ilan Ben Zion, "Rockets Found in UNRWA School, for Third Time," *Times of Israel* (July 30, 2014).

56. Noam Rotenberg, "Exclusive: Hamas Threatened UNRWA Personnel at Gun Point during Gaza War," *Jerusalem Post* (September 11, 2014).

57. "Syria's Army Can Learn a Lot about Morality from the IDF, Al-Jazeera Host Says," *Jerusalem Post* (July 15, 2014).

58. David Bernstein, "Joint Chiefs Chairman Dempsey Undermines Obama Administration Criticism of Israeli Actions in Gaza," *Washington Post* (November 10, 2014); "US Military Chiefs Back Israel on Gaza Tactics," *VOA* (November 10, 2014).

59. Benjamin Wittes and Yishal Schwartz, "What to Make of the UN's Special Commission Report on Gaza?" *Lawfare* (June 24, 2015).

60. "Israelis Protest Hate Crimes in Wake of Baby's Death," *Al-Jazeera* (August 2, 2015).

61. "Glorifying Terrorists and Terror," *Palestinian Media Watch* [Undated]; Itamar Marcus and Nan Jacques Zilberdik, "PA Schools Named after Terrorists by PA Ministry of Education," *Palestinian Media Watch* (September 10, 2015).

62. Metropolitan State University of Denver, "Selected Quotes from Golda Meir," *MSU Denver.*

63. "In Memory of the Victims of Palestinian Violence and Terrorism in Israel," Israel Ministry of Foreign Affairs.

64. Bassam Tawil, "Muslim Blood and Al-Aqsa," Gatestone Institute (October 31, 2015).

65. Bassam Tawil, "Palestinians: A World of Lies, Deception, and Fabrications," *Gatestone Institute* (November 7, 2015).

66. "Abbas Calls Terror Attacks 'Justified Popular Uprising,'" *Ynet News* (December 14, 2015).

67. Bassam Tawil, "Palestinians: A World of Lies, Deception, and Fabrications," *Gatestone Institute* (November 7, 2015).

68. "Rocket Attacks on Israel from Gaza," Israel Defense Forces.

69. Jonathan Zalman, "Hamas Leader: Peace Process Is Futile. There Is Only Jihad, Sacrifice, and Blood," *Tablet* (December 16, 2015).

70. "PA Documents Detail Payments to Terrorists," *The Investigative Project on Terrorism* (January 15, 2015).

71. Edwin Black, "PA Studies Details of Each Terrorist Act before Issuing Salaries," *Times of Israel* (February 6, 2015); Itamar Marcus, Nan Jacques Zilberdik, "PA Allocates $46 Million More for Terrorists in 2014," *Palestinian Media Watch* (February 12, 2014).

72. Itamar Marcus and Nan Jacques Zilberdik, "Teams Named after Rabbi Glick's Shooter and Terrorists Abu Jihad, Khaled Nazzal, and Abu Ali Mustafa Participate in Palestinian Football Championship," *Palestinian Media Watch* (June 25, 2015); Itamar Marcus and Nan Jacques Zilberdik, "PA Schools Named after Terrorists by PA Ministry of Education," *Palestinian Media Watch* (September 10, 2015); Itamar Marcus, Nan Jacques Zilberdik, and Alona Burger, "Palestinian Authority Education, a Recipe for Hate and Terror," *Palestinian Media Watch* (July 21, 2015).

73. Itamar Marcus and Nan Jacques Zilberdik, "Abbas Awards 'Military Star of Honor' to Terrorist Who Attempted to Blow Up Cinema in 1967," *Palestinian Media Watch* (June 4, 2015).

74. Douglas Murray, "The Honey-Trap of Moral Equivalence," *The Gatestone Institute* (April 24, 2013).

75. "Abbas Meets Families of Terrorists Just after Deadly Jerusalem Attack," *Times of Israel* (February 4, 2016).

76. "Official Palestinian TV Calls Jaffa Terrorist a 'Martyr,' Victims 'Settlers,'" *Times of Israel* (March 9, 2016).

77. Lee Hockstader, "Terror Strikes Jerusalem," *Washington Post* (August 10, 2001).

78. Ruthie Blum, "Palestinian Authority Funds Mourning Tent for Terrorist Who Stabbed 13-Year-Old Israeli Girl to Death; Fatah Official Arrives to Pay Tribute to Family," *The Algemeiner* (July 4, 2016).

79. "Terrorism against Israel: The Stabbing Intifada," Jewish Virtual Library.

80. Reza Kahlili, "Ayatollah: Kill All Jews, Annihilate Israel," *WorldNetDaily* (February 5, 2012).

81. "The Covenant of the Hamas—Main Points," Federation of American Scientists [No date].

82. "Imam Who Urged Extermination of Jews Indicted for Incitement," *Times of Israel* (November 12, 2015).

83. Nir Hasson, "Jerusalem Muslim Cleric Who Called for Slaughter of Jews Convicted of Incitement," *Haaretz* (March 28, 2016).

84. "Islamic Hate Speech on PA TV: Jews Are 'Most Evil among Creations,' 'Barbaric Apes, Wretched Pigs,'" Palestinian Media Watch video (November 16, 2014).

85. "Palestinian Authority President Mahmoud Abbas at Fatah Conference: We Are All Ready to Sacrifice Ourselves for Al-Aqsa, Jerusalem," *Middle East Media Research Institute* (November 24, 2014).

86. Barak Ravid, "Quartet Releases Report on Impasse in Israeli-Palestinian Peace: 'Two-State Solution in Danger,'" *Haaretz* (July 1, 2016).

87. The Peace Index (June 2016).

88. "Muslim Publics Share Concerns about Extremist Groups," Pew Research Center (September 10, 2013).

89. "Palestinian Public Opinion Poll #60," Palestinian Center for Policy and Survey (June 2016); Daniel Polisar, "Palestinian Public Opinion Is behind Tel Aviv Terror Attack," *Times of Israel* (June 10, 2016).

90. National Security Adviser Interview with Al-Jazeera TV (October 16, 2001).

91. *"Terrorism 2002-2005"* (Washington, DC: FBI, Undated).

10. The United Nations

Israel's acquisition of territory during the 1967 war is "inadmissible."
Resolution 242 requires Israel to return to its pre-1967 boundaries.
Resolution 242 recognizes a Palestinian right to self-determination.
The United Nations plays a constructive role in Middle East affairs.
Israel enjoys the same rights as any other member of the United Nations.
The United States has always supported Israel at the UN.
America's Arab allies routinely support US positions at the UN.
Israel's failure to implement UN resolutions is a violation of international law.

MYTH

Israel's acquisition of territory during the 1967 war is "inadmissible."

FACT

On November 22, 1967, the UN Security Council unanimously adopted Resolution 242, establishing the principles that were to guide the negotiations for an Arab-Israeli peace settlement.

The first point addressed by the resolution is the "inadmissibility of the acquisition of territory by war." Some people take this to mean that Israel is required to withdraw from all the territories it captured. On the contrary, the reference clearly applies only to an offensive war. If not, the resolution would provide an incentive for aggression. If one country attacks another, and the defender repels the attack and acquires territory in the process, the former interpretation would require the defender to return all the land it took. Thus, aggressors would have little to lose because they would be ensured against the main consequence of defeat.

> *This is the first war in history which has ended with the victors suing for peace and the vanquished calling for unconditional surrender.*
>
> **—Abba Eban[1]**

The ultimate goal of 242, as expressed in paragraph 3, is the achievement of a "peaceful and accepted settlement." This means a negotiated agreement based on the resolution's principles rather than one imposed upon the parties. This is also the implication of Resolution 338, according to Arthur Goldberg, the American ambassador who led the delegation to the UN in 1967.[2] That resolution, adopted after the 1973 War, called for negotiations between the parties to start immediately and concurrently with the cease-fire.

MYTH

Resolution 242 requires Israel to return to its pre-1967 boundaries.

FACT

The most controversial clause in Resolution 242 is the call for the "[w]ithdrawal of Israeli armed forces from territories occupied in the recent conflict." This is linked to the second unambiguous clause calling for "termination of all claims or states of belligerency" and the recognition that "every State in the area" has the "right to live in peace within secure and recognized boundaries free from threats or acts of force."

The resolution does not make Israeli withdrawal a prerequisite for Arab action. Moreover, it does not specify how much territory Israel is required to give up. The Security Council did not say Israel must withdraw from "all the" territories captured during the Six-Day War. This was quite deliberate. The Soviet delegate wanted the inclusion of those words and said that their exclusion meant "that part of these territories can remain in Israeli hands." The Arab states pushed for the word "all" to be added; when the Council rejected their idea, they read the resolution as if it were included. The British ambassador who drafted the approved resolution, Lord Caradon, declared after the vote: "It is only the resolution that will bind us, and we regard its wording as clear."[3]

This literal interpretation, without the implied "all," was repeatedly declared to be the correct one by those involved in drafting the resolution. On October 29, 1969, for example, the British foreign secretary told the House of Commons the withdrawal envisaged by the resolution would *not* be from "all the territories."[4] When asked to explain the British position later, Lord Caradon said: "It would have been wrong to demand that Israel return to its positions of June 4, 1967, because those positions were undesirable and artificial."[5]

Similarly, US ambassador Arthur Goldberg explained, "The notable omissions—which were not accidental—in regard to withdrawal are the words 'the' or 'all' and the 'June 5, 1967 lines' . . . the resolution speaks of withdrawal from occupied territories without defining the extent of withdrawal."[6]

The resolutions clearly call on the Arab states to make peace with Israel. The principal condition is that Israel withdraw from "territories occupied" in 1967. Since Israel withdrew from approximately 94 percent of the territories when it gave up the Sinai, the Gaza Strip, and portions of the West Bank, it has already partially, if not wholly, fulfilled its obligation under 242.

The Arab states also objected to the call for "secure and recognized boundaries" because they feared this implied they would be expected to negotiate with Israel. The Arab League explicitly ruled this out at Khartoum in August 1967, when it proclaimed the three "noes."

Ambassador Goldberg explained that this phrase was specifically included because the parties were expected to make "territorial adjustments in their peace settlement encompassing less than a complete withdrawal of Israeli forces from occupied territories, inasmuch as Israel's prior frontiers had proved to be notably insecure." The question, then, is whether Israel has to give up any additional territory. After signing peace treaties with Egypt and Jordan, and withdrawing to the international border with Lebanon, the only remaining territorial disputes are with the Palestinians (who are not mentioned in 242) and Syria.

The dispute with Syria is over the Golan Heights. Israel repeatedly expressed a willingness to negotiate a compromise in exchange for peace; however, Syria refused to consider even a limited peace treaty unless Israel first agreed to a complete withdrawal. Under 242, Israel has no obligation to withdraw from any part of the Golan in the absence of a peace accord with Syria.

Meanwhile, other Arab states—such as Saudi Arabia, Lebanon, and Libya refused to grant Israel diplomatic recognition, even though they have no territorial disputes with Israel. These states have nevertheless conditioned their relations (at least rhetorically) on an Israeli withdrawal to the pre-1967 borders.

There are some who have urged, as a single, simple solution, an immediate return to the situation as it was on June 4 . . . [T]his is not a prescription for peace but for renewed hostilities.

—President Lyndon Johnson, speech on June 19, 1967[7]

MYTH

Resolution 242 recognizes a Palestinian right to self-determination.

FACT

The Palestinians are not mentioned anywhere in Resolution 242. They are only alluded to in the second clause of the second article of 242, which calls for "a just settlement of the refugee problem." Nowhere does it require that Palestinians be given any political rights or territory.

MYTH

The United Nations plays a constructive role in Middle East affairs.

FACT

Starting in the mid-1970s, an Arab-Soviet bloc joined to form what amounted to a pro-Palestinian lobby at the United Nations. This was particularly true in the General Assembly where these countries—nearly all dictatorships or autocracies—frequently voted together to pass resolutions attacking Israel and supporting the PLO.

In 1975, at the instigation of the Arab states and the Soviet Bloc, the Assembly approved Resolution 3379, which slandered Zionism by branding it a form of racism. US ambassador Daniel Moynihan called the resolution an "obscene act." Israeli ambassador Chaim Herzog told his fellow delegates the resolution was "based on hatred, falsehood and arrogance." Hitler, he declared, would have felt at home listening to the UN debate on the measure.[8]

On December 16, 1991, the General Assembly voted 111–25 (with thirteen abstentions and seventeen delegations absent or not voting) to repeal Resolution 3379. No Arab country voted for repeal. The PLO denounced the vote and the US role.

> *What takes place in the Security Council more closely resembles a mugging than either a political debate or an effort at problem-solving.*
>
> **—Former UN ambassador Jeane Kirkpatrick[9]**

Israel is the object of more investigative committees, special representatives, and rapporteurs than any other state in the UN system. The UN Human Rights Council (HRC) has condemned Israel in sixty-seven individual resolutions since its inception in 2006; more than half of the 128 total resolutions the council has considered.[10]

In March 2016, for example, the HRC condemned Israel five times more often than the other 192 UN member states. In that month alone, five resolutions were devoted to Israel, while Iran, Syria, and North Korea were subjects of one each. Other paragons of human rights, such as Russia, China, Saudi Arabia, and Sudan were never mentioned. The votes against Israel also took place against the backdrop of dozens of stabbings, shootings, and other attacks by Palestinian terrorists against Israelis.

At the same time, the UN Commission on the Status of Women concluded its annual meeting by singling out only one country in the world as a violator of women's rights; Israel was condemned for its alleged mistreatment of Palestinian women. No mention was made of the discrimination against women in the Muslim world, the honor killings, or the gender apartheid of Saudi Arabia.

In March 2005, the Security Council issued an unprecedented condemnation of a suicide bombing in Tel Aviv carried out by Islamic Jihad. Unlike Israeli actions that provoke resolutions, the Security Council issued only a "policy statement" urging the Palestinian Authority to "take immediate, credible steps to find those responsible for this terrorist attack" and bring them to justice. The statement required the consent of all fifteen members of the Security Council. The one Arab member, Algeria, signed on after a reference to Islamic Jihad was deleted.[11] The Council has never adopted a resolution condemning a terrorist atrocity committed against Israel.

In August 2005, just as Israel was prepared to implement its disengagement from the Gaza Strip, the Palestinian Authority produced materials to celebrate the Israeli withdrawal. These included banners that read, "Gaza Today. The West Bank and Jerusalem Tomorrow." News agencies reported that the banners were produced with funds from the UN Development Program and were printed with the UNDP's logo.[12]

In 2016, the UN Educational, Scientific, and Cultural Organization (UNESCO) condemned Israeli actions in Jerusalem, Hebron, and the Tomb of Rachel and called for protecting the cultural heritage of "Palestine." Proposed by several Muslim states, and surprisingly backed by Western friends of Israel such as France, Spain, and Sweden, UNESCO erased the centuries-old linkage between Jews and the Tomb of the Patriarchs in Hebron, the tomb of Rachel near Bethlehem, and even the Western Wall plaza, which UNESCO referred to by the Arabic name "Al-Buraq Plaza." In October 2016, UNESCO erased the Jewish history of Jerusalem by declaring the Temple Mount holy only to Muslims.[13] This was just one more instance where the Palestinians and their supporters have sought to delegitimize Israel and lay the groundwork for its destruction. How they may now ask, can Jews claim territory where the UN's Orwellian historians say they never lived?

History has proven that the path to peace is through direct negotiations between the parties; however, the UN constantly undercuts this principle. The General Assembly routinely adopts resolutions that attempt to impose solutions disadvantageous to Israel on critical issues such as Jerusalem, the Golan Heights, and settlements. Ironically, UN Security Council Resolutions 242 and 338 proposed the bilateral negotiations that are consistently undermined by the General Assembly resolutions.

Thus, the record to date indicates the UN has not played a useful role in resolving the Arab-Israeli conflict.

MYTH

Israel enjoys the same rights as any other member of the United Nations.

FACT

For forty years, Israel was the only UN member excluded from a regional group. Geographically, it belongs in the Asian Group; however, the Arab states barred its membership. Without membership in a regional group, Israel cannot sit on the Security Council or other key UN bodies.

A breakthrough in Israel's exclusion from UN bodies occurred in 2000, when Israel accepted temporary membership in the Western European and Others (WEOG) regional group. The WEOG is the only regional group that is geopolitical rather than purely geographical. WEOG's 27 twenty-seven members—the West European states, Australia, Canada, New Zealand, and the United States—share a Western-Democratic common denominator. This historic step opened the door to Israeli participation in the Security Council. Israel formally applied for membership to the Council in 2005, but the next seat will not be available until 2019.

> [The treatment Israel receives at the United Nations] is obsessive, ugly, bad for the United Nations and bad for peace.
>
> **—UN ambassador Susan Rice**[14]

MYTH

The United States has always supported Israel at the UN.

FACT

Many people believe the United States can always be relied upon to support Israel with its veto in the UN Security Council. The historical record, however, shows that the United States has often opposed Israel in the Council.

The United States did not cast its first veto until 1972, on a Syrian-Lebanese complaint against Israel. From 1967 to 1972, the United States supported or abstained on 24 resolutions, most critical of Israel. From 1973–2015, the Security Council adopted approximately 173 resolutions on the Middle East, most of which were critical of Israel.

The US vetoed a total of forty-four resolutions and, hence, supported the Council's criticism of Israel by its vote of support, or by abstaining, roughly two-thirds of the time.[15]

American officials also often try to convince sponsors to change the language of a resolution to allow them to either vote for, or abstain from a resolution. These resolutions are still critical of Israel, but may not be so one-sided that the United States feels obligated to cast a veto. In 2011, for example, the Palestinians called on the Security Council to label Israeli settlements illegal and to call for a construction freeze. The US ambassador to the UN tried to convince the Palestinians to change the wording, but they refused. After vetoing the resolution, US ambassador Susan Rice still criticized Israeli policy.[16]

In July 2002, the United States shifted its policy and announced that it would veto any Security Council resolution on the Middle East that did not condemn Palestinian terror and name Hamas, Islamic Jihad, and the Al-Aqsa Martyrs Brigade as the groups responsible for the attacks. The United States also said that resolutions must note that any Israeli withdrawal is linked to the security situation and that both parties must be called on to pursue a negotiated settlement.[17] The Arabs can still get around the United States by taking issues to the General Assembly, where nonbinding resolutions pass by majority vote and support for almost any anti-Israel resolution is assured.

The UN has the image of a world organization based on universal principles of justice and equality. In reality, when the chips are down, it is nothing other than the executive committee of the Third World dictatorships.

—Former UN ambassador Jeane Kirkpatrick[18]

MYTH

America's Arab allies routinely support US positions at the UN.

FACT

In 2015, ninety votes were held in the UN General Assembly, eighteen of which were characterized as anti-Israel by the United States. Among the Arab states, Tunisia voted most frequently with the United States (36 percent). Meanwhile, America's Arab allies voted with the United States on less than one-third of the votes. As a group, in 2015, the Arab states voted *against* the United States on 70 percent of the resolutions. Syria and Somalia were at the bottom of the list, opposing the United States 87 percent of the time. By contrast, Israel has consistently been second only to Micronesia as America's top UN ally. Israel voted with the United States 93 percent of the time in 2015, tied with Canada, but outpacing the support levels of major US allies such as Great Britain, and France, which voted with the United States on only 79 percent of the resolutions.[19]

MYTH

Israel's failure to implement UN resolutions is a violation of international law.

FACT

UN resolutions are documents issued by political bodies and need to be interpreted in light of the constitution of those bodies. Votes at the UN are not based on legal principles, but the self-interest of the member states; therefore, UN resolutions represent political rather than legal viewpoints. Resolutions can have moral and political force when they are perceived as expressing the agreed view of the international community, or the views of leading, powerful, and respected nations.

The UN Charter (Articles 10 and 14) specifically empowers the General Assembly to make only nonbinding "recommendations." Assembly resolutions are only considered binding in relation to budgetary and internal procedural matters.

The legality of Security Council resolutions is more ambiguous. There is no consensus as to whether all Security Council resolutions are binding or only those adopted under Chapter 7 of the Charter.[25] Under Article 25 of the Charter, UN member states are obligated to carry out "decisions of the Security Council in accordance with the present Charter," but it is unclear which kinds of resolutions are covered by the term "decisions." These resolutions remain political statements by nation states and not legal determinations by international jurists.

Israel has not violated any Security Council resolutions, and the Council has never sanctioned Israel for noncompliance.

Notes, Chapter 10

1. Abba Eban, *Abba Eban* (NY: Random House, 1977), 446.
2. "Middle East Peace Prospects," *Christian Science Monitor* (July 9, 1985).
3. Security Council Official Records, 1382nd Meeting (S/PV 1382), United Nations, (November 22, 1967).
4. Eban, 452.
5. *Beirut Daily Star* (June 12, 1974).
6. Arthur Goldberg speech to AIPAC Policy Conference (May 8, 1973).
7. "Address by President Johnson at National Foreign Policy Conference of Educators" (June 19, 1967).
8. Chaim Herzog, *Who Stands Accused?* (NY: Random House, 1978), 4-5.
9. *New York Times* (March 31, 1983).

10. "Reform or Regression? Ten Years of the UN Human Rights Council," Testimony of Hillel C. Neuer, Executive Director, United Nations Watch, Washington, DC (May 17, 2016); "Human Rights Actions," Eye on the UN, accessed on April 27, 2011; "Anti-Israel Resolutions at the HRC," UN Watch, accessed on April 27, 2011.

11. "Policy Statement by Security Council on Terrorist Attack in Israel," Press Release SC/8325, United Nations (February 28, 2005).

12. "U.N. Funds Palestinian Campaign," Fox News (August 17, 2005).

13. "UNESCO Erases Jewish Connection to Temple Mount, Kotel" CAMERA (April 19, 2016); "UNESCO Adopts Controversial Jerusalem Resolution," Associated Press (October 18, 2016).

14. Natasha Mozgovaya, "Israel's Treatment at the UN 'Obsessive' and 'Ugly,' US Diplomat Says," *Haaretz* (December 15, 2011).

15. US State Department.

16. Richard Grenell, "Susan Rice Fails to Convince the Palestinians, and Offers a Rebuke to Israel," *Huffington Post* (February 17, 2011), accessed April 27, 2011; "United States vetoes Security Council resolution on Israeli settlements," UN News Centre (February 18, 2011).

17. *Washington Post* (July 26, 2002).

18. Jeremy Havardi, *Refuting the Anti-Israel Narrative: A Case for the Historical, Legal, and Moral Legitimacy of the Jewish State* (McFarland, March 2016), 223.

19. *"Voting Practices at the United Nations, 2015,"* US State Department.

11. Refugees

One million Palestinians were expelled by Israel from 1947 to 1949.
Palestinians were the only refugees of the Arab-Israeli conflict.
The Jews had no intention of living peacefully with their Arab
  neighbors.
The Jews created the refugee problem by expelling the Palestinians.
The Arab invasion had little impact on the Palestinian Arabs.
Arab leaders never encouraged the Palestinians to flee.
The Palestinian Arabs fled to avoid being massacred.
Israel refused to allow Palestinians to return to their homes so Jews could
  steal their property.
The UN called for Israel to repatriate all Palestinian refugees.
Palestinians who wanted to return to their homes posed no danger to
  Israeli security.
The Palestinian refugees were ignored by an uncaring world.
The Arab states have always welcomed the Palestinians.
Millions of Palestinians are confined by Israel to refugee camps.
The Palestinians are the only refugee population barred from returning
  to their homes.
All Palestinian refugees must be given the option to return to
  their homes.

MYTH

One million Palestinians were expelled
by Israel from 1947 to 1949.

FACT

Many Arabs claim that eight hundred thousand to one million Palestinians became refugees during 1947-1949. The last census taken by
the British in 1945 found approximately 1.2 million permanent Arab
residents in *all* of Palestine. A 1949 census conducted by the government of Israel counted 160,000 Arabs living in the new state after
the war. In 1947, a total of 809,100 Arabs lived in the same area.[1] This
meant no more than 650,000 Palestinian Arabs could have become
refugees. A report by the UN Mediator on Palestine arrived at an even
lower refugee figure—472,000.[2]

The Palestinians left their homes for a variety of reasons. Thousands of wealthy Arabs left in anticipation of a war, thousands more
responded to Arab leaders' calls to get out of the way of the advancing

Map 25 Jewish Refugees from Arab States
1948–1972

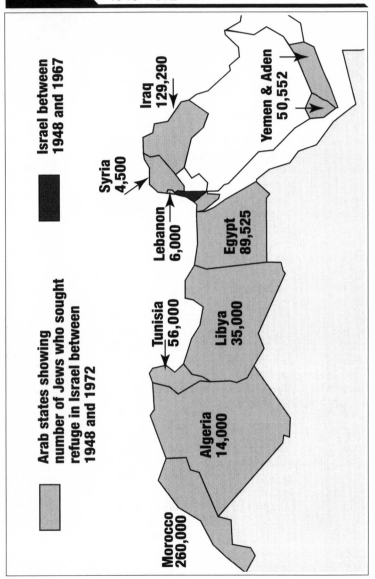

Israel between 1948 and 1967

Arab states showing number of Jews who sought refuge in Israel between 1948 and 1972

Yemen & Aden 50,552

Iraq 129,290

Syria 4,500

Lebanon 6,000

Egypt 89,525

Tunisia 56,000

Libya 35,000

Algeria 14,000

Morocco 260,000

armies, a handful were expelled, but most simply fled to avoid being caught in the cross fire of a war.

MYTH

Palestinians were the only refugees of the Arab-Israeli conflict.

FACT

Although much is heard about the plight of the Palestinian refugees, little is said about the Jews who fled from Arab states. Their situation had long been precarious. During the 1947 UN debates, Arab leaders threatened them. For example, Egypt's delegate told the General Assembly: "The lives of one million Jews in Muslim countries would be jeopardized by partition."[3]

The number of Jews fleeing Arab countries for Israel in the years following Israel's independence was nearly double the number of Arabs leaving Palestine. Many Jews were allowed to take little more than the shirts on their backs. These refugees had no desire to be repatriated. Little is heard about them because they did not remain refugees for long. Of the 820,000 Jewish refugees between 1948 and 1972, 586,000 were resettled in Israel at great expense, and without any offer of compensation from the Arab governments who confiscated their possessions.[4] Israel has consequently maintained that any agreement to compensate the Palestinian refugees must also include Arab reparations for Jewish refugees. To this day, the Arab states have refused to pay anything to the hundreds of thousands of Jews who were forced to abandon their property before fleeing those countries.

As of 2016, at least 170 out of more than seven hundred UN General Assembly resolutions on the Middle East conflict referred directly to Palestinian refugees.[5] The Jewish refugees from Arab countries, however, were not mentioned in any UN resolution.

The contrast between the reception of Jewish and Palestinian refugees is even starker when one considers the difference in cultural and geographic dislocation experienced by the two groups. Most Jewish refugees traveled hundreds—some thousands—of miles to a tiny country whose inhabitants spoke a different language. Most Arab refugees never left Palestine at all; they traveled a few miles to the other side of the truce line, remaining inside the vast Arab nation that they were part of linguistically, culturally, and ethnically.

While Palestinians consider the refugee issue to be among the most important issues for them, the Jewish refugees from Arab countries should not be forgotten. Moreover, the basis for Israeli-Palestinian negotiations, UN Security Council Resolution 242, does not mention Palestinians at all and can apply equally to Jewish refugees.

Jewish Populations in the Arab World

	1948	1958	1968	1978	2011	2014
Algeria	140,000	130,000	1,500	1,000	<50	<50
Egypt	75,000	40,000	1,000	400	100	<40
Iraq	135,000	6,000	2,500	350	7	5-7
Libya	38,000	3,750	100	40	0	0
Morocco	265,000	200,000	50,000	18,000	4,000	2,000
Syria	30,000	5,000	4,000	4,500	100	17
Tunisia	105,000	80,000	10,000	7,000	1,500	1,500
Yemen/Aden	63,000	4,300	500	500	250	<90
Total	851,000	469,060	69,600	31,790	~6,200	3,704

In 2014, the Israeli government dedicated November 30 of every year as a day to honor and remember the refugees to make sure the younger generation is aware of this chapter of Jewish history. Israeli officials hope that this national recognition will spark international acknowledgment of the plight of these refugees and support for compensating them (and their descendants) for their hardships.

MYTH

The Jews had no intention of living peacefully with their Arab neighbors.

FACT

Contrary to the specious claims that the Zionists were interested in driving the Palestinians from their land, the Zionist movement always expected to have a significant Arab population in a future state. In fact, Ze'ev Jabotinsky wrote in the '20s and '30s that Arabs should be treated equally in all sectors of public life and that nothing should be done to force them out. In a draft constitution he worked on, he foresaw Hebrew and Arabic as official languages, Arabs and Jews serving together in the military, and an Arab vice-minister in every cabinet where the prime minister is a Jew.[6]

In numerous instances, Jewish leaders urged the Arabs to remain in Palestine and become citizens of Israel. The Assembly of Palestine Jewry issued this appeal on October 2, 1947:

> We will do everything in our power to maintain peace, and establish a cooperation gainful to both [Jews and Arabs]. It is

now, here and now, from Jerusalem itself, that a call must go
out to the Arab nations to join forces with Jewry and the des-
tined Jewish State and work shoulder to shoulder for our common good, for the peace and progress of sovereign equals.[7]

On November 30, the day after the UN partition vote, the Jewish
Agency announced: "The main theme behind the spontaneous celebrations we are witnessing today is our community's desire to seek
peace and its determination to achieve fruitful cooperation with the
Arabs."[8]

Israel's Proclamation of Independence, issued May 14, 1948, also
invited the Palestinians to remain in their homes and become equal
citizens in the new state:

In the midst of wanton aggression, we yet call upon the
Arab inhabitants of the State of Israel to preserve the ways of
peace and play their part in the development of the State, on
the basis of full and equal citizenship and due representation
in all its bodies and institutions . . . We extend our hand in
peace and neighborliness to all the neighboring states and
their peoples, and invite them to cooperate with the independent Jewish nation for the common good of all.

MYTH

The Jews created the refugee problem by expelling the Palestinians.

FACT

Had the Arabs accepted the 1947 UN resolution, not a single Palestinian would have become a refugee. An independent Arab state would
now exist beside Israel. The responsibility for the refugee problem
rests with the Arabs.

The beginning of the Arab exodus can be traced to the weeks immediately following the announcement of the UN partition resolution.
The first to leave were roughly thirty thousand wealthy Arabs who
anticipated the upcoming war and fled to neighboring Arab countries
to await its end. Less affluent Arabs from the mixed cities of Palestine
moved to all-Arab towns to stay with relatives or friends.[9] By the end
of January 1948, the exodus was so alarming that the Palestine Arab
Higher Committee asked neighboring Arab countries to refuse visas to
these refugees and to seal their borders against them.[10]

A British document indicates officials were aware of the reason
Palestinians were fleeing:

The [Palestine] Arabs have suffered a series of overwhelming
defeats . . . Jewish victories . . . have reduced Arab morale to

zero and, following the cowardly example of their inept leaders, they are fleeing from the mixed areas in their thousands. It is now obvious that the only hope of regaining their position lies in the regular armies of the Arab states.[11]

On January 30, 1948, the Jaffa newspaper, *Ash Sha'ab,* reported, "The first of our fifth-column consists of those who abandon their houses and businesses and go to live elsewhere . . . At the first signs of trouble they take to their heels to escape sharing the burden of struggle."[12]

Another Jaffa paper, *As Sarih* (March 30, 1948) excoriated Arab villagers near Tel Aviv for "bringing down disgrace on us all by 'abandoning the villages.'"[13]

Meanwhile, a leader of the Arab National Committee in Haifa, Hajj Nimer el-Khatib, said Arab soldiers in Jaffa were mistreating the residents. "They robbed individuals and homes. Life was of little value, and the honor of women was defiled. This state of affairs led many [Arab] residents to leave the city under the protection of British tanks."[14]

John Bagot Glubb, the commander of Jordan's Arab Legion, said, "Villages were frequently abandoned even before they were threatened by the progress of war."[15]

Contemporary press reports of major battles in which large numbers of Arabs fled conspicuously fail to mention any forcible expulsion by the Jewish forces. The Arabs are usually described as "fleeing" or "evacuating" their homes. While Zionists are accused of "expelling and dispossessing" the Arab inhabitants of such towns as Tiberias and Haifa, the truth is much different. Both of those cities were within the boundaries of the Jewish State under the UN partition scheme and both were fought for by Jews and Arabs alike.

Jewish forces seized Tiberias on April 19, 1948, and the entire Arab population of six thousand was evacuated under British military supervision. The Jewish Community Council issued a statement afterward: "We did not dispossess them; they themselves chose this course . . . Let no citizen touch their property."[16]

In early April, an estimated twenty-five thousand Arabs left the Haifa area following an offensive by the irregular forces led by Fawzi al-Qawukji, and rumors that Arab air forces would soon bomb the Jewish areas around Mt. Carmel.[17] On April 23, the Haganah captured Haifa. A British police report from Haifa, dated April 26, explained that "every effort is being made by the Jews to persuade the Arab populace to stay and carry on with their normal lives, to get their shops and businesses open and to be assured that their lives and interests will be safe."[18] In fact, David Ben-Gurion sent Golda Meir to Haifa to try to persuade the Arabs to stay, but she was unable to convince them because of their fear of being judged traitors to the Arab cause.[19] By the end of the battle, more than fifty thousand Palestinians had left.

> *Tens of thousands of Arab men, women and children fled toward the eastern outskirts of the city in cars, trucks, carts, and afoot in a desperate attempt to reach Arab territory until the Jews captured Rushmiya Bridge toward Samaria and Northern Palestine and cut them off. Thousands rushed every available craft, even rowboats, along the waterfront, to escape by sea toward Acre.*
>
> **—*New York Times* (April 23, 1948)**[20]

Syria's UN delegate, Faris el-Khouri, interrupted the UN debate on Palestine to describe the seizure of Haifa as a "massacre" and said this action was "further evidence that the 'Zionist program' is to annihilate Arabs within the Jewish state if partition is effected."[21]

The following day, however, the British representative at the UN, Sir Alexander Cadogan, told the delegates that the fighting in Haifa had been provoked by the continuous attacks by Arabs against Jews a few days before and that reports of massacres and deportations were erroneous.[22]

The same day (April 23, 1948), Jamal Husseini, the chairman of the Palestine Higher Committee, told the UN Security Council that instead of accepting the Haganah's truce offer, the Arabs "preferred to abandon their homes, their belongings, and everything they possessed in the world and leave the town."[23]

The US consul general in Haifa Aubrey Lippincott wrote on April 22, 1948, for example, that "local mufti-dominated Arab leaders" were urging "all Arabs to leave the city, and large numbers did so."[24]

Before the Arab invasion in mid-May, Radio Baghdad reported, "Fright has struck the Palestinian Arabs and they fled their country."[25]

Meanwhile, an Israeli army order issued July 6, 1948, made clear that Arab towns and villages were not to be demolished or burned, and that Arab inhabitants were not to be expelled from their homes.[26]

The Haganah did employ psychological warfare to encourage the Arabs to abandon a few villages. Yigal Allon, the commander of the *Palmach,* said he had Jews talk to the Arabs in neighboring villages and tell them a large Jewish force was in Galilee with the intention of burning all the Arab villages in the Lake Hula region. The Arabs were told to leave while they still had time and, according to Allon, they did exactly that.[27]

In the most dramatic example, in the Ramle-Lod area, Israeli troops seeking to protect their flanks and relieve the pressure on besieged Jerusalem, forced a portion of the Arab population to go to an area a few miles away that was occupied by the Arab Legion. "The two towns had served as bases for Arab irregular units, which had frequently attacked Jewish convoys and nearby settlements, effectively barring the main road to Jerusalem to Jewish traffic."[28]

As was clear from the descriptions of what took place in the cities with the largest Arab populations, these cases were clearly the exceptions, accounting for only a small fraction of the Palestinian refugees. The expulsions were not designed to force out the entire Arab population; the areas where they took place were strategically vital and meant to prevent the threat of any rearguard action against the Israeli forces, and to ensure clear lines of communication. Historian Benny Morris notes that "in general, Haganah and IDF commanders were not forced to confront the moral dilemma posed by expulsion; most Arabs fled before and during the battle, before the Israeli troops reached their homes and before the Israeli commanders were forced to confront the dilemma."[29]

MYTH

The Arab invasion had little impact on the Palestinian Arabs.

FACT

The Arabs of Palestine expected the Arab armies to drive the Jews into the sea for their benefit. The Arab leaders, however, were motivated by their own interests and each hoped to grab their own piece of Palestine.

Once the invasion began in May 1948, most Arabs remaining in Palestine left for neighboring countries. Rather than acting as a strategically valuable "fifth-column" that would fight the Jews from within the country, the Palestinians chose to flee to the safety of the other Arab states, still confident of being able to return. A leading Palestinian nationalist of the time, Musa Alami, revealed the attitude of the fleeing Arabs:

> The Arabs of Palestine left their homes, were scattered, and lost everything. But there remained one solid hope: [t]he Arab armies were on the eve of their entry into Palestine to save the country and return things to their normal course, punish the aggressor, and throw oppressive Zionism with its dreams and dangers into the sea. On May 14, 1948, crowds of Arabs stood by the roads leading to the frontiers of the former British Mandate of Palestine and enthusiastically welcomed the advancing armies. Days and weeks passed, but the Arab armies did not defeat the Israelis. Instead, they lost

Acre, Sarafand, Lydda, Ramleh, Nazareth, most of the south and the rest of the north. Then hope fled.[30]

As the fighting spread into areas that had previously remained quiet, the Arabs began to see the possibility of defeat. As that possibility turned into reality, the flight of the Arabs increased—more than three hundred thousand departed after May 15—leaving approximately 160,000 Arabs in the State of Israel.[31]

Although most of the Arabs had left by November 1948, there were still those who chose to leave even after hostilities ceased. An interesting case was the evacuation of three thousand Arabs from Faluja, a village between Tel Aviv and Beersheba:

> Observers feel that with proper counsel after the Israeli-Egyptian armistice, the Arab population might have advantageously remained. They state that the Israeli Government had given guarantees of security of person and property. However, no effort was made by Egypt, Transjordan or even the United Nations Palestine Conciliation Commission to advise the Faluja Arabs one way or the other.[32]

MYTH

Arab leaders never encouraged the Palestinians to flee.

FACT

Despite revisionist attempts to deny that Palestinians were encouraged to leave their homes, a plethora of evidence demonstrates that the Palestinians who later became refugees were indeed told to leave their homes to make way for the invading Arab armies. In fact, in recent years, more Palestinians have come forward to candidly admit this truth.

The Economist, a frequent critic of the Zionists, reported on October 2, 1948:

> Of the 62,000 Arabs who formerly lived in Haifa not more than 5,000 or 6,000 remained. Various factors influenced their decision to seek safety in flight. There is but little doubt that the most potent of the factors were the announcements made over the air by the Higher Arab Executive, urging the Arabs to quit . . . It was clearly intimated that those Arabs who remained in Haifa and accepted Jewish protection would be regarded as renegades.[33]

Time's report of the battle for Haifa (May 3, 1948) was similar: "The mass evacuation, prompted partly by fear, partly by orders of Arab leaders, left the Arab quarter of Haifa a ghost city . . . By withdrawing Arab workers their leaders hoped to paralyze Haifa."[34]

Starting in December 1947, historian Benny Morris said, "Arab officers ordered the complete evacuation of specific villages in certain areas, lest their inhabitants 'treacherously' acquiesce in Israeli rule or hamper Arab military deployments." He concluded, "There can be no exaggerating the importance of these early Arab-initiated evacuations in the demoralization, and eventual exodus, of the remaining rural and urban populations."[35]

> *The [refugee] problem was a direct consequence of the war that the Palestinians—and . . . surrounding Arab states—had launched."*
>
> **—Historian Benny Morris[36]**

The Arab National Committee in Jerusalem, following the March 8, 1948, instructions of the Arab Higher Committee, ordered women, children, and the elderly in various parts of Jerusalem to leave their homes: "Any opposition to this order . . . is an obstacle to the holy war . . . and will hamper the operations of the fighters in these districts." The Arab Higher Committee also ordered the evacuation of "several dozen villages, as well as the removal of dependents from dozens more" in April-July 1948. "The invading Arab armies also occasionally ordered whole villages to depart, so as not to be in their way."[37]

Morris also said that in early May, units of the Arab Legion ordered the evacuation of all women and children from the town of Beisan. The Arab Liberation Army was also reported to have ordered the evacuation of another village south of Haifa. The departure of the women and children, Morris says, "tended to sap the morale of the menfolk who were left behind to guard the homes and fields, contributing ultimately to the final evacuation of villages. Such two-tier evacuation— women and children first, the men following weeks later—occurred in Qumiya in the Jezreel Valley, among the Awarna Bedouin in Haifa Bay and in various other places."

Who gave such orders? Leaders such as Iraqi prime minister Nuri Said, who declared, "We will smash the country with our guns and obliterate every place the Jews seek shelter in. The Arabs should conduct their wives and children to safe areas until the fighting has died down."[38]

Edward Atiyah, the secretary of the Arab League office in London, wrote in his book, *The Arabs*: "This wholesale exodus was due partly to the belief of the Arabs, encouraged by the boastings of an unrealistic Arabic press and the irresponsible utterances of some of the Arab leaders that it could be only a matter of weeks before the Jews were defeated by the armies of the Arab States and the Palestinian Arabs enabled to re-enter and retake possession of their country."[39]

"The refugees were confident their absence would not last long, and that they would return within a week or two," Monsignor George Hakim, a Greek Orthodox Catholic Bishop of Galilee told the Beirut newspaper, *Sada al-Janub* (August 16, 1948). "Their leaders had promised them that the Arab Armies would crush the 'Zionist gangs' very quickly and that there was no need for panic or fear of a long exile."[40]

In his memoirs, Haled al-Azm, the Syrian Prime Minister in 1948–49, also admitted the Arab role in persuading the refugees to leave:

"Since 1948 we have been demanding the return of the refugees to their homes. But we ourselves are the ones who encouraged them to leave. Only a few months separated our call to them to leave and our appeal to the United Nations to resolve on their return."[41]

"The Arab States encouraged the Palestine Arabs to leave their homes temporarily in order to be out of the way of the Arab invasion armies," according to the Jordanian newspaper *Filastin* (February 19, 1949).[42]

One refugee quoted in the Jordan newspaper, *Ad Difaa* (September 6, 1954), said, "The Arab government told us: Get out so that we can get in. So we got out, but they did not get in."[43]

"The Secretary-General of the Arab League, Azzam Pasha, assured the Arab peoples that the occupation of Palestine and Tel Aviv would be as simple as a military promenade," said Habib Issa in the New York Lebanese paper, *Al-Hoda* (June 8, 1951). "He pointed out that they were already on the frontiers and that all the millions the Jews had spent on land and economic development would be easy booty, for it would be a simple matter to throw Jews into the Mediterranean . . . Brotherly advice was given to the Arabs of Palestine to leave their land, homes and property and to stay temporarily in neighboring fraternal states, lest the guns of the invading Arab armies mow them down."[44]

The Arabs' fear was exacerbated by stories of Jewish atrocities following the attack on Deir Yassin. The native population lacked leaders who could calm them; their spokesmen were operating from the safety of neighboring states and did more to arouse their fears than to pacify them. Local military leaders were of little or no comfort. In one instance, the commander of Arab troops in Safed went to Damascus.

The following day, his troops withdrew from the town. When the residents realized they were defenseless, they fled in panic. Palestinian Authority president Mahmoud Abbas, the last person you might expect to confirm this story, admitted that Arabs began emigrating from Safed when the Arab Liberation Army retreated. "In Safed, just like Hebron, people were afraid that the Jews would take revenge for the massacre in 1929" during which sixty-five Jews were killed by Arabs in Hebron and eighteen in Safed.[45]

"As Palestinian military power was swiftly and dramatically crushed, and the Haganah demonstrated almost unchallenged superiority in successive battles," Benny Morris noted, "Arab morale cracked, giving way to general, blind, panic, or a 'psychosis of flight,' as one IDF intelligence report put it."[46]

Dr. Walid al-Qamhawi, a former member of the Executive Committee of the PLO, agreed "it was collective fear, moral disintegration and chaos in every field that exiled the Arabs of Tiberias, Haifa and dozens of towns and villages."[47]

As panic spread throughout Palestine, the early trickle of refugees became a flood, numbering more than two hundred thousand by the time the provisional government declared the independence of the State of Israel.

Even Jordan's King Abdullah, writing in his memoirs, blamed Palestinian leaders for the refugee problem:

"The tragedy of the Palestinians was that most of their leaders had paralyzed them with false and unsubstantiated promises that they were not alone; that 80 million Arabs and 400 million Muslims would instantly and miraculously come to their rescue."[48]

These accounts have been bolstered by more recent statements by Palestinians who have become fed up with the phony narrative concocted by some Palestinian and Israeli academics. Asmaa Jabir Balasimah, for example, recalled her flight from Israel in 1948:

> We heard sounds of explosions and of gunfire at the beginning of the summer in the year of the "Catastrophe" [1948]. They told us: The Jews attacked our region and it is better to evacuate the village and return, after the battle is over. And indeed there were among us [who fled Israel] those who left a fire burning under the pot, those who left their flock [of sheep] and those who left their money and gold behind, based on the assumption that we would return after a few hours.[49]

An Arab resident of a Palestinian refugee camp explained why his family left Israel in 1948:

> The radio stations of the Arab regimes kept repeating to us: "Get away from the battle lines. It's a matter of ten days or two weeks at the most, and we'll bring you back to Ein-Kerem [near Jerusalem]." And we said to ourselves, "That's a very long time. What is this? Two weeks? That's a lot!" That's what we thought [then]. And now 50 years have gone by.[50]

Mahmoud al-Habbash, a Palestinian journalist wrote in the Palestinian Authority's official newspaper:

> The leaders and the elites promised us at the beginning of the "Catastrophe" in 1948, that the duration of the exile will not be long, and that it will not last more than a few days or months, and afterwards the refugees will return to their homes, which most of them did not leave only until they put their trust in those "Arkuvian" promises made by the leaders and the political elites. Afterwards, days passed, months, years and decades, and the promises were lost with the strain of the succession of events [Arkuvian" is a reference to Arkuv, a figure from Arab tradition known for breaking promises and lying.][51]

Another Palestinian journalist, Jawad al-Bashiti, explained the cause of the "Catastrophe":

> The following happened: the first war between Arabs and Israel had started and the "Arab Salvation Army" came and told the Palestinians: "We have come to you in order to liquidate the Zionists and their state. Leave your houses and villages, you will return to them in a few days safely. Leave them so we can fulfill our mission (destroy Israel) in the best way and so you won't be hurt." It became clear already then, when it was too late, that the support of the Arab states (against Israel) was a big illusion. Arabs fought as if intending to cause the "Palestinian Catastrophe."[52]

The Arab armies entered Palestine to protect the Palestinians from the Zionist tyranny but, instead, they abandoned them, forced them to emigrate and to leave their homeland, and threw them into prisons similar to the ghettos in which the Jews used to live.

—Palestinian Authority prime minister Mahmoud Abbas[53]

MYTH

The Palestinian Arabs fled to avoid being massacred.

FACT

The United Nations resolved that Jerusalem would be an international city apart from the Arab and Jewish states demarcated in the partition resolution. The 150,000 Jewish inhabitants were under constant military pressure; the twenty-five hundred Jews living in the Old City were victims of an Arab blockade that lasted five months before they were forced to surrender on May 29, 1948. Prior to the surrender, and throughout the siege on Jerusalem, Jewish convoys tried to reach the city to alleviate the food shortage, which, by April, had become critical.

Meanwhile, the Arab forces, which had engaged in sporadic and unorganized ambushes since December 1947, began to make an organized attempt to cut off the highway linking Tel Aviv with the city's only supply route. The Arabs controlled several strategic vantage points, which overlooked the highway and enabled them to fire on the convoys trying to reach the beleaguered city with supplies. Deir Yassin was situated on a hill, about twenty-six hundred feet high, which commanded a wide view of the vicinity and was located less than a mile from the suburbs of Jerusalem.[54]

On April 6, Operation Nachshon was launched to open the road to Jerusalem. The village of Deir Yassin was included on the list of Arab villages to be occupied as part of the operation. The following day Haganah commander David Shaltiel wrote to the leaders of the Lehi and Irgun:

> I learn that you plan an attack on Deir Yassin. I wish to point out that the capture of Deir Yassin and its holding are one stage in our general plan. I have no objection to your carrying out the operation provided you are able to hold the village. If you are unable to do so I warn you against blowing up the village which will result in its inhabitants abandoning it and its ruins and deserted houses being occupied by foreign forces . . . Furthermore, if foreign forces took over, this would upset our general plan for establishing an airfield.[55]

The Irgun decided to attack Deir Yassin on April 9, while the Haganah was still engaged in the battle for Kastel. This was the first major Irgun attack against the Arabs. Previously, the Irgun and Lehi had concentrated their attacks against the British.

According to Irgun leader Menachem Begin, the assault was carried out by one hundred members of his organization; other authors say it was as many as 132 men from both groups. Begin stated that a small open truck fitted with a loudspeaker was driven to the entrance of the village before the attack and broadcast a warning for civilians to evacuate the area, which many did.[56] Other writers say the warning was never issued because the truck with the loudspeaker rolled into a ditch before it could broadcast the warning.[57] One of the fighters said the ditch had been filled in and that the truck had continued on to the village. "One of us called out on the loudspeaker in Arabic, telling the inhabitants to put down their weapons and flee. I don't know if they heard, and I know these appeals had no effect."[58]

Contrary to revisionist histories that say the village was filled with peaceful innocents, evidence shows that both residents and foreign troops opened fire on the attackers. One Irgun fighter described his experience:

> My unit stormed and passed the first row of houses. I was among the first to enter the village. There were a few other guys with me, each encouraging the other to advance. At the top of the street I saw a man in khaki clothing running ahead. I thought he was one of ours. I ran after him and told him, "advance to that house." Suddenly he turned around, aimed his rifle and shot. He was an Iraqi soldier. I was hit in the foot.[59]

The battle was ferocious and took several hours. The Irgun suffered forty-one casualties, including four dead.

Surprisingly, after the "massacre," the Irgun escorted a representative of the Red Cross through the town and held a press conference. The *New York Times*' subsequent description of the battle was essentially the same as Begin's. The *Times* said more than two hundred Arabs were killed, forty captured, and seventy women and children were released. No hint of a massacre appeared in the report.[60]

"Paradoxically," historian Dan Kurzman observed, "the Jews say about 250 out of 400 village inhabitants [were killed], while Arab survivors say only 110 of 1,000."[61] A study by Bir Zeit University, based on discussions with each family from the village, arrived at a figure of 107 Arab civilians dead and twelve wounded, in addition to thirteen "fighters," evidence that the number of dead was smaller than claimed and that the village did have troops based there.[62] Other Arab sources have subsequently suggested the number may have been even lower.[63]

In fact, the attackers left open an escape corridor from the village and more than two hundred residents left unharmed. For example, at nine thirty in the morning, about five hours after the fighting started, the Lehi evacuated forty old men, women, and children on trucks and took them to a base in Sheik Bader. Later, the Arabs were taken to East

Jerusalem. Seeing the Arabs in the hands of Jews also helped raise the morale of the people of Jerusalem who were despondent from the setbacks in the fighting to that point.[64] Another source says seventy women and children were taken away and turned over to the British.[65] If the intent was to massacre the inhabitants, no one would have been evacuated.

After the remaining Arabs feigned surrender and then fired on the Jewish troops, some Jews killed Arab soldiers and civilians indiscriminately. None of the sources specify how many women and children were killed (the *Times* report said it was about half the victims; their original casualty figure came from the Irgun source), but there were some among the casualties.

> An interesting footnote to the Deir Yassin story is that the survivors of the battle found refuge in the nearby village of Silwan but, just five days after they arrived, a delegation of the villagers demanded that the survivors be sent somewhere else.[66]

At least some of the women who were killed became targets because of men who tried to disguise themselves as women. The Irgun commander reported, for example, that the attackers "found men dressed as women and therefore they began to shoot at women who did not hasten to go down to the place designated for gathering the prisoners."[67] Another story was told by a member of the Haganah who overheard a group of Arabs from Deir Yassin who said, "The Jews found out that Arab warriors had disguised themselves as women. The Jews searched the women too. One of the people being checked realized he had been caught, took out a pistol and shot the Jewish commander. His friends, crazed with anger, shot in all directions and killed the Arabs in the area."[68]

Arab propagandists at the time claimed Jews raped some of the women in the village; however, every villager interviewed denied these allegations. Like many of the claims, this was a deliberate propaganda ploy, but one that backfired. Hazam Nusseibeh, who worked for the Palestine Broadcasting Service in 1948, admitted being told by Hussein Khalidi, a Palestinian Arab leader, to fabricate the atrocity claims. Abu Mahmud, a Deir Yassin resident in 1948 told Khalidi that "there was no rape," but Khalidi replied, "We have to say this, so the Arab armies will come to liberate Palestine from the Jews." Nusseibeh told the BBC fifty years later, "This was our biggest mistake. We did not realize how our people would react. As soon as they heard that women had been raped at Deir Yassin, Palestinians fled in terror."[69]

The Jewish Agency, upon learning of the attack, immediately expressed its "horror and disgust." It also sent a letter expressing the Agency's shock and disapproval to Transjordan's King Abdullah.

Arab radio stations broadcast accounts of what happened over the days and weeks that followed, and the Arab Higher Committee hoped exaggerated reports about a "massacre" at Deir Yassin would shock the population of the Arab countries into bringing pressure on their governments to intervene in Palestine. Instead, the immediate impact was to stimulate a new Palestinian exodus.

Just four days after the reports from Deir Yassin were published, an Arab force ambushed a Jewish convoy on the way to Hadassah Hospital, killing seventy-seven Jews, including doctors, nurses, patients, and the director of the hospital. Another twenty-three people were injured. This premeditated massacre attracted little attention and is never mentioned by those who are quick to bring up Deir Yassin. Moreover, despite attacks that killed more than five hundred Jews in the first four months after the partition decision alone, Jews did not flee.

The Palestinians knew the Jews were not trying to annihilate them; otherwise, they would not have been allowed to evacuate Tiberias, Haifa, or any of the other towns captured by Jewish forces. By contrast, secretary-general of the Arab League Abd al-Rahman Azzam Pasha made clear the Arabs' intent in an interview with an Egyptian newspaper (October 11, 1947): "Personally, I hope that the Jews will not force this war upon us, because it will be a war of annihilation. It will be a momentous massacre in history that will be talked about like the massacres of the Mongols or the Crusades."[70]

References to Deir Yassin have remained a staple of anti-Israel propaganda for decades because the incident was unique.

MYTH

Israel refused to allow Palestinians to return to their homes so Jews could steal their property.

FACT

Israel could not simply agree to allow all Palestinians to return, but consistently sought a solution to the refugee problem. Israel's position was expressed by David Ben-Gurion (August 1, 1948):

> When the Arab states are ready to conclude a peace treaty with Israel this question will come up for constructive solution as part of the general settlement, and with due regard to our counter-claims in respect of the destruction of Jewish life and property, the long-term interest of the Jewish and

Arab populations, the stability of the State of Israel and the durability of the basis of peace between it and its neighbors, the actual position and fate of the Jewish communities in the Arab countries, the responsibilities of the Arab governments for their war of aggression and their liability for reparation, will all be relevant in the question whether, to what extent, and under what conditions, the former Arab residents of the territory of Israel should be allowed to return.[71]

The Israeli government was not indifferent to the plight of the refugees; an ordinance was passed creating a Custodian of Abandoned Property "to prevent unlawful occupation of empty houses and business premises, to administer ownerless property, and also to secure tilling of deserted fields, and save the crops."[72]

The implied danger of repatriation did not prevent Israel from allowing some refugees to return and offering to take back a substantial number as a condition for signing a peace treaty. In 1949, Israel offered to allow families that had been separated during the war to return, to release refugee accounts frozen in Israeli banks (eventually released in 1953), to pay compensation for abandoned lands and to repatriate one hundred thousand refugees.[73]

The Arabs rejected all the Israeli compromises. They were unwilling to take any action that might be construed as recognition of Israel. They made repatriation a precondition for negotiations, something Israel rejected. The result was the confinement of the refugees in camps.

Despite the position taken by the Arab states, Israel did release the Arab refugees' blocked bank accounts, which totaled more than $10 million, paid thousands of claimants cash compensation, and granted thousands of acres as alternative holdings.

MYTH

The UN called for Israel to repatriate all Palestinian refugees.

FACT

The United Nations took up the refugee issue and adopted Resolution 194 on December 11, 1948. This called on the Arab states and Israel to resolve all outstanding issues through negotiations either directly or with the help of the Palestine Conciliation Commission established by this resolution. Furthermore, Point 11 resolves:

that refugees wishing to return to their homes *and live at peace* with their neighbors should be permitted to do so at the earliest practicable date, and that compensation should be paid for property of those choosing not to return and for loss of or damage to property which under principles of international law or in equity should be made good by Governments or authorities responsible. Instructs the Conciliation Commission to facilitate the repatriation, *resettlement* and economic and social rehabilitation of refugees and payment of compensation (emphasis added).

The emphasized words demonstrate that the UN recognized that Israel could not be expected to repatriate a hostile population that might endanger its security. The solution to the problem, like all previous refugee problems, would require at least some Palestinians to be resettled in Arab lands. Furthermore, the resolution uses the word "should" instead of "shall," which, in legal terms, is not mandatory language.

The resolution met most of Israel's concerns regarding the refugees, whom they regarded as a potential fifth-column if allowed to return unconditionally. The Israelis considered the settlement of the refugee issue a negotiable part of an overall peace settlement. As President Chaim Weizmann explained, "We are anxious to help such resettlement provided that real peace is established and the Arab states do their part of the job. The solution of the Arab problem can be achieved only through an all-around Middle East development scheme, toward which the United Nations, the Arab states and Israel will make their respective contributions."[74]

The Palestinian demand for the "right of return" is totally unrealistic and would have to be solved by means of financial compensation and resettlement in Arab countries.

—Egyptian president Hosni Mubarak[75]

At the time, the Israelis did not expect the refugees to be a major issue; they thought the Arab states would resettle the majority and that some compromise on the remainder could be worked out in the context of an overall settlement. The Arabs were no more willing to compromise in 1949, however, than they had been in 1947. In fact, they unanimously rejected the UN resolution.

The UN discussions on refugees had begun in the summer of 1948, before Israel had completed its military victory; consequently, the Arabs still believed they could win the war and allow the refugees to return triumphant. The Arab position was expressed by Emile Ghoury, the secretary of the Arab Higher Committee:

It is inconceivable that the refugees should be sent back to their homes while they are occupied by the Jews, as the lat-

ter would hold them as hostages and maltreat them. The very
proposal is an evasion of responsibility by those responsible.
It will serve as a first step towards Arab recognition of the
State of Israel and partition.[76]

The Arabs demanded that the United Nations assert the "right" of
the Palestinians to return to their homes and were unwilling to accept
anything less until after their defeat had become obvious. The Arabs
then reinterpreted Resolution 194 as granting the refugees the absolute right of repatriation and have demanded that Israel accept this
interpretation ever since. Regardless of the interpretation, 194, like
other General Assembly resolutions, is not legally binding.

MYTH

*Palestinians who wanted to return to their homes
posed no danger to Israeli security.*

FACT

When plans for setting up a state were made in early 1948, Jewish
leaders in Palestine expected the new nation to include a significant
Arab population. From the Israeli perspective, the refugees had been
given an opportunity to stay in their homes and be a part of the new
state. Approximately 160,000 Arabs had chosen to do so. To repatriate
those who had fled would be, in the words of Foreign Minister Moshe
Sharett, "suicidal folly."[77]

In the Arab world, the refugees were viewed as a potential fifth-
column within Israel. As one Lebanese paper wrote:

The return of the refugees should create a large Arab majority that would serve as the most effective means of reviving
the Arab character of Palestine, while forming a powerful
fifth-column for the day of revenge and reckoning.[78]

The Arabs believed the return of the refugees would virtually guarantee the destruction of Israel, a sentiment expressed by Egyptian foreign minister Muhammad Salah al-Din:

It is well-known and understood that the Arabs, in demanding the return of the refugees to Palestine, mean their return
as masters of the Homeland and not as slaves. With a greater
clarity, they mean the liquidation of the State of Israel.[79]

The plight of the refugees remained unchanged after the Suez War.
In fact, even the rhetoric stayed the same. In 1957, the Refugee Conference at Homs, Syria, passed a resolution stating:

Any discussion aimed at a solution of the Palestine problem which will not be based on ensuring the refugees' right to annihilate Israel will be regarded as a desecration of the Arab people and an act of treason.[80]

A parallel can be drawn to the time of the American Revolution, during which many colonists who were loyal to England fled to Canada. The British wanted the newly formed republic to allow the loyalists to return to claim their property. Benjamin Franklin rejected this suggestion in a letter to Richard Oswald, the British negotiator, dated November 26, 1782:

Your ministers require that we should receive again into our bosom those who have been our bitterest enemies and restore their properties who have destroyed ours: and this while the wounds they have given us are still bleeding![81]

MYTH

The Palestinian refugees were ignored by an uncaring world.

FACT

The General Assembly voted on November 19, 1948, to establish the United Nations Relief for Palestinian Refugees (UNRPR) to dispense aid to the refugees. Since then, more than 150 resolutions have been adopted that refer to Palestinian refugees, roughly 17 percent of all the resolutions on the conflict.[82]

The UNRPR was replaced by the United Nations Relief and Works Agency (UNRWA) on December 8, 1949. UNRWA was designed to continue the relief program initiated by the UNRPR, substitute public works for direct relief, and promote economic development. The proponents of the plan envisioned that direct relief would be almost completely replaced by public works, with the remaining assistance provided by the Arab governments.

UNRWA had little chance of success, however, because it sought to solve a political problem using an economic approach. By the mid-1950s, it was evident neither the refugees nor the Arab states were prepared to cooperate on the large-scale development projects originally foreseen by the Agency as a means of alleviating the Palestinians' situation. The Arab governments, and some of the refugees themselves, were unwilling to contribute to any plan that could be interpreted as fostering resettlement. They preferred to cling to their interpretation of Resolution 194, which they believed would eventually result in repatriation.

Palestinian Refugees in UNRWA Camps
(January 2016)[83]

Field of Operations	Official Camps	Registered Refugees	Registered Refugees in Camps
Jordan	10	2,117,361	369,949
Lebanon	12	449,957	238,528
Syria	9	526,744	159,303
West Bank	19	774,167	216,403
Gaza Strip	8	1,258,559	540,515
Agency Total	58	5,126,788	1,524,698

MYTH

The Arab states have always welcomed the Palestinians.

FACT

No one expected the refugee problem to persist after the 1948 war. John Blandford Jr., the director of UNRWA, wrote in his report on November 29, 1951, that he expected the Arab governments to assume responsibility for relief by July 1952. Moreover, Blandford stressed the need to end relief operations: "Sustained relief operations inevitably contain the germ of human deterioration."[84] In 1952, the UNRWA set up a fund of $200 million to provide homes and jobs for the refugees, but it went untouched.

Meanwhile, Jordan was the only Arab country to welcome the Palestinians and grant some citizenship (Gazans were excluded). King Abdullah considered the Palestinian Arabs and Jordanians one people. By 1950, he annexed the West Bank and forbade the use of the term Palestine in official documents.[85] In 2004, Jordan began revoking the citizenship of Palestinians who do not have the Israeli permits that are necessary to reside in the West Bank.[86]

Although demographic figures indicated ample room for settlement existed in Syria, Damascus refused to accept any refugees, except those who might refuse repatriation. Syria also declined to resettle eighty-five thousand refugees in 1952-54, though it had been offered international funds to pay for the project. Iraq was also expected to accept a large number of refugees but proved unwilling. Likewise, Lebanon insisted it had no room for the Palestinians.

After the 1948 war, Egypt controlled the Gaza Strip and its more than two hundred thousand inhabitants but refused to allow the Palestinians into Egypt or permit them to move elsewhere. Saudi Arabian radio compared Egypt's treatment of Palestinians in Gaza to Hitler's rule in occupied Europe.[87]

Little has changed in succeeding years. Arab governments have frequently offered jobs, housing, land, and other benefits to Arabs and non-Arabs, *excluding* Palestinians. For example, Saudi Arabia chose not to use unemployed Palestinian refugees to alleviate its labor shortage in the late 1970s and early 1980s; instead, thousands of South Koreans and other Asians were recruited to fill jobs.

The situation grew even worse in the wake of the 1991 Gulf War. Kuwait, which employed large numbers of Palestinians but denied them citizenship, expelled more than three hundred thousand Palestinians. "If people pose a security threat, as a sovereign country we have the right to exclude anyone we don't want," said Kuwaiti ambassador to the United States Saud Nasir al-Sabah.[88] This expulsion drew no media attention, provoked no UN resolutions condemning Kuwait, and was ignored by pro-Palestinian activists.

The Arab States do not want to solve the refugee problem. They want to keep it as an open sore, as an affront to the United Nations and as a weapon against Israel. Arab leaders don't give a damn whether the refugees live or die.

**—Sir Alexander Galloway,
former head of UNRWA in Jordan (April 1952)[89]**

Today, Palestinian refugees in Lebanon do not have social and civil rights, are prevented from owning property, and have very limited access to public health or educational facilities. The majority relies entirely on UNRWA for education, health, and social services. Considered foreigners, Palestinian refugees are prohibited by law from working in more than seventy trades and professions. Most are restricted to manual and clerical work.[90]

The Palestinian refugees held the UN responsible for ameliorating their condition; nevertheless, many Palestinians were unhappy with the treatment they were receiving from their Arab brethren. Some, like Palestinian nationalist leader Musa Alami were incredulous: "It is shameful that the Arab governments should prevent the Arab refugees from working in their countries and shut the doors in their faces and imprison them in camps."[91] Most refugees, however, focused their discontentment on "the Zionists," whom they blamed for their predicament rather than the vanquished Arab armies.

I briefly visited the Balata refugee camp with its 20,000 residents. The camp is inside the West Bank city of Nablus—that is, within the jurisdiction of the Palestinian Authority (PA)...Balata's children, like the children in similar camps in Gaza and neighboring Arab countries, are nurtured on the myth that someday soon they will return in triumph to their ancestors' homes by the Mediterranean Sea. While awaiting redemption, Balata's residents are prohibited, by the Palestinian Authority, from building homes outside the camp's official boundaries.

—Sol Stern[92]

MYTH

Millions of Palestinians are confined by Israel to refugee camps.

FACT

By 2016, the number of Palestinian refugees on UNRWA rolls had risen to 5.2 million, several times the number that left Palestine in 1948. Nearly one-third of the registered Palestine refugees, more than 1.5 million individuals, live in fifty-eight recognized refugee camps in Jordan, Lebanon, Syria, the West Bank, and the Gaza Strip. The other two-thirds of the registered refugees live in and around the cities and towns of the host countries, and in the West Bank and the Gaza Strip, often in the environs of official camps.[93]

During the years that Israel controlled the Gaza Strip, a consistent effort was made to get the Palestinians into permanent housing. The Palestinians opposed the idea because the frustrated and bitter inhabitants of the camps provided the various terrorist factions with their manpower. Moreover, the Arab states routinely pushed for the adoption of UN resolutions demanding that Israel desist from the removal of Palestinian refugees from camps in Gaza and the West Bank.[94] They preferred to keep the Palestinians as symbols of Israeli "oppression."

Journalist Netty Gross visited Gaza and asked an official why the camps there hadn't been dismantled. She was told the Palestinian Authority had made a "political decision" not to do anything for the more than 650,000 Palestinians living in the camps until the final-status talks with Israel took place.[95]

The Palestinians have received billions of dollars in international aid since 1993, but have not moved the refugees into permanent housing. The refugees who remain in camps are there only because the host Arab governments, Hamas, and the Palestinian Authority keep them there.

MYTH

The Palestinians are the only refugee population barred from returning to their homes.

FACT

After World War II, 12.5 million Germans in Poland and Czechoslovakia were expelled and allowed to take only those possessions they could carry. They received no compensation for confiscated property. World War II's effects on Poland's boundaries and population were considered "accomplished facts" that could not be reversed after the war. No one in Germany petitions today for the right of these millions of deportees and their children to return to the countries they were expelled from despite the fact that they and their ancestors had lived in those places for hundreds of years.

> *If refugees return to Israel, Israel will cease to exist.*
>
> **—Gamal Nasser**[96]

Another country seriously affected by World War II was Finland, which was forced to give up almost one-eighth of its land and absorb more than four hundred thousand refugees (11 percent of the nation's population) from the Soviet Union. Unlike Israel, these were the *losers* of the war. There was no aid for their resettlement.

Perhaps an even better analogy can be seen in Turkey's integration of 150,000 Turkish refugees from Bulgaria in 1950. The difference between the Turks' handling of their refugees and the Arab states' treatment of the Palestinians was the attitude of the respective governments. As the *Des Moines Register* noted:

> Turkey has had a bigger refugee problem than either Syria or Lebanon and almost as big as Egypt has . . . But you seldom hear about them because the Turks have done such a good job of resettling them . . . The big difference is in spirit. The Turks, reluctant as they were to take on the burden, accepted it as a responsibility and set to work to clean it up as fast as possible.[97]

Had the Arab states wanted to alleviate the refugees' suffering, they could easily have adopted an attitude similar to Turkey's.

Another massive population transfer resulted from the partition of India and Pakistan in 1947. The eight *million* Hindus who fled Pakistan and the six *million* Muslims who left India were afraid of becoming a minority in their respective countries. Like the Palestinians, these people wanted to avoid being caught in the middle of the violence that engulfed their nations. In contrast to the Arab-Israeli conflict, however, the exchange of populations was considered the best solution to the problem of communal relations within the two states. Despite the enormous number of refugees and the relative poverty of the two nations involved, no special international relief organizations were established to aid them in resettlement.

> *If there were a Palestinian state, why would its leaders want their potential citizens to be repatriated to another state? From a nation-building perspective it makes no sense. In fact, the original discussions about repatriation took place at a time that there was no hope of a Palestinian state. With the possibility of that state emerging, the Palestinians must decide if they want to view themselves as a legitimate state or if it is more important for them to keep their self-defined status as oppressed, stateless refugees. They really can't be both.*
>
> **—Fredelle Spiegel**[98]

MYTH

All Palestinian refugees must be given the option to return to their homes.

FACT

According to the UN, more than five million Palestinians are refugees. Does Israel have any obligation to take in some or all of those people?

The current Israeli population is approximately 8.46 million, of which 6,119,000 are Jews. If every Palestinian refugee were allowed to move to Israel, the population would exceed thirteen million, and the Jewish proportion would shrink from 75 percent to 46 percent. The Jews would be a minority in their own country, the very situation they fought to avoid in 1948, and which the UN expressly ruled out in deciding to partition Palestine.

> *The demand that the refugees be returned to Israeli territory must be rejected, because if that were to happen, there would be two Palestinian states and no state at all for the Jewish people.*
>
> **—Amos Oz**[99]

It is often forgotten that most Palestinians now live in historic Palestine, which is an area including the Palestinian Authority and Jordan.

When Palestinians demand to return to Palestine they are referring not just to the area, but to the houses they lived in prior to 1948. These homes are either gone or inhabited now.

Even respected Palestinian leaders acknowledge that it is a mistake to insist that millions of refugees return to Israel. Palestinian intellectual Sari Nusseibeh, for example, said the refugees should be resettled in a future Palestinian state, "not in a way that would undermine the existence of the State of Israel as a predominantly Jewish state. Otherwise, what does a two-state solution mean?"[92] In leaked cables from the Palestinian negotiating team, PA president Mahmoud Abbas admitted this as well. "On numbers of refugees," he said, "it is illogical to ask Israel to take 5 million, or indeed 1 million—that would mean the end of Israel."[100]

In the context of a peace settlement, Israel has offered to accept some refugees, as Ben-Gurion said he would do more than fifty years ago. If and when a Palestinian state is created, the refugees should be allowed to move there; however, the Palestinian leadership has shown little interest in absorbing its own people and still believes it can weaken, if not destroy Israel, by overwhelming the country with refugees.

Notes, Chapter 11

1. Arieh Avneri, *The Claim of Dispossession* (New Brunswick, NJ: Transaction Books, 1984), 272; Benjamin Kedar, *The Changing Land Between the Jordan and the Sea* (Israel: Yad Izhak Ben-Zvi Press, 1999), 206; Paul Johnson, *A History of the Jews* (NY: Harper & Row, 1987), 529. Efraim Karsh analyzed rural and urban population statistics and concluded the total number of refugees was 583,000–609,000. Karsh, "How Many Palestinian Refugees Were There?" *Israel Affairs* (April 2011).

2. Progress Report of the United Nations Mediator on Palestine, Submitted to the Secretary-General for Transmission to the Members of the United Nations, General Assembly Official Records: Third Session, Supplement No. 11 (A/648), Paris, 1948, 47 and Supplement No. 11A (A/689 and A/689/Add.1, 5; and "Conclusions from Progress Report of the United Nations Mediator on Palestine" (September 16, 1948), UN doc. A/648 (part 1, 29; part 2, 23; part 3, 11), (September 18, 1948).

3. "Ad Hoc Committee on Palestine—30th Meeting," United Nations Press Release GA/PAL/84 (November 24, 1947).

4. Avneri, 276.

5. United Nations General Assembly Resolutions as recorded in the Jewish Virtual Library.

6. Efraim Karsh, "1948, Israel, and the Palestinians—The True Story," *Commentary online* (May 2008).

7. David Ben-Gurion, *Rebirth and Destiny of Israel* (NY: Philosophical Library, 1954), 220.

8. Atalia Ben Meir, "The Palestinian Refugee Issue and the Demographic Aspect," in *Israel and a Palestinian State: Zero Sum Game?* (ACPR Publishers: 2001), 215.

9. Joseph Schechtman, *The Refugee in the World* (NY: A. S. Barnes and Co., 1963), 184.

10. I. F. Stone, *This is Israel* (NY: Boni and Gaer, 1948), 27.

11. Barry Rubin, "How the Palestinians Trap Themselves and Drag the West Along," PJ Media (May 5, 2013).

12. Shmuel Katz, *Battleground: Fact & Fantasy in Palestine* (Montgomery, TX: Taylor Publications Ltd., 2002), 10.

13. Ibid.

14. Avneri, 270

15. *London Daily Mail* (August 12, 1948), cited in Shmuel Katz, *Battleground: Fact & Fantasy in Palestine* (Montgomery, TX: Taylor Publications Ltd., 2002), 13.

16. Randall Price, *Unholy War: America, Israel, and Radical Islam* (Eugene, OR: Harvest House, November 2001), 166.

17. Dana Adams Schmidt, "Jews Seize Haifa in Furious Battle; Arabs Agree to Go," *New York Times* (April 23, 1948).

18. Secret memo dated April 26, 1948, from the Superintendent of Police, regarding the general situation in Haifa, cited in Shmuel Katz, *Battleground: Fact & Fantasy in Palestine* (Montgomery, TX: Taylor Publications Ltd., 2002), 13.

19. Golda Meir, *My Life* (NY: Dell, 1975), 267-68.

20. Dana Adams Schmidt, "Jews Seize Haifa in Furious Battle; Arabs Agree to Go," *New York Times* (April 23, 1948).

21. Ibid.

22. *London Times* (April 24, 1948).

23. Schechtman, 190.

24. *Foreign Relations of the U.S., 1948*, Vol. V, (DC: GPO, 1976), 838.

25. Efraim Karsh, "1948, Israel, and the Palestinians—The True Story," *Commentary online* (May 2008).

26. Tom Segev, *1949: The First Israelis* (NY: The Free Press, 1986), 27-28.

27. Yigal Allon in *Sefer ha-Palmach*, quoted in Larry Collins and Dominique Lapierre, *O Jerusalem!* (NY: Simon and Schuster, 1972), 337; Yigal Allon, *My Father's House* (NY: W. W. Norton and Company, Inc., 1976), 192.

28. Benny Morris, *The Birth of the Palestinian Refugee Problem Revisited* (Cambridge, MA: Cambridge University Press, 2004), 592.

29. Ibid.

30. Cecil Hourani, *Middle East Journal*, 3, no. 4 (1949): 469-70.

31. Terence Prittie, "Middle East Refugees," cited in Michael Curtis, et al., *The Palestinians* (New Brunswick, NJ: Transaction Books, 1975), 52.

32. Gene Currivan, "Faluja Refugees Swell Arab Total," *New York Times* (March 4, 1949).

33. *The Economist*, (October 2, 1948).

34. "International: On the Eve?" *Time Magazine* (May 3, 1948).

35. *Middle East Studies* (January 1986); See also, Morris, *Birth*, 263, 590-92.

36. Morris, *The Birth of the Palestinian Refugee Problem Revisited*, (Cambridge, MA: Cambridge University Press, 2004), 590.

37. *Middle East Studies* (January 1986); See also, Morris, *Birth*, 263, 590-92.

38. Myron Kaufman, *The Coming Destruction of Israel* (NY: The American Library Inc., 1970), 26-27.

39. Edward Atiyah, *The Arabs* (London: Penguin, 1955), 183.

40. El-Asmar, *supra* note 13, page 7, via *Palestine and Israel: A Challenge to Justice* by John B. Quigley (Durham and London: Duke University Press, 1990).

41. *The Memories of Haled al Azm* (Beirut, 1973), Part 1, 386-87.

42. Jordanian Newspaper *Filastin* (February 19, 1949), quoted in Samuel Katz, *Battleground* (NY: Bantam Books, 1985), 16-17.

43. *Ad Difaa*, Jordan (September 6, 1954).

44. Habib Issa in the New York Lebanese newspaper *Al-Hoda* (June 8, 1951), quoted in Samuel Katz, *Battleground* (NY: Bantam Books, 1985), 17.

45. Itamar Marcus, "Abbas' UN Speech Contradicts His 'Refugee' History," Palestinian Media Watch (October 10, 2013).

46. Morris, *The Birth of the Palestinian Refugee Problem Revisited* (Cambridge, MA: Cambridge University Press, 2004), 591.

47. Yehoshafat Harkabi, *Arab Attitudes to Israel* (Jerusalem: Israel Universities Press, 1972), 364.

48. King Abdallah, *My Memoirs Completed* (London: Longman Group, Ltd., 1978), xvi.

49. *Al-Ayyam* (May 13, 2008), quoted in Itamar Marcus and Barbara Cook, "The Evolving Palestinian Narrative: Arabs Caused the Refugee Problem," *Palestinian Media Watch* (May 20, 2008).

50. Palestinian Authority TV (July 7, 2009), quoted in *Palestinian Media Watch Bulletin* (July 23, 2009).

51. *Al-Hayat al-Jadida* (December 13, 2006), quoted in Itamar Marcus and Barbara Cook, "The Evolving Palestinian Narrative: Arabs Caused the Refugee Problem," *Palestinian Media Watch* (May 20, 2008).

52. *Al-Ayyam* (May 13, 2008), quoted in Itamar Marcus and Barbara Cook, "The Evolving Palestinian Narrative: Arabs Caused the Refugee Problem," *Palestinian Media Watch* (May 20, 2008).

53. *Falastin a-Thaura* (March 1976).

54. Walid Khalidi, *Palestine Reborn* (I. B. Tauris: 1992), 289.

55. Dan Kurzman, *Genesis 1948* (OH: New American Library Inc., 1970), 141.

56. Menachem Begin, *The Revolt* (NY: Nash Publishing, 1977), xx-xxi, 162-63.

57. See, for example, Amos Perlmutter, *The Life and Times of Menachem Begin* (NY: Doubleday, 1987), 214; J. Bowyer Bell, *Terror Out of Zion* (NY: St. Martin's Press, 1977), 292-96; Kurzman, 142.

58. Uri Milstein, *History of Israel's War of Independence, Vol IV,* (Lanham: University Press of America, 1999), 262.

59. Ibid.

60. Dana Adams Schmidt, "200 Arabs Killed, Stronghold Taken," *New York Times* (April 10, 1948).

61. Kurzman, 148.

62. Sharif Kanaana and Nihad Zitawi, "Deir Yassin," Monograph No. 4, Destroyed Palestinian Villages Documentation Project, (Bir Zeit: Documentation Center of Bir Zeit University, 1987), 55.

63. Sharif Kanaana, "Reinterpreting Deir Yassin," *Bir Zeit University* (April 1998).

64. Milstein, 267.

65. Rami Nashashibi, "Dayr Yasin," *Bir Zeit University* (June 1996).

66. Efraim Karsh, "1948, Israel, and the Palestinians—The True Story," *Commentary online* (May 2008).

67. Sharif Kanaana and Nihad Zitawi, "Deir Yassin," Monograph No. 4, Destroyed Palestinian Villages Documentation Project, (Bir Zeit: Documentation Center of Bir Zeit University, 1987), 55.

68. Milstein, 276.

69. "Israel and the Arabs: The 50 Year Conflict," BBC Television Series (1998).

70. "Interview with Abd al-Rahman Azzam Pasha," *Akhbar al-Yom* (Egypt), (October 11, 1947), translated by R. Green.

71. Howard Sachar, *A History of Israel: From the Rise of Zionism to Our Time* (NY: Alfred A. Knopf, 1979), 335.

72. Schechtman, 268.

73. Prittie in Curtis, 66-67.

74. Gene Currivans, "Weizmann Urges Homes for Arabs," *New York Times* (July 17, 1949).

75. *Jerusalem Post* (January 26, 1989).

76. *Telegraph* (Beirut), (August 6, 1948), quoted in Schechtman, 210-11.

77. Moshe Sharett, "Israel's Position and Problems," *Middle Eastern Affairs* (May 1952), 136.
78. *Al-Said* (Lebanon), (April 6, 1950), cited by Prittie in Curtis, 69.
79. *Al-Misri* (October 11, 1949), cited in Nathan Feinberg, *The Arab-Israeli Conflict in International Law* (Jerusalem: Magnes Press, 1970), 109.
80. *Beirut al-Massa* (July 15, 1957), cited in Katz, 21.
81. Benjamin Franklin, *Memoirs of Benjamin Franklin, Vol 1,* (M'Carty & Davis: 1834), 463.
82. Melissa Radler, "UN Marks Partition Plan Anniversary with anti-Israel Fest," *Jerusalem Post* (December 4, 2003).
83. UNRWA.
84. Schechtman, 220.
85. "Speech to Parliament—April 24, 1950," Abdallah, 16-17; Aaron Miller, *The Arab States and the Palestine Question* (Washington, DC: Center for Strategic and International Studies, 1986), 29.
86. Khaled Abu Toameh, "Amman Revoking Palestinians Citizenship," *Jerusalem Post,* (July 20, 2009).
87. Isi Leibler, *The Case for Israel* (Australia: The Globe Press, 1972), 48.
88. *Jerusalem Report* (June 27, 1991).
89. Alexander H. Joffe and Asaf Romirowsky, "A Tale of Two Galloways: Notes on the Early History of UNRWA and Zionist Historiography," *Middle Eastern Studies* (September 2010).
90. *UNRWA* Report of the Commissioner-General of the United Nations Relief and Works Agency for Palestine Refugees in the Near East (January 1-31, 2007).
91. Ibid.
92. Sol Stern, "Mr. Abbas, Tear Down This Wall!" *Jewish Ideas Daily* (September 28, 2010).
93. UNRWA.
94. Arlene Kushner, "The UN's Palestinian Refugee Problem," *Azure* (Autumn 2005).
95. *Jerusalem Report* (July 6, 1998).
96. Katz, 21.
97. Editorial, *Des Moines Register* (January 16, 1952).
98. *Jerusalem Report* (March 26, 2001).
99. Amos Oz, "Israel Partly at Fault," *Ynet News* (March 29, 2007).
100. "Meeting Minutes: President Abbas Meeting with the Negotiations Support Unit" (March 24, 2009).

12. Human Rights

Arabs cannot be anti-Semitic because they are Semites.
Jews who lived in Islamic countries were well treated.
As "People of the Book," Jews and Christians are protected under Islamic law.
Modern Arab nations have never been anti-Jewish.
Israel discriminates against its Arab citizens.
Israeli Arabs are barred from buying land in Israel.
Arabs held in Israeli jails are tortured, beaten, and killed.
Israel treats Palestinians the way the Afrikaner government treated blacks in South Africa.
Israel's policy toward Palestinians is comparable to the Nazis' treatment of the Jews.
Israel uses checkpoints to deny Palestinians their rights and to humiliate them.
Israeli checkpoints prevent Palestinians from receiving medical attention.
Israeli textbooks are just as hateful as those in the Palestinian Authority.
Israel is a theocracy and should not be a Jewish State.
Israel persecutes Christians.
Hamas respects the rights of Palestinian Christians.
Israel denies Palestinians basic rights and freedoms.
The Goldstone Report proved Israel was guilty of war crimes in Gaza.
Israel's blockade of Gaza is collective punishment.
Human rights activists care deeply about the Palestinian people.

MYTH

Arabs cannot be anti-Semitic because they are Semites.

FACT

The term "anti-Semite" was coined in Germany in 1879 by Wilhelm Marr to refer to the anti-Jewish manifestations of the period and to give the previously used term, "Judenhass"—or "Jew-hatred"—a more scientific sounding name.[1] "Anti-Semitism" has been accepted and understood to mean hatred of the Jewish people. Dictionaries define the term as: "Theory, action, or practice directed against the Jews" and "Hostility towards Jews as a religious or racial minority group, often accompanied by social, economic and political discrimination."[2]

The claim that Arabs cannot be anti-Semitic because they are also a Semitic people is a semantic distortion that ignores the history of Arab discrimination and hostility toward Jews. Arabs, like any other people, can indeed be anti-Semitic.

The Arab world is the last bastion of unbridled, unashamed, unhidden and unbelievable anti-Semitism. Hitlerian myths get published in the popular press as incontrovertible truths. The Holocaust either gets minimized or denied... How the Arab world will ever come to terms with Israel when Israelis are portrayed as the devil incarnate is hard to figure out.

—Columnist Richard Cohen[3]

MYTH

Jews who lived in Islamic countries were well treated.

FACT

While Jewish communities in Islamic countries fared better overall than those in Christian lands in Europe during the nearly thirteen hundred years of the Muslim Empire, Jews were no strangers to persecution and humiliation among the Arabs. As Princeton University historian Bernard Lewis has written: "The Golden Age of equal rights was a myth, and belief in it was a result, more than a cause, of Jewish sympathy for Islam."[4]

Muhammad, the founder of Islam, traveled to Medina in AD 622 to attract followers to his new faith. When the Jews of Medina refused to recognize Muhammad as their prophet, two of the major Jewish tribes were expelled. In 627, Muhammad's followers killed between six hundred and nine hundred of the men and divided the surviving Jewish women and children among themselves.[5]

The Muslim attitude toward Jews is reflected in various verses throughout the Koran, the holy book of the Islamic faith. "They [the Children of Israel] were consigned to humiliation and wretchedness. They brought the wrath of God upon themselves, and this because they used to deny God's signs and kill His Prophets unjustly and because they disobeyed and were transgressors" (Sura 2:61). According to the Koran, the Jews try to introduce corruption (5:64), have always been disobedient (5:78), and are enemies of Allah, the Prophet, and the angels (2:97–98).

Jews were generally viewed with contempt by their Muslim neighbors; peaceful coexistence between the two groups involved the subordination and degradation of the Jews. In the ninth century, Baghdad's Caliph al-Mutawakkil designated a yellow badge for Jews, setting a precedent that would be followed centuries later in Nazi Germany.[6]

When Jews were perceived as having achieved too comfortable a position in Islamic society, anti-Semitism would surface, often with devastating results. On December 30, 1066, Joseph HaNagid, the Jewish vizier of Granada, Spain, was crucified by an Arab mob that proceeded to raze the Jewish quarter of the city and slaughter its five thousand inhabitants. The riot was incited by Muslim preachers who had angrily objected to what they saw as inordinate Jewish political power.

Similarly, in 1465, Arab mobs in Fez slaughtered thousands of Jews, leaving only eleven alive, after a Jewish deputy vizier treated a Muslim woman in "an offensive manner." The killings touched off a wave of similar massacres throughout Morocco.[7]

Other mass murders of Jews in Arab lands occurred in Morocco in the eighth century, where whole communities were wiped out by the Muslim ruler Idris I; North Africa in the twelfth century, where the Almohads either forcibly converted or decimated several communities; Libya in 1785, where Ali Burzi Pasha murdered hundreds of Jews; Algiers, where Jews were massacred in 1805, 1815, and 1830; and Marrakesh, Morocco, where more than three hundred Jews were murdered between 1864 and 1880.[8] When Jewish people were not being slaughtered in Morocco, they were subject to heavy taxes and lived in destitute poverty.

Decrees ordering the destruction of synagogues were enacted in Egypt and Syria (1014, 1293-94, 1301-02), Iraq (854-859, 1344) and Yemen (1676). Despite the Koran's prohibition, Jews were forced to convert to Islam or face death in Yemen (1165 and 1678), Morocco (1275, 1465, and 1790-92), and Baghdad (1333 and 1344).[9]

The situation of Jews in Arab lands reached a low point in the nineteenth century. Jews in most of North Africa (including Algeria, Tunisia, Egypt, Libya, and Morocco) were forced to live in ghettos. In Morocco, which contained the largest Jewish community in the Muslim Diaspora, Jews were made to walk barefoot or wear shoes of straw when outside the ghetto. Even Muslim children participated in the degradation of Jews by throwing stones at them or harassing them in other ways. The frequency of anti-Jewish violence increased, and many Jews were executed on charges of apostasy. Ritual murder accusations against the Jews became commonplace in the Ottoman Empire.[10]

As distinguished Orientalist G. E. von Grunebaum observed:

> It would not be difficult to put together the names of a very sizeable number of Jewish subjects or citizens of the Islamic area who have attained to high rank, to power, to great financial influence, to significant and recognized intellectual attainment; and the same could be done for Christians. But it would again not be difficult to compile a lengthy list of persecutions, arbitrary confiscations, attempted forced conversions, or pogroms.[11]

MYTH

*As "People of the Book," Jews and Christians
are protected under Islamic law.*

FACT

This argument is rooted in the traditional concept of the "dhimma"
("writ of protection"), which was extended by Muslim conquerors to
Christians and Jews in exchange for their subordination to the Muslims. Yet, as French authority Jacques Ellul has observed, "One must
ask: 'protected against whom?' When this 'stranger' lives in Islamic
countries, the answer can only be: against the Muslims themselves."[12]

Peoples subjected to Muslim rule often faced a choice between
death and conversion, but Jews and Christians, who adhered to the
Scriptures, were usually allowed, as *dhimmis* (protected persons), to
practice their faith. This "protection" did little, however, to ensure
that Jews and Christians were treated well by the Muslims. On the
contrary, an integral aspect of the *dhimma* was that, being an infidel,
he had to acknowledge openly the superiority of the true believer—
the Muslim.

In the early years of the Islamic conquest, the "tribute" (or *jizya*),
paid as a yearly poll tax, symbolized the subordination of the *dhimmi*.[13]
Later, the inferior status of Jews and Christians was reinforced through
a series of regulations that governed the behavior of the *dhimmi*. For
example, *dhimmis,* on pain of death, were forbidden to mock or criticize the Koran, Islam, or Muhammad, to proselytize among Muslims,
or to touch a Muslim woman (though a Muslim man could take a non-
Muslim as a wife). *Dhimmis* were excluded from public office and
armed service, and were forbidden to bear arms. They were not allowed to ride horses or camels, to build synagogues or churches taller
than mosques, to construct houses higher than those of Muslims, or
to drink wine in public. They were forced to wear distinctive clothing
and were not allowed to pray or mourn in loud voices—as that might
offend the Muslims.

The *dhimmi* also had to show public deference toward Muslims;
for example, always yielding them the center of the road. The *dhimmi*
was not allowed to give evidence in court against a Muslim, and his
oath was unacceptable in an Islamic court. To defend himself, the
dhimmi would have to purchase Muslim witnesses at great expense.
This left the *dhimmi* with little legal recourse when harmed by a Muslim.[14]

By the twentieth century, the status of the *dhimmi* in Muslim lands
had not significantly improved. H. E. W. Young, British vice consul in
Mosul, wrote in 1909:

The attitude of the Muslims toward the Christians and the Jews is that of a master towards slaves, whom he treats with a certain lordly tolerance so long as they keep their place. Any sign of pretension to equality is promptly repressed.[15]

MYTH

Modern Arab nations have never been anti-Jewish.

FACT

Arab leaders have repeatedly made clear their animosity toward Jews and Judaism. For example, on November 23, 1937, Saudi Arabia's King Ibn Saud told British Colonel H. R. P. Dickson, "Our hatred for the Jews dates from God's condemnation of them for their persecution and rejection of Isa (Jesus) and their subsequent rejection of His chosen Prophet." He added "that for a Muslim to kill a Jew, or for him to be killed by a Jew ensures him an immediate entry into Heaven and into the august presence of God Almighty."[16]

When Hitler introduced the Nuremberg racial laws in 1935, he received telegrams of congratulation from all corners of the Arab world.[17] Later, during the war, one of his most ardent supporters was the Mufti of Jerusalem.

Jews were never permitted to live in Jordan. Civil Law No. 6, which governed the Jordanian-occupied West Bank, states explicitly, "Any man will be a Jordanian subject if he is not Jewish."[18]

Public school textbooks used to educate children in the West Bank have been found replete with racist and hateful portrayals of Jews.[19]

According to a study of Syrian textbooks, "the Syrian educational system expands hatred of Israel and Zionism to anti-Semitism directed at all Jews. That anti-Semitism evokes ancient Islamic motifs to describe the unchangeable and treacherous nature of the Jews. Its inevitable conclusion is that all Jews must be annihilated."[20]

An Arabic translation of Adolf Hitler's *Mein Kampf* was distributed in East Jerusalem and the territories controlled by the Palestinian Authority (PA) and became a bestseller. The official website of the Palestinian State Information Service also published an Arabic translation of the "Protocols of the Elders of Zion."[21]

Arab officials have also resorted to blood libels. King Faisal of Saudi Arabia, for example, said that Jews "have a certain day on which they mix the blood of non-Jews into their bread and eat it. It happened that two years ago, while I was in Paris on a visit, that the police discovered five murdered children. Their blood had been drained, and it turned out that some Jews had murdered them in order to take their blood and mix it with the bread that they eat on this day."[22]

Syrian President Bashar Assad on Saturday [May 5] offered a vivid, if vile, demonstration of why he and his government are unworthy of respect or good relations with the United States or any other democratic country. Greeting Pope John Paul II in Damascus, Mr. Assad launched an attack on Jews that may rank as the most ignorant and crude speech delivered before the pope in his two decades of travel around the world. Comparing the suffering of the Palestinians to that of Jesus Christ, Mr. Assad said that the Jews "tried to kill the principles of all religions with the same mentality in which they betrayed Jesus Christ and the same way they tried to betray and kill the Prophet Muhammad." With that libel, the Syrian president stained both his country and the pope.

—Washington Post **editorial**[23]

In June 2016, Abbas declared from the rostrum of the European Parliament that Israeli rabbis called on their government to poison the water used by Palestinians.[24] Other scurrilous allegations made by Palestinian officials include claims that Israel dumped toxic waste in the West Bank, marketed carcinogenic juice to Palestinians, released wild pigs to destroy crops in the West Bank, and infected Palestinians with the AIDS virus. Palestinian officials also have claimed that Israel dropped poison candy for children in Gaza from airplanes, conducted medical experiments on prisoners and poisoned them, used a "radial spy machine" at checkpoints that killed a Palestinian woman, and spread drugs among young Palestinians to distract them from fighting Israel.[25]

The Arab/Muslim press, which is almost exclusively controlled by the governments in each Middle Eastern nation, regularly publish anti-Semitic articles and cartoons. Today, it remains common to find anti-Semitic publications in Egypt. For example, *Al-Ahram*—the most widely circulated Egyptian newspaper—published an article in 2000 accusing Israel of using the blood of Palestinian children to bake matzos.[26]

Anti-Semitic articles also regularly appear in the press in Jordan and Syria. Many of the attacks deal with denial of the Holocaust, the "exploitation" of the Holocaust by Zionism, and the odious comparison of Zionism to Nazism.

As violence in Israel escalated during the "stabbing intifada" in late 2015, content urging Palestinian violence against Israelis began appearing on social media with increasing frequency. The Anti-Defamation League published a selection of this content in October 2015, including diagrams of the body's circulatory system with instructions on where to stab to cause the most damage, and videos in Arabic showing various stabbing techniques, titled "learn how to stab a Jew."[27]

The Palestinian Authority's media have also contained inflammatory and anti-Semitic material. Here is an example of a sermon broadcast on Palestinian Authority television in 2010:

> The loathsome occupation in Palestine—its land and its holy places—by these new Mongols and what they are perpetrating upon this holy, blessed and pure land—killing, assassination, destruction, confiscation, Judaization, harassment and splitting the homeland—are clear proof of . . . incomparable racism, and of Nazism of the 20th century. The Jews, the enemies of Allah and of His Messenger! Enemies of humanity in general, and of Palestinians in particular.[28]

Even Palestinian crossword puzzles are used to delegitimize Israel and attack Jews, providing clues, for example, suggesting that a Jewish trait is "treachery."[29]

MYTH

Israel discriminates against its Arab citizens.

FACT

Israel does not discriminate against its Arab citizens. To the contrary, they enjoy the same rights guaranteed to Jews and all other citizens of Israel.

Arabs in Israel have equal voting rights; in fact, it is one of the few places in the Middle East where Arab women may vote. In 2015, a coalition of Arab parties, called The Joint List, won thirteen seats in the 120-seat Knesset, making it the third biggest party. In addition to members of The Joint List, there are five other Israeli-Arab members of the Knesset (two Muslims and three Druze) who belong to other factions. Two Arab women are also Members of Knesset, Hanin Zoabi of Balad and Aida Touma Suleiman of Hadash.

Israeli Arabs have also held government posts such as ambassador to Finland and the deputy mayor of Tel Aviv. Oscar Abu Razaq was appointed director general of the Ministry of Interior, the first Arab citizen to become chief executive of a key government ministry. Ariel Sharon's original cabinet included the first Arab minister, Salah Tarif, a Druze who served as a minister without portfolio. An Arab is also a Supreme Court justice. Arabic, like Hebrew, is an official language in Israel. More than three hundred thousand Arab children attend Israeli schools. At the time of Israel's founding, there was one Arab high school in the country. Today, there are hundreds of Arab schools.[30] In October 2005, an Arab professor was named vice president of Haifa University, and in 2015, 14.4 percent of bachelor's degree students in Israel were Arabs.[31]

The sole legal distinction between Jewish and Arab citizens of Israel is that the latter are not required to serve in the Israeli army. This is to spare Arab citizens the need to take up arms against their brethren. Nevertheless, Bedouins have served in paratroop units and other Arabs have volunteered for military duty. Compulsory military service is applied to the Druze and Circassian communities at their own request.

Although there have been some Israeli Arabs involved in terrorist attacks, they are by far the exception to the rule. During the 1967, 1973, and 1982 wars, none engaged in any acts of violence against Israelis. Sometimes, Arabs volunteered to take over civilian functions for reservists. During the Palestinian War that began in September 2000, Israeli Arabs engaged in widespread, but short-lived protests for the first time.

Some economic and social gaps between Israeli Jews and Arabs result from the latter not serving in the military. Veterans qualify for many benefits that are not available to nonveterans. Moreover, the army aids in the socialization process. On the other hand, Arabs do have an advantage in obtaining some jobs during the years Israelis are in the military. In addition, industries like construction and trucking have come to be dominated by Israeli Arabs.

Recognizing that Arab communities were not receiving adequate funding, the Israeli government approved in December 2015 a historic five-year economic package of roughly $6.6 billion to close the gaps and promote equality. In addition, twenty different budget areas, including infrastructure, employment, transportation, and education will be allocated based on the Arab proportion of the population (approximately 20 percent). Joint Arab List Party leader Ayman Odeh said the plan "could be a first step to reduce economic and social disparities of the country's Arab population."[32]

Investing in the Arab sector is expected to boost Israel's economy, give Israeli Arabs a greater sense of equality, reinforce Israel's commitment to democracy and pluralism, and show Arabs in the region that making peace with Israel can be beneficial.[33]

The United States has been independent for 240 years and still has not integrated all of its diverse communities. Even today, nearly half a century after civil rights legislation was adopted, discrimination has not been eradicated. It should not be surprising that Israel has not solved all of its social problems in only sixty-eight years.

MYTH

Israeli Arabs are barred from buying land in Israel.

FACT

In the early part of the century, the Jewish National Fund was established by the World Zionist Congress to purchase land in Palestine for

Jewish settlement. This land, and that acquired after Israel's War of Independence, was taken over by the government. Of the total area of Israel, 92 percent belongs to the State and is managed by the Land Management Authority. It is not for sale to anyone, Jew or Arab. The remaining 8 percent of the territory is privately owned. The Arab Waqf (the Muslim charitable endowment), for example, owns land that is for the express use and benefit of Muslim Arabs. All Arab citizens of Israel are eligible to lease government land, regardless of race, religion, or sex.

In 2002, the Israeli Supreme Court also ruled that the government cannot allocate land based on religion or ethnicity, and may not prevent Arab citizens from living wherever they choose.[34]

Meanwhile, in 1996, the Palestinian Authority (PA) Mufti, Ikrima Sabri, issued a *fatwa* (religious decree), banning the sale of Arab and Muslim property to Jews. Anyone who violated the order was to be killed. At least seven land dealers were killed that year.[35]

On May 5, 1997, Palestinian Authority justice minister Freih Abu Middein announced that the death penalty would be imposed on anyone convicted of ceding "one inch" to Israel. Later that month, two Arab land dealers were killed. A year later, another Palestinian suspected of selling land to Jews was murdered. The PA has also arrested suspected land dealers for violating the Jordanian law (in force in the West Bank), which prohibits the sale of land to foreigners.[36] In 2015, Abbas amended the law to impose "life imprisonment with forced labor for the duplicitous transfer, leasing or selling of lands to a hostile country or its citizens" while the Palestinians Supreme Fatwa Council declared that selling land to Israelis also violates Islamic law.[37]

In January 2016, an Israeli news program aired secretly recorded footage showing a prominent Israeli activist, Ezra Nawi, saying that he had turned in Palestinians who wanted to sell West Bank land to Jews to the Palestinian security services, who then killed them.[38]

MYTH

Arabs held in Israeli jails are tortured, beaten, and killed.

FACT

Prison is not a pleasant place for anyone, and complaints about the treatment of prisoners in American institutions abound. Israel's prisons are probably among the most closely scrutinized in the world. One reason is that the government has allowed representatives of the Red Cross and other groups to inspect them regularly.

Israeli law prohibits the arbitrary arrest of citizens. In addition, defendants are considered innocent until proven guilty and have the right to writs of *habeas corpus* and other procedural safeguards. Israel holds no political prisoners and maintains an independent judiciary.

Years ago, some prisoners, particularly Arabs suspected of involvement in terrorism, were interrogated using severe methods that were criticized as excessive. Israel's Supreme Court issued a landmark ruling in 1999 prohibiting the use of a variety of practices that were considered abusive.[39]

The death penalty has been applied just once,[40] in the case of Adolf Eichmann, the man largely responsible for the "Final Solution." No Arab has ever been given the death penalty, even after the most heinous acts of terrorism.

Meanwhile, torture is routinely practiced in the Palestinian Authority and Gaza. A Palestinian human rights organization, the Independent Commission for Human Rights, reported a dramatic rise in the number of complaints about torture in Palestinian prisons run by the Palestinian Authority and Hamas in 2014 and 2015. Prisoners are subject to whippings, verbal abuse, sleep deprivation, and other physical assaults.[41] Many Palestinians are also put to death, often summarily without trial, for angering the leaders of one faction or another, being suspected of collaboration with Israel, or as an excuse to settle scores.

> *The charge that Israel is [like old South Africa] is a false and malicious one that precludes, rather than promotes, peace and harmony.*
>
> **—Richard Goldstone, former justice of the**
> **South African Constitutional Court[42]**

MYTH

Israel treats Palestinians the way the Afrikaner government treated blacks in South Africa.

FACT

Even before the State of Israel was established, Jewish leaders consciously sought to avoid the situation that prevailed in South Africa. As David Ben-Gurion told Palestinian nationalist Musa Alami in 1934:

> We do not want to create a situation like that which exists in South Africa, where the whites are the owners and rulers, and the blacks are the workers. If we do not do all kinds of work, easy and hard, skilled and unskilled, if we become merely landlords, then this will not be our homeland.[43]

Today, within Israel, Jews are a majority, but the Arab minority are full citizens who enjoy equal rights and are represented in all the branches of government. Arabs are represented in the Knesset, and have served in the Cabinet, high-level foreign ministry posts (e.g., ambassador to Finland), and on the Supreme Court.

Unlike Israel, under the discriminatory policies of old South Africa, skin color determined every aspect of your life from birth until death. Black South Africans could not vote and were not citizens of the country in which they formed the overwhelming majority of the population. Laws dictated where they could live, work, attend school, and travel. And, in South Africa, the government killed blacks who protested against its policies. By contrast, Israel allows freedom of movement, assembly, and speech. Some of the government's harshest critics are Israeli Arabs who are members of the Knesset.

"To be sure, there is more de facto separation between Jewish and Arab populations than Israelis should accept," observed Richard Goldstone, former justice of the South African Constitutional Court. "Much of it is chosen by the communities themselves. Some results from discrimination." But, he added this is nothing like the situation in South Africa where separation was considered an ideal. "In Israel," Goldstone added, "equal rights are the law, the aspiration and the ideal; inequities are often successfully challenged in court."[44]

The difference between the current Israeli situation and ... [Afrikaner ruled] South Africa is emphasized at a very human level: Jewish and Arab babies are born in the same delivery room, with the same facilities, attended by the same doctors and nurses, with the mothers recovering in adjoining beds in a ward. Two years ago I had major surgery in a Jerusalem hospital: the surgeon was Jewish, the anesthetist was Arab, the doctors and nurses who looked after me were Jews and Arabs. Jews and Arabs share meals in restaurants and travel on the same trains, buses and taxis, and visit each other's homes.

Could any of this possibly have happened under apartheid? Of course not.

—Benjamin Pogrund[45]

The situation of Palestinians in the territories is different. The security requirements of the nation, and a violent insurrection in the territories, forced Israel to impose restrictions on Arab residents of the West Bank and Gaza Strip that are not necessary inside Israel's pre-1967 borders. Israeli policy is not based on race, but is a result of Palestinian animosity. Palestinians in the territories dispute Israel's right to exist, whereas blacks did not seek the destruction of South Africa, only that of the discriminatory regime.

Despite security concerns and the hostile attitude of many Palestinians, by the summer of 2016, more than one hundred thousand Palestinians from the territories went to work in Israel every day (fifty-eight thousand legally with Israeli work permits). Another twenty-five thousand work in those "obstacles to peace"—Jewish settlements.[46] People who are allegedly so persecuted they live in a constant state of fear, anger, and humiliation work side by side with Israelis, earning more money and enjoying superior benefits to what they would receive from Palestinian employers. According to the Palestinian Authority's official newspaper, *Al-Hayat al-Jadida* (September 21, 2014):[47]

- "The only cases in which a Palestinian worker does not receive the salary his Israeli [employer] determined for him are those cases in which the middleman is Palestinian."

- "Whenever Palestinian workers have the opportunity to work for Israeli employers, they are quick to quit their jobs with their Palestinian employers for reasons having to do with salaries and other rights."

- "The salaries of workers employed by Palestinians amount to less than half the salaries of those who work for Israeli employers in the areas of the Israel-occupied West Bank."

- "The [Israeli] work conditions are very good, and include transportation, medical insurance and pensions. These things do not exist with Palestinian employers."

Many people discovered some of these facts when actress Scarlett Johansson was attacked for being the spokesperson for SodaStream because the company's factory was in Maale Adumim. This city of roughly forty thousand people, ten minutes from downtown Jerusalem, is considered a "settlement." Ironically, Palestinian peace negotiators agreed the city would remain part of Israel if a Palestinian state is established. More to the point, the company employed hundreds of Palestinians, several of whom spoke out against the call to boycott the company: "Before boycotting, they should think of the workers who are going to suffer," a young SodaStream worker said. He now earns nearly ten times what he earned before joining SodaStream, which also provides transportation, breakfast, and lunch for its employees.[48] Though the owners of SodaStream denied the boycott had any effect, they decided to move the plant to Lehavim, near Beersheba, and, sadly, five hundred Palestinian Arabs lost their jobs.

Israel could offer Palestinians in the territories full citizenship, but this would require the annexation of the West Bank and Gaza and the end of the two-state solution. Palestinians vigorously oppose this idea and demand full independence.

Paradoxically, despite their criticism, when asked what governments they admire most, more than 80 percent of Palestinians said

Israel because they can observe its thriving democracy, and the rights the Arab citizens enjoy there. By contrast, Palestinians place Arab regimes, including their own Palestinian Authority, at the bottom of the list.[49]

One other glaring example of Palestinian hypocrisy in condemning Israel's treatment of Arabs is the fact that Mahmoud Abbas and other officials send their family members to Israel when they have serious health problems. Abbas's brother-in-law, for example, underwent life-saving heart surgery in the Assuta Medical Center in Tel Aviv. A year earlier, Abbas's wife was also hospitalized in Assuta. Hamas leaders calling for Israel's destruction also send their loved ones to be saved by Israeli doctors. For example, the daughter, granddaughter, and mother-in-law of Hamas leader Ismail Haniyeh received medical treatment in Israel, as did the sister of Moussa Abu Marzouk.[50]

The glaring differences in the way Israel treats its citizens and the way that the Palestinian Authority, Hamas, and Arab governments treat theirs has led growing numbers of Palestinians in East Jerusalem to apply for Israeli citizenship. When given the choice, many say they would rather live in Israel than Palestine. For example, 54 percent of Arabs living in East Jerusalem said that if their neighborhood were part of Israel, they would not move to Palestine.[51]

There is still one other question arising out of the disaster of nations which remains unsolved to this day, and whose profound tragedy, only a Jew can comprehend. This is the African question. Just call to mind all those terrible episodes of the slave trade, of human beings who, merely because they were black, were stolen like cattle, taken prisoner, captured and sold. Their children grew up in strange lands, the objects of contempt and hostility because their complexions were different. I am not ashamed to say, though I may expose myself to ridicule for saying so, that once I have witnessed the redemption of the Jews, my people, I wish also to assist in the redemption of the Africans.

—Theodor Herzl[52]

MYTH

Israel's policy toward Palestinians is comparable to the Nazis' treatment of the Jews.

FACT

This is perhaps the most odious claim made by Israel's detractors. The Nazis' objective was the systematic extermination of every Jew in Europe. Israel is seeking peace with its Palestinian neighbors. More than one million Arabs live as free and equal citizens in Israel. Of the Palestinians in the territories, 98 percent live under the civil administration of the Palestinian Authority. Israeli policies are designed to protect Israeli citizens—Jews and non-Jews—from the incessant campaign of terror. There has never been a plan to persecute, exterminate, or expel the Palestinian people.

In response to one such comparison, by a poet who referred to the "Zionist SS," the *New Republic*'s literary editor Leon Wieseltier observed:

> The view that Zionism is Nazism—there is no other way to understand the phrase "Zionist SS"—is not different in kind from the view that the moon is cheese. It is not only spectacularly wrong, it is also spectacularly unintelligent. I will not offend myself (that would be self-hate speech!) by patiently explaining why the State of Israel is unlike the Third Reich, except to say that nothing that has befallen the Palestinians under Israel's control may responsibly be compared to what befell the Jews under Germany's control, and that a considerable number of the people who have toiled diligently to find peace and justice for the Palestinians, and a solution to this savage conflict, have been Israeli, some of them even Israeli prime ministers. There is no support for the Palestinian cause this side of decency that can justify the locution "Zionist SS."[53]

Historian Hillel Cohen observed that "there is no non-anti-Semitic way to think or say Israel is carrying out genocide against the Palestinians."[54] The absurdity of the charge is clear from the demography of the disputed territories. While detractors make outrageous claims about Israel engaging in ethnic cleansing, the Palestinian population has continued to grow exponentially. In the ten years prior to 2008, Palestinian population growth in the territories was 30 percent, one of the highest rates in the world and, from 1990 to 2008, the population doubled.

According to the CIA Factbook, the population in Gaza by July 2015 was approximately two million. Twenty years earlier the figure was around 730,000. Similarly, the July 2015 population in the West Bank was nearly 2.8 million, double the figure in 1994.[55] "These numbers demonstrate," Cohen says, "that Israel, a militarily potent and effective country, could not possibly be trying to *exterminate* the Palestinians. Only deeply prejudiced people, either cynically lying or out of touch with Middle Eastern reality, could say that Israel is conducting a war of extermination against Palestinians" (emphasis in the original).[56]

I am a proud Israeli—along with many other non-Jewish Israelis such as Druze, Baha'i, Bedouin, Christians and Muslims, who live in one of the most culturally diversified societies and the only true democracy in the Middle East. Like America, Israeli society is far from perfect, but... By any yardstick you choose—educational opportunity, economic development, women and gay's rights, freedom of speech and assembly, legislative representation—Israel's minorities fare far better than any other country in the Middle East.

—Ishmael Khaldi, a Bedouin in Israel's Diplomatic corps.[57]

MYTH

Israel uses checkpoints to deny Palestinians their rights and to humiliate them.

FACT

It is not unusual for nations to guard their borders and to establish checkpoints to prevent people from illegally entering their countries. The United States has checkpoints at its borders and airports, and as Americans saw on September 11, these are necessary but not foolproof security precautions.

In the case of Israel, the necessity for checkpoints has been created by the Palestinians. By pursuing a violent campaign of terror against Israel's citizens, they have forced Israel to set up barriers to make it as difficult as possible for terrorists to enter Israel to carry out acts of violence. The checkpoints are an inconvenience to innocent Palestinians, but they save lives.

For example, on October 5, 2008, two pipe bombs were found in a parcel carried by a Palestinian man at the Hawara checkpoint near Nablus. On June 8, 2008, an eighteen-year-old Palestinian was arrested at the same checkpoint carrying six pipe bombs, an ammunition cartridge, bullets, and a bag of gunpowder. "It's routine to find bombs at this checkpoint . . . every day, we find knives and other weapons," said Cpl. Ron Bezalel of the military police. Just three weeks earlier, another Palestinian was arrested at Hawara carrying five pipe bombs, which he had attached and strapped to his chest to act as an explosives belt.[58]

The following are just a few other examples of how checkpoints prevent terrorism:

■ On October 23, 2012, a nineteen-year-old Palestinian was caught at the Kalandiya check point with eight pipe bombs he was trying to bring into Jerusalem.[59]

- On July 27, 2014, police stopped a suspicious vehicle at a checkpoint near Beitar Illit and discovered a large explosive device attached to gas cylinders inside the car.[60]

- On June 29, 2015, a female soldier was stabbed at a checkpoint between Jerusalem and Bethlehem.[61]

- On May 10, 2016, an Israeli officer was seriously wounded by an explosive device at the Hizme checkpoint near Jerusalem. Five other explosives were found at the scene.[62]

Barriers are not set up to humiliate Palestinians, but to ensure the safety of Israeli citizens. Frequently, when Israel has relaxed its policy and withdrawn checkpoints, Palestinian terrorists have taken advantage of the opportunity to launch new attacks on innocent Israelis. Still, Israel has dismantled most of its unmanned checkpoints, reduced the number of manned checkpoints, and streamlined the entry process.[63]

One does not judge a democracy by the way its soldiers immediately react, young men and women under tremendous provocation. One judges a democracy by the way its courts react, in the dispassionate cool of judicial chambers. And the Israeli Supreme Court and other courts have reacted magnificently. For the first time in Mideast history, there is an independent judiciary willing to listen to grievances of Arabs—that judiciary is called the Israeli Supreme Court.

—Alan Dershowitz[64]

MYTH

Israeli checkpoints prevent Palestinians from receiving medical attention.

FACT

Israel has instituted checkpoints for one reason—to prevent Palestinian terrorists from infiltrating Israel. If the Palestinian Authority dismantled the terrorist networks, disarmed the terrorists, and prevented Palestinians from planning and launching attacks, Israel would dismantle the checkpoints. Israel tries to balance its security concerns with the welfare of the Palestinians, with specific regard to the medical needs of Palestinians. According to IDF guidelines, any Palestinian in need of urgent medical care is allowed passage through checkpoints. Palestinians are also allowed to enter Israel for routine medical care unless there is a security problem. Even then, Palestinians can appeal decisions and are also offered other options, such as transfer to neighboring states.

Israeli hospitals extend humanitarian treatment to Palestinians from the Gaza Strip and West Bank. These efforts continued when all other cooperation between Palestinians and Israelis came to a halt during the most recent intifada.

—Palestinian obstetrician and gynecologist, Dr. Izzeldin Abuelaish[65]

Ambulances are stopped and searched at Israeli checkpoints because they have frequently been used to transport terrorist bombs, and many of the murderers who have triggered suicide bombings in Israel gained access by driving or riding in Red Crescent ambulances. For example:

- During Operation Protective Edge in 2014, the Israeli Defense Forces reported Hamas operatives taking shelter from Israeli airstrikes in ambulances.[66]

- On May 17, 2002, an explosive belt was found in a Red Crescent ambulance at a checkpoint near Ramallah. The bomb, the same type generally used in suicide bombings, was hidden under a gurney on which a sick child was lying. The driver, Islam Jibril, was already wanted by the IDF, and admitted that this was not the first time that an ambulance had been used to transport explosives or terrorists. In a statement issued the same day, the International Committee of the Red Cross said that it "understands the security concerns of the Israeli authorities, and has always acknowledged their right to check ambulances, provided it does not unduly delay medical evacuations." The sick passengers in the ambulance were escorted by soldiers to a nearby hospital.[67]

- On June 30, 2002, Israeli troops found ten suspected Palestinian terrorists hiding in two ambulances in Ramallah. They were caught when soldiers stopped the vehicles for routine checks.[68]

- In December 2003, Rashed Tarek al-Nimr, who worked as a chemist in hospitals in Nablus and Bethlehem, supplied chemicals from the hospitals to Hamas for use in making bombs and admitted he used ambulances to transport the chemicals. He also said the Hamas commanders would hide in hospitals to avoid arrest.[69]

- In December 2004, a Hamas agent with forged documents claiming that he was a cancer patient in need of medical treatment from an Israeli hospital was arrested by security forces. Hamed A-Karim

Hamed Abu Lihiya was to meet up with another terrorist, obtain weapons from allies inside Israel, and carry out an attack. That same month, a man recruited by the Al-Aqsa Martyrs Brigade to plant a bomb on the railway tracks near Netanya tried to use false papers indicating he needed hospital treatment to enter Israel. Another Hamas terrorist planning a suicide bombing was arrested in March 2005 after pretending to be a kidney donor.[70]

On June 20, 2005, Wafa Samir Ibrahim Bas was arrested attempting to smuggle an explosives belt through the Erez crossing. Bas aroused the suspicion of soldiers at the checkpoint when a biometric scanner revealed she was hiding explosives. When she realized they had discovered the explosive belt, she attempted unsuccessfully to detonate it.[71]

Bas had been admitted on humanitarian grounds to Soroka Medical Center in Beersheva several months earlier for treatment of massive burns she received as a result of a cooking accident. After her arrest, she admitted that the Fatah al-Aqsa Martyrs Brigade had instructed her to use her personal medical authorization documents to enter into Israel to carry out a suicide attack. In an interview shown on Israeli television, Bas said her "dream was to be a martyr" and that her intent was to kill forty or fifty people—as many young people as possible.

Since its founding in 1996, Save a Child's Heart, an Israeli humanitarian group that treats children suffering from heart problems, has treated more than four thousand children worldwide.[72]

Dr. Izzeldin Abuelaish, a Palestinian obstetrician and gynecologist from the Jabalya refugee camp in the Gaza Strip, who has worked at the Soroka Hospital, wrote that he was "outraged at the cynical and potentially deadly suicide bombing attempt." Dr. Abuelaish said he does research at the hospital's Genetic Institute and has warm relations with his colleagues. "I make a point, whenever I'm at the hospital, of visiting Palestinian patients," he said. "I also schedule appointments for other Gaza residents, and even bring medication from Soroka to needy patients in the Strip. On the very day that she planned to detonate her bomb, two Palestinians in critical condition were waiting in Gaza to be taken for urgent treatment at Soroka."

Dr. Abuelaish added, "Wafa was sent to kill the very people in Israel who are healing Palestinians from the Gaza Strip and West Bank. What if Israeli hospitals now decide to bar Palestinians seeking treatment? How would those who sent Bas feel if their own relatives, in need of medical care in Israel, are refused treatment?"[73]

By using this tactic, the Palestinians have reinforced the necessity of retaining checkpoints and forced Israel to carry out more stringent inspections, yet another example of how terrorists are making life unnecessarily difficult for innocent Palestinians.

Despite a number of other cases where Palestinian terrorists tried to take advantage of the "medical route" to infiltrate Israel, tens of thousands of Palestinians from Gaza and the West Bank are allowed to travel each year to hospitals in Israel to receive treatment from some of the finest medical facilities in the world. This includes thousands of children. Many of these patients, including family members of Hamas leaders, receive life-saving treatments that are not available in the Palestinian territories.[74]

In fact, the official PA daily newspaper reported in 2013 that during a visit to Hadassah Hospital in Jerusalem, the PA minister of health estimated that 30 percent of the child patients were Palestinians and that the hospital was training sixty Palestinian medical interns and specialist physicians (including a special program to train Palestinian doctors to treat children with cancer) who would return to work in the PA.[75] Meanwhile, in Gaza, many hospitals and people go without medicine or supplies because they are stolen by Hamas officials concerned only with their organization's welfare.[76]

Case Study

Picture a nineteen-year-old soldier commanding a checkpoint when an ambulance arrives. Inside is a woman who is seemingly pregnant and who appears to be in pain; her husband is also highly anxious.

But the soldier has been warned about an ambulance bearing a pregnant woman who is not really pregnant. The intelligence said that underneath the ambulance's stretcher a wanted terrorist is hiding with an explosive belt for a suicide attack.

It is a hot day, and there is a long line of cars. His commanders are yelling at him on the two-way radio, "Do not let ambulances through without being thoroughly checked, there may very well be terrorists inside!" To complicate the picture, a news video crew is present.

The soldier has to make an incredible number of decisions in a very short time. He is only nineteen and has no medical training. He knows that if he lets the ambulance go through and it contains a terrorist, then innocent people will die and he will have failed in his mission. On the other hand, if there is not a terrorist in this particular ambulance, and he delays a truly pregnant woman from reaching a hospital, the lives of the mother and baby could be endangered.

What would you do?

MYTH

Israeli textbooks are just as hateful as those in the Palestinian Authority.

FACT

The best hope for the future is that Israeli and Arab children grow up with a greater understanding and tolerance of one another. Unfortunately, the textbooks in Arab countries, and the Palestinian Authority, in particular, do not promote coexistence. By contrast, Israeli textbooks are oriented toward peace and tolerance. The Palestinians are accepted as Palestinians. Islam and Arab culture are referred to with respect. Islamic holy places are discussed along with Jewish ones. Stereotypes are avoided to educate against prejudice.

More than twenty years ago, it was true that some Israeli textbooks used stereotyped images of Arabs; however, the books in use in public schools today are very different. Israeli texts go out of their way to avoid prejudices and to guard against generalizations.

Contrary to suggestions that Israelis do not accept the idea that Palestinians are a people, Israeli textbooks explain the origins of Palestinian nationalism. For example, a ninth grade text observes that "during the 1930s, Arab nationalist movements evolved all over the Middle East. Many of the Arabs of Eretz Yisrael also began formulating a national consciousness—in other words, the perception that they are not just part of the larger Arab nation, but are also Palestinians."[77]

While Palestinian texts omit references to Jewish contributions to the world, the Israeli books recognize the achievements of Arabs and Muslims. One text highlights the Arab role as creators of culture: "[T]hey were the first to discover the existence of infectious diseases. They were also the first to build public hospitals. Because of their considerable contribution to various scientific fields, there are disciplines that to this day are called by their Arabic names, such as algebra." Islam's contributions are also acknowledged in the same passage: "The Islamic religion also influenced the development of culture. The obligation to pray in the direction of Mecca led to the development of astronomy, which helped identify the direction according to the heavenly bodies. The duty to make a pilgrimage developed geography and gave a push to the writing of travel books. These books, and the Arabs' high capability in map drawing, helped develop trade. To this day, merchants use Arabic words, such as bazaar, check and tariff."[78]

Palestinian textbooks also negate the Jewish connection to the Holy Land while Israeli texts show respect for the Arab/Muslim attachment to the land. "The Land of Israel in general, and Jerusalem in particular, have been sanctified more and more in Islamic thought—as Islam has developed and spread, both religiously and geographically.

As Islam absorbed more and more of the world conquered by it, so it adapted and Islamized the values that it absorbed, including the holiness of the Land of Israel, its flora and its water, living in it, the sanctity of being buried in it and the like. All these became from that time onwards part of orthodox Islam."[79]

Israeli textbooks contain a plurality of views, including those that conflict with conventional research and are critical of Israeli policies. Controversial topics, such as the disputed territories, the refugee issue, and the status of Israeli Arabs are covered from multiple viewpoints.[80]

The content of the peace treaties between Israel and Egypt and Jordan is detailed, along with the implications of those agreements. Agreements with the Palestinians are discussed as well, and the atlas used in Israeli schools shows the Palestinian Authority.[81]

While Palestinian textbooks do not have maps of Israel; they replace the Jewish State with "Palestine," Israeli texts typically provide clear boundary demarcations, including the designation of parts of the West Bank as Areas A, B, and C as agreed in the Oslo Accords. Israeli textbooks acknowledge the Palestinian presence in Israel prior to the First Aliyah in the 1800s, discuss how Palestinians became refugees and the hardships they have encountered, provide the Palestinian position on the Arab-Israeli conflict, and promote a peaceful resolution to the dispute. As two members of the Institute for Monitoring Peace and Cultural Tolerance in School Education concluded: "Although textbooks are predominantly interested in presenting the Israeli position, its history and narrative—a clear effort is made to add balance and to promote the values of peace and tolerance, as well as to exclude any text promoting racism or violence."[82]

Israel is not perfect, and exceptions do exist. Some generalizations and patronizing terminology are found in textbooks used in the ultra-Orthodox schools. These schools comprise less than 10 percent of the Israeli educational system, and the same Israeli watchdog organizations that have pointed out problems in Palestinian textbooks have also publicized the need to remove inappropriate references from school books in that system.[83]

MYTH

Israel is a theocracy and should not be a Jewish State.

FACT

It often makes people uncomfortable to refer to Israel as "the Jewish State" because it suggests a theocracy and, therefore, the demise of Israel as a Jewish state is viewed by some people as a positive development. Israel is not a theocracy; it is governed by the rule of law as drafted by a democratically elected parliament. It is informed by Jewish values and adheres to many Jewish religious customs (such as holidays), but this is similar to the United States and other nations that also have expressly religious elements (e.g., church-state separation in the United States does not preclude the recognition of Christmas as a holiday). Israel has no state religion, and all faiths enjoy freedom of worship; yet, it is attacked for its Jewish character, whereas the Arab states that all have Islam as their official religion are regarded as legitimate.

Why shouldn't the Jews have a state? The Jewish people are a nation with a shared origin, religion, culture, language, and history. No one suggests that Arab peoples are not entitled to nations of their own (and they have not one, but twenty-one), or that Swedes, Germans, Nigerians, and Tanzanians should be denied states. To suggest that Zionism, the nationalist movement of the Jewish people, is the only form of nationalism that is illegitimate is pure hypocrisy. It is especially ironic that the Jewish nation should be challenged given that Jewish statehood and national identity preceded the emergence of most modern nation-states by thousands of years.

It is also not unusual that one community should be the majority within a nation and seek to maintain that status. In fact, this is true in nearly every country in the world. Moreover, societies usually reflect the cultural identity of the majority. India and Pakistan were established at the same time as Israel through a violent partition, but no one believes those nations are illegitimate because one is predominantly Hindu and the other has a Muslim majority or that these nations shouldn't be influenced by those communities.

In the United States, a vigorous debate persists over the boundaries between church and state. Similar discussions regarding "synagogue and state" are ongoing in Israel, with philosophical disagreements over whether Israel can be a Jewish and a democratic state, and practical arguments over Sabbath observance, marriage and divorce laws, and budgets for religious institutions. Nevertheless, most Jews take for granted that Israel is, and must remain, a Jewish state. Arab citizens also understand that Israel is a Jewish state and, while they might prefer that it was not, they have still chosen to live there (nothing prevents Arabs from moving to any of the 190-odd non-Jewish states in the world). Both Jews and Arabs realize that if Israel loses its Jewish majority, Israel will no longer have a Jewish character or serve as a haven for persecuted Jews.

MYTH

Israel persecutes Christians.

FACT

While Christians are unwelcome in Islamic states such as Saudi Arabia, and most have been driven out of their longtime homes in Lebanon, Christians continue to be welcome in Israel. Christians have always been a minority in Israel, but it is the only Middle East nation where the Christian population has grown in the last half century (from 34,000 in 1948 to 158,000 today), in large measure because of the freedom to practice their religion.

By their own volition, the Christian communities have remained the most autonomous of the various religious communities in Israel, though they have increasingly chosen to integrate their social welfare, medical, and educational institutions into state structures. The ecclesiastical courts of the Christian communities maintain jurisdiction in matters of personal status, such as marriage and divorce. The Ministry of Religious Affairs deliberately refrains from interfering in their religious life, but maintains a Department for Christian Communities to address problems and requests that may arise. In 2014, 17 percent of all Israeli university students were Christians. They also have the highest representation—as a percentage of total population—in white-collar jobs.

In Jerusalem, the rights of the various Christian churches to custody of the Christian holy places were established during the Ottoman Empire. Known as the "status quo arrangement for the Christian holy places in Jerusalem," these rights remain in force today in Israel.

It was during Jordan's control of the Old City from 1948 until 1967 that Christian rights were infringed and Israeli Christians were barred from their holy places. The Christian population declined by nearly half, from 25,000 to 12,646. Since then, the population has slowly been growing.

Some Christians have been among those inconvenienced by Israel's construction of the security fence, but they have not been harmed because of their religious beliefs. They simply live in areas where the fence needs to be built. Like others who can show they have suffered some injury, Christians are entitled to compensation.

Meanwhile, Israel has taken measures to minimize the impact of the fence on Christians. For example, a special terminal was built to facilitate security checks for those traveling between Bethlehem and Jerusalem. Special gates were built in other areas allowing pilgrims to visit religious sites on the Palestinian side of the fence. Israel often moved the fence route to accommodate requests of Christians, as in the case of the Rosary School that was moved to the Israeli side in response to requests from the Mother Superior. Ultimately, nineteen of twenty-two Christian sites in and around Jerusalem were brought inside the fence, with the exceptions primarily due to the desire to avoid moving the fence deep into the West Bank or compromising Muslim property rights.[84]

Meanwhile, Israel's detractors ignore the precarious plight of Christians under Arab rule, especially under the Palestinian Authority, where approximately fifty thousand Christians live among three million Muslims. The total number of Christians in the Palestinian territories has remained stable since 1967; however, the proportion has dropped from 15 percent of the Arab population in 1950 to just over 1 percent today. Three-fourths of all Bethlehem Christians now live abroad, and the overwhelming majority of the city's population is Muslim. By contrast, Israel's Christian population grew by approximately 114 percent since 1967.[85]

Jonathan Adelman and Agota Kuperman noted that Yasser Arafat "tried to erase the historic Jesus by depicting him as the first radical Palestinian armed *fedayeen* (guerrilla). Meanwhile, the Palestinian Authority has adopted Islam as its official religion, applied strict Islamic codes, and allowed even officially appointed clerics to brand Christians (and Jews) as infidels in their mosques." The authors add that the "militantly Islamic rhetoric and terrorist acts of Hamas, [and] Islamic Jihad . . . offer little comfort to Christians."

David Raab observed that "Palestinian Christians are perceived by many Muslims—as were Lebanon's Christians—as a potential fifth column for Israel. In fact, at the start of the Palestinian War in 2000, Muslim Palestinians attacked Christians in Gaza." Raab also wrote that "anti-Christian graffiti is common in Bethlehem and neighboring Beit Sahur, proclaiming: 'First the Saturday people (the Jews), then the Sunday people (the Christians),'" and that "Christian cemeteries have been defaced, monasteries have had their telephone lines cut, and there have been break-ins at convents." In 2002, Palestinian terrorists holed up in the Church of the Nativity in Bethlehem, endangering the shrine and provoking a tense standoff with Israeli troops.

When Arafat died, Vatican Radio correspondent Graziano Motta said, "The death of the president of the Palestinian National Authority has come at a time when the political, administrative and police structures often discriminate against [Christians]." Motta added that Christians "have been continually exposed to pressures by Muslim activists, and have been forced to profess fidelity to the intifada." In addition, he reported, "Frequently, there are cases in which the Muslims expropriate houses and lands belonging to Catholics, and often the intervention of the authorities has been lacking in addressing acts of violence against young women, or offenses against the Christian faith."[86]

It certainly wouldn't be difficult for critics to find evidence of mistreatment of Christians in the PA if they were interested, but unlike Christians who enjoy freedom of speech and religion in Israel, beleaguered Palestinian Christians rarely speak out. "Out of fear for their safety, Christian spokesmen aren't happy to be identified by name when they complain about the Muslims' treatment of them . . . [O]ff the record they talk of harassment and terror tactics, mainly from the gangs of thugs who looted and plundered Christians and their property, under the protection of Palestinian security personnel."[87]

"Christian Arabs," Adam Garfinkle noted, "see Israel as protection against the rising sea of Islam in which they live." Christians also rarely publicly complain, Garfinkle says, "because Arab Christians are somewhat marginalized in majority Islamic culture, they have often gone out of their way to act more Arab than the Arabs, and that has sometimes meant taking the lead in anti-Western and anti-Israel advocacy."[88]

One Christian who went public is Samir Qumsiyeh, a journalist from Beit Sahur who told the Italian newspaper *Corriere della Sera* that Christians were being subjected to rape, kidnapping, extortion, and expropriation of land and property. Qumsiyeh compiled a list of ninety-three cases of anti-Christian violence between 2000 and 2004 and specifically mentioned the case of a seventeen-year-old girl from his town who was raped by members of Fatah. "Even though the family protested," he said, "none of the four was ever arrested. Because of the shame, her family was forced to move to Jordan." He added that "almost all 140 cases of expropriation of land in the last three years were committed by militant Islamic groups and members of the Palestinian police," and that the Christian population of Bethlehem has dropped from 75 percent in 1950 to 12 percent today. "If the situation continues," Qumsiyeh warned, "we won't be here anymore in 20 years."[89]

In 2015, the tiny minority of Christians remaining in Bethlehem learned that the Palestinian Authority decided to limit celebrations of religious observance after Muslim extremists threatened to target Christians and their holy places. The situation was so dangerous that the PA rounded up Islamists in the West Bank. Nevertheless, on Christmas day, Muslim Palestinians threw stones at the car taking the Latin Patriarch of Jerusalem to Bethlehem. Equally dangerous, but more bizarre, was the spectacle of Palestinians dressed in Santa Claus suits throwing rocks at Israeli soldiers. [90]

MYTH

Hamas respects the rights of Palestinian Christians.

FACT

In Gaza, approximately thirteen hundred Christians live among more than one million Muslims. The population has declined as Hamas persecution has intensified.

On June 14, 2007, the Rosary Sisters School and Latin Church in the Gaza Strip were ransacked, burned, and looted by Hamas gunmen who stormed the buildings. Father Manuel Musalam, leader of the Latin community in Gaza, expressed outrage that copies of the Bible were burned, crosses destroyed, and computers and other equipment stolen. The same year, the owner of Gaza's only Christian bookstore was murdered.[91]

"I expect our Christian neighbors to understand the new Hamas rule means real changes. They must be ready for Islamic rule if they want to live in peace in Gaza," said Sheik Abu Saqer, leader of Jihadia Salafiya, an Islamic outreach movement that opened a "military wing" to enforce Islamic law in Gaza. The application of Islamic law, he said, includes a prohibition on alcohol and a requirement that women be covered at all times while in public.[92]

The Christian position throughout the territories has always been precarious, which is why many have fled the Palestinian Authority. Meanwhile, individuals and organizations who profess concern for Christians ignore the persistent discrimination and abuse of Christians by Muslims throughout the Middle East. It is therefore not surprising that they have remained silent while Palestinian Muslims persecute Christians.

MYTH

Israel denies Palestinians basic rights and freedoms.

FACT

Palestinians are deprived of the freedoms in the West Bank and Gaza that Americans and Israelis take for granted, namely, freedom of religion, freedom of the press, freedom of speech, freedom of assembly, gay rights, and women's rights. Israel has nothing to do with the denial of these rights; however, they are all blocked by the Palestinian Authority.

Non-Muslims regularly face discrimination, and Christians have been driven out of Gaza by Hamas. Journalists are not allowed to report freely, and critics of the leadership are harassed, jailed, or prevented from reporting. In a December 2010 poll, only 27 percent of Palestinians in the West Bank and 19 percent in Gaza said they could criticize officials without fear.[93]

Gay Palestinians are not tolerated, and many have fled to Israel for sanctuary. Women are routinely discriminated against, and honor killings are still practiced. A UN organization reported in 2014 that violence against women was on the rise and that fourteen women were killed in just the first five months alone. In 2013, the total was twenty-eight. A 2012 survey by the Palestinian Central Bureau of Statistics found that 37 percent of Palestinian women were victims of some form of violence by their husbands; the figure in Gaza was 58 percent.[94]

While human rights groups obsessively focus on Israel's treatment of Palestinians, they routinely ignore abuses by Palestinians against their own people. While Israel may be blamed for hardships faced by Palestinians, the denial of these basic civil and human rights in the territories has been the sole responsibility of the Palestinian leadership.

MYTH

The Goldstone Report proved Israel was guilty of war crimes in Gaza.

FACT

The Goldstone Commission was created to conduct a fact-finding mission and to investigate whether any violations of international humanitarian law took place during the conflict between Israel and Hamas during Israel's Operation Cast Lead in Gaza in December 2008/January 2009. No one was surprised when the Commission issued a report highly critical of Israel given that it was created by the UN Human Rights Council, an organization long ago discredited for its obsessive and biased focus on Israel, and that one of the Commission members, Christine Chinkin, had previously accused Israel of war crimes.[95]

Following the report's release, Susan Rice, the US ambassador to the United Nations, said, "The mandate was unbalanced, one-sided and unacceptable . . . The weight of the report is something like 85% oriented towards very specific and harsh condemnation and conclusions related to Israel and very lightly treats without great specificity Hamas' terrorism and its own atrocities."[96]

The four-person panel, led by Judge Richard Goldstone, based virtually all of its 575-page report on unverified accounts by Palestinians and NGOs. The Goldstone Commission fixated on Israel's incursion into Gaza while failing to adequately address the provocation—three years of Hamas rocket bombardment of Israeli towns and villages—that led to the Israeli operation. The Israeli government did not cooperate with the Commission because of its one-sided mandate that presumed Israel was guilty of war crimes from the outset.[97]

While ignoring journalistic accounts of the activities of Hamas, the Commission relied on critical reports, which had already been disputed, of Israeli actions by groups such as Human Rights Watch (HRW). HRW, in particular, has been discredited by revelations that it tried to raise money from Saudi Arabia by touting its history of anti-Israel reportage and that its "senior military expert," Marc Garlasco, collected Nazi memorabilia.[98]

When interviewing Gazans, the Commission was chaperoned by Hamas officials to ensure members saw and heard only what Hamas approved.[99] Hence, it was not surprising that investigators made little effort to investigate Hamas activities before or during Operation Cast Lead. It was equally unremarkable for the commission to report that it found no evidence that Hamas had fired rockets from civilian homes, that terrorists had hid among the civilian population, fired mortars, anti-tank missiles, and machine guns into Palestinian villages when IDF forces were in proximity, or that they had seized and booby-trapped Palestinian civilian houses to ambush IDF soldiers. In fact, the report refers to Hamas "police" as civilians, absolving them of terrorist rocket attacks against Israeli civilians and their illegal actions in Gaza during the conflict.[100] This directly contradicts the ample photos, video, and reports by journalists that depict Hamas militants participating in all of these illegal activities.[101]

For the Palestinian people, death has become an industry at which women excel, and so do all the people living on this land. The elderly excel at this, and so do the mujahedeen and the children. This is why they have formed human shields of the women, the children, the elderly, and the mujahedeen, in order to challenge the Zionist bombing machine. It is as if they are saying to the Zionist enemy: We desire death like you desire life.

—Hamas parliamentarian Fathi Hammad[102]

One postwar study rebutting Goldstone's conclusions found that many Hamas fighters were dressed as civilians; some were seen in videos firing mortars and rocket-propelled grenades at troops. The report also documented the use by Hamas of dozens of mosques as armories, command centers, and launching areas for rockets. Evidence was also found of Hamas fighters using civilians as shields.[103]

Ironically, Hamas undermined claims by Goldstone and other critics of Israel who insisted the victims of the war were mostly innocent civilians when Hamas interior minister Fathi Hammad admitted in 2010 that it lost more than six hundred men during the war. This is relatively consistent with the figure of 709 calculated by the IDF after it released an official list of the 1,166 names of Palestinians killed during the war.[104]

Even the UN's Humanitarian Affairs chief, John Holmes, had criticized Hamas for "the reckless and cynical use of civilian installations . . . and indiscriminate firing of rockets against civilian populations," which he characterized as "clear violations of international law."[105]

By not holding Hamas accountable for targeting Israeli civilians, the report essentially legitimizes terrorism and criminalizes self-defense.

Goldstone recognized after the report was lambasted that it was inaccurate. In an April 1, 2011, editorial published by the *Washington Post*, Goldstone retracted his accusations that Israel intentionally targeted civilians and was guilty of war crimes during the fighting. Furthermore, he conceded that "if I had known then what I know now, the Goldstone Report would have been a different document."[106]

The report, which erroneously claimed that Israel led a "deliberately disproportionate attack designed to punish, humiliate and terrorize a civilian population," became a tool for Israel's detractors to demonize the Jewish state and denigrate its right to self-defense.[107] Goldstone now acknowledges that "civilians were not intentionally targeted [by Israel] as a matter of policy" and that in the aftermath of having thousands of rockets and missiles fired at its cities, Israel had the "right and obligation to defend itself and its citizens against such attacks."[108]

In fact, as Colonel Richard Kemp, former commander of British Forces in Afghanistan, testified to the Goldstone committee in 2009, "The IDF did more to safeguard the rights of civilians in a combat zone than any other army in the history of warfare."[109]

Everything that we said proved to be true. Israel did not intentionally target civilians and it has proper investigatory bodies. In contrast, Hamas intentionally directed strikes towards innocent civilians and did not conduct any kind of probe . . . The fact that Goldstone changed his mind must lead to the shelving of [the Goldstone Report] once and for all.

—Benjamin Netanyahu, Israeli prime minister[110]

Israel's claims regarding casualties also proved correct, Goldstone concedes. "The Israeli military's numbers have turned out to be similar to those recently furnished by Hamas." He is referring to the Hamas admission that, as Israel maintained, most of the Palestinians who were killed in the fighting were terrorists and not bystanders.[111]

Goldstone also takes the UN Human Rights Council to task, noting that its original mandate was "skewed against Israel." He said he "hoped that our inquiry into all aspects of the Gaza conflict would begin a new era of evenhandedness at the UN Human Rights Council, whose history of bias against Israel cannot be doubted."[112]

Goldstone focused his criticism on Hamas in a way the report did not. "That comparatively few Israelis have been killed by the unlawful rocket and mortar attacks from Gaza," Goldstone wrote, "in no way minimizes their criminality."[113] He added that Hamas's actions during the conflict were intentional and "purposefully indiscriminate," and he excoriated them for failing to investigate any of the war crimes accusations. By contrast, Goldstone acknowledged that Israel has "dedicated significant resources to investigate" allegations of misconduct.

Goldstone's retraction came too late to mitigate the damage caused to Israel by the Goldstone Report as the "evidence" released in the report continues to be used to smear Israel and its brave soldiers.

MYTH

Israel's blockade of Gaza is collective punishment.

FACT

International law requires that Israel permit passage of food, clothing, and medicines intended for children under fifteen, expectant mothers, and maternity cases. If Israel has reason to believe Hamas will intercept these goods and the enemy will benefit, even these provisions may be prohibited. Israel also need not provide these supplies; it is obligated only to allow others to transfer provisions.

Furthermore, the law does not prohibit Israel from cutting off fuel supplies and electricity to Gaza, withholding commercial items, or sealing its border. Israel also is not obligated to provide any minimum supplies to prevent a "humanitarian crisis."

Some detractors call Israel's actions "collective punishment"; however, this refers to the "imposition of criminal-type penalties to individuals or groups on the basis of another's guilt." Israel has done no such thing. Israel has no obligation to maintain open borders with a hostile territory. The suspension of trade relations or embargoes is a frequent tool of international diplomacy and has never been regarded as "collective punishment."[114]

Israel complied with—and exceeded—international law by delivering humanitarian supplies it was not required to provide.

It is also important to recognize that Israel cannot impose a blockade on its own. Egypt controls the southern border of the Gaza Strip and has maintained its own blockade. In fact, in October 2014, and then again in March 2015, Egypt demolished dozens of homes along its border with Gaza to create a buffer zone to stop smugglers and extremists from crossing in either direction.[115]

Furthermore, the international community, with the possible exception of Turkey, has not opposed the actions of Israel and Egypt because Hamas has refused to meet the conditions of ending terror attacks, recognizing Israel's right to exist, and agreeing to abide by past Israeli-Palestinian agreements.

MYTH

Human rights activists care deeply about the Palestinian people.

FACT

In the media, reports from human rights organizations, and on college campuses there is a steady drumbeat of criticism of Israel for both real and imagined abuses of Palestinians in the disputed territories. While Israel may be legitimately criticized when abuses are documented, what is shocking is the utter hypocrisy of the critics who proclaim concern for Palestinian welfare, but express it only if Israel can be blamed. This raises the question as to whether the concern for Palestinians is genuine or simply a propaganda tool by which to tarnish Israel's image.

It is a legitimate question given the near total silence regarding the treatment and ethnic cleansing of Palestinians living in the Arab world. Palestinians have lived as second- or third-class citizens in Arab countries for decades, but since the Arab Spring, thousands have been tortured, murdered, and expelled by their fellow Muslims for alleged involvement in terrorism, for being Sunnis in areas of Shiite control, or for being deemed disloyal.

According to journalist Khaled Abu Toameh, the plight of the Palestinians in Arab countries became increasingly tenuous long before the Arab Spring.[116] Following the Iraqi invasion of Kuwait, the Palestinians cheered on Saddam Hussein. Fearing their disloyalty, Kuwait expelled more than two hundred thousand Palestinians living and working there. When Hussein was finally driven from power in the second Gulf War, Iraqi Shiites began to take revenge and drove most Palestinians from the country (approximately nineteen thousand out of a population of twenty-five thousand).

Palestinian refugees are not welcome anywhere in the region. And the number has swelled due to the Syrian civil war where thousands of Palestinians have been killed. The lucky ones who escaped to Lebanon or Jordan are unwelcome and confined to refugee camps.

Despite the hardships, Palestinians are far safer in the disputed territories than anywhere else in the region. Hence, while Israel's critics accuse Israel of "ethnic cleansing," the truth is the Palestinian population has grown exponentially in the disputed territories while it is being gradually wiped out in the Arab world. This is tragic. The fact that campaigners for Palestinian human rights and the media ignore what is happening before their eyes is appalling.

Notes, Chapter 12

1. Vamberto Morais, *A Short History of Anti-Semitism*,(NY: W. W. Norton and Co., 1976), 11; Bernard Lewis, *Semites & Anti-Semites* (NY: W. W. Norton & Co., 1986), 81.

2. "Anti-Semitism," *Oxford English Dictionary*; *Webster's Third International Dictionary*.

3. Richard Cohen, "Where Bigotry Gets a Hearing," *Washington Post* (October 30, 2001).

4. Bernard Lewis, *Islam in History: Ideas, People, and Events in the Middle East* (Chicago, IL: Open Court, 2001), 148.

5. Bat Ye'or, *The Dhimmi*, (Rutherford, NJ: Fairleigh Dickinson University Press, 1985), 43-44.

6. Bat Ye'or, *The Dhimmi*, 185-86, 191, 194.

7. Norman Stillman, *The Jews of Arab Lands* (Philadelphia, PA: The Jewish Publication Society of America, 1979), 81; Maurice Roumani, The Case of the Jews from Arab Countries: A Neglected Issue (Tel Aviv: World Organization of Jews from Arab Countries, 1977), 26-27; Bat Ye'or, 72.

8. Stillman, 59, 284.

9. Roumani, 26-27.

10. Bernard Lewis, *The Jews of Islam* (NJ: Princeton University Press, 1984), 158.

11. G. E. Von Grunebaum, "Eastern Jewry Under Islam," *Viator* (1971), 369.

12. Bat Ye'or, *The Dhimmi*, 30.

13. Bat Ye'or, *The Dhimmi*, 14.

14. Bat Ye'or, *The Dhimmi*, 56-57.

15. Bat Ye'or, *Islam and Dhimmitude: Where Civilizations Collide* (Rutherford, NJ: Farleigh Dickinson University Press, 2002), 107.

16. Official British document, Foreign Office File No. 371/20822 E 7201/22/31; Elie Kedourie, *Islam in the Modern World* (London: Mansell, 1980), 69-72.

17. Howard Sachar, *A History of Israel: From the Rise of Zionism to Our Time* (NY: Alfred A. Knopf, 1979), 196.

18. Jordanian Nationality Law, Official Gazette, No. 1171, Article 3(3) of Law No. 6, 1954 (February 16, 1954), 105.

19. Modern World History, Jordanian Ministry of Education, 1966, 150.

20. Meyrav Wurmser, The Schools of Ba'athism: A Study of Syrian Schoolbooks, (Washington, DC: Middle East Media and Research Institute (MEMRI), 2000), xiii.

21. Aaron Klein, "Official PA Site Publishes 'Protocols' in Arabic," *WorldNetDaily* (May 21, 2005); Itamar Marcus and Nan Jacques Zilberdik, "Old Antisemitic Forgery Alive and Well in the PA: The Protocols of the Elders of Zion," *Palestinian Media Watch* (February 25, 2013).

22. *Al-Mussawar* (August 4, 1972).

23. "Vile Words," Editorial in the *Washington Post* (May 8, 2001).

24. Diaa Hadid, "Mahmoud Abbas Claims Rabbis Urged Israel to Poison Palestinians' Water," *New York Times* (June 23, 2016).

25. Middle East Media and Research Institute (MEMRI); *Al-Hayat al-Jadeeda* (May 15, 1997); *Jerusalem Post* (May 23, 2001); Palestine News Agency WAFA (April 28, 2005); Itamar Marcus and Nan Jacques Zilberdik, "PA Official Repeats Libel: 'Zionist policy' Is to Cause Drug Addiction among Palestinian Youth," *Palestinian Media Watch*.

26. "Leading Egyptian Newspaper Raises Blood Libel," *MEMRI* (November 6, 2000).

27. "Instructional Content on How to Stab Jews Spreads on Social Media," ADL Official Blog (October 15, 2015).

28. Palestinian Authority television (January 29, 2010), cited in "PATV Sermon: Jew Are Enemies," *Palestinian Media Watch* (February 1, 2010).

29. Jonathan Krashinsky, "Even Palestinian Crosswords Reject Israel," *Palestinian Media Watch* (March 15, 2001).

30. Israeli Central Bureau of Statistics.

31. Yarden Skop, "More Arab Students in Israel Attending University in New Academic Year," *Haaretz* (October 15, 2015).

32. Ariel Ben Solomon, "Israeli Government Reaches Historic Budget Deal for Arab Sector," *Jerusalem Post* (December 30, 2015).

33. Ariel Ben Solomon, Gil Stern, and Stern Hoffman, "Government in Talks to Invest Billions in Arab Sector," *Jerusalem Post* (October 29, 2015).

34. Ariel Ben Solomon, Gil Stern, and Stern Hoffman, "Government in Talks to Invest Billions in Arab Sector," *Jerusalem Post* (October 29, 2015).

35. Alan Dershowitz, *The Case for Israel* (NY: John Wiley & Sons, 2003), 157.

36. US State Department, Human Rights Report for the Occupied Territories, 1997, 1998.

37. Official PA TV, October 21 and 23, 2014, translated by Itamar Marcus and Nan Jacques Zilberdik, "Abbas Decrees Life Imprisonment for Selling Land to Israelis," *Palestinian Media Watch* (January 6, 2015).

38. "Israeli Leftist Taped Trying to Set Up Palestinians Who Seek to Sell Land to Jews," *Haaretz* (January 8, 2016).

39. "Torture and Ill Treatment as Perceived by Israel's High Court of Justice," *B'Tselem* (May 6, 2010).

40. In June 1948, before most state institutions were established, Meir Tobianski was executed as a traitor based on circumstantial evidence presented at an ad hoc court martial that he gave information to the enemy. He was exonerated by a posthumous inquiry. David B. Green, "This Day in Jewish History 1948: An Israeli Army Captain Is Wrongly Charged With Treason and Shot," *Haaretz* (June 30, 2016).

41. Khaled Abu Toameh, "Palestinian Authority, Hamas, Responsible for Torture," *Gatestone Institute* (January 2016).

42. Richard Goldstone, "Israel and the Apartheid Slander," *New York Times* (October 31, 2011).

43. Shabtai Teveth, Ben-Gurion, and the Palestinian Arabs: From Peace to War (London: Oxford University Press, 1985), 140; *Haaretz* (September 23, 2003).

44. Richard Goldstone, "Israel and the Apartheid Slander," *New York Times* (October 31, 2011).

45. Benjamin Pogrund, "Israel is a Democracy in Which Arabs Vote," *Focus*, 40—(2005).

46. Khaled Abu Toameh, "20,000 Palestinians Working in Settlements, Survey Finds," *Jerusalem Post* (August 15, 2013).

47. Itamar Marcus, Nan Jacques Zilberdik, "Official PA Daily Lauds Israel's Treatment of Palestinian Workers," *Palestinian Media Watch* (September 23, 2014).

48. Christa Case Bryant, "Palestinian Workers Back Scarlett Johansson's Opposition to SodaStream Boycott," *Christian Science Monitor* (January 30, 2014).

49. James Bennet, "Letter from the Middle East; Arab Showplace? Could It Be the West Bank?" *New York Times* (April 2, 2003). The last time the question was asked was in 2002.

50. Ido Efrati. "Hamas Leader's Daughter Received Medical Treatment in Israel," *Haaretz* (October 19, 2014).

51. Daniel Estrin, "Jerusalem Palestinians Taking Israeli Citizenship," *Associated Press* (January 12, 2011); Jackson Diehl, "Why Palestinians Want to Be Israeli Citizens," *Washington Post* (January 12, 2011).

52. Golda Meir, *My Life* (NY: Dell Publishing Co., 1975), 308-09.

53. *New Republic* (December 30, 2002).

54. Hillel Cohen, *Army of Shadows* (Berkeley: University of California Press, 2008), 274.

55. *The World Factbook* (Washington, DC: Central Intelligence Agency, 1994 and 2016).

56. Hillel Cohen, *Army of Shadows* (Berkeley: University of California Press, 2008), 274.

57. Ishmael Khaldi, "Lost in the Blur of Slogans," *SFGate.com* (March 4, 2009).

58. Efrat Weiss, "IDF Thwarts Smuggling of Pipe Bombs," *Ynet News* (October 5, 2008); Yaakov Katz and jpost.com Staff, "Palestinian Bomber Arrested Near Nablus," *Jerusalem Post* (June 8, 2008).

59. Yaakov Lapin, "'Palestinian with Explosives Was Heading for J'lem,'" *Jerusalem Post* (October 23, 2012).

60. Ben Hartman, "Border Police Stop Suspected Bombing Attack during Arrest at West Bank Checkpoint" *Jerusalem Post* (July 28, 2014).

61. Avi Lewis, "Female Soldier Wounded in Bethlehem Stabbing Attack," *Times of Israel* (June 29, 2015).

62. Gili Cohen, "Israeli Army Officer Seriously Wounded in Blast at West Bank Checkpoint," *Haaretz* (May 11, 2016).

63. "UN: Israel Has Dismantled 20 percent of West Bank Checkpoint," *Associated Press* (June 16, 2010); "Israel, the Conflict and Peace: Answers to Frequently Asked Questions," Israel Ministry of Foreign Affairs (December 30, 2009).

64. Speech to AIPAC Policy Conference (May 23, 1989), cited in *Near East Report* (October 16, 1989).

65. "Behind the Headlines: Abortive Suicide Attack at Erez," Ministry of Foreign Affairs (June 22, 2005).

66. Yaakov Lappin, "Fighting Terrorists Who Move around in Ambulances," *Jerusalem Post* (July 20, 2014).

67. "Palestinian Use of Ambulances for Terror," Ministry of Foreign Affairs (December 22, 2003); Amos Harel, Amira Hass, and Yosef Algazy, "Bomb Found in Red Crescent Ambulance," *Haaretz* (March 29, 2002).

68. Ibid.

69. Matthew Levitt, *Hamas: Politics, Charity, and Terrorism in the Service of Jihad* (New Haven, CT: Yale University Press, 2006), 100.

70. "Attack by Female Suicide Bomber Thwarted at Erez Crossing," Ministry of Foreign Affairs (June 20, 2005).

71. "Attack by Female Suicide Bomber Thwarted at Erez Crossing," Ministry of Foreign Affairs (June 20, 2005).

72. "Sanusey, 4, Is 4,000th Helped by Save a Child's Heart," *Times of Israel* (June 17, 2016).

73. "Behind the Headlines: Abortive Suicide Attack at Erez," Ministry of Foreign Affairs (June 22, 2005).

74. "Hamas Leader's Daughter Received Medical Treatment in Israel: Sources," *Reuters* (October 19, 2014).

75. Itamar Marcus and Nan Jacques Zilberdik, "Official PA Daily Acknowledges Israel's Hadassah Hospital's Treatment of Palestinians," *Palestinian Media Watch* (May 22, 2013).

76. "PA: Gaza Officials Stealing Medication," *Ma'an News* (December 7, 2014).

77. *Jerusalem Post* (July 1, 2005); BBC (June 21, 2005).

78. From Exile to Independence—The History of the Jewish People in Recent Generations, vol. 2, 1990, 312.

79. Center for the Monitoring of Peace, "Newsletter" (December 2003).

80. K. Tabibian, *Journey to the Past—The Twentieth Century, By Dint of Freedom*, 1999, 294.

81. Yohanan Manor, "The Future of Peace in the Light of School Textbooks," Center for Monitoring the Impact of Peace (March, 7 2002).

82. Yael Teff-Seker and Nir Boms, "Incitement or Peace Education?" *Jerusalem Post* (June 29, 2015).

83. Alex Safian, "*New York Times* Omits Major Reason Christians Are Leaving Bethle-

hem" (December 24, 2004), *CAMERA*; "The Palestinian Christian Population," JCPA Background Paper (2011).

84. Danny Tirza, "The Influence of Christian Interests in Setting the Route of the Security Fence in Jerusalem," Jerusalem Viewpoints, *JCPA*,(November–December 2008).
85. Alex Safian, *"New York Times* Omits Major Reason Christians Are Leaving Bethlehem" (December 24, 2004), *CAMERA*; "The Palestinian Christian Population," JCPA Background Paper (2011).
86. "Christians in Palestine Concerned about Their Future," *Zenit News Agency* (November 14, 2004).
87. David Raab, "The Beleaguered Christians of the Palestinian-Controlled Areas," *JCPA* (January 15, 2003).
88. Adam Garfinkle, *Politics and Society in Modern Israel: Myths and Realities* (NY: M. E. Sharpe, 1997), 108, 110.
89. Harry de Quetteville, "'Islamic Mafia' Accused of Persecuting Holy Land Christians," *Telegraph* (September 9, 2005).
90. "Palestinian Protestors Dressed as Santa Claus Clash with IDF," *Jerusalem Post* (December 23, 2014).
91. Khaled Abu Toameh, "Gaza's Christians Fear for Their Lives," *Jerusalem Post* (June 18, 2007); "Catholic Compound Ransacked in Gaza," *Associated Press* (June 19, 2007).
92. Aaron Klein, "Christians Must Accept Islamic Rule," *Ynet News* (June 19, 2007).
93. Palestinian Center for Policy and Survey Research, December 16–18, 2010; see also "Palestinian Public Opinion Poll #38."
94. Palestinian Central Bureau of Statistics.
95. "The Goldstone Report: The UN Blood Libel," Human Rights Voices [No Date].
96. "Excerpts from Interview with U.N. Ambassador Susan E. Rice," *Washington Post* (September 22, 2009); "Israel's Bombardment of Gaza Is Not Self-Defense—It's a War Crime," *The Sunday Times* (January 11, 2009).
97. "Israel's Initial Reaction to the Report of the Goldstone Fact-Finding Mission," Israel Ministry of Foreign Affairs (September 15, 2009).
98. Gerald M. Steinberg, "UN Smears Israeli Self-Defense as War Crimes," *Wall Street Journal* (September 16, 2009).
99. "Israel's Analysis and Comments on the Gaza Fact-Finding Mission Report," Israel Ministry of Foreign Affairs (September 15, 2009).
100. Jonathan D. Halevi, "Blocking the Truth of the Gaza War: How the Goldstone Commission Understated the Hamas Threat to Palestinian Civilians," *JCPA* (September 21, 2009).
101. "Hamas and the Terrorist Threat from the Gaza Strip: The Main Findings of the Goldstone Report versus the Factual Findings," Intelligence & Terrorism Information Center (March 2010).
102. "Hamas MP Fathi Hammad: We Used Women and Children as Human Shields," Al-Aqsa TV, cited in Dispatch #1710, *MEMRI* (February 29, 2008).
103. "Hamas and the Terrorist Threat from the Gaza Strip: The Main Findings of the Goldstone Report versus the Factual Findings," Intelligence & Terrorism Information Center (March 2010).
104. "IDF Releases Cast Lead Casualty Numbers," *Jerusalem Post* (March 28, 2009).
105. "Top UN Official Blasts Hamas for 'Cynical' Use of Civilian Facilities," *Haaretz* (January 28, 2009).
106. Richard Goldstone, "Reconsidering the Goldstone Report on Israel and War Crimes," *Washington Post* (April 1, 2011).
107. Ibid.
108. Ibid.

109. "UN Watch Briefing," UN Watch (October 16, 2009).

110. Barak Ravid, "Netanyahu to UN: Retract Gaza War Report in Wake of Goldstone's Comments," *Haaretz* (April 2, 2011).

111. Richard Goldstone, "Reconsidering the Goldstone Report on Israel and War Crimes," *Washington Post* (April 1, 2011).

112. Ibid.

113. Richard Goldstone, "Reconsidering the Goldstone Report on Israel and War Crimes," *Washington Post* (April 1, 2011).

114. Abraham Bell, "International Law and Gaza: The Assault on Israel's Right to Self-Defense," *JCPA* (January 28, 2008); "Is Israel Bound by International Law to Supply Utilities, Goods, and Services to Gaza?" *JCPA* (February 28, 2008).

115. "Egypt Demolishes Sinai Homes for Gaza Border Buffer," *BBC* (October 29, 2014); "Egypt Demolishes 1,020 Rafah Homes for Gaza Buffer Zone," *Maan News Agency* (March 19, 2015).

116. Khaled Abu Toameh, "The Secret Ethnic Cleansing of Palestinians," *Gatestone Institute* (August 10, 2015).

13. Jerusalem

Jerusalem is an Arab City.

The Temple Mount has always been a Muslim holy place.

Jerusalem need not be the capital of Israel.

The Arabs were willing to accept the internationalization of Jerusalem.

Internationalization is the best solution to resolve the conflicting claims over Jerusalem.

While in control of Jerusalem, Jordan ensured freedom of worship for all religions.

Jordan safeguarded Jewish holy places.

Under Israeli rule, religious freedom has been curbed in Jerusalem.

Israel denies Muslims and Christians free access to their holy sites.

Israel has refused to discuss a compromise on the future of Jerusalem.

Israel has restricted the political rights of Palestinian Arabs in Jerusalem.

Under UN Resolution 242, East Jerusalem is considered "occupied territory."

East Jerusalem should be part of a Palestinian state because no Jews have ever lived there.

The United States recognizes Jerusalem as Israel's capital.

The Israeli government wants to destroy the Al-Aqsa Mosque.

Muslims treat the Al-Aqsa Mosque with the reverence it deserves.

MYTH

Jerusalem is an Arab City.

FACT

Jews have been living in Jerusalem continuously for three millennia. They have constituted the largest single group of inhabitants there since the 1840s. Jerusalem contains the Western Wall of the Temple Mount, the holiest site in Judaism.

Jerusalem was never the capital of any Arab entity. In fact, it was a backwater for most of Arab history, and never served as a provincial capital under Muslim rule. While the entirety of Jerusalem is holy to Jews, Muslims only revere one site—the Al-Aqsa Mosque. "To a Muslim," observed British writer Christopher Sykes, "there is a profound difference between Jerusalem and Mecca or Medina. The latter are holy places containing holy sites."[1]

Jerusalem's Population[2]

Year	Jews	Muslims	Christians	Total
1844	7,120	5,000	3,390	**15,510**
1876	12,000	7,560	5,470	**25,030**
1896	28,112	8,560	8,748	**45,420**
1922	33,971	13,411	4,699	**52,081**
1931	51,222	19,894	19,335	**90,451**
1948	100,000	40,000	25,000	**165,000**
1967	195,700	54,963	12,646	**263,309**
1987	340,000	121,000	14,000	**475,000**
1990	378,200	131,800	14,400	**524,400**
2009	476,000	247,800	15,200	**760,800**
2011	648,900	302,600	16,400	**967,900**
2012	660,200	310,700	16,500	**987,400**

MYTH

The Temple Mount has always been a Muslim holy place.

FACT

During the 2000 Camp David Summit, Yasser Arafat said that no Jewish Temple ever existed on the Temple Mount.[3] A year later, the Palestinian Authority–appointed Mufti of Jerusalem, Ikrima Sabri, told the German publication *Die Welt*, "There is not [even] the smallest indication of the existence of a Jewish temple on this place in the past. In the whole city, there is not even a single stone indicating Jewish history."[4]

> The Zionist movement has invented that this was the site of Solomon's Temple. But this is all a lie.
>
> **—Sheik Raed Salah, a leader of the Islamic movement in Israel[5]**

These views are contradicted by a book entitled *A Brief Guide to al-Haram al-Sharif,* published by the Supreme Moslem Council in 1930. The Council, the principal Muslim authority in Jerusalem during the British Mandate, wrote in the guide that the Temple Mount site "is one of the oldest in the world. Its sanctity dates from the earliest times. Its identity with the site of Solomon's Temple is beyond dispute. This, too, is the spot, according to universal belief, on which David built there an altar unto the Lord, and offered burnt offerings and peace offerings."

In a description of the area of Solomon's Stables, which Islamic Waqf officials converted into a new mosque in 1996, the guide states: "little is known for certain about the early history of the chamber itself. It dates probably as far back as the construction of Solomon's Temple . . . According to Josephus, it was in existence and was used as a place of refuge by the Jews at the time of the conquest of Jerusalem by Titus in the year 70 A.D."[6]

More authoritatively, the Koran—the holy book of Islam—describes Solomon's construction of the First Temple (34:13) and recounts the destruction of the First and Second Temples (17:7).

The Jewish connection to the Temple Mount dates back more than three thousand years and is rooted in tradition and history. When Abraham bound his son Isaac upon an altar as a sacrifice to God, he is believed to have done so atop Mount Moriah, today's Temple Mount. The First Temple's Holy of Holies contained the original Ark of the Covenant, and both the First and Second Temples were the centers of Jewish religious and social life until the Second Temple's destruction by the Romans. After the destruction of the Second Temple, control of the Temple Mount passed through several conquering powers. It was during the early period of Muslim control, in the seventh century, that the Dome of the Rock was built on the site of the ancient temples.

> *For three thousand years, Jerusalem has been the center of Jewish hope and longing. No other city has played such a dominant role in the history, culture, religion and consciousness of a people as has Jerusalem in the life of Jewry and Judaism. Throughout centuries of exile, Jerusalem remained alive in the hearts of Jews everywhere as the focal point of Jewish history, the symbol of ancient glory, spiritual fulfillment and modern renewal. This heart and soul of the Jewish people engenders the thought that if you want one simple word to symbolize all of Jewish history, that word would be "Jerusalem."*
>
> **—Teddy Kollek**[7]

MYTH

Jerusalem need not be the capital of Israel.

FACT

Ever since King David made Jerusalem the capital of Israel more than three thousand years ago, the city has played a central role in Jewish existence. The Temple Mount in the Old City is the object of Jewish veneration and the focus of Jewish prayer. Three times a day, for thousands of years, Jews have prayed "To Jerusalem, thy city, shall we return with joy," and have repeated the Psalmist's oath: "If I forget thee, O Jerusalem, let my right hand forget her cunning."

MYTH

The Arabs were willing to accept the internationalization of Jerusalem.

FACT

When the United Nations took up the Palestine question in 1947, it recommended that all of Jerusalem be internationalized. The Vatican and many predominantly Catholic delegations pushed for this status, but a key reason for the UN decision was the Soviet Bloc's desire to embarrass Transjordan's King Abdullah and his British patrons by denying Abdullah control of the city.

The Jewish Agency, after much soul-searching, agreed to accept internationalization in the hope that in the short run it would protect the city from bloodshed and the new state from conflict. Since the partition resolution called for a referendum on the city's status after ten years, and Jews comprised a substantial majority, the expectation was that the city would later be incorporated into Israel. The Arab states were as bitterly opposed to the internationalization of Jerusalem as they were to the rest of the partition plan.

In May 1948, Jordan invaded and occupied East Jerusalem, dividing the city for the first time in its history, and driving thousands of Jews—whose families had lived in the city for centuries—into exile. Consequently, the UN partition plan, including its proposal that Jerusalem be internationalized, was overtaken by events.

> *You ought to let the Jews have Jerusalem; it was they who made it famous.*
>
> **—Winston Churchill**[8]

MYTH

Internationalization is the best solution to resolve the conflicting claims over Jerusalem.

FACT

The seeming intractability of resolving the conflicting claims to Jerusalem has led some people to resurrect the idea of internationaliz-

Map 26 Divided Jerusalem, 1948–1967

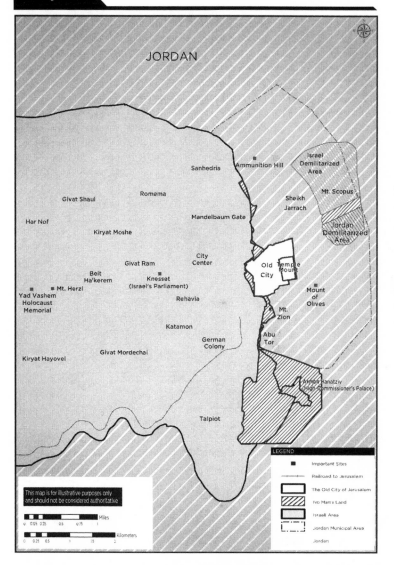

JORDAN

Sanhedria

Ammunition Hill

Israel
Demilitarized
Area

Mt. Scopus

Romema

Givat Shaul

Sheikh
Jarrach

Jordan
Demilitarized
Area

Har Nof

Mandelbaum Gate

Kiryat Moshe

City
Center

Givat Ram

Old
City

Temple
Mount

Beit
Ha'kerem

Knesset
(Israel's Parliament)

Mount
of
Olives

Yad Vashem
Holocaust
Memorial

Mt. Herzl

Rehavia

Mt.
Zion

Katamon

Abu
Tor

German
Colony

Kiryat Hayovel

Givat Mordechai

Armon Hanatziv
(High-Commissioner's Palace)

Talpiot

LEGEND

■ Important Sites

Railroad to Jerusalem

The Old City of Jerusalem

No Man's Land

Israeli Area

Jordan Municipal Area

Jordan

This map is for illustrative purposes only
and should not be considered authoritative

Miles
0   0.125 0.25   0.5   0.75   1

Kilometers
0   0.25   0.5   1   1.5   2

ing the city. Curiously, the idea had little support during the nineteen years Jordan controlled the Old City and barred Jews and Israeli Muslims from their holy sites.

The fact that Jerusalem is disputed, or that it is of importance to people other than Israeli Jews, does not mean the city belongs to others or should be ruled by some international regime. There is no precedent for such a setup. The closest thing to an international city was post-war Berlin when the four powers shared control of the city, and that experiment proved to be a disaster.

Even if Israel were amenable to such an idea, what conceivable international group could be entrusted to protect the freedoms Israel already guarantees? Surely not the United Nations, which has shown no understanding of Israeli concerns since partition.

MYTH

While in control of Jerusalem, Jordan ensured freedom of worship for all religions.

FACT

From 1948 to 1967, Jerusalem was divided between Israel and Jordan. Israel made western Jerusalem its capital; Jordan occupied the eastern section. Because Jordan maintained a state of war with Israel, the city became two armed camps, replete with concrete walls and bunkers, barbed-wire fences, minefields and other military fortifications.

Under paragraph eight of the 1949 Armistice Agreement, Jordan and Israel were to establish committees to arrange the resumption of the normal functioning of cultural and humanitarian institutions on Mt. Scopus, use of the cemetery on the Mount of Olives, and free access to holy places and cultural institutions. Jordan violated the agreement, however, and denied Israelis access to the Western Wall and to the cemetery on the Mount of Olives, where Jews have buried their dead for more than twenty-five hundred years.

Under Jordanian rule, "Israeli Christians were subjected to various restrictions during their seasonal pilgrimages to their holy places" in Jerusalem, noted Teddy Kollek. "Only limited numbers were grudgingly permitted to briefly visit the Old City and Bethlehem at Christmas and Easter."[9]

In 1955 and 1964, Jordan passed laws imposing strict government control on Christian schools, including restrictions on the opening of new schools, state control over school finances, the appointment of teachers, and the requirement that the Koran be taught. In 1953 and 1965, Jordan adopted laws abrogating the right of Christian religious and charitable institutions to acquire real estate in Jerusalem.

In 1958, police seized the Armenian Patriarch-elect and deported him from Jordan, paving the way for the election of a patriarch supported by King Hussein's government. Because of these repressive policies, many Christians emigrated from Jerusalem. Their numbers declined from twenty-five thousand in 1949 to fewer than thirteen thousand in June 1967.[10]

These discriminatory laws were abolished by Israel after the city was reunited in 1967.

MYTH

Jordan safeguarded Jewish holy places.

FACT

Jordan desecrated Jewish holy places during its occupation in 1948–67. King Hussein permitted the construction of a road to the Intercontinental Hotel across the Mount of Olives cemetery. Hundreds of Jewish graves were destroyed by a highway that could have easily been built elsewhere. The gravestones, honoring the memory of rabbis and sages, were used by the engineer corps of the Jordanian Arab Legion as pavement and latrines in army camps (inscriptions on the stones were still visible when Israel liberated the city).

The ancient Jewish Quarter of the Old City was ravaged, fifty-eight Jerusalem synagogues—some centuries old—were destroyed or ruined, others were turned into stables and chicken coops. Slum dwellings were built abutting the Western Wall.[11]

MYTH

Under Israeli rule, religious freedom has been curbed in Jerusalem.

FACT

After the 1967 War, Israel abolished all the discriminatory laws promulgated by Jordan and adopted its own tough standard for safeguarding access to religious shrines. "Whoever does anything that is likely to violate the freedom of access of the members of the various religions to the places sacred to them," Israeli law stipulates, is "liable to imprisonment for a term of five years." Israel also entrusted administration of the holy places to their respective religious authorities. Thus, for example, the Muslim Waqf has responsibility for the mosques on the Temple Mount.

The State Department notes that Israeli law provides for freedom of worship, and the Government respects this right.[12]

I also respect the fact that Israel allows for a multifaith climate in which every Friday a thousand Muslims pray openly on the Temple Mount in Jerusalem. When I saw that, I had to ask myself, where in the Islamic world can 1,000 Jews get together and pray in full public view?

—Muslim author Irshad Manji[13]

MYTH

Israel denies Muslims and Christians free access to their holy sites.

FACT

Since 1967, hundreds of thousands of Muslims and Christians—many from Arab countries that remain in a state of war with Israel—have come to Jerusalem to see their holy places.

According to Islam, the prophet Muhammad was miraculously transported from Mecca to Jerusalem, and it was from there that he made his ascent to heaven. The Dome of the Rock and Al-Aqsa Mosque, both built in the seventh century, made definitive the identification of Jerusalem as the "Remote Place" that is mentioned in the Koran and, thus a holy place after Mecca and Medina. Muslim rights on the Temple Mount, the site of the two shrines, have not been infringed.

There is only one Jerusalem. From our perspective, Jerusalem is not a subject for compromise. Jerusalem was ours, will be ours, is ours and will remain as such forever.

—Prime Minister Yitzhak Rabin[14]

After reuniting Jerusalem during the Six-Day War, Defense Minister Moshe Dayan permitted the Islamic authority, the Waqf, to continue its civil authority on the Temple Mount even though it is part of the holiest site in Judaism. The Waqf oversees all day-to-day activity there. An Israeli presence is in place at the entrance to the Temple Mount to ensure access for people of all religions.

Arab leaders are free to visit Jerusalem to pray, just as Egyptian president Anwar Sadat did at the Al-Aqsa Mosque in 1977. For security reasons, restrictions are sometimes temporarily imposed on the Temple Mount, but the right to worship has never been abridged, and other mosques remain accessible even in times of high tension.

For Christians, Jerusalem is the place where Jesus lived, preached, died, and was resurrected. While it is the heavenly rather than the earthly Jerusalem that is emphasized by the Church, places mentioned in the New Testament as the sites of Jesus's ministry have drawn pilgrims and devoted worshipers for centuries. Among these sites are the Church of the Holy Sepulcher, the Garden of Gethsemane, the site of the Last Supper, and the Via Dolorosa with the fourteen Stations of the Cross.

The rights of the various Christian churches to custody of the Christian holy places in Jerusalem were defined in the course of the nineteenth century, when Jerusalem was part of the Ottoman Empire. Known as the "status quo arrangement for the Christian holy places in Jerusalem," these rights remained in force during the period of the British Mandate and are still upheld today in Israel.

MYTH

Israel has refused to discuss a compromise on the future of Jerusalem.

FACT

Jerusalem was never the capital of any Arab entity. Palestinians have no special claim to the city; they simply demand it as their capital. Nevertheless, Israel has recognized that the city has a large Palestinian population, that the city is important to Muslims, and that making concessions on the sovereignty of the city might help minimize the conflict with the Palestinians. The Palestinians, however, have shown no reciprocal appreciation for the Jewish majority in the city, the significance of Jerusalem to the Jewish people, or the fact that it is already the nation's capital.

> *Anyone who relinquishes a single inch of Jerusalem is neither an Arab nor a Muslim.*
>
> **—Yasser Arafat**[15]

The Israeli-Palestinian Declaration of Principles (DoP) signed in 1993 left open the status of Jerusalem. Article V said only that Jerusalem is one of the issues to be discussed in the permanent status negotiations.

Most Israelis oppose dividing Jerusalem; still, efforts have been made to find some compromise that could satisfy Palestinian interests. For example, while the Labor Party was in power, deputy foreign minister and Knesset member Yossi Beilin reportedly reached a tentative agreement that would allow the Palestinians to claim the city as their capital without Israel sacrificing sovereignty over its capital. Beilin's idea was to allow the Palestinians to set up their capital in a West Bank suburb of Jerusalem—Abu Dis. The PA subsequently constructed a building for its parliament in the city.

Prime Minister Ehud Barak offered dramatic concessions that would have allowed the Arab neighborhoods of East Jerusalem to become the capital of a Palestinian state, and given the Palestinians control over the Muslim holy places on the Temple Mount. These ideas were discussed at the White House Summit in December 2000, but rejected by Yasser Arafat.

In 2008, Prime Minister Ehud Olmert offered a peace plan that included the partitioning of Jerusalem on a demographic basis. Abbas rejected the offer.

MYTH

Israel has restricted the political rights of Palestinian Arabs in Jerusalem.

FACT

Along with religious freedom, Palestinian Arabs in Jerusalem have unprecedented political rights. Arab residents were given the choice of whether to become Israeli citizens. Most chose to retain their Jordanian citizenship, but, in recent years, increasing numbers have applied for Israeli citizenship.[16] Even if a Palestinian state were created, most Palestinians would choose to live in Israel according to a poll conducted by the Palestinian Center for Public Opinion in June 2015. The poll found that 52 percent of Palestinians living in East Jerusalem would prefer to be citizens of Israel compared with 42 percent who would choose citizenship in a Palestinian state.[17] Regardless of whether they are citizens, Jerusalem Arabs are permitted to vote in municipal elections and play a role in the administration of the city.

I'll urge the Muslims to launch jihad and to use all their capabilities to restore Muslim Palestine and the holy al-Aqsa Mosque from the Zionist usurpers and aggressors. The Muslims must be united in the confrontation of the Jews and those who support them.

—Saudi king Fahd[18]

MYTH

*Under UN Resolution 242, East Jerusalem is
considered "occupied territory."*

FACT

One drafter of the UN Resolution was US ambassador to the UN Arthur Goldberg. According to Goldberg, "Resolution 242 in no way refers to Jerusalem, and this omission was deliberate . . . Jerusalem was a discrete matter, not linked to the West Bank." In several speeches at the UN in 1967, Goldberg said, "I repeatedly stated that the armistice lines of 1948 were intended to be temporary. This, of course, was particularly true of Jerusalem. At no time in these many speeches did I refer to East Jerusalem as occupied territory."[19]

Because Israel was defending itself from aggression in the 1948 and 1967 wars, former president of the International Court of Justice Steven Schwebel wrote, it has a better claim to sovereignty over Jerusalem than its Arab neighbors.[20]

> *The basis of our position remains that Jerusalem must never again be a divided city. We did not approve of the status quo before 1967; in no way do we advocate a return to it now.*
>
> **—President George H. W. Bush[21]**

MYTH

*East Jerusalem should be part of a Palestinian
state because no Jews have ever lived there.*

FACT

Before 1865, the entire population of Jerusalem lived behind the Old City walls (what today would be considered part of the eastern part of the city). Later, the city began to expand beyond the walls because of population growth, and both Jews and Arabs began to build in new areas of the city.

By the time of partition, a thriving Jewish community was living in the eastern part of Jerusalem, an area that included the Jewish Quarter of the Old City. This area of the city also contains many sites of importance to the Jewish religion, including the City of David, the Temple Mount, and the Western Wall. In addition, major institutions such as Hebrew University and the original Hadassah Hospital are on Mount Scopus—in eastern Jerusalem.

The only time that the eastern part of Jerusalem was exclusively Arab was between 1949 and 1967, and that was because Jordan occupied the area and forcibly expelled all the Jews.

MYTH

The United States recognizes Jerusalem as Israel's capital.

FACT

"International law makes states the sole determinants of their own capital."[22] Nevertheless, of the 190 nations with which America has diplomatic relations, Israel is the only one whose capital is not recognized by the US government. The US embassy, like most others, is in Tel Aviv, forty miles from Jerusalem. The United States does maintain a consulate in East Jerusalem, however, that deals with Israeli Jews in Jerusalem and Palestinians in the territories. The office works independent of the embassy, reporting directly to Washington, and the consul general is not accredited to Israel. His residence is in West Jerusalem. A whole set of rules (e.g., not allowing official cars to fly the US flag in the city, and marking the birthplace of Americans born in Jerusalem as Jerusalem rather than Israel) were established to do everything possible to avoid the appearance of US legitimation of Israel's capital. The United States not only refused to locate its embassy in Jerusalem, but also pressured others not to do so.[23]

In 1990, Congress passed a resolution declaring that "Jerusalem is and should remain the capital of the State of Israel" and "must remain an undivided city in which the rights of every ethnic and religious group are protected." During the 1992 presidential campaign, Bill Clinton said, "I recognize Jerusalem as an undivided city, the eternal capital of Israel, and I believe in the principle of moving our embassy to Jerusalem." He never reiterated this view as president; consequently, official US policy remained that the status of Jerusalem is a matter for negotiations.

I would be blind to disclaim the Jewish connection to Jerusalem.

—Sari Nusseibeh, president of Al-Quds University[24]

In an effort to change this policy, Congress overwhelmingly passed The Jerusalem Embassy Act of 1995. This landmark bill declared that, as a statement of official US policy, Jerusalem should be recognized as the undivided, eternal capital of Israel and required that the US embassy in Israel be established in Jerusalem no later than May 1999. The law also included a waiver that allowed the president to essentially ignore the legislation if he deemed doing so to be in the best interest of the United States. President Clinton and all of his successors have exercised that option.

While critics of congressional efforts to force the administration to recognize Jerusalem as Israel's capital insist that such a move would harm the peace process, supporters of the legislation argue the opposite is true. By making clear the United States position that Jerusalem, or at least West Jerusalem, should remain unified under Israeli sovereignty, unrealistic Palestinian expectations regarding the city can be moderated and thereby enhance the prospects for a final agreement.

"There was never a Jewish temple on Al-Aqsa [the mosque compound] and there is no proof that there was ever a temple."

—Former mufti of Jerusalem, Ikrema Sabri[25]

MYTH

The Israeli government wants to destroy the Al-Aqsa Mosque.

FACT

In August 1929, the Mufti of Jerusalem spread rumors of Jews killing Arabs and of a Jewish plot to seize control of Muslim holy places on the Temple Mount in Jerusalem. With a rallying cry to defend the Al-Aqsa Mosque, Arab mobs looted Jewish shops and attacked Jewish men, women, and children throughout the country. By the end of the rioting, 135 Jews (including eight Americans) were killed and more than three hundred wounded.

This was the first time during the British Mandate that religion played a direct role in stoking the conflict in Palestine. It would not be the last, however, as Muslim leaders have found it advantageous to make similar accusations to arouse the local population and the Muslim faithful worldwide.

We all know perfectly well that Al-Aqsa mosque is in no danger. Ironically—I am ashamed to admit it—thanks to the Israel Police, Al-Aqsa is the safest mosque in the Middle East.

—Bassam Tawil[26]

In recent years, the calls to liberate Al-Aqsa from the Jews have become more common. On September 29, 2000, the Voice of Palestine, the Palestinian Authority's official radio station, called on "all Palestinians to come and defend Al-Aqsa mosque." The PA closed its schools and bused Palestinian students to the Temple Mount to participate in premeditated riots that escalated into the Palestinian War—popularly known as the Al-Aqsa Intifada.

It is not surprising that Muslims outside Israel have also used Al-Aqsa as a rallying point. The Muslim Brotherhood's Sheikh Yusuf al-Qaradawi, for example, said "the danger to Al-Aqsa is now greater than ever . . . and hence the Muslims of the world must arise and defend it because it is not the property of the Palestinians alone but of the whole Muslim nation."[27]

One of the most frequent uses of the "Al-Aqsa is in danger libel" occurs when Israel engages in any archaeological activity in Jerusalem. Dating back more than three thousand years, the city has a rich past that was unexplored for centuries. In fact, prior to 1967, few excavations were done in the city. After the Muslim Waqf was given responsibility for the Temple Mount, this policy was continued. The authorities are concerned about damage to the Muslim sites. Given the care taken by archaeologists to protect the area, the more likely objection is the fear that researchers will make discoveries that support existing evidence of the long-standing Jewish association with Jerusalem, which would contradict Muslim propaganda claims denying such a connection.

Due to Muslim objections to archaeological research, we know relatively little about the history of the Temple Mount. Worse, actions by the Waqf have contributed to the destruction of evidence from the past, and, ironically, have created the greatest threat to the stability of the Temple Mount. This was especially true when, in the mid-1990s, the Israeli Islamic Movement began the process of converting an area in the southeastern corner of the mount known as Solomon's Stables (so named because the Crusaders had used the area as stables and believed it was located near Solomon's Temple) into a mosque.

Often the Palestinians will regurgitate the libel even when Israel is engaged in activities outside the Temple Mount and nowhere near the mosques. For example, an Islamic group protested Jewish activities in the nearby village of Silwan because it is "the gateway to Al-Aqsa Mosque." The group also believed that the Jews planned to destroy the mosque and rebuild the Temple.[28]

In 2010, Israel restored the Hurva Synagogue in the Jewish Quarter of the Old City, which had been destroyed in 1948 by the Jordanians. Despite its remote location from the Temple Mount, accusations that the reconstruction was part of a plot against Al-Aqsa provoked two days of rioting.

The greatest international uproar occurred in 1996 when Israel completed digging a tunnel along the entire length of the Western Wall, revealing two-thousand-year-old stones where the street had once been. The entire project was completely outside the Temple Mount and nowhere near the mosques. Nevertheless, the Muslim authorities claimed the Jews were digging under the mount with the intention of destroying the mosques, or at least undermining their foundations. While the work had been going on for some time, the spark that led to widespread rioting and international condemnation was Prime Minister Netanyahu's decision to open an exit from what is now referred to as the Western Wall tunnel, at a point along the Via Dolorosa in the Muslim Quarter of the city. Prior to opening the exit, visitors to the tunnel had to walk from the end back the way they came along a narrow corridor that barely had room for people coming from the other direction to pass. The new exit made it possible to avoid backtracking so thousands more visitors could enjoy the site.

The facts were irrelevant to those looking for a reason to criticize Israel and demonstrate sympathy for the Arabs and Muslims. The Arab League falsely claimed "Israel's aim in opening this gate is to cause the collapse of the Al-Aqsa Mosque, so that it can build the Third Temple in its stead."[29] Palestinians rioted, and attacks on soldiers and civilians resulted in the deaths of fifteen Israeli soldiers and dozens of injuries.

Jews, like other non-Muslims, have been visiting the Temple Mount since 1967, but the Israeli government limits visits by non-Jews to specific times and insists that visitors show sensitivity to Muslims by dressing modestly and refraining from bringing any Jewish sacred objects with them. The Israeli Supreme Court has ruled that Jews may pray at the Temple Mount, but police were given the discretion to prevent any provocative activities. Extremist Jewish groups suspected of plotting against Muslim shrines are either prohibited from the Temple Mount altogether or escorted by police. When plots against the mosque have been uncovered, the schemers have been arrested.

Ignoring Jews' right to visit their holiest place, Palestinians routinely turn to violence under the pretense of defending the mosque. In 2013, tensions escalated when Palestinians began to protest and, in some cases, attack Jews visiting the Temple Mount with stones, bottles, and other projectiles, falsely accusing the pilgrims of desecrating Islam's holy place and planning to build the third temple on the site.

The repetition of the libel rarely has anything to do with the behavior of Jews; it inevitably is used for a political purpose, such as rallying the masses, provoking violence, or diverting attention from some unpopular action taken by Palestinian leaders, such as returning to peace talks before Israel satisfies their preconditions.

Protests based on the libel are not restricted to Jerusalem. Israeli Muslims hold an annual "Al-Aqsa Is in Danger" festival. Thousands of people attended the 2013 rally in Umm al-Fahm, where they heard a vitriolic speech by Sheikh Raed Salah, the former mayor of the Israeli Arab town. "Anyone who gives away one stone from al-Aqsa, or one meter of east Jerusalem, or whoever gives up the right of return or the right to free prisoners," Salah thundered, "is a traitor."[30]

With attention focused on Iran and conflagrations throughout the Middle East, the Palestinians are apparently feeling neglected, which is often a good time to trot out the "Al-Aqsa libel." Predictably, PA minister of religious affairs Sheikh Yusuf Ida'is said on official PA TV on July 8, 2015, "the Israeli establishment insists on carrying out its evil plan to destroy the Al-Aqsa Mosque and establish the alleged Temple."

Months before, Palestinian president Mahmoud Abbas had called for a ban on Jews entering the Temple Mount. "This is our Noble Sanctuary," he said. "They have no right to enter and desecrate it."[31]

MYTH

Muslims treat the Al-Aqsa Mosque with the reverence it deserves.

FACT

Many Muslims, with the approval, and sometimes incitement, of the Waqf and Mahmoud Abbas's Palestinian Authority, have desecrated their own holy places by using them as armories and instigating riots against non-Muslim visitors and the police trying to protect them. "We contaminate our mosques with our own hands and feet, and then blame Jews for desecrating Islamic holy sites," according to Middle East scholar Bassam Tawil. "If anyone is desecrating Islamic holy sites, it is those who bring explosives, stones, and firebombs into Al-Aqsa Mosque. The Jews who visit the Temple Mount do not bring with them stones, bombs, or clubs. It is young Muslim men who are desecrating our holy sites with their 'filthy feet'" (a reference to Abbas's slur against Jews visiting the Temple Mount).[32]

One explanation for Palestinian violence on the Temple Mount is that riots are a proven method for provoking an Israeli reaction with the intent of tarring Israel's reputation. Tawil explains:

> Our leaders, who are fully responsible for sending these teenagers to throw stones and firebombs at Jews, are sitting in their luxurious offices and villas in Ramallah and rubbing their hands with deep satisfaction. Abbas and several Palestinian leaders in the West Bank would like to see our youths rioting on the streets of Jerusalem and in the Temple Mount's Al-Aqsa Mosque compound, so that they can hold Israel responsible for cracking down on "innocent" Palestinians. Their main goal is to embarrass Israel and depict it as a state that takes tough measures against Palestinian teenagers, whose only fault is participation in "popular resistance."

Provoking violence and making specious claims about a threat to the Al-Aqsa Mosque also galvanize the Muslim world against Israel and attract attention to Palestinian political demands. In recent years, the Palestinians have resorted to this libel because their plight has been placed on the back burner as far more urgent problems have arisen in the region since the Arab Spring turned into the Islamic Winter. Iran's nuclear program, the advances of ISIS, the Syrian refugee crisis, the Yemeni civil war, and the unrest in Iraq and Libya have all superseded the formerly all-consuming Palestinian issue.

The tragedy for Islam is that the international community and Muslim leaders do not condemn and prevent the defilement of their holy places by Palestinians who are more interested in using Al-Aqsa as a military fort than a place of prayer.

Notes, Chapter 13

1. *Encounter* (February 1968).
2. John Oesterreicher and Anne Sinai, eds., *Jerusalem* (NY: John Day, 1974), 1; Israel Central Bureau of Statistics; Jerusalem Foundation; Municipality of Jerusalem; *JTA* (May 20, 2009). Totals include those classified as "other."
3. Interview with Dennis Ross, Fox News Sunday (April 21, 2002).
4. Sheik 'Ikrima Sabri, PA-appointed Mufti of Jerusalem, Interviewed by German magazine *Die Welt* (January 17, 2001), [Translation by MEMRI].
5. Leon and Jill Uris, *Jerusalem* (New York: Doubleday and Company, 1981), 13.
6. "A Brief Guide to the Haram al-Sharif, Jerusalem," Supreme Muslim Council, (1925).
7. Teddy Kollek, *Jerusalem* (Washington, DC: Washington Institute for Near East Policy, 1990), 19-20.
8. Sir Eveyln Shuckburgh, *Descent to Suez: Diaries 1951-56* (London, 1986).
9. Kollek, 15.
10. Kollek, 16.
11. Kollek, 15.
12. "International Religious Freedom Report for 2015," released by the Bureau for Democracy, Human Rights, and Labor, US Department of State (Washington, DC, April 13, 2016).
13. Pearl Sheffy Gefen, "Irshad Manji, Muslim Refusenik," *Lifestyles Magazine* (Summer 2004), 29.
14. Jerusalem Day Address to Knesset (May 29, 1995).
15. Voice of Palestine, Algiers (September 2, 1993).
16. Maayan Lubell, "Breaking Taboo, East Jerusalem Palestinians Seek Israeli Citizenship," *Haaretz* (August 5, 2015).
17. David Pollock, "Half of Jerusalem's Palestinians Would Prefer Israeli to Palestinian Citizenship," *Fikra Forum* (August 21, 2015).
18. Saudi Press Agency (July 15, 1986).
19. *New York Times* (March 12, 1980).
20. Stephen M. Schwebel, "What Weight to Conquest?" *American Journal of International Law,* vol. 64, no. 2 (April 1970), 346-47.
21. Letter from President George Bush to Jerusalem Mayor Teddy Kollek (March 13, 1990).
22. Avi Bell, "Flaw in U.S. Policy: Even PLO Recognizes Israel's Right to West Jerusalem," *New York Jewish Week* (June 17, 2015).

23. In 1959, for example, Israel complained that two countries (Liberia was one) moved their embassies from Jerusalem to Tel Aviv in response to US pressure. In 2002, Congress passed a law that said that American citizens who wished to do so could have "Israel" listed as their birthplace on US passports. The State Department, however, refused to do so. The parents of Menachem Binyamin Zivotofsky, an American citizen born in Jerusalem, sued the State Department to force the government to enforce the law. The case went all the way to the Supreme Court, which held that the president has an exclusive power of recognition, and, therefore, Congress may not require the State Department to indicate in passports that Jerusalem is part of Israel. "Dismayed: U.S. Court Refuses to Enforce U.S. Law Granting Jerusalem-Born U.S. Citizens Right to Have 'Israel' Listed on Official Documents," Zionist Organization of America (July 15, 2009); instruction from the Department of State to all diplomatic posts, February 20, 1959, in FRUS, 1958-60, vol. 13, 147; memorandum of conversation, March 9, 1959, in FRUS, 1958-60, vol. 13, 151-52; "Supreme Court Strikes Down 'Born in Jerusalem' Passport Law," Associated Press (June 8, 2015).

24. Etgar Lefkovits, "Nusseibeh: Jews Have Bond with Jerusalem," *Jerusalem Post* (November 12, 2001).

25. Mike Seid, "Western Wall Was Never Part of Temple," *Jerusalem Post* (October 25, 2007).

26. Bassam Tawil, "Muslim Blood and Al-Aqsa," Gatestone Institute (October 31, 2015).

27. Nadav Shragai, "The 'Al-Aqsa Is in Danger' Libel: The History of a Lie," *Jerusalem Center for Public Affairs* [No Date].

28. Rafael Israeli, "From Arab Spring to Islamic Winter" (New Brunswick, NJ: Transaction Publishers, 2013), 291.

29. Shragai, "The 'Al-Aqsa Is in Danger' Libel," 2012, 100-101.

30. Yasser Okbi, "Islamic Movement Leaders Warn of Israeli Plan to Destroy Al-Aqsa Mosque," *Jerusalem Post* (September 20, 2013).

31. "Abbas Suggests Ban on Jews at Jerusalem Holy Site," Associated Press (October 17, 2014).

32. Bassam Tawil, "Palestinians: Why Our Leaders Are Hypocrites and Liars," *Gatestone Institute* (October 4, 2015).

14. US Middle East Policy

The creation of Israel resulted solely from US pressure.
The United States favored Israel over the Arabs in 1948 because of the Jewish lobby.
The United States and Israel have nothing in common.
Most Americans oppose a close US relationship with Israel.
US policy has always been hostile toward the Arabs.
The United States always supports Israel.
The United States has always ensured Israel would have a qualitative military edge over the Arabs.
US aid to the Middle East has always been one-sided in favor of Israel.
Israel doesn't need US military assistance.
US aid subsidizes Israeli defense contractors at the expense of American industry.
Israel has no strategic value to the United States.
The attacks on 9/11 were a consequence of US support for Israel.
The United States has the formula to achieve peace between Israelis and Palestinians.

MYTH

The creation of Israel resulted solely from US pressure.

FACT

When the UN took up the question of Palestine, President Harry Truman explicitly said the United States should not "use threats or improper pressure of any kind on other delegations."[1] Some pressure was nevertheless exerted and the United States played a key role in securing support for the partition resolution. US influence was limited, however, as became clear when American dependents such as Cuba and Greece voted against partition, and El Salvador and Honduras abstained.

Many members of the Truman administration opposed partition, including Defense Secretary James Forrestal, who believed Zionist aims posed a threat to American oil supplies and its strategic position in the region. The joint chiefs of staff worried that the Arabs might align themselves with the Soviets if they were alienated by the West. These internal opponents tried to undermine US support for the establishment of a Jewish state.[2]

Meanwhile, the Soviet Union also supported partition—primarily to evict the British—the first foreign policy issue on which the soon-to-be Cold War rivals agreed.

Although much has been written about the tactics of the supporters of partition, the behavior of the Arab lobby has been largely ignored. Arab states and their supporters were, in fact, actively engaged in arm twisting of their own at the UN trying to scuttle partition.[3]

MYTH

The United States favored Israel over the Arabs in 1948 because of the Jewish lobby.

FACT

Truman supported the Zionist movement because he believed the international community was obligated to fulfill the promise of the Balfour Declaration and because he believed that ameliorating the plight of the Jewish survivors of the Holocaust was the humanitarian thing to do. A sense of his attitude can be gleaned from a remark he made with regard to negotiations as to the boundaries of a Jewish state:

> The whole region waits to be developed, and if it were handled the way we developed the Tennessee River basin, it could support from 20 to 30 million people more. To open the door to this kind of future would indeed be the constructive and humanitarian thing to do, and it would also redeem the pledges that were given at the time of World War I.[4]

The American public supported the president's policy. According to public opinion polls, 65 percent of Americans supported the creation of a Jewish state.[5] This public support was reflected in Congress where a resolution approving the Balfour Declaration was adopted in 1922. In 1944, both national parties called for the restoration of the Jewish Commonwealth, and in 1945, a similar resolution was adopted by Congress.

Rather than giving in to pressure, Truman tended to react negatively to the "Jewish lobby." He complained repeatedly about being pressured and talked about putting propaganda from the Jews in a pile and striking a match to it. In a letter to Rep. Claude Pepper, Truman wrote, "Had it not been for the unwarranted interference of the Zionists, we would have had the matter settled a year and a half ago."[6] This was hardly the attitude of a politician overly concerned with Jewish votes.

MYTH

The United States and Israel have nothing in common.

FACT

The US-Israel relationship is based on the twin pillars of shared values and mutual interests. Given this commonality of interests and beliefs, it should not be surprising that support for Israel is one of the most pronounced and consistent foreign policy values of the American people.

Although Israel is geographically located in a region that is relatively undeveloped and closer to the Third World than to the West, Israel has emerged in less than seventy years as an advanced nation with the characteristics of Western society. This is partially attributable to the fact that a high percentage of the population came from Europe or North America and brought with them Western political and cultural norms. It is also a function of the common Judeo-Christian heritage.

Simultaneously, Israel is a multicultural society with people from more than one hundred nations. Today, nearly half of all Israelis are Eastern or Oriental Jews who trace their origins to the ancient Jewish communities of the Islamic countries of North Africa and the Middle East.

While they live in a region characterized by autocracies, Israelis have a commitment to democracy no less passionate than that of Americans. All citizens of Israel, regardless of race, religion, or sex, are guaranteed equality before the law and full democratic rights. Freedom of speech, assembly, and press are embodied in the country's laws and traditions. Israel's independent judiciary vigorously upholds these rights.

The political system differs from America's—Israel's is a parliamentary democracy—but it is still based on free elections with divergent parties. And though Israel does not have a formal constitution, it has adopted "Basic Laws" that establish similar legal guarantees.

Americans have long viewed Israelis with admiration, at least partly because they see much of themselves in their pioneering spirit and struggle for independence. Like the United States, Israel is a nation of immigrants. Despite the burden of spending nearly 23 percent of its budget on defense, it has had an extraordinary rate of growth for most of its history. It has also succeeded in putting most of the newcomers to work. Some immigrants come from relatively undeveloped societies, such as Ethiopia or Yemen, and arrive with virtually no possessions, education, or training and become productive contributors to Israeli society.

In the beginning, Israel had a mixed economy, combining capitalism with socialism similar to the British model. After experiencing serious economic difficulties, created largely in the aftermath of the 1973 Yom Kippur War by increased oil prices and the need to spend a disproportionate share of its gross national product on defense, Israel gradually adopted reforms that reduced the role of the state and shifted the country closer to the free market system of the United States. America has been a partner in this evolution.

The special relationship is also reflected in a variety of *shared value initiatives*, which cover a broad range of common interests, such as the environment, energy, space, education, occupational safety, and health. More than four hundred American institutions in forty-seven states, the District of Columbia, and Puerto Rico have received funds from binational programs with Israel. Little-known relationships like the Free Trade Agreement, the Co-operative Development Research Program, the Middle East Regional Cooperation Program, and various memoranda of understanding with virtually every US governmental agency demonstrate the depth of the special relationship. Even more important may be the broad ties between Israel and each of the individual fifty states and the District of Columbia.

In the 1980s, attention increasingly focused on one pillar of the relationship—shared interests. The Reagan administration saw the Soviet Union as a threat to American Middle East interests and Israel as a bulwark of democracy in the region. Reagan formally recognized Israel's role through agreements for strategic cooperation. After the end of the Cold War, Israel has continued to play a role in joint efforts to protect American interests, including close cooperation in the war on terror. Strategic cooperation has progressed to the point where a de facto alliance now exists and the United States knows it can count on Israel.

MYTH

Most Americans oppose a close US relationship with Israel.

FACT

Support for Israel is not restricted to the Jewish community. Americans of all ages, races, and religions sympathize with Israel. This support is also nonpartisan, with a majority of Democrats and Republicans consistently favoring Israel by large margins over the Arabs.

The best indication of Americans' attitude toward Israel is found in the response to the most consistently asked question about the Middle East: "In the Middle East situation, are your sympathies more with Israel or with the Arab nations?"

In eighty-seven Gallup polls going back to 1967, Israel has had the support of an average of 48 percent of the American people compared to 12 percent for the Arab states/Palestinians. The results are similar (48 percent to 12 percent, respectively) when all 251 polls asking similar questions are included.

> *The allied nations with the fullest concurrence of our government and people are agreed that in Palestine shall be laid the foundations of a Jewish Commonwealth.*
>
> **—President Woodrow Wilson**[7]

Some people have the misperception that sympathy for Israel was once much higher, but the truth is that before the Gulf War the peak had been 56 percent, reached just after the Six-Day War. In January 1991, sympathy for Israel reached a record high of 64 percent, according to Gallup. Meanwhile, support for the Arabs dropped to 8 percent, and the margin was a record 56 points.

In the February 2016 Gallup Poll, 62 percent of Americans sympathized with Israel, just below 2013's all-time high of 64 percent, while only 15 percent expressed support for the Palestinians. Despite the violence of the preceding years, and a steady stream of negative media coverage, this is six points higher than the level of support Israel enjoyed after the 1967 War, when many people mistakenly believe that Israel was overwhelmingly popular.

In recent years, Gallup has noted that many Americans have moved from "no preference" into the pro-Israel column. In the 46 surveys conducted during President Obama's term by multiple pollsters, support for Israel has soared to an average of 55 percent, continuing an upward trend since the 1980s, while sympathy for the Palestinians has sunk to 12 percent, continuing a downward spiral that also began in the 1980s. On average, in all polls, Israel is favored by more than 4 to 1.

Gallup also takes regular polls on world affairs. Overall, favorable ratings of Israel in February 2016 were 71 percent. By contrast, just 19 percent of Americans had a favorable opinion of the Palestinian Authority.

MYTH

US policy has always been hostile toward the Arabs.

FACT

Arabs rarely acknowledge the American role in helping the Arab states achieve independence. President Wilson's stand for self-determination for all nations, and the US entry into World War I, helped cause the dissolution of the Ottoman Empire and stimulate the move toward independence in the Arab world.

Arab leaders assert that Middle East policy must be a zero-sum game whereby support for their enemy, Israel, necessarily puts them at a disadvantage. Thus, Arab states have tried to force the United States to choose between support for them or Israel. The United States has usually refused to fall into this trap. The fact that the United States has a close alliance with Israel while maintaining good relations with several Arab states is proof the two are not incompatible.

The United States has long sought friendly relations with Arab leaders and has, at one time or another, been on good terms with most Arab states. In the 1930s, the discovery of oil led US companies to become closely involved with the Gulf Arabs. In the 1950s, US strategic objectives stimulated an effort to form an alliance with pro-Western Arab states. Countries such as Iraq and Libya were friends of the United States before radical leaders took over those governments. Egypt, which was hostile toward the United States under Nasser, shifted to the pro-Western camp under Sadat.

Since World War II, the United States has poured economic and military assistance into the region and today is the principal backer of nations such as Jordan, Saudi Arabia, Morocco, Egypt, and the Gulf sheikdoms. Although the Arab states blamed the United States for their defeats in wars they initiated with Israel, the truth is most of the belligerents had either been given or offered American assistance at some time.[8]

MYTH

The United States always supports Israel.

FACT

The United States has been Israel's closest ally throughout its history; nevertheless, the United States has acted against the Jewish State's wishes many times.

The US effort to balance support for Israel with placating the Arabs began in 1948 when President Truman showed signs of wavering on partition and advocating trusteeship. After the surrounding Arab states invaded Israel, the United States maintained an arms embargo that severely restricted the Jews' ability to defend themselves.

In October 1953, the United States halted economic aid to Israel for three weeks to protest an Israeli project on the Jordan River in the demilitarized zone.

Ever since the 1948 War, the United States has been unwilling to insist on projects to resettle Arab refugees. The United States has also been reluctant to challenge Arab violations of the UN Charter and resolutions. Thus, for example, the Arabs were permitted to get away with blockading the Suez Canal, imposing a boycott on Israel, and committing acts of terrorism. In fact, the United States has taken positions against Israel at the UN more often than not and did not use its Security Council veto to block an anti-Israel resolution until 1972.

Perhaps the most dramatic example of American policy diverging from that of Israel's came during the Suez War when President Eisenhower took a strong stand against Britain, France, and Israel. After the war, US pressure forced Israel to withdraw from the territory it conquered. David Ben-Gurion relied on dubious American guarantees that sowed the seeds of the 1967 conflict.

At various other times, American presidents have taken action against Israel. In 1981, for example, Ronald Reagan suspended a strategic cooperation agreement after Israel annexed the Golan Heights. On another occasion, he held up delivery of fighter planes because of unhappiness over an Israeli raid in Lebanon.

In 1991, President Bush held a press conference to ask for a delay in considering Israel's request for loan guarantees to help absorb Soviet and Ethiopian Jews because of his disagreement with Israel's settlement policy. In staking his prestige on the delay, Bush used intemperate language that inflamed passions and provoked concern in the Jewish community that anti-Semitism would be aroused.

Though often described as the most pro-Israel president in history, Bill Clinton also was critical of Israel on numerous occasions. George W. Bush's administration was considered equally sympathetic, but also criticized Israel. During the first year of the Palestinian War, the United States imposed an arms embargo on spare parts for helicopters because of anger over the use of US-made helicopters in targeted killings. The Bush administration also punished Israel for agreeing to sell military equipment to China in 2005.[9]

In his first two years in office, Barack Obama was very critical of Israeli policy and publicly demanded a freeze in settlement construction. A number of other confrontations took place publicly and privately, along with reported threats of punitive measures if Israel did not accede to the president's insistence that settlements be frozen. The two countries also bitterly disagreed on how to stop Iran's nuclear program. As a consequence of his approach to Israel and broader Middle East policy, polls in Israel found unprecedented distrust of the president's commitment to Israel. In one 2016 poll, 63 percent of Israelis rated Obama the worst president for Israel in the last thirty years; Jimmy Carter was a distant second at 16 percent.[10]

MYTH

The United States has always ensured Israel would have a qualitative military edge over the Arabs.

FACT

The United States provided only a limited amount of arms to Israel, including ammunition and recoilless rifles, prior to 1962. In that year, President Kennedy sold Israel HAWK antiaircraft missiles, but only after the Soviet Union provided Egypt with long-range bombers. Two years later, Prime Minister Levi Eshkol and President Lyndon Johnson negotiated a deal for 210 Patton tanks based in Germany to be transferred to Israel after being upgraded in Italy.

By 1965, the United States had become Israel's main arms supplier. This was partially necessitated by West Germany's acquiescence to Arab pressure, which led Germany to stop selling tanks to Israel. Throughout most of the Johnson administration, however, the sale of arms to Israel was balanced by corresponding transfers to the Arabs. Thus, the first US tank sale to Israel, in 1965, was offset by a similar sale to Jordan.[11]

The United States did not provide Israel with aircraft until 1966. Even then, secret agreements were made to provide the same planes to Morocco and Libya, and additional military equipment was sent to Lebanon, Saudi Arabia, and Tunisia.[12]

As in 1948, the United States imposed an arms embargo on Israel during the Six-Day War, while the Arabs continued to receive Soviet arms. Israel's position was further undermined by the French decision to embargo arms transfers to the Jewish State, effectively ending their role as Israel's only other major supplier.

It was only after it became clear that Israel had no other sources of arms and that the Soviet Union had no interest in limiting its sales to the region that President Johnson agreed to sell Israel Phantom jets that gave the Jewish State its first qualitative advantage. "We will henceforth become the principal arms supplier to Israel," Assistant Secretary of Defense Paul Warnke told Israeli ambassador Yitzhak Rabin, "involving us even more intimately with Israel's security situation and involving more directly the security of the United States."[13]

From that point on, the United States began to pursue a policy whereby Israel's qualitative edge was maintained. The United States has also remained committed, however, to arming Arab nations, providing sophisticated missiles, tanks, and aircraft to Jordan, Morocco, Egypt, Saudi Arabia, and the Gulf states. Thus, when Israel received F-15s in 1978, so did Saudi Arabia (and Egypt received F-5Es). In 1981, Saudi Arabia, for the first time, received a weapons system that gave it a qualitative advantage over Israel—AWACS radar planes.

Today, Israel buys near top-of-the-line US equipment, but many

Arab states also receive some of America's best tanks, planes, and missiles. In addition to the quality of US weapons sold to Arab states, the quantity also endangers Israel. In 2010, for example, President Obama agreed to the largest arms sale in US history, a $60 billion transaction with Saudi Arabia. The qualitative edge may be intact, but it is undoubtedly narrow.

Our society is illuminated by the spiritual insights of the Hebrew prophets. America and Israel have a common love of human freedom, and they have a common faith in a democratic way of life.

—President Lyndon Johnson[14]

MYTH

US aid to the Middle East has always been one-sided in favor of Israel.

FACT

After Israel's victory in its War of Independence, the United States responded to an appeal for economic aid to help absorb immigrants by approving a $135 million Export-Import Bank loan and the sale of surplus commodities. In those early years of Israel's statehood (also today), US aid was seen as a means of promoting peace.

In 1951, Congress voted to help Israel cope with the economic burdens imposed by the influx of Jewish refugees from the displaced persons camps in Europe and from the ghettos of the Arab countries. Arabs then complained that the United States was neglecting them, though they had no interest in or use for American aid. In 1951, Syria rejected offers of US aid. Oil-rich Iraq and Saudi Arabia did not need US economic assistance (yet the Saudis did get aid and continue to get assistance), and Jordan was, until the late 1950s, the ward of Great Britain. After 1957, when the United States assumed responsibility for supporting Jordan and resumed economic aid to Egypt, assistance to the Arab states soared. Additionally, the United States was by far the biggest contributor of aid to the Palestinians through UNRWA, a status that continues to the present day.

Prior to 1971, Israel received a total of only $277 million in military aid, all in the form of loans. The bulk of the economic aid was also lent to Israel. By comparison, the Arab states received nearly three times as much aid before 1971, $4.4 billion, or $170 million per year. Moreover, unlike Israel, which receives nearly all its aid from the United States, Arab nations have gotten assistance from Asia, Eastern Europe, the Soviet Union, and the European Community.

Israel did not begin to receive large amounts of assistance until 1974, following the 1973 War, and the sums increased dramatically after the Camp David agreements. Altogether, since 1949, Israel has received more than $120 billion in assistance. In 1998, Israel offered to voluntarily reduce its dependence on US aid, and economic assistance was phased out over the next ten years. Israel subsequently signed a new ten-year deal for $30 billion in military assistance and, in 2016, a new ten-year agreement was signed worth $38 billion.

Arab states that have signed agreements with Israel have also been rewarded. Since signing the peace treaty with Israel, Egypt has been the second largest recipient of US foreign aid ($1.5 billion annually, mostly military aid, compared to Israel's $3.1 billion). Jordan has also been the beneficiary of higher levels of aid since it signed a treaty with Israel (increasing from less than $40 million to nearly $1.2 billion in 2015, roughly two-thirds is economic aid). The multibillion dollar debts to the United States of both Arab nations were also forgiven.

It is my responsibility to see that our policy in Israel fits in with our policy throughout the world; second, it is my desire to help build in Palestine a strong, prosperous, free and independent democratic state. It must be large enough, free enough, and strong enough to make its people self-supporting and secure.

—President Harry Truman[15]

After the Oslo agreements, the United States also began providing aid to the Palestinians. Since the mid-1990s, the Palestinians, among the largest per capita recipients of foreign aid worldwide, have received more than $5 billion in US economic assistance. Aid to the Palestinians has grown from an approximate annual average of $70 million between 1994 and 1999 to $170 million between 2000 and 2007. Additionally, since 2008, the average has jumped to roughly $400 million.[16] More than 60 percent of the PA's GNP comes from US, European Union, UN, and World Bank funds. In 2013, the Palestinians received $793 million in international aid or $176 for each Palestinian, by far the highest per capita assistance in the world.[17]

MYTH

Israel doesn't need US military assistance.

FACT

Israel has peace treaties with only two of its neighbors, and the fragility of those agreements came into focus during the "Arab spring" of

2011. The brief reign of the radical Islamic Muslim Brotherhood following the ouster of President Hosni Mubarak posed a threat to the treaty. The takeover of the government by the Egyptian military has, for the time being, actually resulted in a significant improvement in Egyptian-Israeli ties.

Meanwhile, the civil war in Syria threatens to spill over into Israel, and it is unclear who will emerge victorious—Bashar Assad, who kept the peace with Israel—or one of the radical Muslim factions, such as ISIS, fighting to seize control of the country. A radical Islamic government on Israel's border would be a serious threat.

Iran continues to support Hezbollah and can be expected to enhance its capabilities with the financial windfall it receives from the nuclear agreement signed in 2015. As it is, Hezbollah has more than one hundred thousand rockets aimed at Israel.

Despite the nuclear deal, Iran is viewed as a serious danger to Israel. Iran continues to threaten Israel with destruction, and many Israelis fear the nuclear agreement is so flawed that it will not prevent the Iranians from acquiring the capability to carry out their threats.

Today, Israel is primarily concerned with radical Muslims rather than the conventional armies of the Arab states. Nevertheless, Israel must prepare for the worst. It is still conceivable that former enemies will band together, as they have in the past, to endanger its security. Israel must rely, therefore, on its qualitative advantage to ensure it can defeat its enemies, and that can only be guaranteed by the continued purchase of the latest weapons. New tanks, missiles, and planes carry high price tags, however, and Israel cannot afford what it needs on its own, so continued aid from the United States is vital to its security. Furthermore, Israel's enemies have numerous suppliers, but Israel must rely almost entirely on the United States for its hardware.

MYTH

US aid subsidizes Israeli defense contractors at the expense of American industry.

FACT

Contrary to popular wisdom, the United States does not simply write billion-dollar checks and hand them over to Israel to spend as they like. Only about 25 percent of what Israel receives in Foreign Military Financing (FMF) can be spent in Israel for military procurement. The remaining 75 percent is spent in the United States where it generates profits and jobs for Americans. More than one thousand companies in forty-seven states, the District of Columbia, and Puerto Rico have signed contracts worth billions of dollars through this program over the last several years. The figures for the 42 states receiving FMF orders in 2015 are below:

Foreign Military Financing (FMF) Orders by State (2015)[18]

State	Amount	State	Amount
Alabama	$999,546	Mississippi	$98,875
Arkansas	$127,512	Montana	$17,322,802
Arizona	$2,149,206	North Dakota	$44,500
California	$109,994,611	Nebraska	$92,130
Colorado	$18,208,651	Nevada	$954,592
Connecticut	$25,812,009	New Hampshire	$42,503,534
Florida	$66,906,218	New Jersey	$766,500
Georgia	$46,232,283	New Mexico	$74,353,090
Idaho	$1,567,755	New York	$745,883,001
Iowa	$120,530,835	Ohio	$1,065,544
Illinois	$946,762	Oklahoma	$1,207,220
Indiana	$287,027	Oregon	$72,945,751
Kansas	$16,953,641	Pennsylvania	$683,470
Kentucky	$31,428	Rhode Island	$2,784,665
Louisiana	$1,437,152	South Dakota	$1,666,984
Maine	$10,049,549	Tennessee	$177,564,805
Massachusetts	$29,104,199	Texas	$1,820,319
Maryland	$11,943,982	Utah	$6,638,825
Michigan	$13,274,871	Virginia	$3,412,450
Minnesota	$1,122,150	Vermont	$3,783,725
Missouri	$752,814	West Virginia	$15,032,129
Mississippi	$98,875		

According to the terms of the new ten-year aid deal, Israel will have to spend all of the money in the United States.

MYTH

Israel has no strategic value to the United States.

FACT

In 1952, Gen. Omar Bradley, head of the joint chiefs of staff, believed the West required nineteen divisions to defend the Middle East and that Israel could supply two. He also expected only three states to provide the West air power in Middle Eastern defense by 1955: Great Britain, Turkey, and Israel. Bradley's analysis was rejected because the political echelon decided it was more important for the United States to work with Egypt and later Iraq. It was feared that integration of Israeli forces in Western strategy would alienate the Arabs.[19]

After trying unsuccessfully to build an alliance with Arab states, the National Security Council Planning Board concluded in 1958 that "if we choose to combat radical Arab nationalism and to hold Persian Gulf oil by force if necessary, then a logical corollary would be to support Israel as the only pro-West power left in the Near East."[20]

Israel's crushing victory over the combined Arab forces in 1967 reinforced this view. The following year, the United States sold Israel sophisticated planes (Phantom jets) for the first time, and Washington shifted its Middle East policy from seeking a balance of forces to ensuring that Israel enjoyed a qualitative edge over its enemies.

Israel proved its value in 1970 when the United States asked for help in bolstering King Hussein's regime. Israel's willingness to aid Amman, and movement of troops to the Jordanian border, persuaded Syria to withdraw the tanks it had sent into Jordan to support PLO forces challenging the king during "Black September."[21]

By the early 1970s it was clear that no Arab state could or would contribute to Western defense in the Middle East. The Baghdad Pact had long ago expired, and the regimes friendly to the United States were weak compared to the anti-Western forces in Egypt, Syria, and Iraq. Even after Egypt's reorientation following the signing of its peace treaty with Israel, the United States did not count on any Arab governments for military assistance.

The Carter administration began to implement a form of strategic cooperation (it was not referred to as such) by making Israel eligible to sell military equipment to the United States. The willingness to engage in limited, joint military endeavors was viewed by President Carter as a means of rewarding Israel for "good behavior" in peace talks with Egypt.

Though still reluctant to formalize the relationship, strategic cooperation became a major focus of the US-Israel relationship when Ronald Reagan entered office. Before his election, Reagan had written, "Only by full appreciation of the critical role the State of Israel plays in our strategic calculus can we build the foundation for thwarting Moscow's designs on territories and resources vital to our security and our national well-being."[22]

Reagan's view culminated in the November 30, 1981, signing of a Memorandum of Understanding on "strategic cooperation." On November 29, 1983, a new agreement was signed creating the Joint

Political-Military Group (JPMG) and a group to oversee security assistance, the Joint Security Assistance Planning Group (JSAP).

In 1987, Congress designated Israel as a major non-NATO ally. This law formally established Israel as an ally, and allowed its industries to compete equally with NATO countries and other close US allies for contracts to produce a significant number of defense items.

> *Since the rebirth of the State of Israel, there has been an ironclad bond between that democracy and this one.*
>
> **—President Ronald Reagan**[23]

By the end of President Reagan's term, the United States had prepositioned equipment in Israel, regularly held joint training exercises, began codevelopment of the Arrow Anti-Tactical Ballistic Missile, and was engaged in a host of other cooperative military endeavors. In April 1988, Reagan signed another MOU encompassing all prior agreements. This agreement institutionalized the strategic relationship.

US-Israel strategic cooperation has continued to evolve. Israel now regularly engages in joint training exercises with US forces, and in 2005, for the first time, also trained and exercised with NATO forces.

Israeli-developed weapons systems and enhancements are also often adopted by the United States. These include a common laser range finder to assist marines in concealed positions with imaging, range finding, and navigation through combat areas; the Iron Fist Light Configuration active protection system for armored personnel carriers; and Reactive Armor Tiles that protect tanks and the soldiers within them. One of the most recent examples of Israel sharing its technology involves detection equipment to identify tunnels. Israel faces a threat from tunnels dug by Hamas terrorists seeking to infiltrate Israel from the Gaza Strip. The United States is interested in testing the Israeli tunnel-detection system along the US border with Mexico.[24]

In 2007, the United States and Israel signed a new MOU formalizing cooperation in the area of homeland security. Even before that, Israel routinely hosted US law enforcement officers and first responders to share knowledge about prevention of terror attacks and response to emergencies.

Today, strategic ties are stronger than ever and Israel has become a de facto ally of the United States. America purchases innovative and advanced Israeli weapons systems, works together with Israeli companies on missile defense, and shares intelligence. In fact, National Intelligence director James Clapper said in 2015 that intelligence cooperation "was better than at any other time during his 30-year career."[25]

Most important, Israel remains America's only reliable democratic ally in the region.

MYTH

The attacks on 9/11 were a consequence of US support for Israel.

FACT

The heinous attacks against the United States were committed by Muslim fanatics who had a variety of motivations for these and other terrorist attacks. These Muslims have a perverted interpretation of Islam and believe they must attack infidels, particularly Americans and Jews, who do not share their beliefs. They oppose Western culture and democracy and object to any US presence in Muslim nations. They are particularly angered by the existence of American military bases in Saudi Arabia and other areas of the Persian Gulf. This would be true regardless of US policy toward the Israeli-Palestinian conflict. Previous attacks on American targets, such as the USS *Cole* in 2000, and US embassies in Kenya and Tanzania in 1998, were perpetrated by suicide bombers whose anger at the United States was unrelated to Israel.

> *Osama bin Laden made his explosions and then started talking about the Palestinians. He never talked about them before.*
>
> **—Egyptian president Hosni Mubarak**[26]

Osama bin Laden claimed he was acting on behalf of the Palestinians, and that his anger toward the United States was shaped by American support for Israel. This was a new invention by bin Laden clearly intended to attract support from the Arab public and justify his terrorist acts. Bin Laden's antipathy toward the United States was never related to the Arab-Israeli conflict. Though many Arabs were fooled by bin Laden's transparent effort to drag Israel into his war, Dr. Abd al-Hamid al-Ansari, dean of Shar'ia and Law at Qatar University was critical, saying, "In their hypocrisy, many of the [Arab] intellectuals linked September 11 with the Palestinian problem—something that completely contradicts seven years of Al-Qaida literature. Al-Qaida never linked anything to Palestine."[27]

Even Yasser Arafat told the *Sunday Times* of London that bin Laden should stop hiding behind the Palestinian cause. "He never helped us. He was working in another completely different area and against our interests," Arafat said.[28]

MYTH

The United States has the formula to achieve peace between Israelis and Palestinians.

FACT

The European Union, Russia, and the UN all have pursued largely one-sided policies in the Middle East that are detrimental to Israel, which has disqualified them as honest brokers. The United States is the only country that has the trust of both the Israelis and the Arabs and is therefore the only third party that can play a constructive role in the peace process. Historically, however, American peace initiatives always fail.

In his first term, President Barack Obama's initiatives resulted in a loss of Arab and Israeli confidence in the United States and enabled Palestinian president Mahmoud Abbas to avoid negotiations. When John Kerry replaced Hillary Clinton in Obama's second term, the new secretary of state valiantly tried to revive the peace process. Israel repeatedly offered compromises and released dozens of convicted terrorists as a goodwill gesture that was met with more demands from Abbas. Kerry arbitrarily set a nine-month deadline for achieving an agreement, but as in all prior cases, trying to put a time constraint on the parties proved fruitless, and the deadline passed without any agreement.

Obama's effort failed because Kerry could not lure Abbas to the bargaining table or convince him to compromise on the Palestinians' long-standing irredentist positions. By the end of November 2015, Obama sounded prepared to give up trying for a deal for the remainder of his presidency, and his aides admitted a peace agreement was "not in the cards."[29]

Obama is just the latest president to fall short of his ambition to bring peace to the Middle East.

The Eisenhower administration tried to ease tensions by proposing the joint Arab-Israeli use of the Jordan River. The plan would have helped the Arab refugees by producing more irrigated land and would have reduced Israel's need for more water resources. Israel cautiously accepted the plan; the Arab League rejected it.

President Johnson outlined five principles for peace. "The first and greatest principle," Johnson said, "is that every nation in the area has a fundamental right to live and to have this right respected by its neighbors." The Arab response came a few weeks later: "no peace with Israel, no recognition of Israel, no negotiations with it."

President Nixon's secretary of state, William Rogers, offered a plan that sought to "balance" US policy, but leaned on the Israelis to withdraw to the pre-1967 borders, to accept many Palestinian refugees, and to allow Jordan a role in Jerusalem. The plan was totally unacceptable to Israel and, even though it tilted toward the Arab position, was rejected by the Arabs as well.

President Ford's secretary of state, Henry Kissinger, had a little more success in his shuttle diplomacy, arranging the disengagement of forces after the 1973 War. He never put forward a peace plan, however, and failed to move the parties beyond the cessation of hostilities to normalization.

Jimmy Carter was the model for presidential engagement in the conflict. He wanted an international conference at Geneva to produce a comprehensive peace. While Carter spun his wheels trying to organize a conference, Egyptian president Anwar Sadat decided to bypass the Americans and go directly to the Israeli people and address the Knesset. Despite revisionist history by Carter's former advisers, the Israeli-Egyptian peace agreement was negotiated largely *despite* Carter. Menachem Begin and Sadat had carried on secret contacts long before Camp David and had reached the basis for an agreement before Carter's intervention. Carter's mediation helped seal the treaty, but Sadat's decision to go to Jerusalem was stimulated largely by his conviction that Carter's policies were misguided.

The United States was the first country to recognize Israel in 1948, minutes after its declaration of independence, and the deep bonds of friendship between the U.S. and Israel remain as strong and as unshakeable as ever.

—President Barack Obama[30]

In 1982, President Reagan announced a surprise peace initiative that called for allowing the Palestinians self-rule in the territories in association with Jordan. The plan rejected both Israeli annexation and the creation of a Palestinian state. Israel denounced the plan as endangering Israeli security. The plan had been formulated largely to pacify the Arab states, which had been angered by the expulsion of the PLO from Beirut, but they also rejected the Reagan Plan.

George Bush's administration succeeded in convening a historic regional conference in Madrid in 1991, but it ended without any agreements, and the multilateral tracks that were supposed to settle some of the more contentious issues rarely met and failed to resolve anything. Moreover, Bush's perceived hostility toward Israel eroded trust and made it difficult to convince Israelis to take risks for peace.

President Clinton barely had time to get his vision of peace together when he discovered the Israelis had secretly negotiated an agreement with the Palestinians in Oslo. The United States had nothing to do with the breakthrough at Oslo and very little influence on the immediate aftermath. In fact, the peace process became increasingly muddled as the United States got more involved.

Peace with Jordan also required no real American involvement. The Israelis and Jordanians already agreed on the main terms of peace, and the main obstacle had been King Hussein's unwillingness to sign a treaty before Israel had reached an agreement with the Palestinians. After Oslo, he felt safe to move forward, and no American plan was needed.

In a last-ditch effort to save his presidential legacy, Clinton put forward a peace plan to establish a Palestinian state. In this case, it was Prime Minister Ehud Barak's willingness to offer dramatic concessions that raised the prospects for an agreement rather than the president's initiative. Even after Barak agreed to Clinton's "parameters" that would have created a Palestinian state in virtually all the West Bank and Gaza, and to make East Jerusalem their capital, the Palestinians rejected the deal.

President George W. Bush also offered a plan, but it was undercut by Yasser Arafat, who obstructed the required reforms of the Palestinian Authority and refused to dismantle the terrorist infrastructure and stop the violence. Bush's plan morphed into the Road Map, which drew the support of Great Britain, France, Russia, and the United Nations but was never implemented because of continuing Palestinian violence.

The peace process only began to move again when Prime Minister Ariel Sharon made his disengagement proposal, a unilateral approach the State Department had long opposed. Rather than try to capitalize on the momentum created by Israel's evacuation of the Gaza Strip, however, the Bush administration remained wedded to the Road Map that led nowhere.

The United States can play a valuable role as a mediator, but the parties themselves must resolve their differences. History has shown that Middle East peace is not made in America. The obstacle to peace is not the absence of an American framework, a lack of US commitment, or the failure to sufficiently pressure Israel. In fact, the impediments have not changed since the first two-state solution was proposed in 1937; namely, the unwillingness of the Palestinians to agree to live in peace in their own state beside a Jewish state, and the refusal of radical Muslims to contemplate Jews ruling over Muslims or Islamic land.

Notes, Chapter 14

1. *Foreign Relations of the United States, 1947* (DC: GPO, 1948), 1173-74, 1198-99, 1248, 1284 [Henceforth FRUS 1947].

2. Mitchell Bard, *The Water's Edge and Beyond* (New Brunswick, NJ: Transaction Publishers, 1991), 132.

3. FRUS 1947, 1313; see also, Mitchell Bard, *The Arab Lobby: The Invisible Alliance That Undermines America's Interest in the Middle East* (NY: HarperCollins, 2010), 17-36.

4. Harry Truman, *Years of Trial and Hope,* Vol. 2, (NY: Doubleday, 1956), 156.

5. John Snetsinger, *Truman, the Jewish Vote, and the Creation of Israel* (Palo Alto, CA: Hoover Institution Press, 1974), 9-10; David Schoenbaum, "The United States and the Birth of Israel," *Wiener Library Bulletin* (1978), 144n.

6. Michael Cohen, *Truman and Israel* (Berkeley, CA: University of California Press, 1990), 157.

7. Mitchell Bard, "U.S.-Israel Relations: Looking to the Year 2000," AIPAC Papers on US-Israeli Relations (1991), 3.

8. See Bard, *The Arab Lobby,* 41-65.

9. Nathan Guttman, "US Stopped Parts Sales during Intifada," *Jerusalem Post* (September 22, 2005); Ze'ev Schiff, "U.S. Sanctions Still in Place, Despite Deal over Security Exports," *Haaretz* (August 28, 2005).

10. Shmuel Rosner, "How Bad Do Israelis Think Obama Is? As Bad as a US President Can Get," *Jewish Journal* (April 28, 2015).

11. Telegram from the Embassy in Israel to the Department of State (February 25, 1965); Memorandum of conversation between Ambassador Avraham Harman and W. Averill Harriman, ambassador-at-large (March 15, 1965), LBJ Library; Yitzhak Rabin, *The Rabin Memoirs* (Boston, MA: Little, Brown, and Co., 1979), 65-66.

12. Robert Trice, "Domestic Political Interests and American Policy in the Middle East: Pro-Israel, Pro-Arab, and Corporate Non-Governmental Actors and the Making of American Foreign Policy, 1966-1971" (Unpublished PhD Dissertation, University of Wisconsin-Madison, 1974), 226-230.

13. *Foreign Relations of the United States, 1964-1968, Vol. xx,* "Arab-Israeli Dispute 1967-8," Document 306, (Washington, DC: GPO, 1969), 605.

14. "Remarks at the 125th Anniversary Meeting of B'nai B'rith, September 10, 1968," Public Papers of the Presidents of the USA—Lyndon Johnson" (Washington, DC: GPO, 1970), 947.

15. "Address in Madison Square Garden, New York City (October 28, 1948), Public Papers of the President Harry Truman, 1945-1953," *Truman Library,* #262.

16. Jim Zanotti, "U.S. Foreign Aid to the Palestinians," (Washington, DC: Congressional Research Service, March 18, 2016).

17. Tzipi Hotovely, "Where Does All That Aid for Palestinians Go?" *Wall Street Journal* (January 24, 2016).

18. Israeli Ministry of Defense.

19. Dore Gold, *America, the Gulf, and Israel* (Boulder, CO: Westview Press, 1988), 84.

20. "Issues Arising out of the Situation in the Near East" (July 29, 1958), Foreign Relations of the United States, 1958-1960, Vol. XII ("Near East Region; Iraq; Iran; Arabian Peninsula"), (Washington, DC: US Government Printing Office, 1993), 114-124, at 119.

21. Yitzhak Rabin, address to conference on "Strategy and Defense in the Eastern Mediterranean," sponsored by the Washington Institute for Near East Policy and Israel Military Correspondents Association, Jerusalem (July 9-11, 1986).

22. Reagan Address to B'nai B'rith, cited in Mitchell Bard, "U.S.-Israel Relations: Looking to the Year 2000," AIPAC Papers on US-Israel Relations, 6.

23. Ibid.

24. "Israel Shares Anti-Tunnel Tech with U.S.," Middle East Newsline (May 5, 2016).

25. "U.S.-Israel Intel Ties Better Than Ever," Middle East Newsline (November 6, 2015).

26. "We'll Clap Our Hands," *Newsweek* (October 28, 2001).

27. *Al-Raya* (Qatar), (January 6, 2002) cited in "Special Dispatch #337," MEMRI (January 29, 2002).
28. Ian Fisher, "Arafat Disavows bin Laden, Saying 'He Never Helped Us,'" *New York Times* (December 16, 2002).
29. Laura Rozen, "White House Says Israel-Palestine Peace 'Not in the Cards' for Obama," *Al-Monitor* (November 6, 2015).
30. President Barrack Obama, Statement on the 61st Anniversary of Israel's Independence, The White House (Washington, DC, April 28, 2009).

15. The Peace Process

Anwar Sadat deserves all the credit for the Egyptian-Israeli peace treaty.
Solving the Palestinian question will bring peace to the Middle East.
A Palestinian state will pose no danger to Israel.
Jews will be welcome in a future Palestinian state.
If Israel ends the occupation, there will be peace.
The Palestinians have never been offered a state of their own.
Barak's proposals did not offer the Palestinians a viable state.
The Palestinians are asked to accept only 22 percent of Palestine.
Israel should be replaced by a binational state.
The Palestinian education system promotes peace with Israel.
Palestinians no longer object to the creation of Israel.
The Palestinians have given up their dream of destroying Israel.
Palestinians are justified in using violence to achieve their national aspirations.
Palestinians never fabricate stories about Israeli atrocities.
Israel's refusal to withdraw from the Golan Heights prevents peace with Syria.
Israel's occupation of Lebanese territory is the impediment to peace with Lebanon.
Israel's refusal to share water with its neighbors could provoke the next war.
The Arab peace initiative reflects Arab acceptance of Israel and the best hope for peace.
Palestinians would prefer to live in a Palestinian state.
Mahmoud Abbas is a moderate interested in compromise.
Palestinians are driven to terror by poverty and desperation.
Israel must negotiate with Hamas.
The Palestinian Authority believes in a secular Palestinian state.
Netanyahu backtracked on Rabin's positions regarding peace with the Palestinians.
The Palestinians' top priority is peace with Israel.
The Palestinians have recognized Israel as the state of the Jewish people.

MYTH

Anwar Sadat deserves all the credit for the Egyptian-Israeli peace treaty.

FACT

The peace drive did not begin with President Anwar Sadat's November 1977 visit to Jerusalem. Sadat's visit was unquestionably a courageous act of statesmanship, but it came only after more than a half century of efforts by Zionist and Israeli leaders to negotiate peace with the Arabs.

"For Israel to equal the drama," said Simcha Dinitz, former Israeli ambassador to the United States, "we would have had to declare war on Egypt, maintain belligerent relations for years, refuse to talk to them, call for their annihilation, suggest throwing them into the sea, conduct military operations and terrorism against them, declare economic boycotts, close the Strait of Tiran to their ships, close the Suez Canal to their traffic, and say they are outcasts of humanity. Then Mr. Begin would go to Cairo, and his trip would be equally dramatic. Obviously, we could not do this, because it has been our policy to negotiate all along."[1]

Nonetheless, Israeli prime minister Menachem Begin proved that, like Sadat, he was willing to go the extra mile to achieve peace. Despite the Carter administration's tilt toward Egypt during the talks, Begin remained determined to continue the peace process and froze Israeli settlements in the West Bank to facilitate the progress of negotiations.

In the end, Israel made tangible concessions to Egypt in exchange for only promises. Begin agreed to cede the strategically critical Sinai Peninsula—91 percent of the territory won by Israel during the Six-Day War—back to Egypt in exchange for Sadat's pledge to make peace.

In giving up the Sinai, Israel also lost electronic early-warning stations that provided intelligence on Egyptian military movements on the western side of the Suez Canal, as well as the areas near the Gulf of Suez and the Gulf of Eilat, which were vital to defending against an attack from the east. Additionally, Israel relocated more than 170 military installations, airfields, and army bases after it withdrew.

The withdrawal may have also cost Israel its only chance to become energy independent. The Alma oil field in the southern Sinai, discovered and developed by Israel, was transferred to Egypt in November 1979. When Israel gave up this field, it had become the country's largest single source of energy, supplying half the country's energy needs.

Israel also relinquished direct control of its shipping lanes to and from Eilat, as well as one thousand miles of roadways, homes, factories, hotels, health facilities, and agricultural villages. In addition, Egypt insisted that Jewish civilians leave the Sinai, uprooting seven thousand Israelis from their homes and businesses.

In 1988, Israel relinquished Taba—a resort town built by Israel in what had been a barren desert area near Eilat—to Egypt. Taba's status had not been resolved by the Camp David Accords. When an international arbitration panel ruled in Cairo's favor on September 29, 1988, Israel turned the town over to Egypt.

Sadat made a courageous decision to make peace with Israel, but

Begin's decision was no less bold, and the Israeli sacrifices far more substantial than those of the Egyptians.

The state of Israel wants to give the Palestinians what no one else has heretofore given them—the possibility of establishing a state. Neither the Turks, the English, the Egyptians or the Jordanians gave them such a possibility.

—Prime Minister Ariel Sharon[2]

MYTH

Solving the Palestinian question will bring peace to the Middle East.

FACT

The Palestinian question is the result rather than the cause of the Arab-Israeli conflict and stems from the Arabs' unwillingness to accept a Jewish State in the Middle East.

Had Arab governments not gone to war in 1948 to block the UN partition plan, a Palestinian state would now be celebrating more than sixty years of independence. Had the Arab states not supported terrorism directed at Israeli civilians and provoked seven subsequent Arab-Israeli wars, the conflict could have been settled long ago and the Palestinian problem resolved.

From 1948 to 1967, the West Bank and Gaza were under Arab rule, and no Jewish settlements existed there, but the Arabs never set up a Palestinian state. Instead, Gaza was occupied by Egypt, and the West Bank by Jordan. No demands for a West Bank/Gaza independent state were heard until Israel took control of these areas in the Six-Day War.

Meanwhile, the Palestinian problem is but one of many simmering ethnic, religious, and nationalistic feuds plaguing the region. Today, there are civil wars in Syria, Yemen, and Libya; conflicts between Sunni and Shiite Muslims; Iranian threats against its neighbors; a coup attempt in Turkey; and the creation of a caliphate by ISIS to name just a few of the conflicts unrelated to Israel or the Palestinians. "Almost every border in that part of the world, from Libya to Pakistan, from Turkey to Yemen, is either ill-defined or in dispute," scholar Daniel Pipes noted years before the current upheaval. "But Americans tend to know only about Israel's border problems, and do not realize that these fit into a pattern that recurs across the Middle East."[3]

If the Palestinian problem were solved, it would have negligible impact on the region's volatility. It would not bring peace to Israel because radical Muslims such as Hamas, Hezbollah, and the regime in

Iran do not accept the legitimacy of a Jewish state in what they consider the Muslim heartland.

> *In the end we [Israel and the Palestinians] will reach a solution in which there will be a Palestinian state, but it has to be a Palestinian state by agreement and it has to be a demilitarized Palestinian state.*
>
> **—Prime Minister Ariel Sharon[4]**

MYTH

A Palestinian state will pose no danger to Israel.

FACT

For many years, the consensus in Israel was that the creation of a Palestinian state would present a grave risk to Israeli security. These fears were well founded given the long-standing Palestinian commitment to the destruction of Israel, and the later adoption of the phased plan whereby the Palestinians expressed a reluctant willingness to start with a small state in the short term and use it as a base from which to pursue the longer-term goal of replacing Israel.

Starting with the Oslo agreements in the early 1990s, a radical shift in opinion occurred, and most Israelis became reconciled to the idea of living beside a peaceful demilitarized Palestinian state (though Yitzhak Rabin never agreed to establish such a state).

The two-state solution is viewed internationally as the best option for ending the conflict, but Israelis still believe it entails risks, a view reinforced by Palestinian actions since Oslo. Even after returning much of the West Bank and all of Gaza, and allowing the Palestinians to govern themselves, terrorism and incitement against Israelis has continued. So far, no concessions by Israel have been sufficient to prompt the Palestinians to end the violence.

Israelis also fear that a Palestinian state will become dominated by Islamic extremists and serve as a staging area for terrorists, a concern grounded in the experience following the disengagement from Gaza and the efforts of Hamas to take over the West Bank. Another danger, albeit one that has diminished in recent years, is that a Palestinian state could serve as a forward base for Arab nations that have refused to make peace with Israel in a future war.[5]

In an ideal world, a Palestinian state would pose no threat, but history and experience makes Israelis cautious. The level of support for the two-state solution is an indication, however, of the risks Israelis are prepared to take if presented with an agreement that provides peace with security.

MYTH

Jews will be welcome in a future Palestinian state.

FACT

Palestinian officials have made clear that they plan to conduct a policy of ethnic cleansing of Jews reminiscent of Nazi Germany. Abbas said in December 2010, "If there is an independent Palestinian state with Jerusalem as its capital, we won't agree to the presence of one Israeli in it."[6] The PLO's ambassador to the United States, Maen Areikat, said on September 13, 2011, that a future Palestinian state should be free of Jews.[7]

Lest anyone believe such remarks were anomalies, Abbas, the man often referred to as a "moderate," announced on the eve of the resumption of peace talks in 2013 that "in a final resolution, we would not see the presence of a single Israeli—civilian or soldier—on our lands."[8]

These were not the first instances where Palestinian officials have suggested making "Palestine" *judenrein* and that reflect an ugly undercurrent of anti-Semitism within the Palestinian Authority. One might expect such racist and anti-Semitic views to provoke world condemnation, but the media ignores them, and peace activists are so desperate to reach an agreement that they make excuses for the Palestinians. Imagine the uproar if any Israeli official suggested that no Arabs or Muslims should be allowed to live in Israel.

Besides being immoral, the Palestinians' position is also hypocritical: Abbas demands that Palestinian refugees be allowed to move to Israel while simultaneously planning to expel all Jews from territory where they have lived for centuries.

Moreover, while 1.8 million Arabs, more than 20 percent of the population, live peacefully in Israel with full civic rights, no Jew can live in the Palestinian state. "Well, what is that?" Prime Minister Benjamin Netanyahu asked. "There are Arabs who live here, but they can't contemplate Jews living there."[9]

MYTH

If Israel ends the occupation, there will be peace.

FACT

The mantra of the Palestinians and their supporters since 1967 has been, "End the occupation." The assumption underlying this slogan is that peace will follow the end of Israel's "occupation." The equally popular slogan among critics of Israeli policy has been that it should "trade land for peace." Again, the premise being that it is simply Israel's presence on land claimed by the Palestinians that is the impediment to peace.

Map 27 Distances between Israeli Population Centers and Pre-1967 Armistice Lines

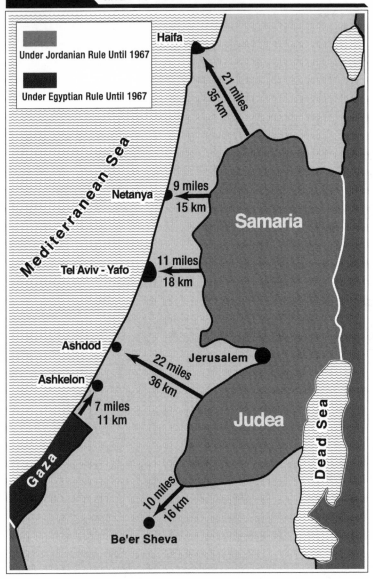

Under Jordanian Rule Until 1967

Under Egyptian Rule Until 1967

Haifa

21 miles
35 km

Mediterranean Sea

9 miles
Netanya
15 km

Samaria

11 miles
Tel Aviv - Yafo
18 km

Ashdod

22 miles
Jerusalem
36 km

Ashkelon

7 miles
11 km

Judea

Gaza

Dead Sea

10 miles
16 km

Be'er Sheva

The experience in Gaza offered a stark case study of the disingenuousness of these slogans. If the Palestinians' fervent desire were really to end Israeli control over their lives, they would have cheered Israel's plan to evacuate the Gaza Strip and done everything possible to make it a success. Instead, they denounced disengagement. Israel still withdrew from every inch of Gaza—not a single Israeli soldier or civilian remains—at great emotional and financial cost.

And what has the end of "the occupation" brought Israel? Has Israel received peace in exchange for the land?

No. To the contrary, the Palestinian answer to meeting their demands was a nearly ten-year barrage of rocket fire and terrorist attacks.[10] Terror and incitement also continued unabated from the West Bank, preempting any possibility that Israelis would support additional territorial concessions. Rather than "end the occupation," Palestinian actions have forced Israel to maintain a presence to ensure the safety of its citizens.

The responsibility for this escalation in the Israeli-Palestinian conflict rests with the Palestinians who have yet again turned their backs on peace. Rather than take the withdrawal of Israel from Gaza as an opportunity to build a future for their children, they instead refused to relinquish their embrace of a culture of hate and death.

—Editorial, *Chicago Sun Times*[11]

Slogans are good for bumper stickers, but they are irrelevant to the future of Israel and its neighbors. Israelis have repeatedly shown a desire for peace, and a willingness to make painful sacrifices, but nothing they do will end the conflict. Peace will be possible only when the Palestinians demonstrate through their actions a willingness to coexist in a state beside Israel.

The events following the disengagement caused Israelis to lose faith that any conceivable compromise would end the conflict with the Palestinians. Consequently, most Israelis are in no hurry to offer new concessions; they now will demand more stringent safeguards before agreeing to any additional withdrawals.

MYTH

The Palestinians have never been offered a state of their own.

FACT

The Palestinians have actually had numerous opportunities to create an independent state, but have repeatedly rejected the offers:

Map 28 Range of Fire from Gaza

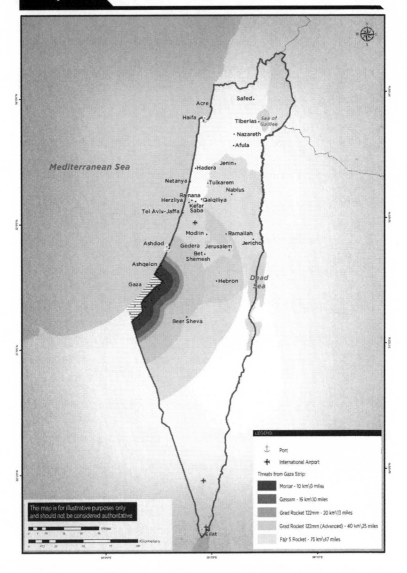

- In 1937, the Peel Commission proposed the partition of Palestine and the creation of an Arab state.

- In 1939, the British White Paper proposed the creation of a unitary Arab state.

- In 1947, the UN would have created an even larger Arab state as part of its partition plan.

- The 1979 Egypt-Israel peace negotiations offered the Palestinians autonomy, which would almost certainly have led to full independence.

- The Oslo agreements of the 1990s laid out a path for Palestinian independence, but the process was derailed by terrorism.

- In 2000, Prime Minister Ehud Barak offered to create a Palestinian state in all of Gaza and 97 percent of the West Bank.

- In 2008, Prime Minister Ehud Olmert offered to withdraw from almost the entire West Bank and partition Jerusalem on a demographic basis.

In addition, from 1948 to 1967, Israel did not control the West Bank. The Palestinians could have demanded an independent state from the Jordanians but never did.

In his last conversation with President Clinton, Arafat told the President that he was "a great man." Clinton responded, "The hell I am. I'm a colossal failure, and you made me one."[12]

The Palestinians have spurned every chance for statehood. A variety of reasons have been given for why the Palestinians have in Abba Eban's words, "never missed an opportunity to miss an opportunity." Historian Benny Morris has suggested that the Palestinians have religious, historical, and practical reasons for opposing an agreement with Israel. He says that "Arafat and his generation [which includes Abbas] cannot give up the vision of the greater land of Israel for the Arabs. [This is true because] this is a holy land, *Dar al-Islam* [the world of Islam]. It was once in the hands of the Muslims, and it is inconceivable [to them] that infidels like us [the Israelis] would receive it."

The Palestinians also believe that time is on their side. "They feel that demographics will defeat the Jews in one hundred or two hundred years, just like the Crusaders." The Palestinians, Morris says, also hope the Arabs will acquire nuclear weapons in the future that will allow them to defeat Israel.[13]

MYTH

Barak's proposals did not offer the Palestinians a viable state.

FACT

In 2000, Israeli prime minister Ehud Barak offered to withdraw from 97 percent of the West Bank and 100 percent of the Gaza Strip. In addition, he agreed to dismantle sixty-three isolated settlements. In exchange for the 3 percent annexation of the West Bank, Israel said it would give up territory in the Negev that would increase the size of the Gaza territory by roughly a third.

Barak also made previously unthinkable concessions on Jerusalem, agreeing that Arab neighborhoods of East Jerusalem would become the capital of the new state. The Palestinians would maintain control over their holy places and have "religious sovereignty" over the Temple Mount.

> Barak made a proposal that was as forthcoming as anyone in the world could imagine, and Arafat turned it down. If you have a country that's a sliver and you can see three sides of it from a high hotel building, you've got to be careful what you give away and to whom you give it.
>
> **—US defense secretary Donald Rumsfeld**[14]

According to US peace negotiator Dennis Ross, Israel offered to create a Palestinian state that was contiguous, and not a series of cantons. Even in the case of the Gaza Strip, which must be physically separate from the West Bank unless Israel were to be cut into noncontiguous pieces, a solution was devised whereby an overland highway would connect the two parts of the Palestinian state without any Israeli checkpoints or interference. The proposal also addressed the Palestinian refugee issue, guaranteeing them the right to live in the Palestinian state and offering reparations from a $30 billion fund that would be collected from international donors to compensate them.

Arafat was asked to agree to Israeli sovereignty over the parts of the Western Wall religiously significant to Jews (i.e., not the entire Temple Mount), and three early warning stations in the Jordan Valley, which Israel would withdraw from after six years. Most important, however, Arafat was expected to agree that the conflict with Israel was over at the end of the negotiations. This was the true deal breaker. Arafat was not willing to end the conflict. "For him to end the conflict is to end himself," said Ross.[15]

The prevailing view of the Camp David/White House negotiations—that Israel offered generous concessions, and that Yasser Arafat rejected them to pursue the war that began in September 2000—was acknowledged for more than a year. To counter the perception that Arafat was the obstacle to peace, the Palestinians and their supporters then began to manufacture a variety of excuses for why Arafat failed to say yes to a proposal that would have established a Palestinian state. The truth is that if the Palestinians were dissatisfied with any part of the Israeli proposal, all they had to do was offer a counterproposal. They never did.

I killed myself to give the Palestinians a state.

—**Bill Clinton**[16]

MYTH

The Palestinians are asked to accept only 22 percent of Palestine.

FACT

The government of Israel has agreed to a two-state solution to the conflict with the Palestinians. Once Israel agreed to give the Palestinians the independence they say they want, the Palestinians shifted their complaint to the *size* of the state they were being offered. Palestinians say Israel is doing them no favors by offering a state in the disputed territories because it is asking them to accept a state in only 22 percent of Palestine while Israel keeps 78 percent. This is a very convincing point to show the unfairness of the Palestinians' plight and to suggest Israel's peace overtures are inconsequential; that is, unless you know the history of Palestine and recognize that the truth is exactly the reverse.

Historic Palestine included not only Israel and the West Bank, but also all of modern Jordan. It is *Israel,* including the disputed territories, that is only 22 percent of "Palestine." If Israel were to withdraw completely from the West Bank and Gaza Strip, it would possess only about 18 percent. And from Israel's perspective, it is the Zionists who have made the real sacrifice by giving up 82 percent of the land of Israel. In fact, by accepting the UN's partition resolution, they were prepared to accept only about 12 percent of historic Israel before the Arab states attacked and tried to destroy the nascent state of Israel.

Meanwhile, of the approximately eleven million Palestinians worldwide, nearly four-fifths live in historic Palestine.

> *To keep 3.5 million people under occupation is bad for us and them ... I want to say clearly that I have come to the conclusion that we have to reach a [peace] agreement.*
>
> **—Prime Minister Ariel Sharon**[17]

MYTH

Israel should be replaced by a binational state.

FACT

The idea of a binational state is not new; it was first proposed by prominent Jews such as Judah Magnes in the 1920s. As is the case today, however, the suggestion enjoyed no popular support.

The utopian view of the advocates of binationalism was that the Jews and Arabs both had legitimate claims to the land and should live in peace together in one state. This idea negated the Jewish right to self-determination in their homeland; ignored the demographic concern that the rapidly growing Arab population would overwhelm that of the Jews, making them a minority in their homeland; and assumed the Arabs were prepared to coexist peacefully with the Jews within the same state. The idealists were proven wrong during two decades of violence by Arabs against Jews in Palestine, and by the Arab rejection of the British White Paper of 1939, which offered them the type of unitary state they proposed.

> *A Palestinian state will never be built on a foundation of violence. Now is the time for every true friend of the Palestinian people, every leader in the Middle East, and the Palestinian people themselves, to cut off all money and support for terrorists and actively fight terror on all fronts. Only then can Israel be secure and the flag rise over an independent Palestine.*
>
> **—President George W. Bush**[18]

As early as 1937, it had become clear that the two peoples could not live together and needed to have states of their own. As a result, the Peel Commission proposed a partition in that year, and the UN approved the same approach a decade later. Nothing has changed since that time to suggest any other solution can end the conflict.

Palestinian Arabs in Israel and the West Bank already constitute approximately 48 percent of the population living between the Mediterranean Sea and the Jordan River. Given their birth rate (even after having slowed in recent years), they would be either a significant minority or the majority of the population in a binational state.[19] The Jewish character of the nation would then erode and disappear, and Israeli Jews would lose political control over the one safe haven for Jews. Moreover, given the historical mistreatment of Jews in Arab lands, creation of a binational state would potentially lead to the persecution of Jews.

No one is born hating another person because of the color of his skin, or his background, or his religion. People must learn to hate, and if they can learn to hate, they can be taught to love, for love comes more naturally to the human heart than its opposite.

—Nelson Mandela[20]

MYTH

The Palestinian education system promotes peace with Israel.

FACT

Rather than use education to promote peace with their Jewish neighbors, the Palestinians have persistently indoctrinated their children with anti-Semitic stereotypes, anti-Israel propaganda, and materials designed to provoke hostility and intolerance rather than coexistence.

For example, a Palestinian children's television show called the "Children's Club" used a "Sesame Street" formula involving interaction between children, puppets, and fictional characters to encourage a hatred for Jews and the perpetration of violence against them in a *jihad* (holy war). In one song, young children were shown singing about their desire to become "suicide warriors" and taking up machine guns against Israelis. Another song features young children singing a refrain, "When I wander into Jerusalem, I will become a suicide bomber."[21]

Another Palestinian TV show featured a Mickey Mouse–like character named Farfour who encouraged children to fight against Israel and to work for "a world led by Islamists." After attracting criticism, the show was canceled, but not before a final episode aired in which Farfour was murdered by Israelis.[22]

PA-run TV also teaches children that all of Israel is "occupied Palestine," referring to Israeli cities such as Haifa and Jaffa, for example, as "occupied Palestinian cities."[23]

Similar messages are conveyed in Palestinian textbooks, many of which were prepared by the Palestinian Ministry of Education. The fifth-grade textbook *Muqarar al-Tilawa Wa'ahkam al-Tajwid* describes Jews as cowards for whom Allah has prepared fires of hell. In a text for eighth graders, *Al-Mutala'ah Wa'alnussus al-Adabia,* Is- raelis are referred to as the butchers in Jerusalem. Stories glorifying those who throw stones at soldiers are also found in various texts. A ninth-grade text, *Al-Mutala'ah Wa'alnussus al-Adabia,* refers to the bacteria of Zionism that has to be uprooted out of the Arab nation.[24]

We have found books with passages that are so anti-Semitic, that if they were published in Europe, their publishers would be brought up on anti-racism charges.

—French lawyer and European Parliament member Francois Zimeray[25]

Newer textbooks are less strident but still problematic. For exam- ple, they describe the Palestinian nation as one comprised of Muslims and Christians. No mention is made of Jews or the centuries-old Jew- ish communities of Palestine. The city of Jerusalem is described as exclusively Arab. Israel is not recognized as a sovereign nation, and all maps are labeled "Palestine." Israel is held responsible for the 1948 War and refugee problem, and a catalog of abuses against the Pales- tinians are attributed to the "occupier." Zionism is depicted as racist and connected to Western imperialism. References to Jews are usu- ally stereotypical and are often related in a negative way to their op- position to Muhammad and refusal to convert to Islam. A lesson on architecture describes prominent mosques and churches, but makes no mention of Jewish holy places.[26] One textbook analysis concludes:

> Despite the evident reduction in anti-Semitic references, com- pared to the old textbooks, the history of the relationship between Muslims, Christians and Jews in the new textbooks strengthen classical stereotypes of Jews in both Islamic and Christian cultures. The linkage of present conflicts with an- cient disputes of the time of Jesus or Muhammad implies that nothing has really changed.[27]

In a 2015 study of textbooks used in the Palestinian Authority, re- searchers concluded that children are taught "through their official communication structures that Jews and Israelis possess inherently evil character traits. Fighting them is therefore said to be heroic and even Allah's will. Terrorists who have murdered dozens of Israeli civil- ians are said to be national heroes and Islamic martyrs." These mes- sages are reinforced by naming schools after terrorists and honoring them in ceremonies that suggest they are role models. The report notes that common PA hate messages include:

Israel has no right to exist.
Israel will disappear and be replaced by "Palestine."
Violence—"armed struggle"—is legitimate to fight Israel.
Muslims must fight an eternal Islamic war against Israel.
Killers of Israelis are heroes and role models.
Martyrdom—death for Allah—is the utmost honor.

Children recited poems on official PA TV children's educational programs in recent years with the following messages:

Jews are "monkeys and pigs."
Jews are "enemies of Allah."
Jews are "most evil of creations."
Zion is "Satan with a tail."[28]

The situation is even worse in the Gaza Strip.

In 2013, Hamas introduced a new youth program for thirty-seven thousand Palestinian boys in Gaza between the ages of fifteen and seventeen. Weekly classes taught first aid, street fighting skills, and how to shoot a Kalashnikov rifle. Another five thousand boys signed up for an optional two-week camp at a Hamas military base. Samar Zakout, from the Gaza-based human rights organization Al-Mezan said "they are trying to create a resistance culture, make our boys stronger to face Israel, but they shouldn't be doing it in schools."[29]

We are teaching the children that suicide bombs make Israeli people frightened . . . We are teaching them that after the suicide attacks, the man who makes it goes to the highest state in paradise.

—Palestinian "Paradise Camp" counselor speaking to
BBC interviewer[30]

The lessons don't end in school. More than one hundred thousand children participate in Hamas summer camps, which "are designed to prepare a generation that carries the Koran and rifle, Hamas official Khalil al-Haya explained. "The camps show that Palestinians support the resistance and the project of liberation of Palestine." The slogan Hamas passes on to campers is the following: "Allah is the goal; Muhammad is its sign; the Koran is its law; *jihad* is its path; and death on behalf of Allah should be their highest aspiration."[31]

With more than 50 percent of the population of Gaza under the age of eighteen, a whole generation is being indoctrinated by Islamic militants. Summer camp teaches Palestinian children how to resist Israelis, stage mock kidnappings, and slit the throats of Israelis. Four

"Paradise Camps" run by Islamic Jihad in the Gaza Strip offered eight-to twelve-year-olds military training and encouraged them to become suicide bombers. During training, children learn to shoot Kalashnikov rifles and antitank weapons and learn to stand in solidarity with the Palestinian terrorists held in Israeli prisons. Gaza's "Pioneers of Liberation program taught 13,000 teens how to emulate 'suicide martyrs.'"[32]

In 2015, Hamas organized military camps for women. According to camp director Rajaa al-Halabi, these camps "teach how to raise a new generation that embraces the culture of liberation and fighting the occupation."[33]

Some parents forbid their children from attending these camps and object to the indoctrination of radical Islamic views that encourage young Palestinians to engage in violence and to support the Islamic State. Nevertheless, tens of thousands of young Palestinians are being groomed to be terrorists.

MYTH

Palestinians no longer object to the creation of Israel.

FACT

To achieve peace, the Palestinians must affirm Israel's right to exist in peace and security. How, then, does one interpret Palestinian Authority Chairman Mahmoud Abbas's description of the establishment of Israel as an unprecedented historic injustice and his vow to never accept it?[34]

While Israelis celebrate their independence, Abbas and other Palestinians mourn the establishment of Israel on what they call Nakba Day. Had the Palestinians and the Arab states accepted the partition resolution in 1947, the State of Palestine would also celebrate its birthday each year, and Palestinians would not be lamenting *Al-Nakba* ("The Catastrophe").

Palestinians are understandably bitter about their history over these last six decades, but we are often told that what they object to today is the "occupation" of the territories Israel captured in 1967. If that is true, then why isn't their Nakba Day celebrated each June on the anniversary of the Arab defeat in the Six-Day War?

Palestine means Palestine in its entirety—from the [Mediterranean] Sea to the [Jordan] River, from Ras al-Naqura to Rafah. We cannot give up a single inch of it. Therefore, we will not recognize the Israeli enemy's [right] to a single inch.

—Hamas leader, Mahmoud Zahar[35]

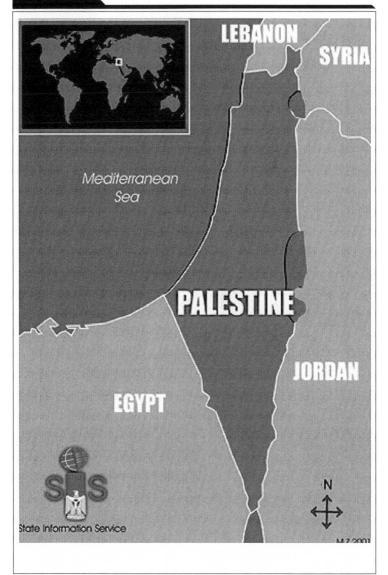

Map 29 The Palestinian Authority's Map of Palestine

The reason is that the Palestinians consider the creation of Israel the original sin, and their focus on that event is indicative of a refusal, even today, to reconcile themselves with the Jewish State. Hamas has never left any doubt about its refusal to accept Israel's existence and unwavering commitment to the Hamas Covenant's call for the destruction of Israel.[36]

As long as the Palestinians treat Israel's creation as a catastrophe on a par with the Holocaust, the prospects for coexistence will remain bleak.

MYTH

The Palestinians have given up their dream of destroying Israel.

FACT

While Israelis have expressed a willingness to live in peace with a Palestinian state beside Israel, the Palestinian Authority continues to promote the maximalist vision in its school textbooks and, especially, its maps. The most dramatic expression of the goal is in the map of Palestine published on its official website (map 29), which showed Palestine as encompassing not only the West Bank and Gaza Strip, but all of Israel as well. Similar maps appear in textbooks.[37] As the map vividly indicates, the Palestinians continue to dream of a Palestinian state that replaces Israel.

MYTH

Palestinians are justified in using violence to achieve their national aspirations.

FACT

The premise from the beginning of the Oslo peace process was that disputes would be resolved by talking, not shooting. The Palestinian leadership has never accepted this most basic of principles for coexistence. The answer to complaints that Israel is not withdrawing far enough or fast enough should be more negotiations, more confidence-building measures, and more demonstrations of a desire to live together without using violence.

To understand why the Oslo process failed, and why Palestinians and Israelis are not living peacefully beside one another, it is useful to look at the first Arab-Israeli peace process that did work: the Egyptian-Israeli negotiations. Though the peace agreement was hammered out in intensive negotiations at Camp David, the route to peace was a long, tortuous one that took years to navigate. What made it possible, however, was the commitment both nations made to peace and the actions they took to ensure it.

Egypt maintained a state of war with Israel for more than twenty-five years before Anwar Sadat seriously talked about peace. Bloody conflicts were fought in 1948, 1956, 1967, 1968–70, and 1973. The anger, heartache, and distrust of a quarter century did not dissipate overnight. The process began after the 1973 War when Henry Kissinger facilitated the negotiation of a disengagement agreement in which both sides made significant concessions.

Egypt had demanded that Israel make a substantial withdrawal from Sinai and commit to abandon all its territorial gains from 1967, but Israel gave up only a tiny area of the Sinai. Rather than resort to violence, the Egyptians engaged in more negotiations.

If the Israelis can make compromises and you can't, I should go home. You have been here 14 days and said no to everything. These things will have consequences. Failure will end the peace process.

—President Clinton to Yasser Arafat[38]

The first agreement was signed in January 1974. It took about a year and a half before a second agreement was reached. Israel was criticized for inflexibility, and the Egyptians were no less difficult. Sadat agreed to limit anti-Israel propaganda in the Egyptian press and to end his country's participation in the Arab boycott. Yitzhak Rabin also made difficult territorial concessions, giving up oil fields and two critical Sinai passes.

After "Sinai II," Egypt still had not recovered all of its territory. Sadat was dissatisfied and was pilloried by the other Arabs for going as far as he did toward peace with Israel. Nevertheless, he did not resort to violence. There was no unleashing of *fedayeen*, as Nasser had done in the 1950s. Instead, he continued talking.

It took three more years before the Camp David Accords were signed and another six months after that before the final peace treaty was negotiated. It took five years to work out issues that were as complex as those in the current impasse.

In return for its tangible concessions, Israel received the promise of a new future of peaceful relations. Israel could take this risk because Egypt had demonstrated over the previous five years that it would resolve disputes with Israel peacefully, and that it no longer wished to destroy its neighbor.

Egypt still wasn't completely satisfied. Sadat demanded a small sliver of land that Israel retained in the Sinai. It took another nine years before international arbitration led Israel to give up Taba. Rather than using this dispute as a pretext for violating the peace treaty, Egypt negotiated.

The lesson for the Palestinians is that they can only achieve their objective through compromise during face-to-face negotiations.

MYTH

Palestinians never fabricate stories about Israeli atrocities.

FACT

To inflame their populations, Palestinian and other Arab leaders routinely use their media outlets to spread outrageous libels against Israel and the Jews. Palestinians have become masters of the technique perfected by Adolf Hitler known as the "big lie." As Hitler explained in *Mein Kampf*:

> The size of a lie is a definite factor in causing it to be believed, for the vast masses of a nation are in the depths of their hearts more easily deceived than consciously and intentionally bad. The primitive simplicity of their minds renders them a more easy prey to a big lie than a small one, for they themselves often tell little lies but would be ashamed to tell big ones.

One example of the Palestinian big lie came on March 11, 1997, when the Palestinian representative to the UN Human Rights Commission claimed the Israeli government had injected three hundred Palestinian children with the HIV virus.[39]

Palestinians claimed in 2002 that Israel was dropping poisoned candies from helicopters in front of schools to poison children. That lie was updated in 2003 with the fabrication that Israel is making "bombs and mines designed as toys" and dropping them into the Palestinian territories from airplanes so children will play with them and be blown up.[40] In 2005, the Palestinians announced that Israel was using a "radial spy machine" at checkpoints, and that the device had killed a fifty-five-year-old Palestinian woman.[41]

The Palestinians also regularly try to inflame the Muslim world by falsely claiming the Jews are going to blow up the Temple Mount or Al-Aqsa Mosque. For example, on September 29, 2000, the Voice of Palestine, the PA's official radio station, sent out calls "to all Palestinians to come and defend Al-Aqsa Mosque." This was the day *after* Ariel Sharon's visit to the Temple Mount, and the subsequent riots marked the unofficial beginning of the Palestinian War.

In the midst of that war, the Palestinian Authority TV "Message to the World" broadcast announced, "The Zionist criminals are planning to destroy Al-Aqsa Mosque on the ground that they are searching for the Holy Temple, which they falsely claim is under the mosque."[42]

In 2013, Abbas complained to a Saudi newspaper that "fanatic Jewish extremists" were part of a scheme to destroy Al-Aqsa Mosque and rebuild the Jewish Temple."[43]

The problem is the same problem that has been there for the three years that I have been working in this account. And that is terrorism, terrorism that still emanates from Hamas, Palestinian Islamic Jihad, and other organizations that are not interested in peace, not interested in a state for the Palestinian people. They're interested in the destruction of Israel.

—Secretary of State Colin Powell[44]

MYTH

Israel's refusal to withdraw from the Golan Heights prevents peace with Syria.

FACT

Given past history, Israel is understandably reluctant to give away the strategic high ground and its early-warning system. Nevertheless, Israel repeatedly expressed a willingness to negotiate the future of the Golan Heights. One possible compromise might be a partial Israeli withdrawal, along the lines of its 1974 disengagement agreement with Syria. Another would be a complete withdrawal, with the Golan becoming a demilitarized zone. In a series of negotiations, both President Hafez Assad and the son who succeeded him, Bashar, always insisted on a total withdrawal with no compromises. They also were unwilling to go beyond agreeing to a far more limited "nonbelligerency" deal with Israel than the full peace treaty Israel has demanded.

The civil war in Syria has provided a vivid reminder of why Israel was so reluctant to give up the Golan Heights. If they had made a deal with Assad, ISIS and other radical groups might be on the shores of the Sea of Galilee and threatening all of northern Israel. After watching the chaos in Syria and the rise of radical Muslims there, it is hard to imagine that Israel would contemplate any compromises on the Golan Heights unless and until a stable, peaceful government emerges in Syria.

MYTH

Israel's occupation of Lebanese territory is the impediment to peace with Lebanon.

FACT

Israel has never had any hostile intentions toward Lebanon but has been forced to fight as a result of the chaotic conditions in southern

Lebanon that have allowed terrorists, first the PLO, and now Hezbollah, to menace citizens living in northern Israel. In 1983, Israel did sign a peace treaty with Lebanon, but Syria forced President Amin Gemayel to renege on the agreement.

Israel pulled all its troops out of southern Lebanon on May 24, 2000. The Israeli withdrawal was conducted in coordination with the UN, and, according to the UN, constituted an Israeli fulfillment of its obligations under Security Council Resolution 425. Still, Hezbollah and the Lebanese government insist that Israel holds Lebanese territory in a largely uninhabited patch called Shebaa Farms. This claim provides Hezbollah with a pretext to continue its belligerency toward Israel. The Israelis maintain, however, that the land was captured from Syria.

Syria, meanwhile, used its influence over Lebanon to discourage any peace negotiations until its claims on the Golan Heights were resolved and supported Hezbollah's efforts to take over Lebanon and threaten Israel. Hezbollah has been weakened by its participation in the Syrian civil war; nevertheless, it remains the dominant political and military force inside Lebanon, continues to receive support from Iran, and has built up an arsenal of more than one hundred thousand rockets aimed at Israel. Given Hezbollah's commitment to Israel's destruction, the only way that peace can be achieved with Lebanon is if Hezbollah is uprooted either by the Lebanese or by Israel.

Palestine is not only a part of our Arab homeland, but a basic part of southern Syria.

—Syrian president Hafez Assad[45]

MYTH

Israel's refusal to share water with its neighbors could provoke the next war.

FACT

The supply of water is a matter of life and death for the peoples of the Middle East. A *Jerusalem Post* headline concisely stated the security threat for Israel: "The hand that controls the faucet rules the country."[46]

King Hussein said in 1990 the one issue that could bring Jordan to war again is water, so it is not surprising that an agreement on water supplies was critical to the negotiation of the peace treaty with Israel. Jordan now receives an annual allotment of water from Israel.[47]

Map 30 Water Resources

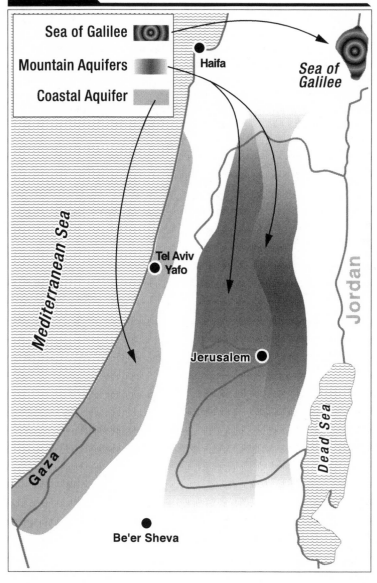

Today, Israel has achieved what was previously thought impossible—water independence. The secret to Israel's success is education and conservation, wastewater reclamation and reuse, legislation that gives the state control over all water resources, new water and agricultural technology, and desalination.

Historically, Israel relied on three main natural water sources: the coastal and mountain aquifers and Lake Kinneret (Sea of Galilee). Each supplied approximately 25 percent of the total consumed. Roughly 20 percent was derived from smaller aquifers. The remaining 5 percent came from recycled sewage. Today, however, five desalination plants provide more than 25 percent of Israel's water supply and 80 percent of household water.[48]

The Palestinians maintain that Israel is stealing their water because the mountain aquifer is partially located in the West Bank. Most of the water extracted by Israel, however, is taken from the portion that is within the pre-1967 border of Israel. The same is true with regard to accusations that Israel provides water to settlements at the expense of the Palestinians; most settlements get their water from inside Israel, not from the West Bank.

In Old Testament times, there were two ways of solving disputes over water, which has always been scarce in our region. One was to fight over it. The other was to jointly place over the mouth of the well, a stone so large that five shepherds were needed to lift it, creating the need for cooperation.

—Former Israeli agriculture minister Yaacov Tzur[49]

Still, the Palestinians argue the water should come under their control while Israel counters that it has a right to the water based on its prior use, its investment in development, and the fact that the water naturally flows inside the Green Line.

According to the Oslo accords, the Palestinians are entitled to 23.6 million cubic centimeters of water a year, but they actually pump, with Israeli consent, 70 million. Israel has also provided additional water to villages that suffer a water shortage.[50]

The Palestinians have exacerbated the situation through mismanagement, neglect, and the failure to build water-treatment facilities. Over the last twenty years, the Palestinians have only drilled in about one-third of the forty sites approved for drilling wells. Furthermore, the failure to fix pipes results in a loss of as much as 33 percent of the city water through leakage. In addition, the Palestinians use water inefficiently, for example, eschewing the proven Israeli practice of using wastewater for irrigation. Israel offered to build a desalination plant in Hadera for the Palestinians in the West Bank, but they rejected the idea. Similarly, Gaza's water problems could be ameliorated by the construction of a desalination plant, but Hamas has refused to accept international offers to build one.[51]

The danger for Israel is that even if a future Palestinian state has peaceful intentions, it could significantly reduce the water available to Israel because of the need to satisfy the needs of its own population, which would quickly swell with the arrival of thousands of refugees. As it is, unauthorized Palestinian drilling of wells in the West Bank has affected the quality of the aquifer. Without any other water source, the Palestinians will be tempted to pump more out of the aquifer to meet their growing needs and thereby could ultimately inundate it with seawater. There would be nothing Israel could do to stop them. Palestinians also steal water by tapping into pipes belonging to the Israeli water company Mekorot.

Additionally, the low priority placed on environmental issues by the PA increases the likelihood that the mountain aquifer will be polluted and its quality reduced perhaps to the point of being undrinkable. This has already occurred in the Gaza Strip where the sole aquifer is unusable because of contamination and salinity.

If Israel gives up control of the mountain aquifer, as is implicit in the proposals made to date, it will depend on the goodwill of the Palestinians to protect the quality of the water and to ensure Israel continues to receive sufficient water to meet its needs.

Israel has no right even to a single drop of water in this region.

—Syrian foreign minister Farouk al-Sharaa[52]

Water is also an issue in negotiations with the Syrians. Syria demanded the full return of the Golan Heights in return for peace with Israel. This means that Israel would face problems regarding the quality and quantity of water that flows into the Kinneret from Syrian-controlled territory. According to water expert Joyce Starr, an Israeli government that concedes territory on the Golan without a guaranteed supply of Yarmuk waters, or some alternative source of water, would be putting the nation in "grave jeopardy."[53]

In 2015, thanks to its desalination plants, Israel doubled its sales of water to Gaza.[54] Desalination could largely solve the Palestinians' water problems if their leaders were more interested in securing water than denying it to their people so they can continue to blame Israel for shortages.

I thank Allah the exalted for His support in the Jihad of our people and for the liberation of the beloved Gaza Strip, and I ask him to help us to liberate Jerusalem and the West Bank, Acre, Haifa, Jaffa, Safed, Nazareth, Ashkelon, and all of Palestine.

—**Muhammad Deif, commander of the**
'Izz al-Din al-Qassam Brigades[55]

MYTH

The Arab peace initiative reflects Arab acceptance of Israel and the best hope for peace.

FACT

In 2002, then crown prince Abdullah of Saudi Arabia told journalist Thomas Friedman his ideas for a comprehensive Mideast peace. Abdullah's ideas were revised and adopted by the Arab League as a peace initiative that offered Israel "normal relations" in exchange for a withdrawal to the 1967 borders and resolution of the Palestinian refugee issue.

The Arab Peace Initiative (API) amounts to nothing more than a restatement of the Arab interpretation of UN Resolution 242. The problem is that 242 does not say what the Saudi plan demands of Israel. The resolution calls on Israel to withdraw from territories occupied during the war, not "all" the territories in exchange for peace.

In addition, Resolution 242 says that every state has the right to live within "secure and recognizable boundaries," which all military analysts have understood to mean the 1967 borders with modifications to satisfy Israel's security requirements. Moreover, Israel is under no obligation to withdraw before the Arabs agree to live in peace.

The Arab plan calls for Israel to withdraw from the Golan Heights. The Israeli government offered to withdraw from most, if not all of the Golan in exchange for a peace agreement; however, Syrian president Bashar Assad was unwilling to make such a deal. The civil war has made the issue moot for the foreseeable future.

The demand that Israel withdraw from "the remaining occupied Lebanese territories in the south of Lebanon" is at odds with the UN conclusion that Israel has completely fulfilled its obligation to withdraw from Lebanese territory.

The Arab initiative calls for a just solution to the Palestinian refugee problem based on the nonbinding UN General Assembly Resolution 194. Under the Arab interpretation, the more than five million refugees should be allowed to live in Israel. This suicidal formula has been rejected by Israel since the end of the 1948 War and is unacceptable to

Israelis today. Israel does, however, recognize a right for all the refugees to live in a future Palestinian state and has agreed to allow some Palestinian refugees to live in Israel on a humanitarian basis, and as part of family reunification.

The refugee issue was not part of Abdullah's original proposal but was added under pressure from other Arab states. Another change from Abdullah's original vision was a retreat from a promise of full normalization of relations with Israel to an even vaguer pledge of "normal relations."

The Arab demand that Israel accept the establishment of a Palestinian state in the West Bank and Gaza with East Jerusalem as its capital has been part of the negotiations since Oslo. Israel's leaders, including Prime Minister Benjamin Netanyahu, have accepted the idea of creating a Palestinian state in part of those territories, and Israel has even offered compromises on the status of Jerusalem, but the Palestinians have rejected them all.

It is also worth noting that most of the Arab League nations have no reason not to be at peace with Israel. Israel holds none of their territory and is willing to make peace with the members of the League. Several members of the League began to improve relations with Israel in the 1990s and maintain low-key informal diplomatic and economic ties today.

Despite Israel's reservations, Israeli president Moshe Katsav agreed to discuss the API in 2002, but the Arabs did not. The fact that the Saudi king who was so gung ho about the plan would neither travel to Israel for talks nor invite an Israeli delegation to Riyadh is evidence that it was nothing but a smoke screen to cover the Saudi role in 9/11 and its ongoing sponsorship of terrorism.[56]

In May 2014, Maj. Gen. Amos Yadlin, the former head of Israeli Military Intelligence met with Prince Turki al-Faisal, son of the late King Faisal, and director of Saudi intelligence for more than two decades. Yadlin suggested that the prince follow in the footsteps of Anwar Sadat and come to Jerusalem. He invited al-Faisal to pray at a mosque in Jerusalem and then address the Israeli people from the Knesset. Alternatively, Yadlin said Prime Minister Benjamin Netanyahu was prepared to go to Riyadh or Jeddah for negotiations. The general said a majority of Israelis would accept the API if al-Faisal spoke to them from Israel's capital.[57] The prince demurred.

Nothing has changed to make the API more palatable to Israel. It relies on the discredited land for peace formula, but, in this case, does not offer peace in exchange for Israeli concessions. Moreover, the Saudis still have no interest in negotiating with Israel even though the two countries have found common cause in fighting Hamas, Hafez Assad in Syria, and preempting the Iranian nuclear program.

If the Arab proponents of the plan were sincere, the response should be that they are prepared to sit down with Israel's leaders and discuss how to overcome the disagreements. But this has not been the Arab response. Rather than accept an Israeli invitation to come to Jerusalem to negotiate, the Arabs have told Israel it must accept the plan or face the threat of war. Here are a few examples:

■ Saudi foreign minister Prince Saud al-Faisal, said: "If Israel refuses, that means it doesn't want peace and it places everything back into the hands of fate. They will be putting their future not in the hands of the peacemakers but in the hands of the lords of war."[58]

■ The Syrian information minister, Muhsen Bilal, declared: "If Israel rejects the Arab League peace proposal, resistance will be the only way to liberate the Golan Heights."[59]

■ The secretary general of the Gulf Cooperation Council, Abdulrahman al-Attiya, said that Israel should respond expeditiously to the Arab peace initiative because the Arabs are in no mood to wait interminably.[60]

Make peace on our terms or else. Is this the rhetoric you would expect from leaders who have moderated their views and want to seek an accommodation with Israel?

Peace plans are not worth the paper they are printed on if the proponents continue to talk about war and pursue policies such as supporting terrorists, arming radical Muslims, inciting their populations with anti-Semitic propaganda, and enforcing boycotts that promote conflict. Progress toward real peace requires the Arab states to show by words *and* deeds that they are committed to finding a formula for coexisting with Israel. The only ultimatum should be that if the first effort to reach an understanding does not succeed, they will try again.

MYTH

Palestinians would prefer to live in a Palestinian state.

FACT

Most Palestinians currently living inside Israel's borders say they would prefer to live in Israel rather than a Palestinian state. One poll found that 62 percent of Israeli Arabs preferred to remain Israeli citizens rather than become citizens of a future Palestinian state. Another poll of East Jerusalemites found that only 30 percent of Palestinians would prefer Palestine over Israel, and, if their neighborhood became an internationally recognized part of Israel, 54 percent said they would not move to Palestine.[61]

Israeli Arabs know that, despite its faults, Israel is still a democratic state that offers them freedom of speech, assembly, religion, and the press and respects human rights in general, and women's rights and gay rights in particular. Palestinians are denied all these rights under Palestinian Authority rule.

The major difficulty is that the Palestinians don't accept Israel's right to exist.

—British prime minister Tony Blair[62]

Residents of East Jerusalem began voting with their feet when politicians began discussing the possibility of dividing Jerusalem prior to the Annapolis Conference in 2007. Only about twelve thousand East Jerusalemites had applied for citizenship since 1967 (out of some 250,000), but three thousand new applications flooded Israel's Ministry of Interior in the four months prior to the meeting.[63]

For the Palestinians of the Ras Hamis and Shuafat refugee camps, which are a part of Jerusalem, but would most likely fall on the side of Jerusalem apportioned to the Palestinian Authority in any future peace agreement, the preference for staying in Israel is clear. They plan to take advantage of their status as Israeli permanent residents, which allows them freedom of movement, and move to a city well within Israel's borders and legal jurisdiction. "If they put a border here, we'll move to Haifa and Tel Aviv. You'll have fifty thousand people who live here leaving East Jerusalem in minutes," declared Jamil Sanduqa, head of the refugee camp's local council.[64]

Many of the 250,000 East Jerusalemites depend heavily on Israel for jobs, health care, and unemployment insurance. They do not foresee having the same opportunities or benefits under the Palestinian Authority. Palestinians living in Israel want to live normal lives and earn a living to help their families and don't want to be involved with extremists. "I don't want to raise my children on throwing stones, or on Hamas," Sanduqa said.[65]

One of the proposals for moving toward a two-state solution is a land swap. The idea is that Israel would evacuate most of the West Bank but keep the large settlement blocs that are home to more than two hundred thousand Jews. This area is estimated to be 3–5 percent of the West Bank. Israel has proposed a land swap of a similar amount of territory now within Israel. One idea is to shift the border so the forty-five thousand residents of Umm el-Fahm, plus an additional 150,000 Israeli Arabs who sit on two hundred square miles of land just northeast of the West Bank, would be a part of a future Palestinian state. The Palestinians swap citizenship; Israel exchanges land. In theory, it's a win-win situation where everyone gets to be citizens of their own nation. But the Israeli Arabs in these towns, especially Umm el-Fahm, the largest Muslim city in Israel, are vehemently opposed to being part of the deal.

> *It's easy enough for global leaders to issue flowery appeals for action on the Middle East or to imply that progress would be possible if only the United States used its leverage with Israel. The stubborn reality is that there can be no movement toward peace until a Palestinian leadership appears that is ready to accept a two-state solution.*
>
> **—Editorial, Washington Post**[66]

"We wish to express our sharp opposition to any initiative taken by the State of Israel and the Palestinian Authority with regard to our civil, political and human rights," the heads of the Arab regional councils and cities wrote to Prime Minister Olmert and his cabinet members in response to the land swap proposal. "We wish to make it clear that as citizens of the State of Israel since 1948-1949 . . . the proposed moving of borders will deprive us of these human rights and tear apart the social and economic ties that have been constructed on the basis of a long and difficult struggle."

One of the first to sign the letter to Prime Minister Olmert was Sheik Hasham Abed Elrahman, Umm el-Fahm mayor and head of the Wadi Ara Forum of Arab and Jewish Mayors. He wrote, "I cannot argue with feelings. I can tell you that we want to work together with the Jewish majority for the betterment of all of Israel. Religiously, politically and socially, we want to remain part of the State of Israel."[67]

Few Palestinians want to move to "Palestine," and many Palestinians now living in the Palestinian Authority would emigrate if they could. According to a December 2007 survey, 34 percent of the residents would like to leave. A June 2015 poll found that 52 percent of Palestinians living in East Jerusalem would prefer to be citizens of Israel.[68]

MYTH

Mahmoud Abbas is a moderate interested in compromise.

FACT

The definition of "moderate" is relative. Compared to the leaders of Hamas and Hezbollah, for example, Mahmoud Abbas can be viewed as a moderate since he does not openly call for Israel's destruction. Abbas, however, has expressed no true willingness to compromise on any substantive issue, balks at true peace efforts, and spews anti-Israel rhetoric that has significantly hampered the peace process.

In November 2010, Abbas spoke at the sixth annual memorial service for Yasser Arafat and definitively announced that he will continue to tow the hard line agenda of his mentor and predecessor.[69] Abbas is holding to Arafat's policies of declaring Jerusalem the capital of Palestine, requiring Israeli withdrawal from all settlements, demanding the full right of return for Palestinian refugees and their descendants, and refusing to acknowledge the Jewish character of the State of Israel. Abbas also publicly glorifies Palestinian martyrs and pays stipends to their families as well as terrorists in Israeli jails.

On the issue of Jerusalem, Abbas said the city would be the capital of a future Palestinian state. "At the Camp David summit, the Palestinian leadership rejected an Israeli proposal to share sovereignty over the Aqsa Mosque," he said. "They wanted to give the Muslims all what is above the mosque, while Israel would control what's under it. We continue to reject this offer. We cannot compromise on Jerusalem."[70] In an interview with the *Washington Post,* Abbas declared, "I say and have always said that East Jerusalem is occupied territory. We have to restore it."[71] Again, in 2010, he said that "the Arab city of Jerusalem, including its holy sites, is an integral part" of the future Palestinian state.[72]

On the subject of Israel's 2005 disengagement from Gaza, Abbas insisted that "the withdrawal from Gaza must only be part of other withdrawals . . . Israel must pull out of all Palestinian lands occupied in 1967."[73] He reiterated again in a letter to Presidents Obama and Medvedev in 2010 that "the shortest way to peace is ending the Israeli occupation of all territory . . . including Jerusalem, occupied Syrian Arab Golan Heights and the remaining Lebanese territories."[74] Abbas refuses to acknowledge Israeli security concerns that would stem from a complete withdrawal and is categorically opposed to land-swap deals to allay those fears.

In the same speech, Abbas said that the refugee issue had to be solved on the basis of UN Resolution 194. According to Abbas, at the time there were 4.7 million Palestinian refugees. In a January 3, 2005, appearance, Abbas said Palestinian refugees and their descendants have the right to return to their original homes. "We will never forget the rights of the refugees, and we will never forget their suffering. They will eventually gain their rights, and the day will come when the refugees return home," Abbas told a cheering crowd.[75] In November 2010, the Fatah Revolutionary Council praised Abbas for standing up to pressure and maintaining his position on the Palestinian right of return.[76]

Abbas has negotiated with Israel in the past, but he rejects its raison d'être as a Jewish state. Speaking to the Palestinian youth parliament in 2009, Abbas declared his refusal to recognize Israel's Jewish character saying, "Call yourselves what you want, but I will not accept it . . . The 'Jewish State' . . . I will not accept it."[77] Abbas backed that statement again in September 2010, when he told members of the Hadash party it was an "unacceptable demand" that he recognize Israel as a Jewish state.[78]

In 2008, Israeli prime minister Ehud Olmert extended a peace proposal to Abbas that would have created two nation-states. Under the plan Israel would have withdrawn from almost the entire West Bank and partitioned Jerusalem on a demographic basis. Abbas rejected the offer and has refused to participate in peace talks with Israel's leaders since that time.[79]

Abbas was supposed to have renounced terror, but on February 28, 2008, he told the Jordanian newspaper *al-Dustur* that he did not rule out returning to the path of armed "resistance" against Israel. In fact, his reason for not engaging in "armed struggle" was not because he disavowed terror, but because he did not believe the Palestinians can achieve their objectives. "At this present juncture, I am opposed to armed struggle because we cannot succeed in it, but maybe in the future things will be different," he said.[80] Earlier, Abbas had launched his presidential election campaign by saying "the use of weapons is unacceptable because it has a negative impact on our image." The *Wall Street Journal* noted afterward that "Mr. Abbas does not reject terrorism because it is immoral, but because it no longer sells the cause abroad."[81]

Abbas was the number two person in the PLO under Arafat and a founder of the Fatah terrorist organization, which makes him responsible for decades of atrocities. In February 2008, he proudly claimed credit for initiating the terror campaign against Israel. "I had the honor of firing the first shot in 1965 and of being the one who taught resistance to many in the region and around the world," Abbas said. The PA president even takes credit for training the Lebanese Shiite terrorists. "We (Fatah) had the honor of leading the resistance and we taught resistance to everyone, including Hezbollah, who trained in our military camps."[82] In 2010, Abbas eulogized the mastermind behind the massacre at the 1972 Munich Olympics, in which eleven Israeli athletes were murdered, as "a leading figure in resistance" who "sacrificed for his people's just causes."[83]

Abbas is also a Holocaust denier. His PhD dissertation suggested that six million Jews did not die at the hands of the Nazis, and he denied that gas chambers were used to murder Jews.[84] Abbas also allows Holocaust denial to spread under his watch. The official PA media outlet airs programs where Palestinian academics teach that Auschwitz and Dachau "never existed," and the Palestinian Ministry of Education produces schoolbooks that teach the history of World War II, yet completely ignore the Holocaust and the extermination of six million Jews.[85]

Abbas also clings to the hope that Israel will be forced to capitulate to his demands by outside powers, a fantasy that is fed by pressure exerted on Israel from the Europeans, the UN, and the US State Department. After refusing to negotiate with the Netanyahu government, Abbas announced plans to make an end-run around peace talks and seek UN recognition of a Palestinian state.

Israelis have no illusions about Abbas and remain skeptical that any agreements can be reached with a man who has shown neither the will nor the ability to carry out any of his promises. Nevertheless, Israeli leaders understand he is the only interlocutor they have for the moment and are willing to pursue negotiations in the hope that Abbas will genuinely moderate his views and compromise on the issues required to reach an agreement.

MYTH

Palestinians are driven to terror by poverty and desperation.

FACT

The situation many Palestinians find themselves in is unfortunate and often quite severe. Many live in poverty, see the future as hopeless, and are unhappy with the way they are treated by Israelis. None of these are excuses for engaging in terrorism. In fact, many terrorists are not poor, desperate people at all. Osama bin Laden, for example, was a Saudi millionaire.

On March 6, 2008, Ala Abu Dhaim murdered eight seminary students and wounded fifteen more at the Merkaz Harav yeshiva in Jerusalem. Dhaim was not poor or desperate. He was engaged to be married, he came from a family that is financially comfortable, and was employed by the yeshiva as a driver. Dhaim also was not suffering under "occupation." In fact, as a resident of the East Jerusalem village of Jabel Mukaber, which lies within Jerusalem's municipal boundaries, he was entitled to all the same social and welfare benefits as Israeli citizens.

The stereotype that Palestinians turn to terrorism out of desperation is simply untrue. "There is no clear profile of someone who hates Israel and the Jewish people. They come in every shape and from every culture. Demonstrators, rioters and stone throwers do tend to be younger, unmarried males. But there's a big difference between the young men who participate in those types of disturbances and terrorists," remarked Aryeh Amit, former Jerusalem District police chief.[86]

A report by the National Bureau of Economic Research concluded, "economic conditions and education are largely unrelated to participation in, and support for, terrorism." The researchers said the outbreak of violence in the region that began in 2000 could not be blamed on deteriorating economic conditions because there is no connection between terrorism and economic depression. Furthermore, the authors found that support for violent action against Israel, including suicide bombing, does not vary much according to social background.[87]

For example, the cousin of one of the two Palestinian suicide bombers who blew themselves up on a pedestrian mall in Jerusalem in 2001, killing ten people between the ages of fourteen and twenty-one, remarked candidly, "These two were not deprived of anything."[88]

The use of suicide bombing is entirely unacceptable. Nothing can justify this.

—UN special representative for the protection of children in armed conflict, Undersecretary-General Olara Otunnu[89]

Though some try to suggest the violence has nothing to do with radical Islam, the reality is that it is only Muslims who have engaged in suicide bombing. Palestinian Christians living in the same situation have not resorted to terror.

Terrorism is not Israel's fault. It is not the result of "occupation." And it certainly is not the only response available to satisfy Palestinian discontent. Palestinians have an option for improving their situation, namely, negotiations. But under the current Hamas regime, this is adamantly rejected. The Palestinians could also choose the nonviolent path emphasized by Martin Luther King, Jr., or Gandhi. Unfortunately, they choose to pursue a war of terror instead of a process for peace. Given that 40 percent of Palestinians think suicide bombing is justified (the highest percentage in a poll of Muslims in twenty-one countries), Israelis have good reason to doubt their intentions.[90]

Israel has proven repeatedly willingness to trade land for peace, but it can never concede land for terror.

MYTH

Israel must negotiate with Hamas.

FACT

Hamas controls the Gaza Strip and, therefore, some people argue that Israel must negotiate with the terror group. Few Israelis seriously believe that Hamas is interested in any lasting peace with Israel, but the advocates for negotiations believe it may be possible to reach a long-term cease-fire agreement in which Hamas promises to stop firing rockets into Israel and Israel ceases its military operations against the group in Gaza.

Hamas cease-fires have resulted from fear that Israel was about to attack them or in response to targeted killings of their leaders. In 2007 and 2008, truces were used by Hamas to rearm and then were subsequently broken when terrorists resumed rocket attacks on southern Israel.

Meanwhile, its spokesmen continue to make belligerent statements. In December 2015, for example, Hamas leader Khaled Meshaal said, "The so-called peace process is futile. There is no peace. Only the path of Jihad, sacrifice, and blood (will bear fruit)."[91] Hamas also remains committed to its covenant that calls for the destruction of Israel.

It is often said that you don't make peace with your friends, you make peace with your enemies, but this assumes the enemy you are negotiating with is not committed to your destruction. Golda Meir said it best when she explained the conflict had nothing to do with territory. "We're the only people in the world where our neighbors openly announce they just won't have us here," she observed. "And they will not give up fighting and they will not give up war as long as we remain alive . . . They say we must be dead. And we say we want to be alive. Between life and death, I don't know of a compromise."

MYTH

The Palestinian Authority believes in a secular Palestinian state.

FACT

Many people have forgotten, or simply chosen to ignore, that one of the reasons that President Clinton's peace summit with Prime Minister Ehud Barak and Yasser Arafat failed was the latter's assertion that Jews had no historical connection to Jerusalem. Israel's top negotiator Shlomo Ben-Ami told Palestinian negotiator Saeb Erekat: "You are barely 4 million Muslim Palestinians and pretend to represent one billion Muslims regarding the Temple Mount. Clinton's proposals are historic and you are about to miss another opportunity." I added that Arafat placed the Muslim agenda before the national Palestinian agenda. "Your national agenda is held hostage in the hands of the Muslim agenda and you will pay a heavy price for this."[92]

The following year Arafat criticized Hamas and Islamic Jihad for acting independently and ignoring his authority. Two days later, Arafat proclaimed:

> With God's help, next time we will meet in Jerusalem, because we are fighting to bring victory to our prophets, every baby, every kid, every man, every woman and every old person and all the young people, we will all sacrifice ourselves

for our holy places and we will strengthen our hold of them and we are willing to give 70 of our martyrs for every one of theirs in this campaign, because this is our holy land. We will continue to fight for this blessed land and I call on you to stand strong.[93]

Hamas, in particular, had forced Arafat and Fatah to eschew political rhetoric for Islamic language that played to the masses. When he agreed to the Oslo agreement with Israel, Arafat alienated the Islamists, who vehemently opposed any accommodation with Israel, which they insisted was a cancer that had to be excised from the region. The PLO responded to criticisms about its lack of commitment to Islam and the growing popularity of Hamas by adopting Islamic references and imagery in its rhetoric. For example, in a speech in Bethlehem, Yasser Arafat aroused his listeners by chanting, "Struggle, struggle, struggle, struggle. Combat, combat, combat, combat. Jihad, Jihad, Jihad, Jihad."[94] Terrorists captured or killed by Israel became martyrs for Islam; calls to liberate al-Aqsa became more common; and the PLO's "military" arm was named the Al-Aqsa Martyrs Brigade, which engaged in terror attacks that were just as heinous as those conducted by Hamas.

Following Arafat's rejection of a Palestinian state at the summit with Clinton, an uprising was launched by Arafat and referred to as the al-Aqsa intifada. This and other references to the al-Aqsa Mosque date back to the 1920s when the Mufti of Jerusalem incited the masses by accusing the Jews of plotting to destroy it. Since then, this libel has been a recurrent theme; whenever a Palestinian leader finds himself in trouble, he need only accuse the Jews of threatening the mosque, and Muslims will riot against Jewish worshippers. In 2013, for example, Abbas hoped publicizing a threat to the mosque would enrage the Muslim world and mobilize a *jihad* against Israel. He complained to a Saudi newspaper that "fanatic Jewish extremists" were entering the Temple Mount "to practice their religion" as part of "an evil and dangerous scheme to destroy [Al-Aqsa] and establish the alleged Temple."[95]

Despite such claims over the last one hundred years, and the fears of American Arabists who justify keeping the US embassy in Tel Aviv out of a misguided fear of a Muslim uproar, the Muslim world has done little more than issue condemnations and ask the UN to censure Israel's actions. While the al-Aqsa Mosque is revered as the third holiest shrine in Islam, no current Muslim leader is prepared to go to war today over the dubious accusations of the Palestinian leaders.

Abbas has followed in his mentor's footsteps in adopting radical Islamic rhetoric and behavior. Examples abound, but here are just a few:

The PA continues to misinform its youth in schools and demonize Jews in textbooks and the media. In a poetry segment on a Friday morning talk show on PA TV (which is controlled by Abbas), a poet recited a poem cursing the Jews as "the most evil among creations," "barbaric monkeys," and "wretched pigs." The poem has been featured several times on PA TV, sometimes recited by young schoolchildren.[96]

The PA minister of religious affairs, Mahmoud al-Habbash, said all of the Western Wall and Jerusalem belong to the Palestinians. He speciously claimed that "no person besides Muslims ever used it [the Western Wall] as a place of worship throughout all of the Jewish nation's history."[97]

Besides the statements, which some might dismiss as rhetoric, the Palestinian Authority has taken the more practical step of establishing Islam as the official religion of "Palestine," which contradicts the fantasies of liberal supporters of the Palestinians who believe their future state, unlike all the other Muslim states, will be a liberal democracy. To the contrary, one need only look at the authoritarian rule of the "moderate" Abbas for a foreshadowing of things to come. Abbas has repeatedly canceled elections, remaining in office more than a decade beyond the end of his term; Abbas does not allow freedom of speech, assembly, or religion. Critics of the regime are jailed or, in some cases, executed. Women's rights are a slight improvement over those in Gaza, but honor killings and other abuses remain common. Similarly, gays are persecuted based on Koranic prohibitions forbidding homosexuality. Putting aside the threat of a radical Islamic state on Israel's border, the threat to the liberties of Palestinians are also at stake if the Palestinians are allowed to create another Sharia-based state.

If anyone doubts the conflict is not primarily religious, with Islamic intolerance the greatest obstacle to peace, simply listen to Abbas. In July 2014, Abbas explicitly said the war with Israel is a "war for Allah," a remark that set off renewed attacks by Palestinians against Jews in Jerusalem.[98]

MYTH

Netanyahu backtracked on Rabin's positions regarding peace with the Palestinians.

FACT

On November 4, 2015, Israelis and all those who long for peace mourned the twentieth anniversary of the assassination of Prime Minister Yitzhak Rabin. The role Rabin played in the defense of his country as a soldier, diplomat, and politician should never be forgotten. In 1993, he took the courageous step of recognizing the PLO and negotiating a peace agreement with Yasser Arafat that for a brief period offered hope for an end to the conflict. Alas, by reneging on the commitment to end terror and, instead, intensifying the murderous attacks on Israeli civilians, the Palestinians squandered perhaps their best chance for achieving their stated goal of independence.

In fact, before his death, Rabin indicated he had lost faith in the peace process and was considering putting an end to Israeli concessions. According to his daughter Dalia, "Many people who were close to father told me that on the eve of the murder he considered stopping the Oslo process because of the terror that was running rampant in the streets and that Arafat wasn't delivering the goods. Father, after all, wasn't a blind man running forward without thought . . . After all he was someone for whom the security of the state was sacrosanct."[99]

Rabin was not naive and did not let his desire for peace blind him to the risks. Rabin's clear-eyed realism has been forgotten, however, by many people who have mythologized Rabin's role in the Oslo process, presenting him as so determined that it was only his death that prevented the implementation of a two-state solution to the conflict. By contrast, Prime Minister Benjamin Netanyahu is internationally vilified as someone who is uncompromising and uninterested in peace. Ironically, a closer examination reveals that their views were remarkably similar—with one notable exception—unlike Rabin, Netanyahu has accepted the eventual creation of a Palestinian state.

The best evidence of Rabin's thinking at the time of his death was his final speech to the Knesset on October 5, 1995, just a month before he was murdered. Compare Rabin's views with those of Netanyahu:

On a Palestinian State

Rabin: We view the permanent solution in the framework of [the] State of Israel, which will include most of the area of the land of Israel as it was under the rule of the British Mandate, and alongside it a Palestinian entity which will be a home to most of the Palestinian residents living in the Gaza Strip and the West Bank. *We would like this to be an entity which is less than a state*, and which will independently run the lives of the Palestinians under its authority."

Netanyahu: "We want a peace that would end the conflict once and for all . . . I don't support a one-state solution; I don't believe that's a solution at all; I support the vision of two states for two peoples."[100]

The 1967 Lines

Rabin: "The borders of the State of Israel, during the permanent solution, will be beyond the lines which existed before the Six Day War. We will not return to the 4 June 1967 lines."

Netanyahu: "For there to be peace, the Palestinians will have to accept some basic realities—the first is that *while Israel is prepared to make generous compromises for peace it cannot go back to the 1967 lines, because these lines are indefensible.*"[101]

Control of the Jordan Valley

Rabin: "*The security border of the State of Israel will be located in the Jordan Valley*, in the broadest meaning of that term."

Netanyahu: "Our strength is the guarantee for our existence and peace. We do not want an Iranian offshoot in Judea and Samaria. *This requires a security border in the Jordan Valley*, as Rabin said in his last speech."[102]

Settlements

Rabin: "I want to remind you: we committed ourselves, that is, we came to an agreement, and committed ourselves before the Knesset, *not to uproot a single settlement in the framework of the interim agreement, and not to hinder building for natural growth.*"

Netanyahu: "*I have no intention of evacuating any settlement or uprooting any Israelis.*"[103]

Jerusalem

Rabin: "*United Jerusalem, which will include both Ma'ale Adumim and Givat Ze'ev*" as the capital of Israel, under Israeli sovereignty, while preserving the rights of the members of the other faiths, Christianity and Islam, to freedom of access and freedom of worship in their holy places, according to the customs of their faiths.

Netanyahu: "We will keep Jerusalem united under Israeli authority."[104]

Rabin took the peace process as far as he could under the circumstances he faced. Had he lived, he may have seen the process through to a successful conclusion, but his daughter's remarks suggest that he did not believe peace could be achieved because of the unceasing Palestinian terrorism.

Netanyahu now faces more grave dangers and yet has been willing to go even further than Rabin in accepting Palestinian independence. That is a significant concession that the Palestinians have ignored. Worse, as they did during the Oslo period, they seem determined to prove through acts of violence that they are not interested in ending the conflict.

MYTH

The Palestinians' top priority is peace with Israel.

FACT

According to a poll conducted in the disputed territories in June 2015, establishing a Palestinian state was not the first or second highest priority for respondents.[105] Making enough money to live comfortably and having a good life were far more important. For example, 44 percent of West Bankers said making money was their top priority, and only 14 percent said it was statehood.

More ominously, the survey found that majorities in both the West Bank and Gaza have not abandoned their dream of liberating "all of historic Palestine." Fifty-eight percent of West Bankers and 65 percent of Gazans said that even if a "two-state solution" is negotiated, "the struggle is not over and resistance should continue until all of historic Palestine is liberated." Toward that end, 56 percent of Palestinians in the West Bank supported "armed struggle and car attacks against the occupation" and 84 percent of Gazans agreed.

These responses come as no surprise to Israelis who have long maintained that the Palestinians have not reconciled themselves to coexisting with Israel, even if Israel withdraws from the disputed territories and an independent state is established in the West Bank and Gaza Strip. Moreover, given the Palestinians' ongoing support for terrorism, it should not be surprising that Israelis are wary of making any territorial concessions that will fuel the Palestinians' belief that time is on their side, and that continued "resistance," combined with international pressure, will allow them to liberate all of Palestine, by which they mean the area currently known as Israel.

MYTH

The Palestinians have recognized Israel
as the state of the Jewish people.

FACT

Prime Minister Benjamin Netanyahu has insisted that one of the most important precursors for achieving a peace agreement with the Palestinians is their recognition of Israel as a Jewish state. In his speech to AIPAC on March 4, 2014, Netanyahu explained:

> Just as Israel is prepared to recognize a Palestinian state, the Palestinians must be prepared to recognize a Jewish state. President Abbas, recognize the Jewish state, and in doing so, you would be telling your people, the Palestinians, that while we might have a territorial dispute, the right of the Jewish

people to a state of their own is beyond dispute. You would be telling Palestinians to abandon the fantasy of flooding Israel with refugees, or amputating parts of the Negev and the Galilee. In recognizing the Jewish state, you would finally [be] making clear that you are truly prepared to end the conflict. So recognize the Jewish state. No excuses, no delays, it's time.[106]

Mahmoud Abbas gave his response three days later when he vowed the Palestinians will never recognize Israel as a Jewish state. "They are pressing and saying, 'no peace without the Jewish state,'" he said, without clarifying if he was referring to Israel or the United States. Regardless, he said, "There is no way. We will not accept." Two days later, the Arab League backed Abbas's stance, emphasizing "its rejection of recognizing Israel as a 'Jewish state.'"[107]

The incessant terrorist attacks provide an almost daily reminder of why Israelis do not take Palestinian rhetoric about peace seriously. Even if the Palestinians recognize Israel as a Jewish state, most Israelis will remain skeptical until they see those words translated into deeds that will permanently end the conflict.

Notes, Chapter 15

1. Speech to AIPAC Policy Conference (May 8, 1978).
2. "Sharon: Israel Wants to Give Palestinians Possibility of a State," *Haaretz* (September 24, 2001).
3. Daniel Pipes, *The Long Shadow: Culture and Politics in the Middle East* (New Brunswick, NJ: Transaction Publishers, 1989), 273-74.
4. "Sharon Reaffirms Stance on Palestinian State," *Hurriyet Daily News* (November 30, 2001).
5. Michael Widlanski, *Can Israel Survive a Palestinian State?* (Jerusalem: Institute for Advanced Strategic and Political Studies, 1990), 10, 35.
6. Khaled Abu Toameh, "Abbas Vows: No Room for Israelis in Palestinian State," *Jerusalem Post* (December 25, 2010).
7. Oren Dorell, "PLO Ambassador Says Palestinian State Should Be Free of Jews," *USA TODAY* (September 18, 2011).
8. Noah Browning, "Abbas Wants 'Not a Single Israeli' in Future Palestinian State," *Reuters* (July 29, 2013).
9. "Netanyahu: Jew Free Palestinian State Would Be Ethnic Cleansing," *Algemeiner* (January 15, 2014).
10. Dore Gold, "Israel's War to Halt Palestinian Rocket Attacks," *JCPA* (March 3, 2008).
11. Editorial, *Chicago Sun Times* (June 27, 2006).
12. Michael Hirsh, "Clinton to Arafat: It's All Your Fault," *Newsweek* (June 26, 2001).
13. Mohammed Salem, "Fatah, Hamas Hold Reconciliation Talks ahead of Possible Peace Negotiations with Israel," *NBC News* (February 8, 2013).
14. *Yediot Aharanot* (August 7, 2002).
15. "Proceedings and Debates of the 107th Congress, 2nd Session, Vol. 148, Part 4," US Congressional Record (April 11-24, 2002), 5174.
16. Jessie Hellmann, "Bill Clinton: 'I Killed Myself to Give Palestinians a State,'" *The Hill* (May 14, 2016).

17. Ian J. Bickerton, *The Arab-Israeli Conflict: A History* (Routledge, October 2015) 195.

18. Richard Stevenson, "Bush Declares Violence in Iraq Tests U.S. Will," *New York Times* (August 27, 2003).

19. Nir Hasson, "Demographic Debate Continues—How Many Palestinians Actually Live in the West Bank?" *Haaretz* (June 30, 2013).

20. Nelson Mandela, *Long Walk to Freedom* (NY: Little, Brown, and Co., 1993).

21. Daniel Pipes, "[Suicide Bombers:] A Father's Pride and Glory," *Jerusalem Post* (August 15, 2001).

22. "Hamas TV Drops Militant Mickey Mouse," *Jerusalem Post* (May 9, 2007); Itamar Marcus and Barbara Cook, "Hamas Steals Mickey Mouse Image to Teach Hate and Islamic Supremacy," *Palestinian Media Watch Bulletin* (May 6, 2007).

23. Itamar Marcus and Nan Jacques Zilberdik, "PA TV to Kids: Israeli Cities, Haifa, Jaffa, Lod, Ramle, Acre Are All 'Occupied Cities,'" Palestinian Media Watch (August 29, 2010).

24. "Sharm el-Sheikh Fact-Finding Committee—First Statement of the Government of Israel" (December 28, 2000).

25. Tal Ben-Shahar, "*A Clash of Values: The Struggle for Universal Freedom*" (iUniverse, May 2002) 134.

26. Lee Hockstader, "At Arab, Israeli Schools, Hatred Is Common Bond," *Washington Post* (September 5, 2001).

27. Goetz Norbruch, *Narrating Palestinian Nationalism: A Study of the New Palestinian Textbooks"* (Washington, DC: MEMRI, 2002).

28. Phoebe Greenwood, "Hamas Teaches Palestinian Schoolboys How to Fire Kalashnikovs," *Telegraph* (April 28, 2013).

29. Ibid.

30. Jeremy Cooke, "School Trains Suicide Bombers," BBC News (July 20, 2001).

31. Itamar Marcus, Nan Jacques Zilberdik, and Alona Berger, "Palestinian Authority Education: A Recipe for Hate and Terror," Palestinian Media Watch (July 21, 2015); Riley Clafton, "At Summer Camp, Hamas Raises the Next Generation of Killers," *The Tower* (August 2016).

32. *Near East Report* (June 25, 2001); Margot Dudkevitch, "Islamic Jihad Summer Camps Teach 'Martyrdom,'" *Jerusalem Post* (July 20, 2001); Michael Morrow, "Hamas Groups Run Brutal Summer Camps for Palestinian Kids," news.com.au (June 11, 2014); Elhanan Miller, "13,000 Teens Complete Hamas Training Camps to Emulate 'Suicide Martyrs,'" *Times of Israel* (January 15, 2014); Elior Levy, "10,000 Palestinian Teens Graduate Hamas Terror Camp," *Ynet News* (January 27, 2015); Riley Clafton, "At Summer Camp, Hamas Raises the Next Generation of Killers," *The Tower* (August 2016).

33. Arnon Ben-Dror, "Welcome to Camp Hamas," *Israel Defense Forces* (August 29, 2009).

34. Efraim Karsh, *The Tail Wags the Dog: International Politics and the Middle East* (London: Bloomsbury, 2015), 151.

35. Joe Kaufman, "Calls for Palestinian Uprising from . . . Miami," *The Gatestone Institute* (May 19, 2011).

36. For example, Hamas foreign minister Mahmoud Zahar, "I dream of hanging a huge map of the world on the wall at my Gaza home which does not show Israel on it," *Xinhua* (April 1, 2006).

37. "Map Erasing Israel on Palestinian Website," *Palestinian Media Watch* (February 1, 2010).

38. *Washington Post* (July 18, 2001), citing an article by Robert Malley and Hussein Agha in the *New York Review of Books* in which they quote the president at the Camp David summit in July 2000.

39. Moshe Zak, "Did Israel Inject AIDS to Palestinian Children?" *Israel Behind the News* (March 30, 1998).

40. Palestinian Authority TV (March 3, 2003).
41. Aaron Klein, "Palestinians Claim Israelis X-Rayed Woman to Death," *WorldNet Daily* (May 2, 2005).
42. Palestinian Authority TV (March 3, 2003).
43. *Al-Watan* (June 2, 2013) translated by *Elder of Zion* (June 3, 2013).
44. "Powell Blames Arafat for Impasse in Israeli-Palestinian Peace Efforts," *VOA News* (October 29, 2009).
45. Radio Damascus, (March 8, 1974) cited in Daniel Pipes, "Palestine for the Syrians?" Commentary (December 1986).
46. *Jerusalem Post* (July 16, 1994).
47. "Main Points: Israel-Jordan Peace Treaty," *Ministry of Foreign Affairs* (October 26, 1994).
48. Oded Distel, "Israel's Water Revolution and Its Overflow for the World," *Times of Israel* (June 27, 2016).
49. "Averting the Middle East Water Crisis," *Link* (May 1995).
50. Israel Harel, "Claims Israel Deprives Palestinians of Water Are Groundless," *Haaretz* (October 29, 2009).
51. Haim Gvirtzman, "The Truth behind the Palestinian Water Libels," Begin-Sadat Center for Strategic Studies (February 24, 2014).
52. *Mideast Mirror* (October 7, 1991).
53. *Washington Post* (September 10, 1995).
54. Christa Case Bryant, "Tap Dance: Water's Effect on Arab-Israeli Relations," *Christian Science Monitor* (June 21, 2015).
55. Audiotape posted August 27, 2005, on the 'Izz al-Din al-Qassam Brigades website, translated by MEMRI.
56. "Saudi Prince Won't Go to Israel," *UPI* (Feb. 28, 2002).
57. Mitch Ginsberg, "Saudi Royal Turns Down Ex-IDF Intel Chief's Invite to the Knesset," *The Times of Israel* (May 26, 2014).
58. David Blair, "Accept Peace Plan or Face War, Israel Told," *Telegraph* (March 28, 2007).
59. Roee Nahmias, "Syria: Without Peace, Resistance Will Liberate Golan Heights," *Ynet News* (April 16, 2007).
60. "Arabs Won't Wait Decades for Israeli Response to Arab Peace Initiative: GCC," Kuwait News Agency (May 3, 2007).
61. KEEVOON Research, Strategy, and Communications (December 26, 2007); "The Palestinians of East Jerusalem: What Do They Really Want?" Pechter Middle East Polls/Council on Foreign Relations (January 12, 2011).
62. Associated Press (December 7, 2006).
63. Ronny Shaked, "Thousands of Palestinians Apply for Israeli Citizenship," *Ynet News*, (November 7, 2007).
64. Joshua Mitnick, "Better the Devil You Know," *The Jerusalem Report* (November 11, 2007).
65. Ibid.
66. "Intransigent Hamas," *Washington Post* (October 11, 2006).
67. Eetta Prince-Gibson, "Land (Swap) for Peace?" *The Jerusalem Report* (November 26, 2007).
68. Near East Consulting, Bulletin # II-12, (December 2007); David Pollock, "Half of Jerusalem's Palestinians Would Prefer Israeli to Palestinian Citizenship," *Fikra Forum* (August 21, 2015).
69. "Abbas Talks Peace Process at Arafat Memorial," *Ma'an News Agency* (November 11, 2010).
70. Tani Goldstein, "Rocket Hits Ashkelon House; Qassams Land in Sderot," *Ynet News* (March 3, 2008).

71. "A Conversation with Mahmoud Abbas," *Washington Post* (September 30, 2007).
72. Khaled Abu Toameh, "Abbas Vows to Walk in Arafat's Footsteps in Palestine," *Jerusalem Post* (November 12, 2010).
73. "Abbas Demands Israeli Pullout, Prisoner Release," *Daily Times* (December 26, 2004).
74. "Erekat Delivers Message from President Abbas to Quarter," *Independent Media Review Analysis* (August 22, 2010).
75. "Abbas: Refugees to Return to their Homes in Israel," *Haaretz* (January 4, 2005).
76. Khaled Abu Toameh, "Fatah: No to Israel as Jewish State, No Land Swaps," *Jerusalem Post* (November 28, 2010).
77. "Abbas Scorns 'Jewish State,'" *Palestinian Media Watch* (April 27, 2009).
78. "Abbas: We Won't Recognize Israel as Jewish State," *Ynet News* (October 15, 2010).
79. Ari Shavit, "The Two Nation-State Solution," *Haaretz* (April 23, 2009).
80. Roee Nahmias, "Report: Abbas Does Not Rule Out Resuming Armed Conflict with Israel," *Ynet News* (February 28, 2008).
81. Editorial, "The End of the Affair," *Wall Street Journal* (December 31, 2004).
82. "Abbas: Armed Resistance Not Ruled Out," *Jerusalem Post* (February 29, 2008).
83. Tzvi Ben Gedalyahu, "Abbas Eulogizes Munich Massacre Mastermind," Arutz Sheva (July 4, 2010).
84. "Palestinian Authority Holocaust Denial and Distortion," *Palestinian Media Watch,* [No Date]
85. Ibid.
86. Interview with Jerusalem District Police Chief Aryeh Amit by Eetta Prince Gibson, "The Back Page," *The Jerusalem Report* (March 31, 2008).
87. Jitka Maleckova and Alan Kreuger, "Education, Poverty, Political Violence and Terrorism: Is There a Causal Connection?" (July 2002), quoted in the *Daily Star* [Lebanon], (August 6, 2002).
88. Lee Hockstader, "Jerusalem Bombers: Little in Common but a Mission," *Washington Post* (December 5, 2001).
89. UN Security Council Statement (January 14, 2003).
90. "Poll: 40% of Palestinians Support Suicide Bombing," *Jerusalem Post* (May 2, 2013).
91. Stuart Winer, "Hamas Political Leader: Stabbers Are 'the Most Exalted, Noblest of People,'" *Times of Israel* (December 15, 2015).
92. Nathan Cheiman, "Palestinian Intransigence Makes Mideast Peace Impossible," *South African Jewish Report* (July 6, 2016).
93. "Israeli Ambassador Blasts Palestinians," *JTA* (December 20, 2001).
94. Yasser Arafat calls for "jihad, struggle, and combat," Palestinian Media Watch (October 21 1996).
95. *Al-Watan* (June 2, 2013), translated by *Elder of Zion* (June 3, 2013).
96. Islamic-based hate speech on PA TV: Jews are "most evil among creations, barbaric apes, wretched pigs," Palestinian Media Watch, September 18, 2014.
97. Itamar Marcus, "PA: The Western Wall . . . No Person besides Muslims Ever Used It as a Place of Worship, throughout All of History." Palestinian Media Watch, January, 15 2013.
98. Itamar Marcus, "Abbas Calls for 'War for Allah,'" Palestinian Media Watch (July 27, 2014).
99. "Dalia Rabin: My Father Might Have Stopped Oslo," *IMRA* (October 20, 2010).
100. Allyn Fisher-Ilan, "Netanyahu Renews Support for Two-State Solution with Palestinians," *Reuters* (May 20, 2015).
101. "Netanyahu Rejects Obama's 1967 Border Proposal," *Fox News* (May 20, 2011).
102. Lahav Harkov, "Netanyahu: Border Must Remain in Jordan Valley—Like Rabin Said," *Jerusalem Post* (October 16, 2013).

103. Tovah Lazaroff, "Netanyahu: I won't Evacuate Settlements," *Jerusalem Post* (January 26, 2014).

104. Oren Lieberman, "Benjamin Netanyahu: Jerusalem Will Remain United City," *CNN* (May 17, 2015); "Yitzhak Rabin Was Not the Blind Peace-Maker That Bubba Clinton Claims He Was," *The Lid* (November 2, 2015).

105. David Pollock, "New Poll Shows Most Palestinians for Practical Progress, Tactical Compromises with Israel," *Fikra Forum* (July 23, 2015).

106. "Full Transcript: Prime Minister Netanyahu's Speech at AIPAC Policy Conference, 2014," *Algemeiner* (March 4, 2014).

107. "Palestinian President Abbas Says There's 'No Way' He'll Recognize Israel as Jewish State," *Fox News* (March 7, 2014).

16. Settlements

Israeli settlements are illegal.

Settlements are an obstacle to peace.

The Geneva Convention prohibits the construction of Israeli settlements.

The size of the Jewish population in the West Bank precludes any territorial compromise.

Israel must dismantle all the settlements for peace.

Settlements make it impossible for a Palestinian state to be contiguous.

MYTH

Israeli settlements are illegal.

FACT

Jews have lived in Judea and Samaria—the West Bank—since ancient times. The only time Jews have been prohibited from living in the territories in recent decades was during Jordan's rule from 1948 to 1967.

Numerous legal authorities dispute the charge that settlements are "illegal." Stephen Schwebel, formerly president of the International Court of Justice, notes that a country acting in self-defense may seize and occupy territory when necessary to protect itself. Schwebel also observes that a state may require, as a condition for its withdrawal, security measures designed to ensure its citizens are not menaced again from that territory.[1]

According to Eugene Rostow, a former undersecretary of state for political affairs in the Johnson administration, Resolution 242 gives Israel a legal right to be in the West Bank. "Israel is entitled to administer the territories" it captured in 1967, Rostow observed, until "a just and lasting peace in the Middle East" is achieved.[2] Though critical of Israeli policy, the United States does not consider settlements illegal.

MYTH

Settlements are an obstacle to peace.

FACT

Settlements have never been an obstacle to peace.

■ From 1949 to 1967, when Jews were forbidden to live on the West Bank, the Arabs refused to make peace with Israel.

- From 1967 to 1977, the Labor Party established only a few strategic settlements in the territories, yet the Arabs were unwilling to negotiate peace with Israel.

- In 1977, months after a Likud government committed to greater settlement activity took power, Egyptian president Sadat went to Jerusalem and later signed a peace treaty with Israel. Incidentally, Israeli settlements existed in the Sinai, and those were removed as part of the agreement with Egypt.

- One year later, Israel froze settlement building for three months, hoping the gesture would entice other Arabs to join the Camp David peace process, but none would.

- In 1994, Jordan signed a peace agreement with Israel, and settlements were not an issue; if anything, the number of Jews living in the territories was growing.

- Between June 1992 and June 1996, under Labor Party–led governments, the Jewish population in the territories grew by approximately 50 percent. This rapid growth did not prevent the Palestinians from signing the Oslo accords in September 1993 or the Oslo 2 agreement in September 1995.

- In 2000, Prime Minister Ehud Barak offered to dismantle dozens of settlements, but the Palestinians still would not agree to end the conflict.

- In August 2005, Israel evacuated all of the settlements in the Gaza Strip and four in Northern Samaria, but terror attacks continued.

- In 2008, Prime Minister Ehud Olmert offered to withdraw from approximately 94 percent of the West Bank, but the deal was rejected.

- In 2010, Prime Minister Benjamin Netanyahu froze settlement construction for ten months, and the Palestinians refused to engage in negotiations until the period was nearly over. After agreeing to talk, they walked out when Netanyahu ended the freeze.

Settlement activity may be a *stimulus* to peace because it forced the Palestinians and other Arabs to reconsider the view that time is on their side. Arabic writings frequently reference how long it took to expel the Crusaders and how it might take a similar length of time to do the same to the Zionists. The growth in the Jewish population in the territories forced the Arabs to question this tenet. "The Palestinians now realize," said Bethlehem Mayor Elias Freij, "that time is now on the side of Israel, which can build settlements and create facts, and that the only way out of this dilemma is face-to-face negotiations."[3]

Even though settlements are not an obstacle to peace, many Israelis still have concerns about the expansion of settlements. Some consider them provocative, others worry that the settlers are particularly vulnerable, and note they have been targets of repeated Palestinian terrorist attacks. To defend them, large numbers of soldiers are deployed who would otherwise be training and preparing for a possible future conflict with an Arab army. Some Israelis also object to the amount of money that goes to communities beyond the Green Line, and special subsidies that have been provided to make housing there more affordable. Still others feel the settlers are providing a first line of defense and developing land that rightfully belongs to Israel.

The disposition of settlements is a matter for the final status negotiations. The question of where the final border will be between Israel and a Palestinian entity will likely be influenced by the distribution of these Jewish towns in Judea and Samaria (the border with Gaza was unofficially defined following Israel's withdrawal). Israel wants to incorporate as many settlers as possible within its borders while the Palestinians want to expel all Jews from the territory they control.

If Israel withdraws toward the 1949 armistice line unilaterally, or as part of a political settlement, many settlers will face one or more options: remain in the territories (the disengagement from Gaza suggests this may not be possible), expulsion from their homes, or voluntary resettlement in Israel (with financial compensation).

The impediment to peace is not the existence of Jewish communities in the disputed territories; it is the Palestinians' unwillingness to accept a state next to Israel instead of one replacing Israel.

MYTH

The Geneva Convention prohibits the construction of Israeli settlements.

FACT

The Fourth Geneva Convention prohibits the *forcible* transfer of people of one state to the territory of another state that it has occupied as a result of a war. The intention was to ensure that local populations who came under occupation would not be forced to move. This is in no way relevant to the settlement issue. Jews are not being forced to go to the West Bank; on the contrary, they are voluntarily moving back to places where they, or their ancestors, once lived before being expelled by others.

In addition, those territories never legally belonged to either Jordan or Egypt, and certainly not to the Palestinians, who were never the sovereign authority in any part of Palestine. "The Jewish right of settlement in the area is equivalent in every way to the right of the local population to live there," according to Professor Eugene Rostow, former undersecretary of state for political affairs.[4]

The settlements do not displace Arabs living in the territories. The media sometimes gives the impression that for every Jew who moves to the West Bank, several hundred Palestinians are forced to leave. The truth is that the majority of settlements have been built in uninhabited areas, and even the handful established in or near Arab towns did not force any Palestinians to leave.

MYTH

The size of the Jewish population in the West Bank precludes any territorial compromise.

FACT

Altogether, built-up settlement area is less than 2 percent of the disputed territories. An estimated 70 percent of the settlers live in what are in effect suburbs of major Israeli cities such as Jerusalem. These are areas that—virtually the entire Jewish population believes—Israel must retain to ensure its security, and presidents Clinton and Bush anticipated would remain under permanent Israeli sovereignty.[5]

Strategic concerns have led both Labor and Likud governments to establish settlements. The objective is to secure a Jewish majority in key strategic regions of the West Bank, such as the Tel Aviv–Jerusalem corridor, the scene of heavy fighting in several Arab-Israeli wars. Still, when Arab-Israeli peace talks began in late 1991, more than 80 percent of the West Bank contained no settlements or only sparsely populated ones.[6]

> *If settlement-building is now concentrated in areas that the Palestinians themselves acknowledge will remain part of Israel in any future peace agreement, why the obsessive focus on settlements as an "obstacle to peace?"*
>
> **—Yossi Klein Halevi[7]**

Today, approximately four hundred thousand Jews live in 127 communities in the West Bank. Nearly half of these settlements have fewer than one thousand citizens, 30 percent have fewer than five hundred, and only 11 percent have more than five thousand. Contrary to Palestinian-inspired hysteria about settlement expansion, only nine settlements were built in the 1990s and only five since then.[8] Analysts have noted that 70–80 percent of the Jews could be brought within Israel's borders with minor modifications of the "Green Line."

Ironically, while Palestinians complain about settlements, an estimated thirty-six thousand work in them and support a population of more than two hundred thousand.[9]

MYTH

Israel must dismantle all the settlements for peace.

FACT

When serious negotiations begin over the final status of the West Bank, battle lines will be drawn over which settlements should be incorporated into Israel, and which must be evacuated. In August 2005, Prime Minister Ariel Sharon acknowledged that "not all the settlements that are today in Judea and Samaria will remain Israeli," while leaked Palestinian negotiating documents indicate the Palestinians were prepared to accept that some settlements will be incorporated into Israel.[10]

In Gaza, Israel's intent was to withdraw completely, and no settlements were viewed as vital to Israel for economic, security, or demographic reasons. The situation in the West Bank is completely different because Jews have strong historic and religious connections to the area stretching back centuries. Moreover, the West Bank is an area with strategic significance because of its proximity to Israel's heartland and the fact that roughly one-quarter of Israel's water resources are located there.

The disengagement from Gaza involved only twenty-one settlements and approximately eighty-five hundred Jews; more than one hundred settlements with a population of roughly 370,000 are located in Judea and Samaria.[11] Any new evacuation from the West Bank will involve another gut-wrenching decision that most settlers and their supporters will oppose with even greater ferocity than the Gaza disengagement. Most Israelis, however, favor withdrawing from all but the largest communities.

Approximately 60 percent of the Jews in the West Bank live in five settlement "blocs" that are all near the 1967 border. Most Israelis believe these blocs should become part of Israel when final borders are drawn. The table below lists the "consensus" settlements:

As the table shows, these are large communities with thousands of residents. Evacuating them would be the equivalent of dismantling major American cities such as Annapolis, Maryland; Olympia, Washington; or Carson City, Nevada.

Ma'ale Adumim is a suburb of Israel's capital, barely three miles outside Jerusalem's city limits and a ten-minute drive away. Ma'ale Adumim is not a recently constructed outpost on a hilltop; it is a thirty-five-year-old community that is popular because it is clean, safe, and close to where many residents work. It is also the third largest

Jewish city in the territories, with a population of 40,710. Approximately eight thousand people live in surrounding settlements that are included in the Ma'ale bloc. Israel has long planned to fill in the gap of approximately 3,250 acres between Jerusalem and this bedroom community (referred to as the E1 project). According to the Clinton plan, Ma'ale was to be part of Israel.

Bloc	No. of Communities	Population	Approximate. Area (sq. miles)
Ma'ale Adumim	4	48,468	28
Modiin Illit	4	72,313	2
Ariel	11	56,207	47
Gush Etzion	13	30,268	10
Givat Ze'ev	5	17,257	3
Total	37	224,513	90

The Gush Etzion Bloc consists of thirteen communities with a population of roughly thirty thousand just ten minutes from Jerusalem. Jews lived in this area prior to 1948, but the Jordanian Legion destroyed the settlements and killed 240 women and children during Israel's War of Independence. After Israel recaptured the area in 1967, descendants of those early settlers reestablished the community. The largest of the settlements is the city of Betar Illit with nearly thirty-five thousand residents.

The Givat Ze'ev bloc includes five communities just northwest of Jerusalem. Givat Ze'ev, with a population of just under eleven thousand, is the largest.

Modiin Illit is a bloc with four communities. The city of Modiin Illit is the largest in all the disputed territories, with more than sixty-five thousand people situated just over the Green Line, about twenty-three miles northwest of Jerusalem and the same distance east of Tel Aviv.

Ariel is now the heart of the second most populous bloc of settlements (56,207). The city is located just twenty-five miles east of Tel Aviv and thirty-one miles north of Jerusalem. Ariel and the surrounding communities expand Israel's narrow waist (which was just nine miles wide prior to 1967) and ensure that Israel has a land route to the Jordan Valley in case Israel needs to fight a land war to the east. It is more controversial than the other consensus settlements because it is the furthest from the 1949 Armistice Line, extending approximately twelve miles into the West Bank. Nevertheless, Barak's proposal at Camp David included Ariel among the settlement blocs to be annexed to Israel, and the Clinton plan also envisioned incorporating Ariel within the new borders of Israel.

Most peace plans, including Clinton's, assumed that Israel would annex sufficient territory to incorporate 75–80 percent of the Jews currently living in the West Bank. Using the figures in the table above, however, it appears that Israel would fall short of that demographic goal even if these five blocs were annexed. The total population of these communities is approximately 225,000, which is roughly 60 percent of the estimated 370,000 Jews living in Judea and Samaria. The expectation, however, is that roughly one-third of the Jews living in other settlements will move into these blocs, which would bring the total closer to 87 percent but still require Israel to evacuate approximately fifty thousand people.

> *Clearly, in the permanent agreement we will have to give up some of the Jewish settlements.*
>
> **—Prime Minister Ariel Sharon**[12]

At Camp David, Israel insisted that 80 percent of the Jewish residents of Judea and Samaria would be in settlement blocs under Israeli sovereignty. President Clinton agreed and proposed that Israel annex 4–6 percent of the West Bank for three settlement blocs to accomplish this demographic objective and swap some territory within Israel in exchange.

Recognizing the demographics of the area, President Bush acknowledged the inevitability of some Israeli towns in the West Bank being annexed to Israel in his 2004 letter to Prime Minister Sharon. In his meeting a year later with Palestinian Authority president Abbas, however, he seemed to hedge his support by saying that any such decision would have to be mutually agreed to by Israelis and Palestinians. The Obama administration subsequently repudiated Bush's commitment.[13]

Regardless, the future border is likely to approximate the route of the security fence, given the Israeli prerequisite of incorporating most settlers within Israel. Ultimately, Israel may decide to unilaterally disengage from the West Bank and determine which settlements it will incorporate within the borders it delineates. Israel would prefer, however, to negotiate a peace treaty with the Palestinians that would specify which Jewish communities will remain intact within the mutually agreed border of Israel and which will need to be evacuated. Israel will undoubtedly insist that some or all of the "consensus" blocs become part of Israel.

Map 31 The Future Borders of Israel and Palestine?

MYTH

Settlements make it impossible for a
Palestinian state to be contiguous.

FACT

As map 31 indicates, it is possible to create a contiguous Palestinian state in the West Bank even if Israel incorporates the major settlement blocs. The total area of these communities is only about 1.5 percent of the West Bank. A kidney-shaped state linked to the Gaza Strip by a secure passage would be contiguous. Some argue that the E1 project linking Ma'ale Adumim to Jerusalem would cutoff East Jerusalem, but even that is not necessarily true as Israel has proposed constructing a four-lane underpass to guarantee free passage between the West Bank and the Arab sections of Jerusalem.

Notes, Chapter 16

1. Stephen M. Schwebel, "What Weight to Conquest?" *American Journal of International Law* (April, 1970), 345–46.
2. Eugene Rostow, "Bricks and Stones: Settling for Leverage," *New Republic* (April 23, 1990).
3. Charles Krauthammer, "The Settlements Are a Spur to Peace," *Washington Post* (November 1, 1991).
4. Eugene Rostow, "Bricks and Stones: Settling for Leverage," *New Republic* (April 23, 1990).
5. Ari Shavit, "End of a Journey," *Haaretz* (September 13, 2001); President George W. Bush's Letter to Prime Minister Ariel Sharon (April 14, 2004).
6. *Jerusalem Post* (October 22, 1991).
7. Yossi Klein Halevi, "The Great Israeli Settlement Myth," *Los Angeles Times* (June 20, 2001).
8. Tovah Lazaroff, "Frontlines: Is Settlement Growth Booming?" *Jerusalem Post* (December 30, 2010); "Statistics on Settlements and Settler Population," B'Tselem (May 11, 2015).
9. Avi Issacharoff, "PA Lightens Ban on Working in Settlements to Ease Palestinian Unemployment," *Haaretz* (December 28, 2010); Ali Sawafta, "For Many Palestinians, Israel Settlement Work the Only Option," *Reuters* (February 22, 2016); Itamar Marcus and Nan Jacques Zilberdik, "Why Palestinians Prefer to Work for Israeli Employers," Palestinian Media Watch (July 25, 2016).
10. Greg Myre, "Middle East: Sharon Sees More West Bank Pullouts," *New York Times* (August 30, 2005).
11. "Report of the Middle East Quartet" (July 1, 2016).
12. Prime Minister Ariel Sharon, Address to the Likud Central Committee (January 5, 2004).
13. Steven J. Rosen, "Abrams: Israel Is Right That There Were Settlement Agreements," *Middle East Forum* (June 25, 2009).

17. The Nuclear Issue

Israel's refusal to sign the NPT allows it to threaten its neighbors.

Iran has no ambition to become a nuclear power.

Israel has nothing to fear from a nuclear Iran.

Iran's nuclear program threatens only Israel.

Iran has signed an agreement that will prevent it from building a nuclear bomb.

Negotiators achieved the best possible deal with Iran.

Iran's breakout time for building a weapon is now one year instead of three months.

The only alternative to the nuclear deal was war.

Military force could not have stopped Iran's nuclear program.

The United States did not go to war against Iran.

Iran will be prevented from building a bomb by an "unprecedented" verification regime.

If Iran cheats, sanctions can be easily reimposed.

The Iran deal eliminates the danger of nuclear proliferation.

The agreement put an end to Iran's ballistic missile research.

Iran's attitude toward the United States and Israel has moderated.

Iran is an ally in the fight against ISIS.

Unfrozen assets will aid the Iranian economy but not its hostile activities.

MYTH

Israel's refusal to sign the NPT allows it to threaten its neighbors.

FACT

Though Israel does not formally acknowledge that it has a nuclear capability, it has been widely reported that Israel has been a member of the nuclear club for a number of years. During that time, Israel has never tested, used, or threatened the use of nuclear weapons. Israel, has in fact, pledged never to be the first to introduce nuclear weapons into the region and proven through the wars since acquiring a bomb that it will use only conventional weapons to defend its security.

Like India, Israel has not signed the Non-Proliferation Treaty (NPT). Israel's decision is based largely on the grounds that the treaty has done little to stem nuclear proliferation in the region. Iraq is a signatory to the NPT and yet was able to amass a large amount of nuclear material without the knowledge of the International Atomic Energy Agency prior to the Israeli attack on its reactor in 1981.

Iran is also a signatory to the NPT and was discovered to have had a secret nuclear weapons program for more than a decade. Even after the disclosure, Iran defied the international community and continued to enrich uranium for the purpose, most believe, of building a nuclear weapon.

Another signatory to the treaty, Syria, was accused of pursuing a nuclear weapon after Israel bombed a suspected weapons facility in 2007. The CIA subsequently said it was a plutonium reactor being built with the help of North Korea.[1]

I wish Israel did not need defensive weapons of mass destruction or the region's most powerful defense forces. I wish the world had not driven the Jewish State into allocating its limited resources away from its universities and toward its military, but survival must come first, and Israel's military strength is the key to its survival. Anyone who believes that survival can be assured by moral superiority alone must remember the Warsaw Ghetto and the Treblinka gas chambers.

—Alan Dershowitz[2]

MYTH

Iran has no ambition to become a nuclear power.

FACT

Few people were aware of Iran's nuclear program or worried until the election of President Mahmoud Ahmadinejad. His belligerent rhetoric, explicit threats against Israel, and Holocaust denial attracted worldwide attention. Iran's desire to build nuclear weapons predated his regime, however, and becoming a nuclear power became a matter of national pride. Furthermore, the nuclear threat from Iran did not disappear when he was replaced.

American intelligence assessments estimated that, before signing the nuclear agreement, Iran had the capability to build a nuclear weapon within two to three months.[3] If they had no interest in a bomb, why did they acquire the means to build one within such a short period?

Evidence of Iran's pursuit of nuclear weapons was revealed in 2002 with the discovery of two previously unknown nuclear facilities in Arak and Natanz. This was followed by the admission by Pakistan's top nuclear scientist, Abdul Qadeer Khan, that he provided nuclear weapons expertise and equipment to Iran.[4]

Secretary of State Colin Powell said US intelligence indicated Iran was trying to fit missiles to carry nuclear weapons. "There is no doubt in my mind—and it's fairly straightforward from what we've been saying for years—that they have been interested in a nuclear weapon that has utility, meaning that it is something they would be able to deliver, not just something that sits there," Powell said.[5]

Iranian president Mahmoud Ahmadinejad defended his country's right to produce nuclear fuel in a fiery speech to the UN General Assembly in 2005 and later said he was prepared to transfer Iran's nuclear knowledge to other Islamic countries.[6]

The international consensus opposing Iran's pursuit of nuclear weapons was reflected by multiple UN Security Council measures starting with Resolution 1696 in July 2006. This resolution gave Iran a deadline to suspend its uranium enrichment. In December, the UN adopted a similar measure (Resolution 1737), which added prohibitions on Iran's ability to acquire nuclear material and equipment. On February 22, 2007, the IAEA announced that Iran had not complied with the resolutions, prompting Iranian foreign minister Manouchehr Mottaki to declare that Iran would never suspend uranium enrichment.[7]

In February 2010, President Obama announced new unilateral sanctions by the United States. In yet another act of defiance, Iran announced the next day it had begun enriching uranium to a higher level of purity, 20 percent, moving a step closer to producing weapons-grade uranium.[8] By May, the IAEA reported that Iran had produced a stockpile of nuclear fuel that, with further enrichment, would be sufficient to build two nuclear weapons.[9]

MYTH

Israel has nothing to fear from a nuclear Iran.

FACT

Jews have learned from painful history that when someone threatens to kill them, they should take it seriously. Therefore, no one should be surprised at the alarm expressed by Israel after hearing Iranian president Mahmoud Ahmadinejad proclaim, "This origin of corruption [Israel] will soon be wiped off the Earth's face!"[10] and Ayatollah Ali Khamenei, Iran's supreme leader, declaring that Israel is a "cancerous tumor that should be cut and will be cut."[11]

Would Iran launch a nuclear attack against Israel and take the risk of an Israeli counterstrike that might destroy the country? Perhaps, Middle East expert Bernard Lewis observed, because what matters to the Islamists in Iran is that infidels go to hell and believers go to heaven. As evidence, Lewis quotes a passage from Ayatollah Khomeini, cited in an eleventh-grade Iranian schoolbook:

> I am decisively announcing to the whole world that if the world-devourers [the infidel powers] wish to stand against

our religion, we will stand against the whole world and will not cease until the annihilation of all of them. Either we all become free, or we will go to the greater freedom, which is martyrdom. Either we shake one another's hands in joy at the victory of Islam in the world, or all of us will turn to eternal life and martyrdom. In both cases, victory and success are ours.[12]

Iranian president Mahmoud Ahmadinejad believed the most important task of the Iranian Revolution was to prepare the way for the return of the Twelfth Imam, who disappeared in 874, bringing an end to Muhammad's lineage. Shiites believe this imam, the Mahdi or "divinely guided one," will return in an apocalyptic battle in which the forces of righteousness will defeat the forces of evil and bring about a new era in which Shi'a Islam ultimately becomes the dominant religion throughout the world. The Shiites have been waiting patiently for the Twelfth Imam for more than a thousand years, but some feared that Ahmadinejad believed he could hasten the return through a nuclear war. It is this apocalyptic worldview, Lewis notes, that distinguishes Iran from other governments with nuclear weapons.

There are those who think that Iran would never use such weapons against Israel because innocent Muslims would be killed as well; however, Ayatollah Ali Akbar Hashemi-Rafsanjani, Ahmadinejad's predecessor, explicitly said he wasn't concerned about fallout from an attack on Israel. "If a day comes when the world of Islam is duly equipped with the arms Israel has in its possession," he said, "the strategy of colonialism would face a stalemate because application of an atomic bomb would not leave anything in Israel but the same thing would just produce damages in the Muslim world." As one Iranian commentator noted, Rafsanjani apparently wasn't concerned that the destruction of the Jewish State would also result in the mass murder of Palestinians as well.[13]

During negotiations with Iran, President Obama repeated the falsehood that Iran's Supreme Leader had issued a *fatwa* [religious edict] against the development of nuclear weapons.[14] Besides minimizing the Iranian threat, the claim raised the question: Why is it necessary to sanction or negotiate with Iran if Obama believed they will not develop nuclear weapons because of this *fatwa*?

The president was misinformed. After an exhaustive investigation into the question of whether or not a *fatwa* regarding nuclear weapons was ever issued, the Middle East Media Research Institute (MEMRI) concluded the *fatwa* "does not exist."[15]

Iran will not have to use nuclear weapons to influence events in the region. By possessing a nuclear capability, the Iranians can deter

Israel or any other nation from attacking Iran or its allies. When Hezbollah attacked Israel in 2006, for example, a nuclear Iran could have threatened retaliation against Tel Aviv if Israeli forces bombed Beirut. The mere threat of using nuclear weapons would be sufficient to drive Israelis into shelters and could cripple the economy.

Israel's prime minister must contemplate the following questions: Will immigrants want to come to a country that lives in the shadow of annihilation? Will companies want to do business under those conditions? Will Israelis be willing to live under a nuclear cloud?

If you were the prime minister of Israel, would you take seriously threats to destroy Israel by someone who might obtain the capability to carry them out? Could you afford to take the risk of allowing Iran to acquire nuclear weapons? How long would you wait for sanctions or other international measures to work before acting unilaterally to defend your country?

MYTH

Iran's nuclear program threatens only Israel.

FACT

Israel is not alone in its concern about Iran's nuclear weapons program. In fact, the nations most worried about Iran are its immediate neighbors who have no doubts about the hegemonic ambitions of the radical Islamists in Tehran.

Iran's Arab neighbors have accused it of threatening the sovereignty and independence of the Kingdom of Bahrain and territories of the United Arab Emirates, "issuing provocative statements against Arab states," and interfering in the affairs of the Palestinians, Iraq, and Morocco.[16]

In statements challenging Bahrain's sovereignty, Iranian officials renewed claims that the kingdom was actually a part of the Persian Empire. The effect of Iran's saber rattling, journalist Giles Whittell wrote, "is especially chilling in Bahrain as the only Sunni-led country with a Shia majority that is not at war or on the brink of war."[17] Arab League Deputy Secretary-General Ahmad Bin Hali angrily denounced Iran's claims to Bahrain while former Bahraini army chief of staff Sheik Maj.-Gen. Khalifa ibn Ahmad al-Khalifa said Iran stirs trouble in many Gulf nations. "[Iran] is like an octopus," he observed. "It is rummaging around in Iraq, Kuwait, Lebanon, Gaza and Bahrain."[18]

The crown prince of Bahrain was the first Gulf leader to explicitly accuse Iran of lying about its weapons program. "While they don't have the bomb yet, they are developing it, or the capability for it," Salman bin Hamad bin Isa al-Khalifa said.[19]

Iran also reasserted its authority over three islands of the United Arab Emirates that it forcibly seized in the early 1970s and continues to occupy. While joint sovereignty was maintained between Iran and the UAE over the Abu Musa and Greater and Lesser Tunbs islands until 1994, Iran significantly increased its military capabilities on Abu Musa, stationed Islamic Revolutionary Guard Corps soldiers there, and expelled foreign workers in attempts to assert full control of the island. The United Nations General Assembly, the Arab League, and the Arab Parliamentary Union have all affirmed their support for the UAE's claim and determined that Iran illegally occupies the islands.[20]

The United States and the international community are determined to prevent Iran from acquiring nuclear weapons.

—President Barrack Obama[21]

The Iranian threat is felt in Arab states beyond the Gulf as well. Morocco severed diplomatic relations with Iran in response to the inflammatory statements concerning Bahrain and hostile activity by Iranians inside Morocco. Morocco's foreign ministry accused the Iranian diplomatic mission in Rabat of interfering in the internal affairs of the kingdom and attempting to spread Shi'a Islam in the nation where 99 percent of the population are Sunni Muslims.[22]

European leaders also see Iran as a threat to their interests. French president Nicolas Sarkozy said, for example, "Iran is trying to acquire a nuclear bomb. I say to the French, it's unacceptable."[23] German chancellor Angela Merkel stated, "I'm emphatically in favor of solving the problem through negotiations, but we also need to be ready to impose further sanctions if Iran does not give ground."[24] "Iran is trying to get a nuclear weapon," British prime minister David Cameron declared. "It's in the interests of everyone here and everyone in the world that we don't get a nuclear arms race."[25] Similarly, Europe's neighbor, Turkey, has also expressed alarm at Iran's actions. Turkish president Abdullah Gül declared that "Turkey will not accept a neighboring country possessing weapons not possessed by Turkey herself."[26]

The international concern that prompted a series of UN resolutions and condemnation of Iranian behavior has nothing to do with Israel. Most of the world understands that a nuclear Iran poses a direct threat to countries inside and outside the Middle East, raises the specter of nuclear terrorism, increases the prospects for regional instability, and promotes proliferation.

Given the threat posed by Iran, the Arab states, not Israel, aggressively lobbied the US government to launch a military attack against Iran. The king of Saudi Arabia, for example, said the United States should put an end to its nuclear programs and "cut off the head of the snake."[27]

MYTH

Iran has signed an agreement that will prevent it from building a nuclear bomb.

FACT

On July 14, 2015, the P5+1 (USA, Germany, France, the United Kingdom, China, and Russia) announced they had agreed with Iran on the Joint Comprehensive Plan of Action (JCPOA) on Iran's nuclear program with the aim of preventing Iran from acquiring nuclear weapons. The deal is complex; however, the main points are:

1. Iran claims its nuclear program is for peaceful purposes. Most power reactors in the West use uranium enriched to 5 percent; however, Iran had been processing ore to 20 percent enrichment, with the possibility of increasing this to the 90 percent level required to build a bomb. Under the agreement, Iran agreed to limit enrichment to 3.7 percent and to cap its stockpile of low-enriched uranium at 300 kilograms, or 660 pounds, for 15 years.

2. Israel had called for the destruction of Iran's nuclear facilities and centrifuges. Iran agreed, however, only to turn its underground plant at Fordo into a center for science research, and to reduce the number of centrifuges for enriching uranium at its Natanz plant from about nineteen thousand to roughly five thousand. A third reactor being constructed at Arak is to be redesigned so it cannot produce weapons-grade plutonium, and the reactor's spent fuel, which could also be used to produce a bomb, will be shipped out of the country. Iran will not build any additional heavy water reactors for fifteen years.

3. The agreement allows the International Atomic Energy Agency (IAEA) greater access and information regarding Iran's nuclear program; however, it may not conduct "anywhere, anytime" inspections as originally demanded by President Obama. Iran also refused to allow the IAEA to investigate Iran's past efforts to build a nuclear weapon.

4. The provisions of the deal relating to uranium enrichment, research, and development will expire in fifteen years. Some inspections and transparency measures will remain in place for as long as twenty-five years.

5. The agreement increases the "breakout" time—the amount of time it would take Iran to produce enough bomb-grade material for a singular nuclear weapon—to at least one year.

6. Iran will be permitted to buy ballistic missiles within eight years and conventional weapons within five years. In the meantime, Iran continues to build and test its own missiles.

7. A variety of sanctions are to be gradually lifted with the possibility of Iran reaping a windfall of more than $100 billion. In the event of Iran failing to comply with the agreement, Obama insisted sanctions could be reimposed.

Many observers are skeptical that the JCPOA will prevent Iran from building a bomb, though there is disagreement as to whether it may be possible for Iran to do this before or after the deal expires. Director of National Intelligence James Clapper told the Senate Armed Services Committee that "Iran does not face any insurmountable technical barriers to producing a nuclear weapon," contradicting the Obama administration's claim that the nuclear deal blocks all of Iran's pathways to a nuclear bomb.[28]

Clapper reiterated the Obama administration's controversial assertion, which has been questioned by outside experts,[29] that it would now take Iran about a year to build a nuclear weapon. He also said the US intelligence community does not know "whether Iran will build a nuclear weapon in the wake of last summer's nuclear deal," adding that the question is whether Iran has the "political will" to pursue the bomb. "Iran probably views the Joint Comprehensive Plan of Action (JCPOA) as a means to remove sanctions while preserving some of its nuclear capabilities, as well as the option to eventually expand its nuclear infrastructure," Clapper testified.

MYTH

Negotiators achieved the best possible deal with Iran.

FACT

Iranians have centuries of experience negotiating in the bazaar and knowing how to get the best deal for themselves. Former Israeli ambassador to the United States Michael Oren put it this way in the context of the Iran negotiations:

> In reaching the parameters agreement, international negotiators were worn down by the protracted talks. They were persuaded by Iran's displays of warmth and earnestness, and accepted its claim that the nuclear program was a matter of national pride similar to America's moon landing. Most dam-

agingly, when asked by the Iranians "how much do you want to spend?" the P5+1 replied by recognizing the Islamic Republic's right to enrich and to maintain its nuclear facilities. This became the new baseline and the only remaining questions were: How much enrichment and how many facilities? The haggling had scarcely begun and already the merchant profited.[30]

How did Iran benefit? Consider some of the most serious holes in the Iranian deal:

1. The IAEA has been repeatedly rebuffed in its efforts to inspect Iranian facilities and to obtain information about Iran's past military nuclear work. The agreement does not require Iran to comply with IAEA requests until after sanctions have been eased, at which point Iran will have no incentive to cooperate.

2. Not one nuclear facility will be destroyed, including the Fordow center buried under a mountain (which Obama previously insisted be closed) and the Arak heavy-water nuclear facility, which appears to have no other purpose than to produce plutonium for a bomb. At the end of ten years, a nanosecond in Persian history, Iran can build as many heavy water reactors as it wants.

3. The *Washington Post* noted that "not one of the country's 19,000 centrifuges will be dismantled," and that, contrary to Obama's 2012 pledge, "enrichment will continue with 5,000 centrifuges for a decade, and all restraints on it will end in 15 years."[31]

4. Additionally, at odds with expectations, the *Post* reported that Iran's "existing stockpile of enriched uranium will be 'reduced' but not necessarily shipped out of the country" to Russia for reprocessing.

5. *The Post* added, "The proposed accord will provide Iran a huge economic boost that will allow it to wage more aggressively the wars it is already fighting or sponsoring across the region."

6. The president originally insisted on anytime, anywhere inspections, but Iran would not agree, leaving open the possibility that nuclear programs may be concealed.

Ultimately, Secretary of State John Kerry's hands were tied in the negotiations, as were those of representatives of France, Germany, and England. The reason, Ed Rogers, noted was two-fold: First, Obama was afraid that a breakdown in talks would allow Iran to move ahead and build a bomb. Second, Obama needed an agreement he could sell as a guaranteed means of cutting off all paths to an Iranian bomb because he was unwilling to use force if negotiations failed, and the Iranians knew it.[32]

MYTH

*Iran's breakout time for building a weapon is
now one year instead of three months.*

FACT

The nuclear deal was predicated on the idea that the agreement would
push back the time required for Iran to produce enough fissile material for a weapon from two months or less to one year. Doubts were
expressed about this during the negotiations. "It remains to be seen,"
editorialized the *Washington Post*, "whether the limits on enrichment
and Iran's stockpile will be judged by independent experts as sufficient to meet that standard."[33]

Obama subsequently set off alarm bells by saying in an interview that
"in year 13, 14, 15 [of the proposed deal], they [Iran] have advanced centrifuges that enrich uranium fairly rapidly, and at that point the breakout times would have shrunk *almost down to zero* (emphasis added)."[34]

"By making the central measure by which to judge the effectiveness of the deal a one-year breakout time," Ambassador Dennis Ross
explained, "the administration has made verification the most important part of the agreement. It must be in a position to show that it can
detect what the Iranians are doing, when they are doing it. International Atomic Energy Agency (IAEA) inspectors must have access to
declared and undeclared sites—even if it is at a military or Revolutionary Guard facility."[35] Ross expressed skepticism that the Iranians
would agree and, indeed, Iranian officials have repeatedly said they
will not allow inspections of military sites. In fact, shortly after the
agreement was signed, Foreign Minister Mohammad Javad Zarif said
Iran had made access to military sites a "red line."[36]

If Iran's ability to build a bomb were reduced to one year, why
would this ease the concerns of countries in the region? Obama
claims that safeguards would allow the detection of any Iranian effort
to "breakout"; however, given the failure to detect and stop nuclear
programs in North Korea, Pakistan, and India, the record on nonpro-
liferation is not encouraging.

Even if an agreement pushes the breakout time to a year, that may
not be enough time "for the intelligence community to identify the
development, attempt to persuade Iran to refrain from making it, and
take action to stop it."[37]

Meanwhile, countries in the region may be unwilling to trust
Obama's claim to have cut off all of Iran's avenues to building a
bomb. They may not want to risk the possibility that Iran will obtain
a weapon in less time or, later, when the agreement expires. Saudi
Arabia, for example, has repeatedly stated it would obtain a nuclear
bomb if Iran did, and may want to act preemptively to acquire one.[38]

MYTH

The only alternative to the nuclear deal was war.

FACT

This straw man was cynically used by the Obama administration to suggest that anyone who opposed their policy wanted a war with Iran because that was the only alternative to the agreement. Israeli prime minister Benjamin Netanyahu and other opponents of the deal were subsequently painted as warmongers; however, Netanyahu repeatedly said the alternative to a bad deal was not war, but a better deal. Moreover, by taking what he claimed was the only alternative to talks off the table, Obama weakened his bargaining position and virtually guaranteed that the ultimate agreement would not meet all his demands.

MYTH

Military force could not have stopped Iran's nuclear program.

FACT

Former Israeli defense and prime minister Ehud Barak noted that in the last generation, six countries have pursued nuclear weapons programs. "Two were persuaded to surrender their ambition voluntarily: Libya and South Africa. Two were stopped by surgical airstrikes: Iraq and Syria. The final two—Pakistan and North Korea—got the bomb, and got it following a path not so different than the one the ayatollahs are treading today."[39]

The truth is that no one could be sure what impact a military operation would have on Iran's nuclear program. Would it knock out some, all, or none of the research facilities? If it only knocked out some of them, would that slow down Iran's progress toward building a bomb? And, the question asked most frequently: At best, wouldn't a military operation delay Iran's ability to build a bomb by only a few years?

Let's take the last question first. Depending on the effectiveness of the military operation, it is possible that the Iranian program would only be delayed; however, the negotiated agreement will do the same. Obama has said that Iran will have a breakout time of zero within fifteen years. A military attack might deter Iran for a shorter period, but as Barak noted, "A surgical strike on key nuclear facilities in Iran can throw them five years backward, and a repetition would become a major Iranian worry. On the spectrum of military actions, this would be closer to the raid that killed Osama bin Laden than to the invasion of Iraq."[40]

Obama insisted the cost of any attack would exceed the benefit of what he believed would result in only a short-term delay in Iran's ability to build a bomb. Prime Minister Benjamin Netanyahu argued the president had it backward. "There's been plenty of talk," he said, "about the costs of stopping Iran. I think it's time we started talking about the costs of not stopping Iran."

"A nuclear-armed Iran," Netanyahu said, "would dramatically increase terrorism by giving terrorists a nuclear umbrella." This would allow Iran's terror proxies—Hezbollah and Hamas—to feel "emboldened to attack the United States, Israel, and other countries because they will be backed by a power that has atomic bombs." Furthermore, Netanyahu warned, "A nuclear-armed Iran could choke off the world's oil supply and could make real its threat to close the Straits of Hormuz."

Proliferation would also be a serious problem because, Netanyahu says, "If Iran gets nuclear weapons, it would set off a mad dash by Saudi Arabia, Turkey, and others to acquire nuclear weapons of their own. The world's most volatile region would become a nuclear tinderbox waiting to go off."

"The worst nightmare of all," he added, is that "Iran could threaten all of us with nuclear terrorism."

Still, Netanyahu said, Israel preferred a peaceful resolution to the issue.[41]

Besides the basic desire to avoid war, a number of factors militated against a military operation. The Europeans were unlikely to act without the United States because they lack the military capability to sufficiently damage the Iranian facilities and, more important, lack the will to use force. It is possible that one (most likely Britain) or more would act in concert with the United States if American forces were deployed.

The United States is the one country that has the military capability to destroy, or at least seriously set back Iran's nuclear program. Nevertheless, the United States had its own reasons to hesitate besides the potential consequences of initiating a war. First, before resorting to military force, the president wanted to demonstrate to the American people that he did everything possible to avoid war. Second, the Obama administration wanted to focus on the economy and domestic issues and become more engaged in Asia. Third, Obama was afraid of starting a third war with a Muslim country after pledging in his first foreign policy address in Cairo in 2009 that he wanted to improve ties with the Muslim world. Fourth, after bringing troops home from Iraq and planning to withdraw those in Afghanistan, he was reticent to risk putting troops in a new theater of conflict. Fifth, Obama disdained unilateral moves and was reluctant to act without a multilateral consensus that there was no other option, and without at least one other major power joining any military operation.

MYTH

The United States did not go to war against Iran.

FACT

The United States did not deploy troops or aircraft to Iran; however, even as negotiations were conducted, a covert war was being waged against Iran's nuclear program. One of its most important components was cyber warfare. This involved efforts to sabotage nuclear-related equipment, both before and after it arrived in Iran.

In 2010, for example, the world learned that a computer worm referred to as Stuxnet wreaked havoc on Iranian computer systems and led to the destruction or damage of hundreds of centrifuges.[42] Two years later, Iran admitted that another cyberattack, "Flame," infected their computers, this time allowing the attackers to use them for surveillance. Iran's oil ministry was hit by the "Wiper" program, which erased its hard drives.

News reports attributed the cyber warfare to a US and Israeli intelligence operation called "Operation Olympic Games," started under President George W. Bush and expanded under Obama.[43]

MYTH

Iran will be prevented from building a bomb by an "unprecedented" verification regime.

FACT

Paradoxically, President Obama claimed the nuclear agreement will cut off all avenues for Iran to achieve a bomb, while also saying that we have measures we can take if they do begin to build one.

The ability to prevent Iran from cheating on the agreement depends on a strict verification regime; however, there is ample reason to be skeptical. Iran has consistently obstructed IAEA investigations, concealed research sites and materials, and offered no reason to trust it to cooperate in the future. The IAEA reported, for example, that Iran refused to disclose information about its past military nuclear work.[44] Iranian foreign minister Muhammad Javad Zarif stressed that Iran would allow no online cameras to be installed in nuclear facilities, and Iranian officials repeatedly said investigators would be barred from military installations.[45]

Iran has also prevented the IAEA from thoroughly investigating the Parchin site where it is suspected that Iran engaged in research and testing related to building a nuclear weapon. The Iranians tried to conceal the work done in the area by removing soil and infrastructure; however, uranium particles discovered at Parchin in 2015, along with satellite imagery and documents from defectors, indicate the base was part of the nuclear program.[46]

Iran has a history of deception that is likely to continue. Former IAEA inspector Olli Heinonen, recalled, for example, that it took six months between the time the Natanz plant was discovered and the IAEA was allowed inside. The delay was designed to conceal another research and development site. The same deceptive policy, he said, was used to develop the secret underground facility at Fordo.[47]

Former Secretaries of State Henry Kissinger and George Shultz pointed out a number of other loopholes in the verification regime. "Iran permanently gives up none of its equipment, facilities or fissile product to achieve the proposed constraints," they note. "It only places them under temporary restriction and safeguard—amounting in many cases to a seal at the door of a depot or periodic visits by inspectors to declared sites. The physical magnitude of the effort is daunting. Is the International Atomic Energy Agency technically, and in terms of human resources, up to so complex and vast an assignment?"[48]

Furthermore, the secretaries note that because Iran is "a large country with multiple facilities and ample experience in nuclear concealment, violations will be inherently difficult to detect." Maintaining constant vigilance will be difficult, and any reported violations will likely be subject to debate that may allow Iran to delay or circumvent any penalties.

Another option for Iran to cheat is to transfer the weapons outside the country. For example, Iran has worked closely with North Korea on ballistic missile development and cofinanced the Koreans' nuclear tests. According to William R. Harris, an international lawyer who formerly took part in drafting and verifying US arms control agreements, Iran could hide its nuclear weapons in that country.[49]

The Obama administration claims that any Iranian breakout will be detectable; however, Kissinger and Shultz point out that it is unlikely "that breakout will be a clear-cut event," so Iran could build a weapon through "the gradual accumulation of ambiguous evasions" that might not attract attention until it is too late.

Furthermore, if there is one thing we have learned over the years, it is the need for a healthy dose of skepticism about what intelligence agencies know and when they know it. We have myriad examples, from the failure to predict the fall of the Soviet Union to the misinformation about Iraq's weapons of mass destruction to the inability to anticipate the Arab Spring. In the case of Iran, the failure of the intelligence community to detect Iran's secret nuclear program should give pause to anyone who wants to trust the future of the Middle East to the analysts in Langley or anywhere else. And what will be the implications if the information is wrong or too late?

The North Korean precedent is hardly reassuring. In that case, IAEA inspectors were given limited access to known nuclear facilities and none whatsoever to suspected sites where nuclear materials were hidden. "The result was that when the so-called Hermit Kingdom decided to sprint for a bomb and violate its negotiated agreements regarding its nuclear program, it could reach breakout more quickly."[50]

MYTH

If Iran cheats, sanctions can be easily reimposed.

FACT

The Obama administration sold the nuclear agreement with a promise to "snapback" penalties if Iran violated the deal.[51] Beyond that, the president leaves open how the West would respond. Based on Obama's failure to enforce his "red line" in Syria, or to show a serious willingness to use force against Iran for previous violations of UN resolutions, Iran may believe it can break the agreement with impunity.

Moreover, sanctions are not like a water spigot; they cannot be easily turned on and off. It took years and multiple UN resolutions to impose sanctions and many countries, including the United States, cheated on them for years. This allowed Iran to sustain its economy at a high enough level to stave off a popular revolt and permitted it to pursue its hegemonic designs on the region.

China and Russia, which both have billion-dollar deals with Iran, were reluctant to support sanctions in the past, threatening to veto more draconian proposals. It is likely they will use their veto power to prevent the reimposition of sanctions in the absence of a threat to their interests.

Once the sanctions were removed, companies from around the world raced to Iran with business proposals and, within weeks, dozens had signed deals worth billions of dollars. Most countries will not want to reverse their policy, and it is likely the current consensus would break down, unless the Iranian breach was so egregious that the international community could be rallied again to act. By that time, however, it may be too late, and the only alternative may then be military action.

MYTH

The Iran deal eliminates the danger of nuclear proliferation.

FACT

One of the most serious but understated threats posed by Iran's nuclear program is the prospect of widespread proliferation. President Obama acknowledged the danger when he stated, "It will not be tolerable to a number of states in that region for Iran to have a nuclear weapon and them not to have a nuclear weapon." He added, "Iran is known to sponsor terrorist organizations, so the threat of proliferation becomes that much more severe." Obama continued, "The dangers of an Iran getting nuclear weapons that then leads to a free-for-all in the Middle East is something that I think would be very dangerous for the world."[52]

In theory, the agreement reduces the danger of proliferation, but, in practice, it will not. Iran's neighbors are unlikely to risk the possibility of Iran cheating and will therefore provoke an arms race as Turkey and several Arab states seek weapons to deter the Iranians. For example, former US diplomat Dennis Ross said he was told by Saudi Arabia's King Abdullah in 2012, before the JCPOA was signed, "If they get nuclear weapons, we will get nuclear weapons."[53] After the agreement was approved, Saudi prince Turki al-Faisal reiterated that one option for responding to Iran's nuclear ambitions would be "the acquisitions of nuclear weapons, to face whatever eventuality might come from Iran."[54]

Most Arab countries say publicly they are only interested in peaceful uses of nuclear technology, but the fear is that some or all will follow the Iranian example and work toward building a bomb. Since 2006, at least thirteen Arab countries (including Saudi Arabia, Egypt, Jordan, Morocco, Turkey, and Syria) have either announced new plans to explore atomic energy or revived preexisting nuclear programs in response to Iran's nuclear program.[55] Several countries have strengthened their nuclear cooperation with other nations, such as the United States, Russia, and France. Both Saudi Arabia and the UAE signed nuclear cooperation accords with the United States while Russia is expected to build Egypt's first civilian nuclear power station. Kuwait, Bahrain, Libya, Algeria, Morocco, and Jordan announced plans to build nuclear plants as well. Even Yemen, one of the poorest countries in the Arab world, announced plans to purchase a nuclear reactor before it disintegrated in civil war.[56]

If Iran has nuclear weapons, it can also pose an indirect threat by sharing the technology, or an actual weapon, with other Muslim countries or terrorists. President Ahmadinejad raised worldwide concern about nuclear proliferation when he told the UN General Assembly in September 2005, "Iran is ready to transfer nuclear know-how to the Islamic countries due to their need."[57] Iran's Supreme Leader, Ayatollah Ali Khamenei, repeated the proliferation threat several months later when he told the president of Sudan, "Iran's nuclear capability is one example of various scientific capabilities in the country . . . The Islamic Republic of Iran is prepared to transfer the experience, knowledge and technology of its scientists."[58]

One major fear is that Iran could provide terrorists access to nuclear material. Former president Bill Clinton noted, "the more of these
weapons you have hanging around, the more fissile material you've
got, the more they're vulnerable to being stolen or sold or just simply
transferred to terrorists." He added, "even if the [Iranian] government
didn't directly sanction it, it wouldn't be that much trouble to get a
Girl Scout cookie's worth of fissile material, which, if put in the same
fertilizer bomb Timothy McVeigh used in Oklahoma City, is enough to
take out 20 to 25 percent of Washington, DC."[59]

A particular concern would be if Iran decided to transfer any of
these materials to Hezbollah. This is a group that is engaged in terror
worldwide, is committed to Israel's destruction, and has killed more
Americans than any terrorist group other than al-Qaeda on 9/11.

The United States has reportedly proposed extending an American
"umbrella" to the Gulf States to reassure them of American support
and discourage their pursuit of a nuclear option. This raises a series of
questions according to Henry Kissinger and George Shultz: "How will
these guarantees be defined? What factors will govern their implementation? Are the guarantees extended against the use of nuclear
weapons—or against any military attack, conventional or nuclear? Is
it the domination by Iran that we oppose or the method for achieving
it? What if nuclear weapons are employed as psychological blackmail?
And how will such guarantees be expressed, or reconciled with public opinion and constitutional practices?"[60]

The region will become far more dangerous as the number of countries engaged in nuclear activities grows. More ominously, the expansion of the Middle East nuclear club will pose a threat to global peace
and stability.

MYTH

The agreement put an end to Iran's ballistic missile research.

FACT

While the focus of the last several years has been on Iran's nuclear
program, the danger of a conventional Iranian attack with advanced
missiles has steadily grown. The National Council of the Resistance of
Iran, an Iranian opposition group, said that North Korea helped Iran
build dozens of underground tunnels and facilities for the construction of nuclear-capable missiles beginning in 1989.[61]

Iran has repeatedly violated UN Security Council Resolution 1929,
which forbids Iran from engaging in "any activity related to ballistic
missiles capable of delivering nuclear weapons, *including launches
using ballistic missile technology*" [emphasis added].[62]

According to the Congressional Research Service (CRS), "Iran's ballistic missiles challenge U.S. military capabilities and U.S. influence in the Middle East." US intelligence indicates that "Iran already has the largest inventory of ballistic missiles in the Middle East, and is expanding the scale, reach, and sophistication of its ballistic missile forces, many of which are inherently capable of carrying a nuclear payload."[63] The Pentagon also believes that Iran's missiles threaten "U.S. forces, allies, and partners in regions where the United States deploys troops and maintains security relationships."

Even without nuclear weapons, CRS noted Iran poses a serious threat to its Arab neighbors because they do not have missile defenses or the ability to deter an Iranian attack. This could allow Iran to "blackmail such states into meeting demands, for example, to raise oil prices, cut oil production, or even withhold cooperation with the U.S. on which their very survival depends."

The CRS study concluded that "Iran has not shown that it is deterred or dissuaded by U.S. conventional military superiority, or by U.S. and international sanctions, or by the deployment of U.S. BMD [ballistic missile defense] capabilities."[64]

In May 2013, Iranian officials unveiled a domestically developed transporter-erecter-launcher (TEL) system for their Shahab-3 missiles, making their missile arsenal more mobile and easily disguised. The development of a multiple reentry vehicle (MRV) attachment for the Shahab-3 missiles and newer longer-range Qiam missiles was unveiled in February 2014. The MRV attachments allow the missiles to carry multiple warheads and strike many different targets at once. Also unveiled in 2014 was the Iranian Kadr F missile, capable of hitting targets up to 1,950 kilometers away.

The range of our missiles covers all of Israel today. That means the fall of the Zionist regime, which will certainly come soon.

—General Mohammad Ali Jafari[65]

In the midst of the nuclear negotiations, Iran's Revolutionary Guard announced the test firing of a new missile, "Great Prophet 9," in the Strait of Hormuz on February 26, 2015, as part of a large-scale naval and air-defense drill. The drill also included an attack on a simulated American aircraft carrier. The Naval Chief of the Revolutionary Guard, Adm. Ali Fadavi, stated after the drill that "the new weapon will have a very decisive role in adding our naval power in confronting threats, particularly by the Great Satan, the United States."[66]

Meanwhile, North Korea reportedly supplied Iran with several shipments of missile components during the nuclear negotiations, violating UN sanctions against both countries.[67]

The Joint Comprehensive Plan of Action (JCPOA) reached between Iran and the P5+1 did not specify any limits on the Iranian ballistic missile program, except that the Iranians cannot develop any missiles capable of carrying a nuclear warhead for the duration of the agreement. Iranian officials insisted the deal did not apply to their missile program because their missiles were not designed to transport nuclear warheads. US officials, however, have repeatedly said that Iranian missiles are capable of carrying nuclear warheads.[68]

Announcing that "we will have a new ballistic missile test in the near future that will be a thorn in the eyes of our enemies," Iranian president Hassan Rouhani unveiled a new missile, known as the Fateh 313 on August 22, 2015. The missile has a range of 310 miles and is one of the most accurate in the Iranian arsenal. Rouhani defiantly added, "We will buy, sell and develop any weapons we need and we will not ask for permission or abide by any resolution for that."[69]

In defiance of a United Nations ban on testing missiles that could possibly deliver a nuclear warhead, Iran tested a new missile known as the Emad in October 2015. The Emad is a precision-guided long-range missile, and is the first guided weapon in Iran's arsenal capable of striking Israel. It is estimated that the missile has a range of more than one thousand miles, and Israeli military analyst Uzi Rubin noted that "the Emad represents a major leap in terms of accuracy."[70]

While agreeing that the missile test violated the UN ban, the White House took no action, insisting, "This is altogether separate from the nuclear agreement that Iran reached with the rest of the world."[71] Iran's defiance of the world in this regard, however, does not bode well for its adherence to the nuclear deal.

In 2016, Iran conducted several ballistic tests involving missiles capable of delivering nuclear weapons in defiance of Security Council Resolution 2231, adopted in July 2015 to ratify the nuclear agreement.[72] Russia promised to veto any new sanctions at the UN; however, anger in Congress over the Iranian violations has provoked bipartisan consideration of new US sanctions. President Obama opposed new congressional sanctions out of fear Iran might withdraw from the nuclear deal (the Treasury Department did impose sanctions on a few individuals and organizations associated with the missile program[73]). In fact, a senior Iranian military commander claimed that US officials were encouraging Iran to keep its illicit ballistic missile tests a secret so as not to provoke opposition.[74]

Iran also reportedly has an arsenal of cruise missiles. In March 2005, Ukraine admitted that it had exported to Iran cruise missiles that are capable of reaching Israel and carrying nuclear weapons. Israel is also concerned that Teheran is developing its own cruise missile to evade interception by the Arrow, the IDF's antiballistic missile defense system.[75]

Yet another concern is Iran's development of a space launch capability. Clapper told the Senate that "Iran's progress on space launch vehicles—along with its desire to deter the United States and its allies—provides Tehran with the means and motivation to develop longer-range missiles, including ICBMs."

Iran became just the ninth country to demonstrate this capability when it launched the Omid satellite from a Safir-2 rocket. Though the satellite ultimately crashed into the ocean, the launch was an indication that Iran was making progress toward developing long-range ballistic missiles. The Congressional Research Service warned that Iran "will use space for a range of military purposes, such as for reconnaissance and communications." The CRS study concluded that "Iran has not shown that it is deterred or dissuaded by U.S. conventional military superiority, or by U.S. and international sanctions, or by the deployment of U.S. BMD [ballistic missile defense] capabilities."[76]

MYTH

Iran's attitude toward the United States and Israel has moderated.

FACT

One rationale for the negotiations with Iran was to improve relations with Iran. Even as Iranians continued to chant "Death to America," President Obama said he hoped the diplomatic arrangement "ushers a new era in US-Iranian relations—and, just as importantly, over time, a new era in Iranian relations with its neighbors."[77]

Meanwhile, as Congress debated the nuclear deal, Iran's Supreme Leader Ayatollah Ali Khamenei called the United States the "Great Satan." He also threatened Israel, declaring, "God willing, there will be no such thing as a Zionist regime in 25 years."[78]

Iran also engaged in a number of provocative actions immediately after the nuclear deal was announced. A *Washington Post* reporter— John Rezaian—was sent to an Iranian prison as a spy on November 22, 2015. He and three other American hostages were essentially ransomed as part of the deal to repeal the sanctions against Iran, the Iranian navy fired rockets near US warships in the Gulf, and two US Navy boats that allegedly strayed inadvertently into Iranian waters were seized. The crew was humiliated on Iranian national television by being forced to kneel with their hands behind their heads, and one sailor was coerced to make a public apology.[79]

MYTH

Iran is an ally in the fight against ISIS.

FACT

The recognition that ISIS is a threat to the Middle East and beyond has led the United States to see Iran as an ally in the battle to destroy the radical Sunni group. Iran, however, is far more dangerous than ISIS.

The regional fight with ISIS is not only about territory and power; it is also a continuation of the centuries-old conflict between Sunnis and Shiites. As a Sunni group, ISIS has naturally drawn the wrath of Shiites, particularly in Iraq and Iran (and by extension their Lebanese proxies, Hezbollah). Even Sunni nations are afraid of ISIS, however, because of its declared goal of establishing a caliphate (which they've already declared in the area they control) with its leaders as rulers.

Iran does have an interest in defeating ISIS because it is threatening Shiite domination of Iraq and Iranian patronage of Bashar Assad's regime in Syria. Nevertheless, this does not change the fact that Iran's leaders are just as brutal and fanatical as ISIS and have for decades sought to spread their revolution across the region as a prelude to what they hope will ultimately result in the global domination of Islam. Unlike ISIS, Iran already controls a large nation with a formidable army, and has spread its influence to Iraq, Syria, Lebanon, Libya, and Yemen. Iran's reach extends even further as one of the leading sponsors of international terror.

Defeating ISIS is vital to preventing the spread of one radical Islamic party, but it will not eliminate the broader Islamist threat posed by Iran and its allies.

MYTH

*Unfrozen assets will aid the Iranian economy
but not its hostile activities.*

FACT

Iran agreed to the nuclear deal because it ended sanctions and unfroze assets that could be worth as much as $150 billion.[80] Administration officials say the figure is much lower. Regardless, those are billions of dollars that Iran will now have to continue and expand its nuclear research; to improve and test its ballistic missiles; to maintain troops in Syria, Libya, Yemen, and Iraq; to threaten Israel and its Gulf neighbors; and to fund Hezbollah and other terrorist organizations.

Notes, Chapter 17

1. Robert Siegel and Tom Gjelten, "CIA: North Korea Helping Syria Build Nuke Reactor," National Public Radio (April 24, 2008).

2. Alan Dershowitz, *Chutzpah* (Boston, MA: Little, Brown, and Co., 1991), 249.

3. "Parameters for a Joint Comprehensive Plan of Action regarding the Islamic Republic of Iran's Nuclear Program," *White House* (April 2, 2015).

4. Dean Nelson, "A. Q. Khan Boasts of Helping Iran's Nuclear Programme," *The Telegraph* (September 10, 2009).

5. Robin Wright and Keith Richburg, "Powell Says Iran Is Pursuing the Bomb," *Washington Post* (November 18, 2004).

6. Associated Press (September 15, 2005).

7. Raheb Homavandi, "Iran Says It Won't Suspend Atomic Work," *Irish Times* (February 27, 2007).

8. Glenn Kessler, "Analysis: Iranian Plan Will Put Nation a Step Closer to Having Material for Bomb," *Washington Post* (February 9, 2010).

9. David E. Sanger and William J. Broad, "U.N. Says Iran Has Fuel for 2 Nuclear Weapons," *New York Times* (May 31, 2010).

10. "Ahmadinejad: Israel Will Disappear from Map," Associated Press (June 3, 2008).

11. "Iran: We Will Help 'Cut Out the Cancer of Israel,'" *The Telegraph* (February 3, 2012).

12. Bernard Lewis, "Does Iran Have Something in Store?" *Wall Street Journal* (August 8, 2006).

13. Iran Press Service (December 14, 2001); see also "Former Iranian President Rafsanjani on Using a Nuclear Bomb against Israel," MEMRI (January 3, 2002).

14. Jed Babbin, "Obama's Iran Speech Deceit," *Washington Post* (August 6, 2015).

15. "Iranian Regime Continues Its Lies and Fabrications about Supreme Leader Khameni's Nonexistent Fatwa Banning Nuclear Weapons," *MEMRI* (April 6, 2015).

16. "AIP Calls on Iran to Respect Int'l Treaties Relevant to Bahrain, UAE," Kuwait News Agency (March 22, 2009).

17. Giles Whittell, "Bahrain Accuses Iran of Nuclear Weapons Lie," *TimesOnline* (November 2, 2007).

18. *Al-Hayat* (London) May 16, 2008, "Arab League Slams Iran's 'Provocation,'" *The Jerusalem Post* (March 22, 2009).

19. Giles Whittell, "Bahrain Accuses Iran of Nuclear Weapons Lie," *TimesOnline* (November 2, 2007).

20. AIP Calls on Iran to Respect Int'l Treaties Relevant to Bahrain, UAE, *Kuwait News Agency* (March 22, 2009); "Abu Musa Island," GlobalSecurity.org (October 15, 2008).

21. "Obama Says New U.S. Sanctions Show International Resolve in Iran issue," *CNN* (July 1, 2010).

22. "Morocco Severs Relations with Iran," *Al-Jazeera* (March 8, 2009).

23. David Jackson, "Iran, Iraq Top Agendas for Meetings with Allies," *USA Today* (November 1, 2007).

24. David Jackson, "Busy Week with World Leaders Planned," *USA Today* (November 9, 2011).

25. "David Cameron Threatens More Iran Nuclear Sanctions," *BBC* (February 23, 2011).

26. "Gül: Turkey Will Not Accept Iran Possessing Nuclear Weapons," Today's Zaman (January 3, 2013).

27. "Saudi King Abdullah and Senior Princes on Saudi Policy toward Iraq," White House for OVP, Department for NEA/ARP and S/I (April 20, 2008).

28. Aaron Kliegman, "Clapper: Iran Views Deal as 'Means to Remove Sanctions while Preserving Nuclear Capabilities,'" *Washington Free Beacon* (February 9, 2016).

29. "Obama's Iran Deal Falls Far Short of His Own Goals," *Washington Post* (April 2, 2015).

30. Ed Rogers, "What Should Republicans Do about the Framework Agreement with Iran?" *Washington Post* (April 3, 2015).

31. Kristina Wong, "5 Key Demands US Dropped in Iran Talks," *The Hill* (April 11, 2015).

32. Josh Lederman, "Obama Admits: Deal Will Give Iran 'Near Zero' Breakout Time in 13 Years," *Times of Israel* (April 7, 2015).

33. Greg Jaffe, "How Long Would an Iran Nuclear Deal Last?" *Washington Post* (April 7, 2015).

34. "Transcript: President Obama's Full NPR Interview on Iran Nuclear Deal," *NPR* (April 7, 2015).

35. Jane Harman, "We've Reached a 'Nuclear Framework' with Iran. So Now What?" *Washington Post* (April 2, 2015).

36. Paul Richter and Ramin Mostaghim, "Iran Can Deny Access to Military Sites, Foreign Minister Says," *Los Angeles Times* (July 22, 2015).

37. Ephraim Kam, "Deal Makes Iran Stronger Than Ever," *Israel Hayom* (April 7, 2015).

38. Ewen MacAskill and Ian Traynor, "Saudis Consider Nuclear Bomb," *The Guardian* (September 18, 2003).

39. Ehud Barak, "Ehud Barak: Iran Has Escaped a Noose," *Time* (April 2, 2015).

40. Ibid.

41. Prime Minister Benjamin Netanyahu Speech at the 2012 AIPAC Policy Conference," Jewish Virtual Library (March 5, 2012).

42. William J. Broad, John Markoff, and David Sanger, "Israeli Test on Worm Called Crucial in Iran Nuclear Delay," *New York Times* (January 15, 2011).

43. Ellen Nakashima and Joby Warrick, "Stuxnet Was Work of U.S. and Israeli Experts, Officials Say," *Washington Post* (June 2, 2012).

44. *New York Times* (June 3, 2004)

45. "No Online Cameras Allowed at Nuclear Sites: Zarif," *Mehr News Agency* (April 7, 2015).

46. William Tobey, "Iran's Parchin Particles: Why Should Two Mites of Uranium Matter?" *Foreign Policy* (July 7, 2016).

47. Rebecca Shimoni Stoil, "Ex-IAEA Deputy: Deal Puts Iran on Nuke Threshold for 10 Years, Then Gets Worse," *Times of Israel* (April 7, 2015).

48. Henry Kissinger and George Shultz, "The Iran Deal and Its Consequences," *Wall Street Journal* (April 7, 2015).

49. Ibid.

50. Rebecca Shimoni Stoil, "Ex-IAEA Deputy: Deal Puts Iran on Nuke Threshold for 10 Years, Then Gets Worse," *Times of Israel* (April 7, 2015).

51. Eric B. Lorber and Peter Feaver, "Do the Iran Deal's 'Snapback' Sanctions Have Teeth?" *Foreign Policy* (July 21, 2015).

52. Jeffrey Goldberg, "Obama to Iran and Israel: 'As President of the United States, I Don't Bluff,'" *Atlantic* (March 2, 2012).

53. Chemi Shalev, "Dennis Ross: Saudi King Vowed to Obtain Nuclear Bomb after Iran," *Haaretz* (May 30, 2012).

54. Nicole Gaouette, "Saudi Prince: Getting Nukes an Option if Iran Breaks Deal," *CNN* (May 7, 2016).

55. Friedrich Steinhausler, "Infrastructure Security and Nuclear Power," Strategic Insights, Volume VIII, Issue 5 (December 2009).

56. "Yemen Signs Agreement with US Firm to Build Nuclear Plant," *Almotamar.net* (September 25, 2007).

57. "Iran's Khamenei Says Willing to Transfer Nuclear Technology to Sudan," *Sudan Tribune* (April 25, 2006).

58. Ibid.

59. Piers Morgan Tonight (September 25, 2012).

60. Henry Kissinger and George Shultz, "The Iran Deal and Its Consequences," *Wall Street Journal* (April 7, 2015).

61. Luis Martinez and Jacqueline Shire, "Iran Is Building Nukes in Underground Locations," ABC News (November 21, 2005).

62. Louis Charonneau, "Iran's October Missile Test Violated U.N. Ban: Expert Panel," *Reuters* (December 16, 2015).

63. Steven A. Hildreth, "Iran's Ballistic Missile and Space Launch Programs," Congressional Research Service (December 6, 2012).

64. Ibid.

65. Mehrdad Balali, "Khamenei Tells Iran Armed Forces to Build Up 'Irrespective' of Diplomacy," *Reuters* (November 30, 2014).

66. Nasser Karimi, "Iran Test Fires New Weapon in Naval Drill," *Military Times* (February 27, 2015).

67. Bill Gertz, "North Korea Transfers Missile Goods to Iran During Nuclear Talks," *Free Beacon* (April 15, 2015).

68. Asa Fitch, "Iran Says Missile Didn't Violate Nuclear Deal," *Wall Street Journal* (October 12, 2015).

69. Bozorgmehr Sharafedin, "Iran Unveils New Missile, Says Seeks Peace through Strength," *Reuters* (August 22, 2015).

70. Sam Wilkin, "Iran Tests New Precision-Guided Ballistic Missile," *Reuters* (October 11, 2015).

71. Carol Lee, "White House Sees Signs Iran Missile Test Violated U.N. Resolution," *Wall Street Journal* (October 13, 2015).

72. Louis Charbonneau, "Exclusive: Iran Missile Tests Were 'in Defiance of' U.N. Resolution—U.S., Allies," *Reuters* (March 30, 2016).

73. "Treasury Sanctions Those Involved in Ballistic Missile Procurement for Iran," US Department of the Treasury (January 17, 2016).

74. Adam Kredo, "Iran: U.S. Encouraging Islamic Republic to Keep Illicit Missile Tests Secret," *Free Beacon* (May 16, 2016).

75. Eliott C. McLaughlin, "Iran's Supreme Leader: There Will Be No Such Thing as Israel in 25 Years," CNN (September 11, 2015).

76. Steven A. Hildreth, "Iran's Ballistic Missile and Space Launch Programs," Congressional Research Service (December 6, 2012).

77. Thomas L. Friedman, "Iran and the Obama Doctrine," *New York Times* (February 5, 2015).

78. Elioh C. McLaughlin, "Iran's Supreme Leader: There Will Be No Such Thing as Israel in 25 Years," CNN (September 11, 2015).

79. Chris Pleasance, Regina F. Graham, and Ollie Gillman, "Obama Under Fire for Historic Prisoner Swap with Iran Which Sees Seven Spies and Hackers Returned to Tehran in Exchange for a U.S. Journalist and Three Other Americans, as Kerry Lifts Economic Sanctions," *Daily Mail* (January 16, 2016).

80. Oren Dorell, "Lawmakers Alarmed over Iranian Nuclear Windfall," *USA Today* (July 5, 2015).

18. The Media

Press coverage of Israel is proportional to its importance in world affairs.
Media coverage of the Arab world is objective.
Journalists covering the Middle East are driven by the search for the truth.
Arab officials tell Western journalists the same thing they tell their own people.
Israelis cannot deny the truth of pictures showing their abuses.
The press makes no apologies for terrorists.
The Palestinian Authority places no restrictions on reporters.
The media carefully investigates Palestinian claims before publicizing them.
Media coverage of Israeli operations in Gaza was fair and accurate.
Journalists are never deceived by Palestinian propaganda.

MYTH

Press coverage of Israel is proportional to its importance in world affairs.

FACT

It is hard to justify the amount of news coverage given to Israel based on that nation's importance in world affairs or American national interests. How is it that a country the size of New Jersey routinely merits top billing over seemingly more newsworthy nations such as Russia, China, and Great Britain?

One reason Americans are so knowledgeable about Israel is the extent of coverage. American news organizations usually have more correspondents in Israel than in any country except Great Britain. For example, when Matti Friedman worked in Israel for the Associated Press, the news agency had more than forty people covering Israel and the territories. "That was more than AP had in China, Russia, or India, or in all of the 50 countries of sub-Saharan Africa combined," he said. Those journalists need to generate copy to justify their postings as well as their egos. Thus, in 2013, when the Israeli-Palestinian conflict claimed forty-two lives, Israel received more publicity than the Syrian civil war in which nearly two hundred thousand people died. According to Friedman:

> News organizations have nonetheless decided that this conflict is more important than, for example, the more than 1,600 women murdered in Pakistan last year (271 after being raped and 193 of them burned alive), the ongoing erasure of

Tibet by the Chinese Communist Party, the carnage in Congo (more than 5 million dead as of 2012) or the Central African Republic, and the drug wars in Mexico (death toll between 2006 and 2012: 60,000), let alone conflicts no one has ever heard of in obscure corners of India or Thailand. They believe Israel to be the most important story on earth, or very close.

Many reporters also suffer from plain ignorance and lack of preparation. Journalist Khaled Abu Toameh recalled one reporter who wanted to set up an interview with Yasser Arafat—only one problem—he was dead. Another was convinced there was a Palestinian state with Jerusalem as its capital in 1948. A third wanted to interview settlers in the Gaza Strip; however, they had all left the area ten years earlier. "Journalists of this type have become quite familiar to me," Abu Toameh relates. "They board a plane, read an article or two in the *Times* and feel ready to be experts on the Israeli-Palestinian conflict."[1]

MYTH

Media coverage of the Arab world is objective.

FACT

When asked to comment on what many viewers regard as CNN's bias against Israel, Reese Schonfeld, the network's first president explained, "When I see them [reporters] on the air I see them being very careful about Arab sensibilities." Schonfeld suggested the coverage is slanted because CNN doesn't want to risk the special access it has in the Arab world.[2] Other networks engage in similar self-censorship.

In Arab countries, journalists are usually escorted to see what the government wants them to see or they are followed. Citizens are warned by security agencies, sometimes directly, sometimes more subtly, that they should be careful what they say to visitors.

In Lebanon during the 1980s, for example, the Palestine Liberation Organization (PLO) had reporters doing their bidding as the price for obtaining interviews and protection. During the Palestinian War, Israeli journalists were warned against going to the Palestinian Authority, and some received telephone threats after publishing articles critical of the PA leadership.[3]

In the case of coverage of the PA, the Western media relies heavily on Palestinian assistants to escort correspondents in the territories. In addition, Palestinians often provide the news that is sent out around the world. For example, at least two journalists working for Agence France-Presse simultaneously worked for PA media outlets. An Associated Press correspondent also worked for the PA's official newspaper.

One veteran journalist said, "It's like employing someone from the [Israeli] Government Press Office or one of the Israeli political parties to work as a journalist."[4]

"By my own estimate," journalist Ehud Yaari wrote, "over 95 percent of the TV pictures going out on satellite every evening to the various foreign and Israeli channels are supplied by Palestinian film crews. The two principal agencies in the video news market, Associated PressTN and Reuters TV, run a whole network of Palestinian stringers, freelancers and fixers all over the territories to provide instant footage of the events. These crews obviously identify emotionally and politically with the intifada and, in the 'best' case, they simply don't dare film anything that could embarrass the Palestinian Authority. So the cameras are angled to show a tainted view of the Israeli army's actions, never focus on the Palestinian gunmen and diligently produce a very specific kind of close-up of the situation on the ground."[5]

We were filming the beginning of the demonstration. Suddenly, a van pulled in hurriedly. Inside, there were Fatah militants. They gave their orders and even distributed Molotov cocktails. We were filming. But these images, you will never see. In a few seconds, all those youngsters surrounded us, threatened us, and then took us away to the police station. There, we identified ourselves but we were compelled to delete the controversial pictures. The Palestinian Police calmed the situation but censored our pictures. We now have the proof that those riots are no longer spontaneous. All the orders came from the Palestinian hierarchy.

—Jean Pierre Martin[6]

A particularly egregious incident occurred in October 2000 when two Israelis were lynched in Ramallah by a Palestinian mob. According to reporters on the scene, the Palestinian police tried to prevent foreign journalists from filming the incident. One Italian television crew managed to film parts of the attack and these shocking images ultimately made headlines around the world. A competing Italian news agency took a different tack, placing an advertisement in the PA's main newspaper, *Al-Hayat-al-Jadidah*, explaining that it had nothing to do with filming the incident.[7]

If a news organization strays from the pro-Palestinian line, it comes under immediate attack. In November 2000, for example, the Palestinian Journalist's Union complained that the Associated Press was presenting a false impression of the Palestinian War. The Union called Associated Press's coverage a conscious crime against the Palestinian people and said it served the Israeli position. The Union threatened to adopt all necessary measures against Associated Press staffers as well as against Associated Press bureaus located in the PA if the agency continued to harm Palestinian interests.[8]

Bias enters coverage in other ways as well. For example, in 2009, journalists learned that Israeli prime minister Ehud Olmert had been negotiating a peace agreement with Palestinian Authority president Mahmoud Abbas. Ultimately, Abbas rejected Olmert's offer. This should have been one of the biggest stories of the year, according to Matti Friedman; however, the top editors at the Associated Press would not publish the story. "This decision taught me a lesson that should be clear to consumers of the Israel story: Many of the people deciding what you will read and see from here view their role not as explanatory but as political. Coverage is a weapon to be placed at the disposal of the side they like." And most journalists prefer the Palestinian narrative. Friedman adds:

> When journalists, the people responsible for explaining the world to the world, cover the Jews' war as more worthy of attention than any other, when they portray the Jews of Israel as the party obviously in the wrong, when they omit all possible justifications for the Jews' actions and obscure the true face of their enemies, what they are saying to their readers— whether they intend to or not—is that Jews are the worst people on earth.[9]

MYTH

Journalists covering the Middle East are driven by the search for the truth.

FACT

It will come as no surprise to learn that journalists in the Middle East share an interest in sensationalism with their colleagues covering domestic issues. The most egregious examples come from television reporters whose emphasis on visuals over substance encourages facile treatment of the issues. For example, when NBC's correspondent in Israel was asked why reporters turned up at Palestinian demonstrations in the West Bank they knew were being staged, he said, "We play along because we need the pictures."[10] The networks can't get newsworthy pictures from closed societies such as Syria, Saudi Arabia, Iran, or Libya, so events in Israel routinely make headlines while the Arab world is ignored.

Israel often faces an impossible situation of trying to counter images with words. "When a tank goes into Ramallah, it does not look good on TV," explains Gideon Meir of the Israeli Foreign Ministry.

"Sure we can explain why we are there, and that's what we do. But it's words. We have to fight pictures with words."[11]

The magnitude of the problem Israel confronts is clear from Tami Allen-Frost, deputy chairman of the Foreign Press Association and a producer for Britain's ITN news, who says "the strongest picture that stays in the mind is of a tank in a city" and that "there are more incidents all together in the West Bank than there are suicide bombings. In the end, it's quantity that stays with you."[12]

One cause of misunderstanding about the Middle East and bias in media reporting is the ignorance of journalists about the region. Few reporters speak Hebrew or Arabic, so they have little or no access to primary sources. They frequently regurgitate stories they read in English language publications from the region rather than report independently. Media outlets also often rely on stringers—local Arabs who help them find stories—whose biases are often interjected into the coverage. When they do attempt to place events in historical context, they often get the facts wrong and create an inaccurate or misleading impression. To cite one example, during a recitation of the history of the holy sites in Jerusalem, CNN's Garrick Utley reported that Jews could pray at the Western Wall during Jordan's rule from 1948 to 1967.[13] In fact, Jews were prevented from visiting their holiest shrine. This is a critical historical point that helps explain Israel's position toward Jerusalem.

The press often makes factual mistakes that place Israel in an unfavorable light. For example, in October 2015, MSNBC aired graphics similar to those used in anti-Israel propaganda that suggested Israel destroyed the country of Palestine. One of the network's broadcasters, Martin Fletcher, said the map and analysis were "dead wrong" and the network subsequently apologized for using maps that were "not factually accurate."[14]

In one remarkable example, a Finnish journalist filed a factual report, but then lashed out against those who used it because it conflicted with her bias. Aishi Zidan of Finland's Helsingin Sanomat reported that a rocket was launched from the backyard of the main hospital in Gaza City (which also served as the Hamas headquarters). This was one of the rare cases where a journalist documented how Hamas used Palestinians, in this case hospital patients, as human shields. When the story was publicized, she criticized the pro-Israel media because it distracted from her goal of covering the "Palestinian civilians who were victims of war."[15] Though rare, a handful of other journalists also reported examples of Hamas using human shields. *Financial Times* Jerusalem Bureau Chief John Reed, for example, saw "two rockets fired toward Israel from near al-Shifa hospital, even as more bombing victims were brought in. Similarly, Peter Stefanovic of Australia's Channel Nine News tweeted: "Hamas rockets just launched over our hotel from a site about two hundred meters away. So a missile launch site is basically next door."[16]

MYTH

Arab officials tell Western journalists the same thing they tell their own people.

FACT

Arab officials often express their views differently in English than they do in Arabic. They express their true feelings and positions to their constituents in their native language. For external consumption, however, Arab officials have learned to speak in moderate tones and often relate very different views when speaking in English to Western audiences. Long ago, Arab propagandists became more sophisticated about how to make their case. They now routinely appear on American television news broadcasts and are quoted in the print media and come across as reasonable people with legitimate grievances. What many of these same people say in Arabic, however, is often far less moderate and reasonable. Since Israelis can readily translate what is said in Arabic, they are well aware of the views of their enemies. Americans and other English speakers, however, can easily be fooled by the slick presentation of an Arab propagandist.

To give just one example, Palestinian peace negotiator Saeb Erekat is frequently quoted by the Western media. After the brutal murder of two Israeli teenagers on May 9, 2001, he was asked for a reaction. The *Washington Post* reported his response:

> Saeb Erekat, a Palestinian official, said in English at a news conference that "killing civilians is a crime, whether on the Palestinian or the Israeli side." The comment was not reported in Arabic-language Palestinian media.[17]

The unusual aspect of this story was that the *Post* reported the fact that Erekat's comment was ignored by the Palestinian press.

In an interview with Israeli TV in March 2011, Palestinian Authority Chairman Mahmoud Abbas condemned the Palestinians' naming of a square after Dalal Mughrabi, the terrorist who led the most lethal terror attack in Israel's history. When speaking to Palestinians in 2010, however, Abbas said, "Of course we want to name a square after her . . . We carried out a military action; can I then later renounce all that we have done?"[18]

Over the years, Yasser Arafat was famous for saying one thing in English to the Western media and something completely different to the Arabic press in his native tongue. This is why the Bush administration insisted that he repeat in Arabic what he said in English, in particular condemnations of terrorist attacks and calls to end violence.

It is more difficult for Arab leaders to get away with doubletalk today because their Arabic remarks are now translated by watchdog organizations and disseminated in English.

Case Study

A *Washington Post* story about the "cycle of death" in the West Bank included an interview with Raed Karmi, an official in Fatah, the dominant faction in Yasser Arafat's Palestine Liberation Organization. The report begins with the observation that Karmi is running out to join a battle against Israeli soldiers and grabs an M-16 assault rifle. What the story fails to mention is that only Palestinian police are supposed to be armed. The report implies that Israeli and Palestinian violence is equivalent in this "cycle" because Karmi said he was acting to avenge the death of a Palestinian who the Israelis assassinated for organizing terrorist attacks. Karmi admits that he participated in the kidnapping and execution-style murder of two Israelis who had been eating lunch in a Tulkarm restaurant. Karmi was jailed by the Palestinian Authority, but he was released after just four months and subsequently killed four more Israelis, including a man buying groceries and a driver who he ambushed. "I will continue attacking Israelis," he told the *Post*.[19]

MYTH

Israelis cannot deny the truth of pictures showing their abuses.

FACT

A picture may be worth a thousand words, but sometimes the picture and the words used to describe it are distorted and misleading. Photographers understandably seek the most dramatic pictures they can find, and those suggesting that brutal Israeli Goliaths are mistreating suffering Palestinian Davids are especially appealing, but the context is often missing.

In one classic example, the Associated Press circulated a dramatic photo of an angry baton-wielding Israeli soldier standing over a bloody young man. It appeared the soldier had just beaten the youth. The picture appeared in the *New York Times* and spurred international outrage because the caption, supplied by Associated Press, said, "An Israeli policeman and a Palestinian on the Temple Mount."[20] It turned out, however, the photo actually showed an incident that might have conveyed almost the exact opposite impression had it been reported correctly. The victim was not a Palestinian beaten by an Israeli soldier, he was a policeman protecting an American Jewish student, Tuvia Grossman, who had been riding in a taxi when it was stoned by Palestinians.

Grossman was pulled out of the taxi, beaten, and stabbed. He broke free and fled toward the Israeli policeman. At that point, a photographer snapped the picture.

Besides getting the victim wrong, the Associated Press also inaccurately reported that the photograph was taken on the Temple Mount. When the Associated Press was alerted to the errors, it issued a series of corrections, several of which still did not get the story straight. As is usually the case when the media makes a mistake, the damage had already been done. Many outlets that had used the photo did not print clarifications. Others issued corrections that did not receive the prominence of the initial story.

Another example of how pictures can be both dramatic and misleading was a Reuters photo showing a young Palestinian being arrested by Israeli police on April 6, 2001. The boy was obviously frightened and wet his pants. The photo attracted worldwide publicity and reinforced the media image of brutal Israelis who abuse innocent children. In this instance, it is the context that is misleading. Another Reuters photographer snapped another picture just before the first one was taken. It showed the same boy participating in a riot against Israeli soldiers. Few media outlets published this photo.

The Palestinians have also learned to use videos and photos, especially on social media, to spread misinformation. In one classic example of Palestinians staging a scene for propaganda purposes, what Professor Richard Landis has labeled "Pallywood," a video shows Palestinians carrying a stretcher with a corpse presumably on the way to the funeral. Suddenly, the pall bearers drop the stretcher and when it hits the ground the "corpse" gets up and runs away.[21]

A BBC investigation during Operation Protective Edge in 2014 found that the hashtag #GazaUnderAttack was used to distribute many bogus photos claiming to show the effects of Israeli air strikes. The BBC reported that some of the pictures dated back to 2009 and others were actually taken in Iraq and Syria.[22]

MYTH

The press makes no apologies for terrorists.

FACT

The media routinely accepts and repeats the platitudes of terrorists and their spokespersons with regard to their agendas. The press gullibly treats claims that attacks against innocent civilians are acts of "freedom fighters." In recent years, some news organizations have developed a resistance to the term "terrorist" and replaced it with euphemisms such as "militant" because they don't want to be seen as taking sides or making judgments about the perpetrators.

For example, after a Palestinian suicide bomber blew up a pizza restaurant in downtown Jerusalem on August 9, 2001, killing fifteen people, the attacker was described as a "militant" (*Los Angeles Times, Chicago Tribune,* NBC Nightly News). When a Palestinian woman walked into a crowded beach restaurant in Haifa on October 4, 2003, and detonated a bomb that killed twenty-one people, including four children, the Reuters account said she had waged an "attack" in retaliation for previous Israeli army actions and that the bombing showed that Palestinian officials had failed to "rein in the militants."[23]

The heinous attack on March 11, 2011, in which two Palestinian terrorists infiltrated the Israeli town of Itamar in the West Bank and brutally murdered a family of five, including a three-month-old infant, was described by the *Los Angeles Times* as part of a "continuing cycle of violence."[24] After terrorists killed eight Israelis and wounded more than thirty in multiple attacks near Eilat, the *New York Times* referred to the perpetrators as "armed attackers" and reported that Israeli counterstrikes killed Palestinians from a "militant group."[25]

After terrorists killed four Israelis in a Tel Aviv market on June 8, 2016, CNN headlined its story, "Two 'Terrorists' Arrested." The BBC didn't mention terrorism at all, referring to a "Tel Aviv Shooting." Sky News referred to the attack as a "mass shooting." *The New York Times* reported that "Palestinian Gunmen Open Fire in Tel Aviv, Leaving Three Dead." By contrast, the Fox News headline was clear and accurate: "Terror in Israel: At Least 3 Dead in Shooting Spree at Tel Aviv Market."[26]

Clifford May, writing for the Middle East Information Network, pointed out the absurdity of the media coverage: "No newspaper would write, 'Militants struck the World Trade Center yesterday,' or say, 'They may think of themselves as freedom fighters, and who are we to judge, we're news people.'"[27]

One of the best examples of how the press sometimes distinguishes terrorist attacks against other nations was a list of "recent terror attacks around the world" disseminated by the Associated Press, probably the most influential news service in the world. The list cited fifteen terrorist incidents during the five-year period between August 1998 and August 2003. During that period, more than eight hundred Israelis were murdered in terrorist attacks, but not one of the incidents in Israel made the list.[28] Similarly, when the Associated Press released its Year in Photos 2003, six of the 130 photos related to human suffering in the Israeli-Palestinian conflict. All six were of Palestinians.

In a memo to the *New York Times* foreign desk, former Jerusalem bureau chief James Bennet criticized his paper's reluctance to use the word "terrorism." He said, "The calculated bombing of students in a university cafeteria, or of families gathered in an ice cream parlor, cries out to be called what it is . . . I wanted to avoid the political meaning that comes with 'terrorism,' but I couldn't pretend that the word had no usage at all in plain English." Bennet acknowledged that not using the term was "a political act in itself."[29] Similarly, an independent inquiry into the BBC's Middle East coverage found that "the BBC should get the language right. We think they should call terrorist acts 'terrorism' because that term is clear and well understood."[30]

Rather than apologize for terrorists, the media sometimes portrays the victims of terror as equivalent to the terrorists themselves. For example, photos are sometimes shown of Israeli victims on the same page with photos of Israelis capturing terrorists, giving the sense, for example, that the Palestinian held in handcuffs and blindfolded by a soldier is as much a victim as the shocked woman being helped from the scene of a suicide bombing.

In one of the most egregious examples, after a suicide bombing in Petah Tikva on May 27, 2002, CNN interviewed the mother of the bomber, Jihad Titi. The parents of a fifteen-month-old girl killed in the attack, Chen and Lior Keinan, were also interviewed. The interviews with the Keinans were not shown on CNN international in Israel or elsewhere around the world until hours after the interview with Titi's mother had been broadcast several times.

This was too much even for CNN, which subsequently announced a policy change whereby it would no longer "report on statements made by suicide bombers or their families unless there seemingly is an extraordinarily compelling reason to do so."[31]

By any logic, militants engaged in warfare don't blow up little babies.

—Tom Fiedler, Executive Editor, *Miami Herald*[32]

MYTH

The Palestinian Authority places no restrictions on reporters.

FACT

A case study of the Palestinian Authority's idea of freedom of the press occurred following the September 11 terrorist attacks against the United States. An Associated Press cameraman filmed Palestinians at a rally in Nablus celebrating the terror attacks and was subsequently summoned to a Palestinian Authority security office and told that the material must not be aired.

Ahmed Abdel Rahman, Arafat's cabinet secretary, said the Palestinian Authority "cannot guarantee the life" of the cameraman if the footage was broadcast.[33] The cameraman requested that the material not be aired and the Associated Press never released the footage.

More than a week later, the Palestinian Authority returned a videotape it confiscated from the Associated Press showing a Palestinian rally in the Gaza Strip in which some demonstrators carried posters supporting Osama bin Laden. The Palestinians, according to an Associated Press official, had erased two separate parts involving "key elements" of the six-minute tape.[34]

In October 2001, after the United States launched attacks against Afghanistan, Palestinians supporting Osama bin Laden staged rallies in the Gaza Strip that were ruthlessly suppressed by Palestinian police. The PA took measures to prevent any media coverage of the rallies or the subsequent riots. The Paris-based Reporters Without Frontiers issued a scathing protest to the PA and also objected to Palestinian orders not to broadcast calls for general strikes, nationalistic activities, demonstrations, or other news without permission from the PA. The aim of the press blackout was expressed by an anonymous Palestinian official, "We don't want anything which could undermine our image."[35]

In August 2002, the Palestinian journalists' union banned journalists from photographing Palestinian children carrying weapons or taking part in activities by terrorist organizations because the pictures were hurting the Palestinians' image. The ban came after numerous photographs were published showing children carrying weapons and dressing up like suicide bombers. Another group, the Palestinian Journalists Syndicate, issued a similar ban that included photographing masked men. The Foreign Press Association expressed "deep concern" over the effort to censor coverage, and the threats of sanctions against journalists who disregarded the ban.[36]

In July 2004, as Gaza became increasingly unstable, and protests were being mounted against corruption in the Palestinian Authority and the leadership of Arafat, Palestinian journalists covering the crisis received death threats.[37] Numerous incidents have also been reported of physical attacks on journalists who offended PA officials. A reporter for a Saudi-owned news channel was wounded by gunfire when he was driving through the Gaza Strip. He was then dragged from his car and beaten because his station had allowed criticism of Yasser Arafat and other officials. A week later, one hundred Palestinian journalists went to Arafat's headquarters in Ramallah to pledge allegiance to him.[38]

The Palestinian Authority and Hamas were accused of systematically abusing Palestinian journalists in a Human Rights Watch report released April 6, 2011. The report documents cases of torture, beatings, and arbitrary detainment of journalists by security forces and says that "severe harassment by Palestinian Authority and Hamas security forces targeting Palestinian journalists in the West Bank and Gaza has had a pronounced chilling effect on freedom of expression."

For example, Hamas security forces detained an Al-Quds radio reporter and attacked him "in a morgue where he had reported on a man, supposedly killed by Israeli military attack, who was discovered still to be alive."[39]

The Center for Development and Media Freedoms, a Palestinian rights group, said that the number of attacks by Palestinians on journalists, arrests, and confiscations of equipment rose by 45 percent in 2010.[40] In a 2014 study, the center found that 80 percent of Palestinian journalists practice self-censorship in their writing largely out of fear of reprisals and death threats from authorities.[41]

In June 2011, the Palestinian Authority banned Palestinian journalists from reporting about the findings of the Ramallah-based Independent Commission for Human Rights concerning abuse of human rights by the PA and Hamas. "Assaults on journalists and censorship and restrictions on freedom of expression are still a dreadful nightmare for the journalists," said Palestinian reporter Mustafa Ibrahim. "Journalists avoid covering events out of fear of being targeted or arrested by [Palestinian] security forces in the West Bank."[42]

In February 2012, the PA arrested two Palestinian journalists supposedly in an attempt to suppress dissent. One of the journalists, Yousef Shayeb, of the Jordanian paper *Al-Ghad*, had reported on corruption in a Palestinian diplomatic mission while the second, Rami Samara, of the Palestinian agency Wafa, had outwardly criticized President Abbas. "Before this detention, I thought that we, the Palestinian people, enjoy wide freedom, but after what I saw, I think I'm being followed by the intelligence in every step of my life," Samara said.[43]

In 2015 alone, a Palestinian human rights group received complaints about the detention of thirty-five Palestinian journalists. At least fifteen more were interrogated or detained for posting controversial statements on social media.[44]

"Freedom of the media exists only when journalists direct their criticism against Israel," journalist Khaled Abu Toameh observed. "The Palestinian journalists know that at the end of the day, they need to go back to their family in the West Bank and Gaza without having to worry about masked men knocking on their doors at night."[45]

Meanwhile, Jewish and Israeli journalists are routinely banned from meetings with Palestinian officials. When Palestinian journalists attempt to arrange meetings for colleagues they are typically told to make sure that none are Jews or Israelis.[46]

MYTH

The media carefully investigates Palestinian claims before publicizing them.

FACT

Palestinians have learned that they can disseminate almost any information to the media and that it will be published or broadcast somewhere. Once it is picked up by one media outlet, it is inevitably repeated by others. Quickly, misinformation can take on the appearance of fact, and while Israel can present evidence to correct the inaccuracies being reported, the damage is already done. Once an image or impression is in someone's mind, it is often difficult, if not impossible to erase it.

For example, a Palestinian boy was stabbed to death in a village near a Jewish settlement. The media repeated Palestinian claims that the boy had been attacked by settlers when in fact he had been killed in a brawl between rival Palestinian clans.[47] On another occasion, a ten-year-old Palestinian girl was allegedly killed by IDF tank fire. This time it turned out she had died as a result of Palestinians shooting in the air to celebrate the return of Muslim worshipers from Mecca.[48]

The media's rush to judge Israel is damaging even when the truth comes out later, because by that time the harm has already been done. For example, during Israel's Operation Pillar of Defense in November 2012, the eleven-month-old son of a BBC journalist was killed allegedly by Israeli shrapnel. Nearly four months later, however, a UN investigation found that the baby had been killed by shrapnel from a Palestinian rocket.[49]

One staple of Palestinian propaganda has been to distribute false statistics in an effort to make Israeli actions look monstrous. For example, if an incident involves some death or destruction, they can grossly exaggerate the figures, and a gullible media will repeat the fabricated data until they become widely accepted as accurate. This occurred, for example, during the Lebanon War when Yasser Arafat's brother claimed that Israel's operations had left six hundred thousand Lebanese homeless. He made the number up, but it was repeated by the International Committee of the Red Cross and publicized in the media. By the time the ICRC repudiated the figure, it was too late to change the impression that Israel's military operation to defend itself from terrorist attacks on its northern border had created an unconscionable refugee problem.[50]

The Palestinians were caught lying again in April 2002 when Palestinian spokesman Saeb Erekat told CNN on April 17 that at least five hundred people were massacred in Jenin and sixteen hundred people, including women and children, were missing. Erekat produced no evidence for his claim, and the Palestinians' own review committee later reported a death toll of fifty-six, of whom thirty-four were combatants. No women or children were reported missing.[51]

What is perhaps more outrageous than the repetition of Erekat's lie is that media outlets continue to treat him as a legitimate spokesperson, giving him access that allows him to disseminate misinformation.

MYTH

*Media coverage of Israeli operations in
Gaza was fair and accurate.*

FACT

Israel's enemies will do everything possible to manipulate the media to influence public opinion. Israel will be accused of massacres, fabricated casualty figures will be distributed, photographs will be doctored, and journalists will be threatened. These and other ploys are used to create sympathy for the Palestinians and cast aspersions on Israeli forces in the hope of turning world opinion against Israel.

Too often, irresponsible journalists have repeated unverified and often inaccurate information in their haste to be the first to report a story. In an effort to present an evenhanded account, some reporters have the mistaken belief that allowing an Arab spokesperson to lie and then giving an Israeli a chance to respond represents a balanced account. This is like allowing a spokesperson to accuse Israelis of beating their spouses and then inviting an Israeli to deny that they beat their husbands and wives.

One of the first examples of this in the Gaza War occurred after Israeli forces fired near a UN-run school on January 6, 2009. The press immediately reported that more than forty Palestinians seeking shelter in the building were killed, and the attack was portrayed as a deliberate assault on innocent people.[52] Hours later, Israeli investigators reported that they had fired after being attacked by Hamas terrorists launching mortars from the area. Witnesses supported the Israeli account, and the UN later claimed a "clerical error" led them to falsely accuse Israel of shelling the school.[53] Additionally, the original casualty figure was fabricated; the death toll was actually twelve, nine of whom were Hamas combatants. The facts came too late, however, to offset the initial impression created and reinforced by repeated claims by UN officials discounting the Israeli version.[54]

France 2, the same television network that broadcast the notoriously inaccurate story about Mohammed al-Dura during the Palestinian War, aired an erroneous report showing dead children allegedly killed in the Gaza fighting. The amateur video of the dead toddlers being laid out on a white sheet was actually shot after they had been killed by the explosion of a Hamas ammunition truck during a parade in Gaza in September 2005.[55]

CNN's Anderson Cooper described one way Hamas manipulated news coverage:

Inside Gaza, press controlled by Hamas is heavy-handed. There are few press freedoms inside Gaza, and Hamas controls who reports from there and where they can go. While pictures of wounded children being brought to hospitals are clearly encouraged, we rarely see images of Hamas fighters or their rockets being fired into Israel.

—CNN's Anderson Cooper[56]

Even before Israel initiated Operation Cast Lead, many journalists were quick to report whatever they were told by Hamas. When Hamas staged blackouts in Gaza, the media incorrectly reported that Israel was preventing the Gazans from obtaining fuel and electricity. Israel was regularly blamed for a "humanitarian crisis" in Gaza while, at the same time, truckloads of goods were sent in from Israel each day. While Israel's air attacks on Gaza immediately made the front page of newspapers around the world, the rocket barrages on southern Israel, and the impact they had had on the population over the preceding three years, were rarely mentioned.

Journalists could not rely on interviews with civilians they met on the street. During the war in July 2014, Polish reporter Wojciech Cegielski said, "I couldn't meet anyone who spoke something other than official propaganda. But some Palestinians, when they were sure my microphone was turned off, told me they have had enough but they are afraid. No one would dare to say publicly that Hamas is creating a hell inside Gaza.[57]

Reporters were equally afraid. For example, journalists knew that Hamas was using Gaza City's biggest hospital, Shifa Hospital, as its command post, and yet the media failed to report that the Hamas leadership was using patients as human shields. Correspondents were forced to play by Hamas rules; they were welcome to take pictures of Palestinians who were killed or wounded, but they were not permitted to show Hamas terrorists carrying weapons in the hospital, the rooms where injured Hamas fighters were being treated, or the bunkers where they hid in the basement. Violations of the rules were not tolerated and journalists dared not cross their Hamas minders.

For example, the *Wall Street Journal's* Nick Casey tweeted that "You have to wonder with the shelling how patients at Shifa hospital feel as Hamas uses it as a safe place to see media." Even though he deleted the tweet, Casey was placed on a list of journalists who "lie/fabricate info for Israel."[58]

After the war, a Hamas spokesperson admitted that some journalists were under surveillance and that those who filmed missile launch locations were forced to stop or face deportation from Gaza. "Hamas security personnel would give journalists 'some time to change their message' and 'one way or another' they would be forced to change their reporting."[59]

The Foreign Press Association complained to Hamas about denied entry to reporters who did not meet Hamas's approval. Several who were allowed into Gaza were threatened, harassed, or questioned. A few journalists did report on Hamas's use of civilian shields, but they did so outside Gaza, because they feared retribution from Hamas.

> "[A] man drove up in a pickup to our tiny street. He placed a rocket launcher outside and fired. But the rocket failed to go upwards and flew along the street at ground level for a long time before destroying a building. It was a miracle that nobody was hurt or killed. When we calmed down, we started to analyze the situation. It became obvious that the man or his supervisor wanted the Israel Defense Forces to destroy civilian houses, which our tiny street was full of.
>
> **—Polish reporter Wojciech Cegielski[60]**

The media often turns conflicts into numbers games, keeping running tallies of casualties. Israel always is accused of disproportionality because fewer Israelis typically die in confrontations. Israelis, however, are under no obligation to take greater casualties for the sake of looking better in the media box score.

MYTH

Journalists are never deceived by Palestinian propaganda.

FACT

The normally skeptical press is remarkably docile and unquestioning when it comes to information coming from Hamas. As we've seen in past conflicts, journalists often check their professional ethics at the door to gain access to areas controlled by terrorists. Unlike journalists in Israel who are free to report whatever they want, the price of admission to Gaza is to go where Hamas wants them to go, see what the terrorists want them to see, and report what they are told.

Hamas spokespeople are articulate and well prepared to present their case to the media. They have also prepped the civilian population on how to respond to media inquiries. The interior ministry published guidelines instructing the civilian population in how to contribute to the Hamas propaganda campaign. For example:

> Anyone killed or martyred is to be called a civilian from Gaza or Palestine, before we talk about his status in jihad or his military rank. Don't forget to always add "innocent civilian" or "innocent citizen" in your description of those killed in Israeli attacks on Gaza.

> Begin [your reports of] news of resistance actions with the phrase "In response to the cruel Israeli attack," and conclude with the phrase, "This many people have been martyred since Israel launched its aggression against Gaza." Be sure to always perpetuate the principle of "the role of the occupation is attack, and we in Palestine are fulfilling [the role of] the reaction."

> Avoid publishing pictures of rockets fired into Israel from [Gaza] city centers. This [would] provide a pretext for attacking residential areas in the Gaza Strip. Do not publish or share photos or video clips showing rocket launching sites or the movement of resistance [forces] in Gaza.

> When speaking to the West, you must use political, rational, and persuasive discourse, and avoid emotional discourse aimed at begging for sympathy. There are elements with a conscience in the world; you must maintain contact with them and activate them for the benefit of Palestine. Their role is to shame the occupation and expose its violations.

> Avoid entering into a political argument with a Westerner aimed at convincing him that the Holocaust is a lie and deceit; instead, equate it with Israel's crimes against Palestinian civilians.

> Do not publish photos of military commanders. Do not mention their names in public, and do not praise their achievements in conversations with foreign friends![61]

Journalists are always looking for the powerful story and photograph. What is startling is the failure to find pictures of Hamas terrorists in the act of firing rockets from civilian areas or those who have been "martyred." A similar pattern emerged during the last Lebanon War when Hezbollah tightly controlled what journalists could see, film, and write. "Foreign correspondents were warned on entry to the tour [of a southern Beirut suburb]," according to a report by Marvin Kalb, "that they could not wander off on their own or ask questions of any residents. They could take pictures only of sites approved by their Hezbollah minders. Violations, they were told, would be treated harshly." He added, "The rarest picture of all was that of a Hezbollah guerilla. It was as if the war on the Hezbollah side was being fought by ghosts."[62] The media is giving the impression Israel is now fighting ghosts in Gaza.

Journalists can be forgiven if they shoot pictures of children; they're emotion-laden photos, which editors readily publish knowing they are contributing to Hamas propaganda. What is more disturbing is the journalists' failure to investigate the claims by Hamas's health minister and others with regard to casualties. We've learned from past conflicts that the Palestinians fabricate Israeli "atrocities," and, as the guidelines cited above indicate, they have been instructed by their leaders to do so.

Palestinian officials, all of whom were employed in Gaza by Hamas, have an incentive to skew casualty numbers to tarnish Israel's image and give the appearance of victimization. Determining how many terrorists are killed is complicated because they are told to take off their uniforms and put on civilian clothing.

Thus, no one seems to ask the obvious question of how many of the dead reported by the Palestinian Health Ministry are members of Hamas. The first guideline makes clear that "anyone killed or martyred is to be called a civilian." Therefore, the widely reported casualty totals coming from the Palestinians do not include any terrorists.

Journalists treat official Israeli sources with skepticism while unquestioningly repeating propaganda from Hamas. This was true during Operation Cast Lead when Israel was charged with using disproportionate force and targeting civilians; however, after the fighting ceased, Hamas interior minister Fathi Hammad admitted Hamas lost more than six hundred men during the war—a figure consistent with the 709 calculated by the IDF. This accounted for a majority of the casualties.[63]

Professor Eytan Gilboa concluded:

> The distorted and misleading coverage of the Gaza conflict contributed to the hasty calls made by political leaders, UN officials and NGOs to prosecute Israel for war crimes. It also contributed to the mass hate demonstrations in Europe and to the sharp rise in anti-Semitic incidents . . . The Western media betrayed their audiences who deserve receiving accu-

rate information on Gaza. They should be held accountable for their skewed coverage, but it is doubtful whether they have the courage to heed to the advice they so often offer to governments—to investigate their professional and ethical failures and put their house in order."[64]

Notes, Chapter 18

1. Khaled Abu Toameh, "Palestinians: Western Media's Ignorance and Bias," Gatestone Institute (January 21, 2016).
2. *New York Jewish Week* (August 31, 2001).
3. *Jerusalem Report* (May 7, 1991).
4. "Where the Reporting Stops," *Jerusalem Post* (January 18, 2005).
5. *Jerusalem Report* (May 7, 1991).
6. Report filed by Jean Pierre Martin on October 5, 2000, a day after his Belgian television team from RTL-TV1 was filming in the area of Ramallah.
7. Judy Lash Balint, "Media Frightened into Self-Censorship," *WordNet Daily* (March 5, 2001).
8. *Al-Hayat al-Jadidah* (November 2, 2001).
9. Matti Friedman, "An Insider's Guide to the Most Important Story on Earth," *Tablet* (August 26, 2014).
10. *Near East Report* (August 5, 1991).
11. *Jerusalem Report* (April 22, 2002).
12. Ibid.
13. CNN (October 10, 2000). Cited in Abraham Foxman, "Letter to Garrick Utley," *Anti-Defamation League* (October 13, 2000).
14. Adam Kredo, "MSNBC Admits Anti-Israel Graphics Were 'Wrong,'" *Washington Free Beacon* (October 18, 2015); Raoul Wootliff, "MSNBC Apologizes for 'Completely Wrong' Maps of Israel," *Times of Israel* (October 20, 2015).
15. Sharona Schwartz, "'Don't Use Me': Reporter Admits Seeing Rocket Fired from Gaza Hospital, then Blasts Pro-Israel Media for Quoting Her," *The Blaze* (August 3, 2014).
16. Lahav Harkov, "Gaza Reporters' Tweets: Hamas Using Human Shields," *Jerusalem Post* (July 24, 2014).
17. Yoav Appel, "Two Israeli Teen-Agers Killed," *Washington Post* (May 10, 2001).
18. *Al-Hayat al-Jadida* (January 17, 2010), cited in Itamar Marcus and Nan Jacques Zilberdik, "Abbas's Duplicity about His Support for Honoring Terrorist Dalal Mughrabi," Palestinian Media Watch (May 27, 2011).
19. Lee Hockstader, "A Cycle of Death in West Bank Town," *Washington Post* (September 7, 2001).
20. *New York Times* (September 30, 2000).
21. Richard Landis, "Pallywood, 'According to Palestinian Sources . . . '" *The 2nd Draft*.
22. "#BBCtrending: Are #GazaUnderAttack Images Accurate?" BBC (July 8, 2014).
23. Tom Fiedler, "Handle with Care: Words like 'Conflict,' 'Terrorist,'" *Miami Herald* (January 4, 2004).
24. Editorial Staff, "A Fatal Israeli-Palestinian Flaw," *Los Angeles Times* (March 14, 2011).
25. Isabel Kershner and David D. Kirkpatrick, "Attacks Near Israeli Resort Heighten Tensions with Egypt and Gaza," *New York Times* (August 18, 2011).
26. "International Coverage of TA Terror Attack Refer to 'Shooting,' but Not Terrorists," *Ynet News* (June 9, 2016).
27. Howard Kurtz, "Commentators Are Quick to Beat Their Pens into Swords," *Washington Post* (September 13, 2001).
28. *WorldnetDaily* (November 24, 2003).

29. Daniel Okrent, "The War of the Words: A Dispatch from the Front Lines," *New York Times* (March 6, 2005).

30. Tom Leonard, "News Chiefs Criticised for Avoiding the Word Terrorism," *Telegraph* (May 3, 2006).

31. Jim Rutenberg, "CNN Executive Issues Apology for Coverage," *New York Times* (June 25, 2002).

32. Tom Fiedler, "Handle with Care: Words like 'Conflict,' 'Terrorist,'" *Miami Herald* (January 4, 2004).

33. Associated Press (September 12, 2001).

34. Jewish Telegraphic Agency (September 18, 2001).

35. *Jerusalem Post* (October 10, 2001).

36. *Jerusalem Post* (August 26, 2002).

37. *Jerusalem Post* (July 25, 2004).

38. *Jerusalem Post* (January 12 and 14, 2004).

39. "West Bank/Gaza: Stop Harassing Journalists," Human Rights Watch (April 6, 2011).

40. Lahav Harkov, "PA, Hamas Systematically Abuse Palestinian Journalists," *Jerusalem Post* (April 6, 2011).

41. Asmaa al-Ghoul, "Threat of Violence Silences Palestinian Journalists," *Al-Monitor* (February 3, 2015).

42. Khaled Abu Toameh, "PA Bans Journalists from Reporting Human Rights Abuses," *Jerusalem Post* (June 8, 2011).

43. Associated Press, "2 Palestinian Journalists Say They Were Questioned after Criticizing Abbas, Government," *Washington Post* (February 1, 2012).

44. Khaled Abu Toameh, "Palestinian Authority, Hamas, Responsible for Torture," Gatestone Institute (January 8, 2016).

45. Khaled Abu Toameh, "Islamic State Joins Hamas, PA in Threatening Palestinian Journalists," Gatestone Institute (February 5, 2015).

46. Khaled Abu Toameh, "Palestinians: 'No Jews Allowed!'" Gatestone Institute (June 25, 2013).

47. Arnon Regular, "Palestinian Boy Likely Stabbed to Death in West Bank Clan Feud," *Haaretz* (July 20, 2005).

48. Margot Dudkevitch, "PA Arrests Suspect in Girl's Murder," *Jerusalem Post* (February 1, 2005).

49. Raphael Ahren, "UN Clears Israel of Charge It Killed Baby in Gaza," *Times of Israel* (March 10, 2013).

50. "Toll of Lebanon Dead and Injured Still Uncertain in Chaos of War," *New York Times* (July 14, 1982).

51. *New York Post* (April 17, 2002). See also myths and facts related to coverage of the Lebanon wars, the Palestinian War, and Operation Cast Lead.

52. Patrick Martin, "Account of Israeli Attack on Gaza School Doesn't Hold Up," *Globe and Mail* (January 29, 2009).

53. Yaakov Katz, "UN: IDF Did Not Shell UNRWA School," *Jerusalem Post* (February 1, 2009).

54. Steven Erlanger "Weighing Crimes and Ethics in the Fog of Urban Warfare," *New York Times* (January 16, 2009).

55. Haviv Rettig Gur and Ehud Zion Waldoks, "'Ask Egypt to Let You into the Gaza Strip,'" *Jerusalem Post* (January 7, 2009).

56. Anderson Cooper, "Covering the Gaza Crisis," *CNN* (January 6, 2009); see also, Eytan Gilboa, "Hamas Cheerleaders: Professional Failures of the Western Media in Gaza," The Begin-Sadat Center for Strategic Studies, Perspectives Paper No. 265 (August 13, 2014).

57. Wojciech Cegielski, "I Saw Hamas' Cruel and Selfish Game in Gaza," *Haaretz* (August 25, 2015).

58. "Top Secret Hamas Command Bunker in Gaza Revealed," *Tablet* (July 29, 2014).

59. Ariel Ben Solomon, "Hamas Spokesperson: We Deported Foreign Journalists for Filming Missile Launches," *Jerusalem Post* (August 15, 2014); Elhanan Miller, "Hamas Provides New Info on Moves to Squeeze Foreign Media," *Jerusalem Post* (August 17, 2014).

60. Wojciech Cegielski, "I Saw Hamas' Cruel and Selfish Game in Gaza," *Haaretz* (August 25, 2015).

61. "Hamas Interior Ministry to Social Media Activists: Always Call the Dead 'Innocent Civilians'; Don't Post Photos of Rockets Being Fired from Civilian Population Centers," MEMRI (July 17, 2014).

62. Mitchell Bard, "Israel's Other Enemy in Lebanon War—the Media," *Jweekly.com* (April 27, 2007).

63. "Hamas MP Fathi Hammad: We Used Women and Children as Human Shields," Al-Aqsa TV, cited in Dispatch #1710, MEMRI (February 29, 2008).

64. Eytan Gilboa, "Hamas Cheerleaders: Professional Failures of the Western Media in Gaza," The Begin-Sadat Center for Strategic Studies, Perspectives Paper No. 265 (August 13, 2014).

19. The Campaign to Delegitimize Israel

Anti-Semitism is a result of Israeli policies.

Supporters of Israel only criticize Arabs and never Israelis.

Academic freedom means any criticism of Israel is permissible in a university.

American universities should divest from companies that do business in Israel.

Advocates for Israel try to silence critics by labeling them anti-Semitic.

The BDS movement originated with Palestinians seeking to promote peace and justice.

Campus delegitimization campaigns are successful.

The BDS movement advocates peace and a two-state solution.

The BDS campaign has succeeded in isolating Israel.

Selective boycotts advance prospects for Palestinian-Israeli peace.

Academic boycotts of Israel are popular in America.

Labeling products manufactured in West Bank settlements promotes peace.

MYTH

Anti-Semitism is a result of Israeli policies.

FACT

Anti-Semitism existed for centuries before the establishment of the State of Israel. Rather than Israel being the cause of anti-Semitism, it is more likely that dissatisfaction with Israeli behavior and the distorted media coverage of Israeli policies are reinforcing latent anti-Semitic views.

As writer Leon Wieseltier observed, "The notion that all Jews are responsible for whatever any Jews do is not a Zionist notion. It is an anti-Semitic notion." Wieseltier adds that attacks on Jews in Europe have nothing whatsoever to do with Israel. To blame Jews for anti-Semitism is similar to saying blacks are responsible for racism.[1]

> *Israel is the only state in the world today, and the Jews the only people in the world today, that are the object of a standing set of threats from governmental, religious, and terrorist bodies seeking their destruction. And what is most disturbing is the silence, the indifference, and some-times even the indulgence, in the face of such genocidal anti-Semitism.*
>
> **—Canadian minister of justice and attorney general Irwin Cotler[2]**

MYTH

Supporters of Israel only criticize Arabs and never Israelis.

FACT

Israel is not perfect. Even the most committed friends of Israel acknowledge that the government sometimes makes mistakes, that it has not solved all the problems in its society, and that it should do better. Supporters of Israel may not emphasize these faults, however, because there is no shortage of groups and individuals who are willing to do nothing but focus on Israel's imperfections. The public usually has much less access to Israel's side of the story in the conflict with the Palestinians or to the positive aspects of its society; therefore, it is often important to put events in context.

Israelis themselves are their own harshest critics. If you want to read criticism of Israeli behavior, you can pick up any Israeli newspaper and find no shortage of news and commentary critical of government policy. The rest of the world's media provides constant attention to Israel, and the coverage is far more likely to be unfavorable than complimentary.

The openness of debate in Israel has led some to conclude that Americans should not feel constrained from expressing similarly critical views. America is not Israel; Israelis have a common narrative and shared experiences. Americans, even American Jews, do not have the same level of knowledge or experience with regard to Israel, so critics should be aware that their criticism may be subject to misinterpretation by those who do not know the history or context of the topic under discussion.

Criticism is also not justified by Israeli encouragement, as Israelis do not understand the American milieu, and typically only bless critics who agree with them (leftist Israelis are happy to encourage American Jews to speak out against rightist governments but are furious with criticism of leftist governments and vice versa).

MYTH

Academic freedom means any criticism of Israel is permissible in a university.

FACT

The one place in America where anti-Semitism is still tolerated is in the university, where "academic freedom" is often used as a cover to sanction anti-Israel teachings and forums that are anti-Semitic.

In an address on the subject of academic freedom, Columbia Uni-

Map 32   Israel: Size and Dimensions

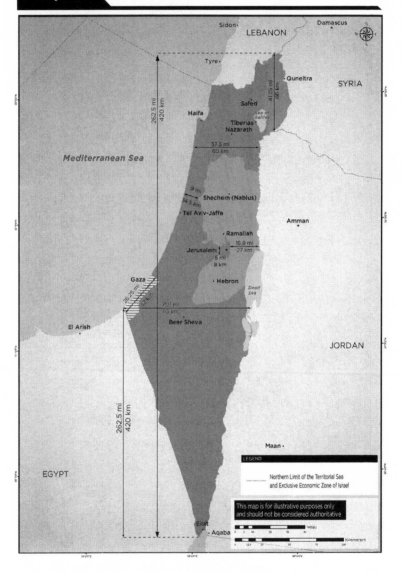

versity president Lee Bollinger quoted from a report that described a professor as someone whom "'no fair-minded person' would even suspect of speaking other than as 'shaped or restricted by the judgment . . . of professional scholars.'"[3] He also spoke about the need for faculty to "resist the allure of certitude, the temptation to use the podium as an ideological platform, to indoctrinate a captive audience, to play favorites with the like-minded, and silence the others."[4]

Many faculty, however, do not resist temptation; rather, they embrace their position as an ideological platform. Those who abuse their rights, and insist they can say what they want, hypocritically denounce others who exercise their right to criticize them. To suggest that a professor's views are inappropriate, or their scholarship is faulty, is to risk being tarred with the charge of McCarthyism.

Legality is not the issue in evaluating the anti-Israel, sometimes anti-Semitic speeches and teachings of faculty and speakers on campus. No one questions that freedom of speech allows individuals to express their views. The issue is whether this type of speech should be given the cover of "academic" freedom, and granted legitimacy by the university through funding, publicity, or use of facilities.

It is sometimes suggested critics seek to stifle legitimate criticism of Israel. There is a clear distinction, however, between criticism of Israeli policy, which you can read in any Israeli newspaper, and anti-Semitism, in which the attacks against Israel challenge its right to exist, or single out Israel among all other nations for opprobrium.

A related question is whether the presentations are in any way academic or scholarly. Few people would claim that a conference in which anti-black, anti-gay, or anti-female sentiments were expressed would be protected by academic freedom, and yet that is the shield used to permit attacks on the Jewish people.

While criticism of Israel is allowed, when it crosses the line into hate speech or anti-Semitism, it may create a hostile environment that violates the civil rights of Jews. The US Department of Education issued policy guidance in October 2010 clarifying that Jews are protected from discrimination and harassment under Title VI of the 1964 Civil Rights Act. The Office of Civil Rights specifies that school districts and institutions of higher education "may violate these civil rights statutes and the Department's implementing regulations when peer harassment based on race, color, national origin, sex, or disability is sufficiently serious that it creates a hostile environment and such harassment is encouraged, tolerated, not adequately addressed, or ignored by school employees."[5]

MYTH

American universities should divest from companies that do business in Israel.

FACT

The word "peace" does not appear in divestment petitions, which makes clear the intent is not to resolve the conflict but to delegitimize Israel. Petitioners blame Israel for the lack of peace and demand that it make unilateral concessions without requiring anything of the Palestinians, not even the cessation of terrorism. Divestment advocates also ignore Israel's efforts to reach historic compromises with the Palestinians that would have created a Palestinian state. Even after Israel completely withdrew from the Gaza Strip, certain individuals and groups persisted in their campaign to undermine Israel, reinforcing their interest in Israel's destruction rather than any territorial compromise.

The divestment campaign against South Africa was specifically directed at companies that were using that country's racist laws to their advantage. In Israel, no such racist laws exist; moreover, companies doing business there adhere to the same standards of equal working rights that are applied in the United States.

Harvard University president Lawrence Summers forthrightly declared that divestment efforts are anti-Semitic. "Profoundly anti-Israel views are increasingly finding support in progressive intellectual communities," said Summers. "Serious and thoughtful people are advocating and taking actions that are anti-Semitic in their effect, if not their intent."[6]

Peace between Israel and its neighbors will come only from direct negotiations between the parties, Arab recognition of Israel's right to exist, and the cessation of terrorism. American universities cannot help through misguided divestment campaigns that unfairly single out Israel as the source of conflict in the region. Divestment proponents hope to tar Israel through an association with the old discriminatory policies of South Africa, an offensive comparison that ignores the fact that all Israeli citizens are equal under the law, unlike nonwhite South Africans who were not allowed to own land or businesses, access education, or speak their native languages.

Honest proponents of BDS realize their action will not change anything about the Israeli-Palestinian conflict and that, even when BDS motions pass, they have no impact on university policy. BDS campaigns do, however, roil the campus, pit students against one another, and often provoke an upsurge of anti-Semitism.

MYTH

*Advocates for Israel try to silence critics
by labeling them anti-Semitic.*

FACT

Criticizing Israel does not necessarily make someone anti-Semitic. The
determining factor is the intent and content of the observer.

■ Legitimate critics accept Israel's right to exist, whereas anti-Semites
do not.

■ Anti-Semites use double standards when they criticize Israel, for example, denying Israelis the right to pursue their legitimate claims
while encouraging the Palestinians to do so.

■ Anti-Semites deny Israel the right to defend itself, and ignore Jewish
victims, while blaming Israel for pursuing their murderers.

■ Anti-Semites rarely, if ever, make positive statements about Israel.

■ Anti-Semites describe Israelis using pejorative terms and hate
speech, suggesting, for example, that they are "racists" or "Nazis."

Natan Sharansky has suggested a "3-D" test for differentiating legitimate criticism of Israel from anti-Semitism. The first "D" is the test
of whether Israel or its leaders are being demonized or their actions
blown out of proportion. Equating Israel with Nazi Germany is one
example of demonization. The second "D" is the test of double standards. An example is when Israel is singled out for condemnation at
the United Nations for alleged human rights abuses while nations that
violate human rights on a massive scale, such as Iran, Syria, and Saudi
Arabia, are not even mentioned. The third "D" is the test of delegitimization. Questioning Israel's legitimacy, that is, its right to exist, is
always anti-Semitic.[7]

*The view of Israel as a monolithic entity composed of racists and brutal
oppressors is a caricature. Israel is a complex society, struggling with
itself. The forces of good and evil, and many in between, are locked in
a daily battle on many different fronts.*

—Uri Avnery[8]

No campaign exists to prevent people from expressing negative
opinions about Israeli policy. In fact, the most vociferous critics of
Israel are Israelis themselves who use their freedom of speech to express their concerns every day. A glance at any Israeli newspaper will

reveal a surfeit of articles questioning particular government policies. Anti-Semites, however, do not share Israelis' interest in improving the society; their goal is to delegitimize the state in the short run and destroy it in the long run. There is nothing Israel could do to satisfy these critics. Jews are also the only group that is not allowed to call out bigotry on college campuses. No one would tell African-Americans what is racist, or women what is sexist, or gays what is homophobic; however, Jews are told by non-Jews what is and is not anti-Semitic.

MYTH

The BDS movement originated with Palestinians seeking to promote peace and justice.

FACT

The Boycott, Divestment, and Sanctions (BDS) campaign is a product of the NGO Forum that was held in parallel to the 2001 UN World Conference against Racism in Durban, South Africa. The NGO Forum was marked by repeated expressions of naked anti-Semitism by nongovernmental organization (NGO) activists and condemned as such by United Nations High Commissioner for Human Rights Mary Robinson who chaired the conference.

The Forum's final declaration described Israel as a state that was guilty of "racist crimes including war crimes, acts of genocide and ethnic cleansing." The declaration established an action plan—the "Durban Strategy"—promoting "a policy of complete and total isolation of Israel . . . the imposition of mandatory and comprehensive sanctions and embargoes, the full cessation of all links (diplomatic, economic, social, aid, military cooperation and training) between all states and Israel" (para. 424).[9]

The BDS movement deliberately draws a false parallel to South Africa. According to BDS proponents, if South Africa was worthy of a boycott and sanctions campaigns that eventually led to the downfall of that despicable system, "Israel should be subject to the same kind of attack, leading to the same kind of result."[10]

> *When people criticize Zionists, they mean Jews. You're talking anti-Semitism.*
>
> **—Martin Luther King[11]**

In 2005, anti-Israel activists issued the "Palestinian Civil Society Call for BDS against Israel" in an effort to create the false impression that BDS is endorsed by all Palestinians. In truth, despite the obvious tensions between Palestinian Arabs and Israelis, a great deal of dialogue and cooperation has been ongoing.

In 2008, the *Histadrut* (Israeli labor union) and the Palestine General Federation of Trades Unions (PGFTU) signed an agreement to base future relations on negotiation, dialogue, and joint initiatives to advance "fraternity and co-existence." Palestinian Arab Universities—despite being hotbeds of anti-Israel activity—maintained links with their Israeli counterparts. Artist, doctors, and businesspeople were among those who formed bonds of mutual benefit, cooperation, and even occasional friendship across the divide of conflict. The severing of these ties was not an objective that Israelis or Palestinian Arabs sought, and the move to isolate the two sides did not spring from popular opinion on the Palestinian Arab side. Rather, it was a strategy of a self-appointed vanguard that expressed itself through a network of NGOs who put pressure on other elements in Palestinian Arab society to fall in behind the "Durban strategy."

Case Study

SodaStream was targeted by boycotters because of its factory in Mishor Adumim, adjacent to the "settlement" of Ma'ale Adumim. The company was the largest employer of Palestinians in the territories with nearly six hundred workers who received the same salary, medical insurance, and conditions as the other workers. BDS activists protested outside stores, intimidated shoppers, and vandalized SodaStream products. As a result of financial losses, partly due to the BDS attacks, the company closed the West Bank factory and replaced it with one in the Negev Desert putting all the Palestinians out of work. Ali Jafar, a shift manager from a West Bank village who worked for SodaStream for two years, said, "All the people who wanted to close [SodaStream's West Bank factory] are mistaken . . . They didn't take into consideration the [Palestinian] families."[12]

MYTH

Campus delegitimization campaigns are successful.

FACT

The campus divestment campaign was initiated in 2001 by Students for Justice in Palestine (SJP), a student group at the University of California, Berkeley, in conjunction with the San Francisco chapter of the American-Arab Anti-Discrimination Committee. A year later, following the Palestine Solidarity Movement's first conference, which was held in Berkeley, the delegitimization movement began to spread to other universities, including the University of Michigan, Yale, Princeton, Harvard, and the Massachusetts Institute of Technology.

Campus divestment failed miserably. A huge blow came in 2002, when Harvard University president and former Treasury secretary Lawrence Summers said the divestment campaign was anti-Semitism. Soon after, Columbia University president Lee Bollinger said he opposed divestment and considered the analogy to South Africa "both grotesque and offensive."[13]

In the 2015–16 school year, eighteen divestment votes were taken (counting only the final votes), down from twenty-seven the year before—a 33 percent decrease. The resolutions were defeated in eleven of the eighteen votes. Of the nine new schools that debated divestment, only four passed. Even more significant were the schools that did not hold votes, which included typical hot spots such as Stanford, UC Davis, UCLA, and Berkeley.

If we look at the results from the 2005–06 through 2015–16 school years, a total of eighty-eight votes have been taken; opponents have defeated divestment by a 64 to 36 percent margin, with this past year's margin 61 to 39 percent. During that time, only four schools—Michigan Dearborn, UC San Diego, UC Irvine, and UC Davis—have voted in favor of divestment more than once. Only one of those voted in the 2015–16 school year, Michigan Dearborn, and divestment lost.

Altogether, fifty-three schools have considered divestment in the last eleven years; only twenty-two have passed resolutions (42 percent). Among elite schools, sixteen of the top fifty schools (32 percent) have considered divestment, and BDS lost 63 percent of the time.

To put this in perspective, these schools comprise fewer than 3 percent of all four-year colleges. Other colleges have anti-Israel activity and BDS rumblings, but those remain a small fraction of all institutions. The important statistic is that 97 percent of schools have not had divestment resolutions, and the overwhelming majority have no anti-Israel activity.[14]

Another effort to push the Durban agenda has been for students to stage Israel hate weeks on campuses around the world. These events typically bring speakers and films to demonize Israel on campus. Meanwhile, pro-Israel students have staged Israel "Peace Week" and related positive programming.

Even when they fail, BDS advocates often claim victory in the hope that the perception of winning will create momentum for their cause. Institutions that allow BDS initiatives to be launched on campus should be aware that BDS supporters may report success even when there is none, to the detriment of the university's reputation.

Perhaps the more serious delegitimization efforts on campus escape public notice because they take place in classrooms where professors around the country—predominantly in Middle East Studies departments—use their positions to advance political agendas that are often hostile toward Israel and selective in their exploration of Islam.[15] As Princeton's Bernard Lewis observed, Middle East Studies programs have been distorted by "a degree of thought control and limitations of freedom of expression without parallel in the Western world since the 18th century, and in some areas longer than that." He added, "It seems to me it's a very dangerous situation because it makes any kind of scholarly discussion of Islam, to say the least, dangerous. Islam and Islamic values now have a level of immunity from comment and criticism in the Western world that Christianity has lost and Judaism never had."[16]

Following a vote in 2007 by a British academic union to boycott Israeli universities (the decision was later rescinded), nearly three hundred university presidents denounced the British boycott in a statement that said, "In seeking to quarantine Israeli universities and scholars, this vote threatens every university committed to fostering scholarly and cultural exchanges that lead to enlightenment, empathy, and a much-needed international marketplace of ideas."[17]

The delegitimization movement on campus has to date had no impact on Israeli policy toward the Palestinians. Nevertheless, the mere discussion of BDS allows Israel's detractors to propagate a negative image of Israel that many fear will take root while, simultaneously, shifting the tenor of debate from the merits of Israeli policies to its right to exist.

Israeli academics have never boycotted Palestinian professors, even in the worst days of terror. To the contrary: if you're organizing a conference in Israel, it's almost obligatory to have a Palestinian professor on the podium. Free exchange is what academic freedom means, and Israeli universities have done an admirable job of upholding it in trying times. In contrast, the academic boycott against Israel is itself a gross violation of academic freedom, because it explicitly imposes a political litmus test on Israelis scholars. It's radical-style McCarthyism."

—Professor Martin Kramer[18]

MYTH

The BDS movement advocates peace and a two-state solution.

FACT

The BDS movement is based on coercion rather than democracy. Proponents imply that Israel is not open to persuasion and that the electorate is too stupid, immature, or evil to know what is best for the society. Unable to convince the Israeli electorate of the merits of their views, BDS proponents demonize Israel and call for outsiders to punish the citizens of Israel until they capitulate to Palestinian demands.

Some students believe that pressure must be applied to stimulate the parties to make concessions that will make a peace agreement possible. While this is a debatable tactic, students genuinely interested in peace recognize that any pressure would have to be directed at both parties. BDS proponents, however, are interested only in pressuring Israel and hold the Palestinians blameless for the conflict.

> *The real aim of BDS is to bring down the state of Israel... That should be stated as an unambiguous goal. There should not be any equivocation on the subject. Justice and freedom for the Palestinians are incompatible with the existence of the state of Israel.*
>
> **—Professor As'ad AbuKhalil[19]**

Many injustices have resulted from the ongoing failure to resolve the Israeli-Palestinian conflict, but seeking to present Palestinian grievances out of context and without consideration of parallel Israeli concerns is neither constructive nor fair. The advancement of Palestinian rights should not negate the legitimate rights of Israelis.

Unlike peace advocates fighting to hasten a two-state solution to the conflict, BDS proponents make partisan political demands that are clearly aimed at a different outcome.

Israel does not need to be coerced to seek peace. The effort to reach a compromise between Jews and Arabs began nearly a century ago. Israel has repeatedly offered a variety of compromises that would have allowed the Palestinians to establish a state. Israelis have already seen the size of the home they were promised reduced to a fraction of its original size. Still, Israelis express a willingness to do more if it will bring peace.

By contrast, the BDS movement rejects the peace process. Its leaders routinely dismiss peace efforts ranging from the 1978 Camp David Peace Accords to the Oslo Process to President Barack Obama's peace initiatives. BDS advocates refuse to contemplate the negative effects their efforts will have on the peace process. With their zero-sum approach to everything Israeli, they make no attempt to address issues of reconciliation and coexistence. Moreover, they do not acknowledge any Palestinian responsibility or accountability.

BDS is modeled on the campaign against South Africa, which was not designed to promote peace, but to dismantle the state. Thus, BDS leaders abhor cooperation between Israelis and Palestinians. Perhaps the best example of their hypocrisy is BDS cofounder, Omar Barghouti, who advocated a boycott against Israeli universities even as he enjoyed the benefits of participating in a PhD program at Tel Aviv University.

The Arab League boycott, which has been in force since 1945, before the creation of the state, did nothing to help the Palestinians achieve independence, nor did it prevent Israel from becoming one of the world's economic success stories. The BDS campaign has been equally ineffective.

Since BDS activities are indiscriminate, they harm those Israelis who are most actively campaigning for peace and strengthen those who are more skeptical of peace initiatives. BDS reinforces the views of the cynics who do not believe that any compromise will satisfy the Palestinians, and undermines the peace activists who believe the Palestinians would trade peace for land. Rather than encourage compromise, efforts to isolate Israel only make its citizens feel more vulnerable and raise the already high level of risk associated with evacuating additional territory.

Our position is based upon the belief that it is through cooperation based on mutual respect, rather than through boycotts or discrimination, that our common goals can be achieved. Bridging political gulfs—rather than widening them further apart—between nations and individuals thus becomes an educational duty as well as a functional necessity, requiring exchange and dialogue rather than confrontation and antagonism. Our disaffection with, and condemnation of acts of academic boycotts and discrimination against scholars and institutions, is predicated on the principles of academic freedom, human rights, and equality between nations and among individuals.

—Joint Hebrew University/Al-Quds University Statement[20]

Under the false premise of being "apolitical," BDS proponents claim they are not advocating any one solution. In reality, this is purposeful ambiguity, as their three demands clearly spell out a "one-state" outcome, which has no basis in international law, and which is code for the destruction of Israel as the nation-state of the Jewish people. While disavowing any interest in a formula for concluding an Israeli-Palestinian agreement, their preconditions make it impossible to see an outcome whereby an independent state of Palestine would coexist beside a secure Jewish state. Meanwhile, BDS proponents use this ambiguity to try to recruit well-meaning people unaware of the movement's true agenda. BDS is, therefore, a recipe for disaster, not coexistence. Creating "one state" with the "right of return" would mean that there would be no Israel and no self-determination for the Jewish people. This is not a basis for peace but a formula for perpetual conflict.

Good riddance! The two-state solution for the Palestinian-Israeli conflict is finally dead. But someone has to issue an official death certificate before the rotting corpse is given a proper burial and we can all move on and explore the more just, moral and therefore enduring alternative for peaceful coexistence between Jews and Arabs in Mandate Palestine: the one-state solution.

—Omar Barghouti, Founder, Palestinian Campaign for the Academic and Cultural Boycott of Israel[21]

The BDS campaign does not advance the cause of Middle East peace but does create unwanted and unnecessary turmoil on campus. At a time when real campus dialogue is needed more than ever, BDS is more of a barrier than a catalyst to such discussions.

Zionist Jews can handle criticism of Israeli policy, just as they are open to hearing criticism of American policy. Demonization, double standards, and delegitimization are a different story. Those who label Israel as a Nazi state, a state like old South Africa, or a colonial state are clearly trying to use these hurtful analogies to malign Israel. These are not criticisms that are aimed at improving the lives of Palestinians or Israelis, but are rather attempts to convince people to ostracize, punish, and impugn the Jewish state. Likewise, questioning the Jewish connection to Israel or the right of the Jewish people to self-determination in their homeland are attacks on the identities of all Jews.

After many of the past campus divestment debates, Jewish students have felt personally attacked by anti-Israel supporters. Many Jewish students feel hurt when their peers become part of a movement that seeks to delegitimize their own identity. The ideas may be abstract, but the emotional alienation that many Jewish students feel from BDS is real.

Honest discussion about Israeli and Palestinian narratives is needed on college campuses. Divestment advocates seek to circumvent a real debate by promoting the Palestinian narrative and delegitimizing Israel's story. BDS proponents preempt dialogue by adopting an inherently anti-Israel position as their starting point. Instead of asking questions such as: "How did things get this way?" or "What should we do?" BDS supporters have adopted the premise that Israel is guilty of misbehavior, and they use any piece of negative news—both real and imagined—to attack the Jewish state. Nations do not lose their right to exist, however, when they fall short of their ideals.

MYTH

The BDS campaign has succeeded in isolating Israel.

FACT

Today, Israel has diplomatic relations with 161 countries, more than ever before, and its trade relations are growing exponentially with countries in Asia. In fact, Israel's trade with Asia made it Israel's second biggest export destination in 2015, surpassing the United States. China is already Israel's third-largest trading partner; in fact, since formally establishing diplomatic relations with China in 1992, trade has increased 220-fold from $50 million in 1992 to $11 billion in 2014. In addition, total trade between Israel and Japan reached $2.2 billion in 2015.

Israel's relations with India have improved dramatically, highlighted by the 2015 visit of Narendra Modi to Israel, the first Indian prime minister to go to Israel. Since the establishment of diplomatic relations between India and Israel in 1992, bilateral trade and economic relations have grown from $200 million in 1992 to $4.2 billion in 2015. Between Modi's election in May 2014 and November 2014, Israel exported $662 million worth of Israeli weapons and defense items to India. This export number alone is greater than the total Israeli exports to India during the previous three years combined.

Overall, Israeli exports have grown from around $5 million in 1948, to more than $47 billion in 2014. Israel's largest single trade partner remains the United States. The total volume of trade in 2015 was $36 billion. In addition, each of the fifty states benefit from their ties with Israel. In 2015 alone, twenty-one states exported more than $100 million worth of goods to Israel, led by New York with exports of more than $5 billion.

Israel's political relations with the European Union have been strained, and yet trade with the EU exceeds that of the United States. Roughly one-third of Israel's imports and exports are a result of trade with the EU. Moreover, total trade with the EU has grown from approximately $21 billion in 2003 to $34 billion in 2013, and Israel is a part of the Euro-Mediterranean free trade area. Even at "ground zero" for the BDS movement—the United Kingdom—relations and commercial exchange are thriving. In 2015, total bilateral trade amounted to nearly $7 billion.

Israel is also expanding ties with Latin America and has been granted observer status in the Pacific Alliance, an economic trade organization of several major Latin and Central American countries.

In addition to trade, foreign investment in Israel has grown rapidly despite a brief global economic downturn in 2014. More than ten thousand US companies do business in or with Israel, including all the major high-tech companies. Intel, for example, which already has a large presence in Israel, invested $6 billion in its plant in Kiryat Gat.

Kristin Lindow, senior vice president at Moody's Investors Service and Moody's lead analyst for Israel, told *Forbes* in February 2015 that "the impact of BDS is more psychological than real so far and has had no discernible impact on Israeli trade or the broader economy."[22] Moody's chief economist, Dr. Mark Zandi, told *Globes* three months later that Israel has "one of the world's best economies." Elaborating, Zandi notes that Israel's "fiscal situation is better than ever, the debt-to-GDP ratio is low and continues to fall, your economy has been growing for 15 straight years, and there's almost no unemployment."[23]

Efforts to compel universities to divest from companies doing business in Israel or boycott Israeli universities have also fallen flat. They've also produced a backlash as many US states, as well as Congress, have either adopted, or are considering legislation, that bans certain boycotts against Israel.

The cultural boycott has been an annoyance, especially when protestors disrupt Israeli cultural events abroad, but A-list celebrities and performers have ignored threats and intimidation to visit Israel. Among the visitors: Paul McCartney, Elton John, Madonna, Bon Jovi, Helen Mirren, Rihanna, Kanye West, Santana, and Alicia Keys.

The principal victims of the anti-Semitic boycott are the Palestinians in the territories who, in some cases, are losing good jobs in Israeli companies targeted by the boycotters. The bigger loss is the prospect for peace. Palestinians and their supporters are naive if they believe the BDS campaign will encourage Israelis to offer them concessions. If they were interested in changing the status quo for the better, this is the time when they should be demonstrating their interest in peaceful coexistence—not economic warfare.

MYTH

Selective boycotts advance prospects for Palestinian-Israeli peace.

FACT

A group of Israeli artists, academics, and authors have called upon actors to avoid performing in a theater in the town of Ariel, which is located in the West Bank, as a form of protest against Israeli settlement policy. While the Israelis boycotting Ariel are primarily Zionists who believe strongly in the right of the Jewish people to self-determination and oppose the BDS agenda and creation of a binational state that replaces Israel, their tactics are identical to those used outside of Israel. The Ariel boycott, and similar targeted boycotts, do nothing to advance the cause of peace, but do punish innocent Jews uninvolved in the political conflict and give unintentional legitimacy to the boycotters seeking to delegitimize Israel. As Rabbi Eric Yoffie, former president of the Reform Judaism movement, and a frequent critic of Israeli policy, observed:

> The most important reason to oppose the boycott, however, is simply that it is impossible to distinguish between different types of boycotts. There is a growing global BDS (boycott, divestment, sanctions) movement whose intention is to isolate and delegitimize Israel. Those who claim that they only support the boycott of [the West Bank settlement] Ariel but oppose the BDS movement are making distinctions that will not be clear to anyone but themselves. If an internal boycott in Israel is the way that Israelis deal with the question of settlement expansion, what is the basis for objecting when countries and groups hostile to Israel call for a boycott of Israel's academic institutions?[24]

The distinction between Israeli businesses and communities in the territories and the rest of their compatriots cannot be applied in practice. Any steps to isolate and exclude Israelis in settlements also impacts Israelis on both sides of the Green Line. Because the economies are interdependent, efforts to punish or damage the settlements also injure the broader economy and all Israelis. Both sweeping and targeted boycott campaigns are a form of collective punishment that is fundamentally unfair.

Boycotts and other punitive measures aimed solely at Israel do not address the real sources of the current political impasse, such as the Palestinian failure to reassure the Israeli public of the peacefulness of their intentions. Punishing Israelis for the "occupation" may even help entrench maximalist Palestinian claims, rather than encourage the moderation needed to reach a fair political accommodation.

The BDS movement is essentially a means of coercion. If it were meant to encourage peace, the measures would be directed against the Palestinians to pressure them to end terrorism and recognize the state of Israel. Peace and a two-state solution are not the intent, however, of most BDS advocates. They want to raise questions about the legitimacy of Israel to generate international pressure to force Israel to capitulate to Palestinian demands and to avoid the necessity of negotiations to arrive at a mutually agreed upon division of the land that will guarantee the rights of both Palestinians and Israelis.

While someone supporting a limited or selective boycott may think they are not engaging in an act of delegitimization, BDS proponents use and abuse any kind of BDS activity to claim support and momentum for their full-blown anti-Semitic version of the strategy. No matter how good the intention may be, associating with BDS strengthens the delegitimizers who seek Israel's demise.

If Amos Oz, David Grossman, Meretz, Peace Now and other Zionist doves want the country to listen to them, they can't slap the settlers in the face, which is what this boycott does. It's not only a mistake, it's an insult. I, too, wish the settlements had never been built, and hope to see many of them evacuated one day, but in the meantime the people living there are entitled to a decent life, which includes such things as culture, entertainment and higher education.

—*Jerusalem Post* **columnist Larry Derfner**[25]

MYTH

Academic boycotts are popular in America.

FACT

In December 2013, the American Studies Association (ASA) passed a resolution calling for an academic boycott of Israel and specifically demanded that American universities end all collaboration with Israeli institutions. Of the ASA's total membership of five thousand, 826 members (17 percent) voted for the resolution; moreover, the ASA itself, and its members, were not required to comply with the resolution. Nevertheless, the Boycott, Divestment, and Sanctions (BDS) movement crowed about the "victory." Israel is the first nation ever boycotted by the ASA in the fifty-two years since the organization's founding.

The call for a boycott is ironic given that Mahmoud Abbas, the president of the Palestinian Authority, told South African journalists, "We do not ask anyone to boycott Israel itself . . . We have relations with Israel, we have mutual recognition of Israel."[26]

Like most campus-related BDS "victories," the ASA vote will have no impact on Israel and do nothing to help the Palestinians, many of whom now benefit from attending Israeli universities and from collaboration between colleges in the West Bank and Israel. In fact, many professors in Israel are very active in the peace camp, and their research often examines issues related to the Israeli-Palestinian dispute from a critical perspective. Furthermore, hundreds of American scholars enjoy fruitful collaboration with Israeli colleagues each year.

The ASA faced a torrent of criticism from the academic community and beyond. Though it may have come as a shock to the ASA, the backlash did not surprise anyone knowledgeable about Israel or committed to the free exchange of ideas. Within a month, more than one hundred universities rejected the idea of boycotting Israel.[27] Another fifty institutions specifically denounced the ASA's decision and the association "lost nearly 20 percent of its affiliated universities."[28] Drew Faust, president of Harvard University, said, "the recent resolution of the ASA proposing to boycott Israeli universities represents a direct threat to [academic freedoms and values], ideals which universities and scholarly associations should be dedicated to defend."[29]

Individual universities were not the only ones to denounce the ASA boycott. The American Council on Education (representing seventeen hundred academic institutions), the Association of Public and Land-Grant Universities (216 institutions), the Association of American Universities (sixty-two institutions), and the American Association of University Professors (forty-eight thousand members) criticized the ASA vote. Not one university defended the ASA resolution, and five universities—Bard College, Brandeis University, Indiana University, Kenyon College, and Penn State Harrisburg—announced they would terminate their membership in the ASA. Thus, roughly two thousand academic institutions representing tens of thousands of faculty disagree with the minority within the ASA that has aligned itself with a movement that openly calls for Israel to be replaced with a Palestinian state.[30]

The principal impact of the ASA action was to give the association a black eye and associate it with other zealots who believe academic freedom does not apply to research or cooperation with Israel.

Far more important than the decisions of a handful of minor associations to call for essentially meaningless boycotts were rejections of similar proposals by the larger and more prestigious American Historical Association and American Anthropological Association.

If we are to look at Israeli society, it is within the academic community that we've had the most progressive pro-peace views and views that have come out in favor of seeing us as equals . . . If you want to punish any sector, this is the last one to approach.

—Al-Quds University president Sari Nusseibeh on academic boycotts of Israel[31]

Walter Reich, the Yitzhak Rabin Memorial professor of international affairs at George Washington University, said, "Boycotting Israeli academic institutions not only trashes the sacrosanct academic principle of the free exchange of ideas; it's also hypocritical and wrong. Most egregiously, it targets Israel to the exclusion of countries with immeasurably worse human-rights records."[32]

Stanley Fish of the *New York Times* said the boycotters' argument was "as pathetic as it is laughable."[33]

Henry Reichman, professor emeritus of history at CSU East Bay, and first vice president of the American Association of University Professors, said the boycott is "at best misguided" and "is the wrong way to register opposition to the policies and practices it seeks to discredit; it is itself a serious violation of the very academic freedom its supporters purport to defend."[34]

The BDS movement may have thought the ASA action would act as a clarion call for academics to join their anti-Semitic campaign; however, it has primarily attracted a small group of faculty extremists committed to demonizing Israel. More seriously, it exposed the large number of professors whose research and teaching is ideologically driven and that may constitute academic malpractice.

MYTH

Labeling products manufactured in West Bank settlements promotes peace.

FACT

The European Union has called for member states to require goods originating from the West Bank to be labeled separately from products from the rest of Israel.[35] Following this move, the Obama administration also announced plans to enforce regulations requiring goods entering the United States from the West Bank to be labeled as such.[36] The EU and Obama mistakenly believe that this will pressure Israel to evacuate the West Bank and capitulate to Palestinian demands. This cynical campaign is blatantly hypocritical and anti-Semitic and will in no way advance the cause of peace.

As Danielle Pletka of the American Enterprise Institute has noted, "Labeling goods made by Israeli businesses in disputed territories, but not goods made in other disputed territories like Kashmir, for example, is an example of blatant anti-Semitism."[37] As is so often the case, it is only Israeli Jews who must be given special treatment while other peoples involved in conflicts are ignored. "What, you say, but there are no Jews occupying those other places? We only condemn the Jews? Well, of course. Because only the Jews are especially worthy of EU condemnation. Next, a yellow star. Now that would be bold," wrote Pletka.[38] Though European leaders claim to oppose the efforts of the BDS (boycott, divestment, and sanctions) movement to boycott and isolate Israel, the labeling campaign supports it.

The labeling idea is also counterproductive because it only hardens the views of Israelis who believe they are under siege and that criticism of their policies are one sided. The principal obstacle to peace today as well as yesterday is the refusal of the Palestinians to accept a Jewish state, and yet no pressure is exerted on them to change their irredentist position. Proponents of labeling also fail to recognize that Israel can and will make concessions only when Israelis feel strong, that their views are understood, and that they have the backing of the United States.

The labeling idea will also have little impact on Israeli trade. A small percentage of Israeli exports are from West Bank companies. In addition, not all EU states are going to adopt this anti-Semitic requirement. Furthermore, Israeli trade with the EU has been expanding even as BDS sympathizers call for boycotting Israel.

Members of Congress responded to the EU decision in December 2015 out of concern that the labeling rule could "promote a de-facto boycott of Israel." Thirty-six senators signed a letter to the EU's top diplomat, "urging the European body to reconsider the discriminatory policy."[39]

When members learned the Obama administration plans to enforce similar anti-Semitic labeling rules, Senator Tom Cotton (R-Ark.) introduced a bill in the Senate and said the administration's "directive plays right into the hands of those who are driving insidious efforts to boycott Israeli goods."[40]

Notes, Chapter 19

1. Leon Wieseltier, "Israel, Palestine, and the Return of the Binational Fantasy," *New Republic* (October 24, 2003).

2. Steve Linde, "Cotler's Call to Action," *Jerusalem Post* (June 2, 2015).

3. "President Bollinger Delivers Cardozo Lecture on Academic Freedom" *Columbia News* (March 24, 2005).

4. Karen W. Arenson, "Columbia Chief Tackles Dispute over Professors" *New York Times* (March 24, 2005).

5. "Dear Colleague Letter," Russlyn Ali—Assistant Secretary for Civil Rights, US Department of Education (October 26, 2010).

6. Address at morning prayers—Memorial Church, Cambridge, Massachusetts, (September 17, 2002), Office of the President, Harvard University.

7. Natan Sharansky, "Antisemitism in 3-D," *Forward* (January 21, 2005), 9.

8. Uri Avnery, "The Boycott Revisited," *Gush-Shalom.org* (September 6, 2009).

9. NGO Forum, "World Conference against Racism—Durban, South Africa," *NGO Monitor* (August 27–September 1, 2001).

10. "NGO 'Apartheid State' Campaign: Deliberately Immoral or Intellectually Lazy," *NGO Monitor* (March 22, 2010).

11. Seymour Martin Lipset, "The Socialism of Fools: The Left, the Jews, and Israel," *Encounter* (December 1969), 24.

12. "SodaStream Leaves West Bank as CEO Says Boycott anti-Semitic and Pointless," *The Guardian* (September 2, 2015).

13. Kim Kirschenbaum, "Israel, Gaza Student Groups Clash on Issues of Divestment, Apartheid," *Columbia Spectator* (March 4, 2009).

14. Mitchell Bard, "#BDSFail on Campus Part 1," *Jerusalem Post* (July 13, 2016).

15. See, for example, Martin Kramer, *Ivory Towers on Sand* (Washington, DC: The Washington Institute for Near East Policy), 2001, 16; Marla Braverman, "The Arabist Predicament," *Azure* (Summer 2003), 176-184; Mitchell Bard, *The Arab Lobby: The Invisible Alliance That Undermines America's Interests in the Middle East* (NY: HarperCollins, 2010), 284-321.

16. Matt Korade, "Lack of Openness Makes Scholarly Discussion of Islam Dangerous, Says Bernard Lewis," *Congressional Quarterly's Homeland Security News and Analysis* (April 26, 2008).

17. Lee C. Bollinger, "Statement by President Lee C. Bollinger on British University and College Union Boycott" *Columbia University* (June 12, 2007).

18. Martin Kramer, "Boycotting Israel at NYU," *Sandbox* (March 31, 2004).

19. As'ad AbuKhalil, "A Critique of Norman Finkelstein on BDS," *Al-Akhbar* (February 17, 2012).

20. Joint Hebrew University/Al-Quds University Statement on Academic Cooperation, signed in London (May 22, 2005), accessed May 9, 2011.

21. Omar Barghouti, "Relative Humanity: The Essential Obstacle to a Just Peace in Palestine," *Counterpunch.org* (December 13-14, 2003).

22. Carrie Sheffield, "Boycott Israel Movement Stunts the Palestinian Economy," *Forbes* (February 22, 2015).

23. Amiram Barkat "Moody's Chief Economist: Israel in Good Shape" *Globes* (May 17, 2015).

24. Eric H. Yoffie, "The Idiocy of the Ariel Boycott," *Jerusalem Post* (November 15, 2010).

25. Larry Derfner, "Rattling the Cage: A little Culture, Comrades," *Jerusalem Post* (September 6, 2010).

26. Yoel Goldman, "Abbas: Don't Boycott Israel," *Times of Israel* (December 13, 2013).

27. William A. Jacobson, "List of Universities Rejecting Academic Boycott of Israel (Update—Over 150)," *Legal Insurrection* (December 22, 2013).

28. American Studies Association, "ASA Turpie Award Winners in Opposition to Israeli Boycott Resolution," *ASA* (January 5, 2014); Yair Rosenberg, "American Historical Association Decisively Rejects Anti-Israel Resolution, 111-51," *Tablet* (January 11, 2016).

29. President of Harvard University, "Statement on ASA Resolution," Harvard University, Office of the President (December 20, 2013).

30. Thomas Doherty, "The Israel Boycott That Backfired" *LA Times* (November 5, 2014).

31. "Palestinian University President Comes Out against Boycott of Israeli Academics," *Associated Press* (June 18, 2006).

32. Walter Reich, "Reject Boycott of Israel," *Philly.com* (January 7, 2014).

33. Stanley Fish, "Academic Freedom against Itself: Boycotting Israeli Universities," *New York Times* (October 28, 2013).

34. Henry Reichman, "Against Academic Boycotts," *Inside Higher Ed* (December 12, 2013).

35. Steven J. Rosen, "The EU's Israel Problem Goes Far Beyond Labels," *The Tower* (January 2016).

36. Jordan Schatchel, "Obama Joins Israel Boycott, Labels West Bank Goods," *Breitbart* (January 28, 2016).

37. Jennifer Rubin, "Why It's Correct to Label the Obama Administration 'Anti-Israel,'" *Washington Post* (January 20, 2016).

38. Danielle Pletka, "The EU Leads Boldly on Israeli-Palestinian Peace," *American Enterprise Institute* (November 12, 2015).

39. "West Bank Country of Origin Marking Requirements," US Customs and Border Protection (January 23, 2016).

40. Patrick Goodenough, "Sen. Cotton Introduces Bill to Rescind 'Nonsensical' Directive to Israel/West Bank Product Labelling," *CNS News* (January 14, 2016).

Index of Myths

13: Jerusalem 207

Alphabetical Index

Suggested Reading

Aumann, Moshe. *Land Ownership in Palestine 1880–1948.* Jerusalem: Academic Committee on the Middle East, 1976.

Avineri, Shlomo. *The Making of Modern Zionism: Intellectual Origins of the Jewish State.* NY Basic Books, 1981.

Avner, Yehuda. *The Prime Ministers: An Intimate Narrative of Israeli Leadership.* NY: Toby Press, 2010.

Avneri, Arieh. *The Claim of Dispossession.* NJ: Transaction Books, 1984.

Bard, Mitchell G. and Moshe Schwartz. *1001 Facts Everyone Should Know About Israel.* NJ: Jason Aronson, 2002.

Bard, Mitchell G. *The Arab Lobby: The Invisible Alliance That Undermines America's Interests in the Middle East.* HarperCollins, 2010.

Bard, Mitchell G. *The Complete Idiot's Guide to Middle East Conflict.* NY: Alpha Books, 2008.

Bard, Mitchell and David Nachmias. *Israel Studies: An Anthology.* MD: American-Israeli Cooperative Enterprise, 2011. http://www.jewishvirtuallibrary.org/jsource/isdf/text/anthologycvr.html.

Bard, Mitchell. *Will Israel Survive?* (NY: Palgrave Macmillan, 2007).

Bass, Warren. *Support Any Friend: Kennedy's Middle East and the Making of the U.S. Israel Alliance.* NY: Oxford University Press, 2003.

Becker, Jillian. *The PLO.* NY: St. Martin's Press, 1985.

Begin, Menachem. *The Revolt.* NY: EP Dutton, 1978.

Bell, J. Bowyer. *Terror Out Of Zion.* NJ: Transaction, 1996.

Bickerton, Ian and Carla Klausner. *A Concise History of the Arab-Israeli Conflict.* NY: Prentice Hall, 2002.

Carter, Jimmy. *Keeping Faith: Memoirs of a President.* AR: University of Arkansas Press, 1995.

Gurion, David. *My Talks with Arab Leaders.* New York: The Third Press, 1973.

Gurion, David. *Rebirth and Destiny of Israel.* NY: Philosophical Library, 1954.

Cohen, Hillel. *Army of Shadows: Palestinian Collaboration with Zionism, 1917–1948.* CA: University of California Press, 2008.

Collins, Larry and Dominique Lapierre. *O Jerusalem!* NY: Simon and Schuster, 1972.

Dayan, Moshe. *Breakthrough: A Personal Account of the Egypt-Israel Peace Negotiations.* NY: Alfred A. Knopf, 1981.

Dershowitz, Alan. *The Case for Israel.* NY: John Wiley & Sons, 2003.

Dowty, Alan. *Israel/Palestine.* Cambridge, UK: Polity Press, 2nd edition, 2008.

Eban, Abba. *Heritage: Civilization and the Jews.* NY: Summit Books, 1984.

Eban, Abba. *My Country: The Story of Modern Israel.* NY: Random House, 1972.

Gilbert, Martin. *Israel: A History.* NY: William Morrow & Co., 1998.

Harel, Amos and Avi Issacharoff. *34 Days: Israel, Hezbollah and the War in Lebanon.* NY: Palgrave Macmillan, 2009.

Hertzberg Arthur. *The Zionist Idea.* PA: Jewish Publications Society, 1997.

Herzl, Theodor. *The Diaries of Theodore Herzl.* NY: Peter Smith Publishers, 1987.

Herzl, Theodor. *The Jewish State.* Dover Publications, 1989.

Herzog, Chaim. *The Arab-Israeli Wars.* NY: Random House, 1984.

Johnson, Paul. *A History of the Jews.* NY: HarperCollins, 1988.

Karsh, Efraim. *Fabricating Israeli History: The "New Historians."* London: Frank Cass, 1997.

Katz, Samuel. *Battleground-Fact and Fantasy in Palestine.* SPI Books, 1986.

Kissinger, Henry. *The White House Years.* MA: Little Brown & Co., 1979.

Kissinger, Henry. *Years of Renewal.* NY: Simon & Schuster, 1999.

Kollek, Teddy. *Jerusalem.* Washington, D.C.: Washington Institute For Near East Policy, 1990.

Lacquer, Walter and Barry Ru bin. *The Israel-Arab Reader.* NY: Penguin, 2001.

Lewis, Bernard. *The Jews of Islam.* NJ: Princeton University Press, 1984.

Lewis, Bernard. *The Middle East: A Brief History of the Last 2000 Years.* NY: Touchstone Books, 1997.

Livingstone, Neil C., and David Halevy. *Inside the PLO.* NY: William Morrow and Co., 1990.

Lorch, Netanel. *One Long War.* NY: Herzl Press, 1976.

Meir, Golda. *My Life.* NY: Dell, 1975.

Morris, Benny. *The Birth of the Palestinian Refugee Problem Revisited.* MA: Cambridge University Press, 2004.

Morris, Benny. *Righteous Victims: A History of the Zionist-Arab Conflict, 1881–1999.* NY: Knopf, 2001.

Netanyahu, Benjamin. *A Place Among Nations: Israel and the World.* NY: Warner Books, 1998.

Oren, Michael. *Six Days of War: June 1967 and the Making of the Modern Middle East.* NY: Oxford University Press, 2002.

Pipes, Daniel. *The Hidden Hand: Middle East Fears of Conspiracy.* Griffin Trade Paperback, 1998.

Porath, Yehoshua. *The Emergence of the Palestinian-Arab National Movement, 1918–1929.* London: Frank Cass, 1996.

Porath, Yehoshua. *In Search of Arab Unity 1930–1945.* London: Frank Cass and Co., Ltd., 1986.

Porath, Yehoshua. *Palestinian Arab National Movement: From Riots to Rebellion: 1929–1939. vol. 2.* London: Frank Cass and Co., Ltd., 1977

Rabin, Yitzhak. *The Rabin Memoirs.* CA: University of California Press, 1996

Rabinovich, Itamar and Jehuda Reinharz. *Israel in the Middle East: Documents and Readings on Society, Politics, and Foreign Relations, Pre-1948 to the Present.* Waltham: Brandeis University Press, 2007

Rosenthal, Donna. *The Israelis: Ordinary People in an Extraordinary Land.* Free Press, 2008.

Ross, Dennis. *Doomed to Succeed: The U.S.-Israel Relationship from Truman to Obama.* NY: Farrar, Straus and Giroux, 2015.

Ross, Dennis. *The Missing Peace: The Inside Story of the Fight for Middle East Peace.* NY: Farrar, Straus and Giroux, 2004.

Sachar, Howard. *A History of Israel: From the Rise of Zionism to Our Time.* NY: Alfred A. Knopf, 1998.

Freedman, Robert O., ed. *The Intifada: Its Impact on Israel, The Arab World and the Superpowers.* Miami: University Press of Florida, 1991.

Schiff, Zeev and Ehud Yaari. *Israel's Lebanon War.* NY: Simon and Schuster, 1984.

Senor, Dan and Saul Singer. *Start-Up Nation: The Story of Israel's Economic Miracle.* Toronto: McClelland & Stewart, Ltd, 2009.

Shapira, Anita. *Israel: A History.* Waltham: Brandeis, 2014.

Stillman, Norman. *The Jews of Arab Lands.* PA: The Jewish Publication Society of America 1989.

Stillman, Norman. *The Jews of Arab Lands in Modern Times.* NY: Jewish Publication Society, 1991.

Truman, Harry. *Years of Trial and Hope. Vol. 2.* NY: Doubleday, 1956.

Weizmann, Chaim. *Trial and Error.* NY: Greenwood Press, 1972.

Ye'or, Bat. *The Dhimmi.* NJ: Associated University Press, 1985.

About the American-Israeli Cooperative Enterprise

The American-Israeli Cooperative Enterprise (AICE) was established in 1993 as a nonprofit 501(c)(3), nonpartisan organization to strengthen the US-Israel relationship by emphasizing the fundamentals of the alliance—the values our nations share.

The objectives and purposes of AICE include:

■ To provide a vehicle for the research, study, discussion, and exchange of views concerning nonmilitary cooperation (Shared Value Initiatives) between the peoples and governments of the United States and Israel.

■ To publicize joint activities and the benefits accruing to America and Israel from them.

■ To explore issues of common historical interest to the peoples and governments of the United States and Israel.

■ To serve as a clearinghouse on joint US-Israeli activities.

■ To provide educational materials on Jewish history and culture.

■ To promote scholarship in the field of Israel studies.

Jewish Virtual Library
The Jewish Virtual Library is the most comprehensive online Jewish encyclopedia in the world, covering everything from anti-Semitism to Zionism. Nearly twenty-five thousand entries and more than ten thousand photographs and maps have been integrated into the site. The Library averages nearly one million visitors per month from more than two hundred countries.

Israel Scholar Development Fund
To address the critical need to develop new scholars and place established Israel scholars on campus, AICE created the project to:

■ Identify Israeli scholars who could be placed in visiting professorships.

■ Offer universities grants to hire a visiting scholar.

■ Offer awards to encourage students to pursue graduate degrees related to Israel.

■ Strategically promote Israel Studies by identifying institutions that can benefit from hosting Israeli scholars.

■ Advise philanthropists on investing in Israel Studies programs.

■ Over eight years, AICE brought more than 100 visiting Israeli professors to teach at 72 different universities.

The Dream-Team Initiative
AICE assembled a "Dream Team" of professionals, faculty, students, and consultants to develop materials (stopbds.com), ideas, and strategies to help students, faculty, administrators, trustees, and community members to preempt and defeat anti-Semitic boycott, divestment, sanctions (BDS) campaigns.

About the Author

Dr. Mitchell Bard is the executive director of the nonprofit American-Israeli Cooperative Enterprise (AICE) and one of the leading authorities on US Middle East policy. Dr. Bard is also the director of the Jewish Virtual Library (www.JewishVirtualLibrary.org), the world's most comprehensive online encyclopedia of Jewish history and culture.

Dr. Bard co-chairs the task force on BDS and Delegitimization for the Global Forum on Combatting Anti-Semitism. For three years, he was the editor of the *Near East Report*, the American Israel Public Affairs Committee's (AIPAC) newsletter on US Middle East policy. He also served as a polling analyst in the 1988 presidential campaign.

In 2013, Dr. Bard was named one of the "top 100 people positively influencing Jewish life" by the Algemeiner newspaper. He has appeared on local and national television and radio outlets. His work has been published in academic journals, magazines, and major newspapers. He has written and edited twenty-four books including:

- *Death to the Infidels: Radical Islam's War against the Jews*
- *After Anatevka: Tevye in Palestine* (fiction)
- *Israel Matters: Understand the Past—Look to the Future*
- *The Arab Lobby: The Invisible Alliance That Undermines America's Interests in the Middle East*
- *Israel Studies: An Anthology* (coeditor with David Nachmias)
- *Will Israel Survive?*
- *The Complete Idiot's Guide to Middle East Conflict* (4th edition)
- *48 Hours of Kristallnacht*
- *The Founding of Israel*
- *The Complete Idiot's Guide to World War II*
- *1001 Facts Everyone Should Know about Israel*
- *Forgotten Victims: The Abandonment of Americans in Hitler's Camps*
- *The Nuremberg Trials (At Issue in History)*
- *From Tragedy to Triumph: The Politics behind the Rescue of Ethiopian Jews*
- *The Complete History of the Holocaust*
- *The Water's Edge and Beyond: Defining the Limits to Domestic Influence on U.S. Middle East Policy*
- *Building Bridges: Lessons for America from Novel Israeli Approaches to Promote Coexistence*
- *On One Foot: A Middle East Guide for the Perplexed or How to Respond on Your Way to Class When Your Best Friend Joins an Anti-Israel Protest*

Bard holds a PhD in political science from UCLA and a master's degree in public policy from Berkeley. He received his BA in economics from the University of California at Santa Barbara.

Made in the USA
Middletown, DE
26 January 2018